The Role of the Judge in International Trade Regulation

SIE *Studies in International Economics* includes works dealing with the theory, empirical analysis, and evaluation of international policies and institutions, in the area of international macroeconomics and finance, international trade theory and policy, as well as international legal and political economy.

Alan V. Deardorff and Robert M. Stern, Editors
Constituent Interests and U.S. Trade Policies

Gary R. Saxonhouse and T. N. Srinivasan, Editors
Development, Duality, and the International Economic Regime: Essays in Honor of Gustav Ranis

Charles P. Kindleberger *Essays in History: Financial, Economic, Personal*

Keith Acheson and Christopher Maule
Much Ado about Culture: North American Trade Disputes

Alan V. Deardorff and Robert M. Stern *Social Dimensions of U.S. Trade Policies*

Thomas Cottier and Petros C. Mavroidis, Editors
Regulatory Barriers and the Principle of Non-Discrimination in World Trade Law, The World Trade Forum, Volume 2

Bernard Hoekman and Jamel Zarrouk, Editors *Catching Up with the Competition: Trade Opportunities and Challenges for Arab Countries*

Jun Fu *Institutions and Investments: Foreign Direct Investment in China during an Era of Reforms*

Robert M. Stern, Editor *Services in the International Economy*

Keith E. Maskus and John S. Wilson, Editors
Quantifying the Impact of Technical Barriers to Trade: Can It Be Done?

Robert M. Stern, Editor *Issues and Options for U.S.-Japan Trade Policies*

Thomas Cottier and Petros C. Mavroidis, Editors
Intellectual Property: Trade, Competition, and Sustainable Development, The World Trade Forum, Volume 3

Andrew G. Brown
Reluctant Partners: A History of Multilateral Trade Cooperation, 1850–2000

Ka Zeng
Trade Threats, Trade Wars: Bargaining, Retaliation, and American Coercive Diplomacy

Thomas Cottier and Petros C. Mavroidis, Editors
The Role of the Judge in International Trade Regulation: Experience and Lessons for the WTO, The World Trade Forum, Volume 4

For a complete list of books in the series, please visit
www.press.umich.edu/subjects/econ.html

THE WORLD TRADE FORUM, VOLUME 4

The Role of the Judge in International Trade Regulation

Experience and Lessons for the WTO

Thomas Cottier and Petros C. Mavroidis,
Editors

Patrick Blatter,
Associate Editor

THE UNIVERSITY OF MICHIGAN PRESS
Ann Arbor

Published in the United States of America by
The University of Michigan Press
Manufactured in the United States of America
♾ Printed on acid-free paper

2006 2005 2004 2003 4 3 2 1

A CIP catalog record for this book is available from the British Library.

Library of Congress Cataloging-in-Publication Data

World Trade Forum (4th : 2000 : Neuchâtel, Switzerland)
The Role of the Judge in International Trade Regulation : Experience and Lessons for the WTO / Thomas Cottier and Petros C. Mavroidis, editors ; Patrick Blatter, associate editor.
p. cm. — (World Trade Forum ; v. 4) (Studies in international economics)
Papers presented at the fourth annual World Trade Forum Conference held in Neuchâtel, Switzerland, on August 21–22, 2000.
ISBN 0-472-11319-4 (cloth : alk. paper)
1. World Trade Organization. Appellate Body—Congresses. 2. Foreign trade regulation—Congresses. 3. Judges. 4. Arbitration, International. I. Cottier, Thomas. II. Mavroidis, Petros C. III. Blatter, Patrick. IV. Title V. World Trade Forum (Series) ; v. 4. VI. Studies in international economics (Ann Arbor, Mich.)

K4603.W67 2003
382'.92—dc21 2003040228

The World Trade Forum

The World Trade Forum was founded in 1997 to offer an opportunity for an international in-depth discussion of issues facing the world trading system. The Forum is organized through the cooperation of the Universities of Berne and Neuchâtel (Switzerland). Since the year 2000, it has been held at the newly-founded World Trade Institute in Berne. Forum participants include academics, practitioners, and professionals from government and from international non-governmental organizations. Representing both the legal and economic communities, the participants bring a wide variety of perspectives to the issues of debate.

Each year, one particular topic is chosen as the focus of that year's forum. The participants invited to the conference are requested to prepare a paper on that topic, and then to present the paper for discussion. Question-and-answer sessions follow each presentation, and a short analysis by an appointed discussant following the presentation of each group of papers allows for a synthesis of the ideas. At the end of all sessions, a roundtable discussion takes place, in which participants may either make comments on the overall problems of the topic or address questions and suggestions to the other participants in light of the entire series of papers presented.

Following the conference, the authors of the papers revise their submissions for publication in the series of books that accompany the World Trade Forum conferences. An introduction and conclusory analysis by the editors further the synthesis of the topic at hand and aid the reader in determining the overall results of the scholarship.

We are most grateful to the Silva Casa Foundation in Berne for its generous financial support that allows the conferences to take place as well as for its encouragement to pursue the idea of the World Trade Forum, and to the Universities of Berne and Neuchâtel.

The World Trade Forum series was founded in order to help spread the ideas that arise from the careful consideration of the issue presented to interested persons throughout the world. We sincerely hope that this volume achieves this goal.

Contents

Part III: The Review of Health Standards in the WTO

Part IV: Where Do We Go from Here?

Appendix

Abbreviations and Acronyms

AB	Appellate Body (WTO)
ACTPN	Advisory Committee for Trade Policy and Negotiations (U.S.)
AD	Antidumping
APEC	Asia-Pacific Economic Cooperation
BISD	Basic Instruments and Selected Documents (GATT/WTO)
BOP	Balance-of-Payment
BSE	Bovine Spongiform Encephalopathy
BTAs	Border Tax Adjustments
CAP	Common Agricultural Policy
CEC	Central European Countries
CIT	Court of International Trade
CJD	Creutzfeld Jakob Disease
CRS	Computer Reservation System
CVD	Countervailing Duty
DCC	Dormant Commerce Clause
DCS	Directly Competitive or Substitutable Products
DDD	Dumb Duck Disease (see Appendix)
DSU	Understanding on Rules and Procedures Governing the Settlement of Disputes (WTO)
EAC	European Accreditation of Certification Bodies
EAL	European Accreditation of Laboratories
EC	European Community
ECJ	European Court of Justice
ECR	European Court Reports
ECSC	European Community of Steel and Coal
ECT	European Community Treaty
EEA	European Economic Area
EEC	European Economic Community
EFTA	European Free Trade Association
Ens	European standards
ESBs	European Standards Bodies
ETSI	European Telecommunications Standards Institute
EU	European Union
FAO	Food and Agriculture Organization
FDA	Food and Drug Administration
FTA	Free Trade Agreement
GATS	General Agreement on Trade in Services (WTO)
GATT	General Agreement on Tariffs and Trade (WTO)
GMO	Genetically Modified Organism

GPA	Agreement on Government Procurement (WTO)
IARC	International Agency for Research on Cancer
ICJ	International Court of Justice
ICSID	International Centre for Settlement of Investment Dispute
IMF	International Monetary Fund
IPCC	Intergovernmental Panel on Climate Change
ISO	International Standard Organization
ITC	International Trade Commission (U.S.)
MCM	Monetary Compensatory Amount
MFN	Most-Favored Nation
MNCs	Multinational Corporations
MRA	Mutual Recognition Agreement
MSOs	Market Surveillance Operators
MSSBs	Member State Standards Bodies
NAFTA	North American Free Trade Agreement
NGO	Non-Governmental Organization
OECD	Organization for Economic Cooperation and Development
OIE	Office International des Epizooties
PPMs	Production and Process Methods
QR(s)	Quantitative Restriction(s)
RBP	Restrictive Business Practice
SCM	Subsidies and Countervailing Measures
SPS	Agreement on Sanitary and Phytosanitary Measures
TED	Turtle Excluder Device
TABD	Transatlantic Business Dialogue
TBT	Technical Barriers to Trade
TEP	Transatlantic Economic Partnership
TRIMs	Agreement on Trade-Related Investment Measures (WTO)
TRIPs	Agreement on Trade-Related Aspects of Intellectual Property Rights (WTO)
TRIS	Technical Regulations and Industry Standards
UNCTAD	United Nations Conference on Trade and Development
UN-ECE	United Nations Economic Commission for Europe
USDA	U.S. Department of Agriculture
VAT	Value Added Tax
VCLT	Vienna Convention on the Law of Treaties
WHO	World Health Organization
WIPO	World Intellectual Property Organization
WTO	World Trade Organization

Authors and Conference Participants

Authors

GEORGE A. BERMANN, Professor, University of Columbia, Law School, New York, USA

STEVE CHARNOVITZ, Attorney, Wilmer, Cutler & Pickering, Washington D.C., USA

THOMAS COTTIER, Professor of European & International Economic Law, University of Berne, Director, World Trade Institute, Berne, Switzerland

WILLIAM DAVEY, Edwin M. Adams Professor of Law, University of Illinois, College of Law. Former Director, WTO Legal Affairs Division (1995 to 1999)

PIET EECKHOUT, Herbert Smith Professor of European Law, King's College, Law School, London, UK

HENRIK HORN, Institute for International Economic Studies, Stockholm University, Sweden

GARY HORLICK, Attorney, O'Melveny and Myers, Washington D.C., USA

ROBERT L. HOWSE, Professor, University of Michigan, Law School, Ann Arbor, USA

MERIT JANOW, Professor in the Practice of International Trade, Columbia University School of International and Public Affairs (SIPA), New York, USA

MITSUO MATSUSHITA, Professor, Seikei University, Law School, Tokyo, Japan

NATALIE MCNELIS, Senior Associate, Wilmer, Cutler & Pickering, Brussels, Belgium, formerly Stibbe, Brussels, Belgium

PETROS C. MAVROIDIS, Professor, University of Neuchâtel, Law School, Neuchâtel, Switzerland

KALYPSO NICOLAIDIS, University Lecturer, Oxford University, and Associate Professor (on leave), Kennedy School of Government, Harvard University, USA

MATTHIAS OESCH, Attorney-at-Law, LL.M., Research Fellow, World Trade Institute, Berne, Switzerland

DAVID PALMETER, Attorney, Powell Goldstein, Washington D.C., USA

JOOST PAUWELYN, WTO Legal Affairs Division, Geneva, Switzerland, currently on leave with the University of Neuchâtel, Switzerland

ERNST-ULRICH PETERSMANN, Professor of Law, European University Institute, Florence, formerly University of Geneva, Switzerland

DONALD H. REGAN, Professor, University of Michigan, Law School, Ann Harbor, USA
JOEL TRACHTMAN, Professor of International Law and Dean ad interim, The Fletcher School of Law and Diplomacy, Tufts University, Medford, USA
MICHEL WAELBROECK, Professor Emeritus, Université libre de Bruxelles, IEE, Brussels, Belgium
DIANE P. WOOD, Judge at the Seventh Circuit Court of Appeals, Chicago, USA

Other Conference Participants

RICHARD BALDWIN, Professor of International Economics, Graduate Institute of International Studies, Geneva, Switzerland
JACQUES BOURGEOIS, Attorney, Akin & Gump, Brussels, Belgium; Professor, College d'Europe, Brugge, Belgium
MARCO BRONCKERS, Attorney, Stibbe, Brussels; Professor, University of Leyden, Law School, Belgium
ALEXANDRA CAPLAZI, Research Fellow, University of Berne, Berne, Switzerland
CLAUS-DIETER EHLERMANN, Professor of Law, Wilmer, Cutler & Pickering, Brussels, Belgium, formerly European University Institute, Florence, Italy, and member of the Appellate Body of the WTO, Geneva, Switzerland
ALVIN KOPŠE, Research Fellow, University of Berne, Berne, Switzerland
INGO MEITINGER, Research Fellow, University of Berne, Berne, Switzerland
FRIEDER ROESSLER, former Director of GATT's Legal Division, Geneva, Switzerland
ANDRE SAPIR, Professor, Université Libre de Bruxelles, IEE and CEPR, Brussels, Belgium
LORENZO SIGISMONDI, Research Fellow, University of Neuchâtel, Neuchâtel, Switzerland
JOSEPH WEILER, Professor, New York University (NYU), Law School, New York, USA
DANIEL WÜGER, Research Fellow, University of Berne, Berne, Switzerland

Preface

On August 21 and 22, 2000, over thirty trade professionals met at the World Trade Institute in Berne, Switzerland, for the fourth annual World Trade Forum. The topic established for the 2000 Conference was the evolution of the role of the judge in the World Trade system, mainly focusing on the work of the Appellate Body during its first five years of operation. Inquiries went along three lines, the first trying to determine whether we could find cases submitted to the WTO after 1995 where the judge would have exceeded its authority, the second comparing the WTO with operations of national judicial systems, specifically from the U.S. and the EC, and the third trying to show directions for the future.

To favor the debate, contributors coming from divergent backgrounds (economics, political science, and law) were confronted with a simulation case, designed to serve as a benchmark and reproduced in the Appendix. They engaged in a series of discussions on the role of the judicial branch of the WTO, notably regarding the level of deference to be granted to national authorities of Member States, with references to particular problems such as the obstruction of trade for health or environmental purposes, the place to be granted to the civic society and various captivating issues.

Debating does not mean reaching unanimity, and thus the result of the conference was a mix of overlaps and divergences. What is important is that progress was made, everybody agreeing the WTO is in need of some form of evolution, the present state being unsatisfactory. In that perspective, the cross-fertilization of ideas occurring in such meetings shows our modest—but hopefully important—involvement in that evolutionary process.

This volume constitutes our contribution to an existing dialogue that has been taking place for some time now in various fora. Our aim was to provide added impetus to continue this dialogue. The fourth World Trade Forum convinced its participants that a multi-disciplinary approach in this context is highly recommended.

The World Trade Forum could not have taken place without the active involvement and support of the participants. Once again, we want to thank the participants and especially the Silva Casa Foundation, which very generously has been supporting our conferences and largely contributing to their success. Last but not least, we would like to thank our associate editor Patrick Blatter for all his work, Wulfhard Stahl, the WTI librarian, and the people at the University of Michigan Press for their commitment to our project.

Papers and discussions reflect the state of play by the end of 2000. Later developments—beyond the first five years of the Appellate Body and the new system—are only referred to incrementally. – The Editors

The Role of the Judge in International Trade Regulation: An Overview

Petros C. Mavroidis and Thomas Cottier

The coming-into-being of the WTO Appellate Body in 1995 itself was not met with enthusiasm in all corners. Expert commentators cast doubt as to the need to have a second look at the same case and there was a feeling that the establishment of the Appellate Body corresponded more to the political need to have a counter-weight against the loss of sovereignty resulting from the passage to negative consensus, implying that the WTO is now the only truly multilateral system where disputes will always be resolved through third party adjudication.

On the other hand, proponents of a two-instances system pointed to the fact that the Appellate Body would be the essential permanent feature in WTO adjudication thereby contributing to more coherence in jurisprudence. It is undeniable that before the Appellate Body came into the picture, the GATT Legal Affairs Division was the only permanent feature in the adjudication process, since the composition of Panels varied over time and over case depending on the preferences of the parties to a dispute. Generally, the most successful, and only a handful of, Panelists were selected four or five times (sometimes more often) in a total of over a hundred and twenty disputes brought before a Panel. With the advent of the Appellate Body, the prospects of continuity and coherence increased.

By August 2000, the Appellate Body had already issued 34 reports (54 by April 2003). The members of the Forum felt that this was a critical mass that now allows commentators to pronounce on the quality of the work done in Geneva. Although contributions focused on both Panel and Appellate Body reports, it is true that the main focus of the discussions evolved around the work of the Appellate Body.

This approach seems warranted for two reasons: first, with very few exceptions, Panel reports were appealed in the first five years; second, the Appellate Body is the last word, the *ultima ratio* in the WTO adjudication process. And since the Appellate Body's review is confined to legal issues only, although its reports bind only their addressees, they inherently carry a message for a wider public.

Having said so, we should quickly point out that there is nothing like binding precedent or *stare decisis* in WTO law. It is, however, an incentive-compatible structure for the Appellate Body to ensure, through its jurisprudence, that it applies the same law to the same issues independently of the parties to the dispute.

One of the rather surprising features of the WTO Dispute Settlement Understanding (DSU) is that, whereas there exists a specific provision (Art. 11 DSU) obliging Panels to always ensure that they make an objective assessment of the matter before them, there is nothing like a corresponding Article to the same effect obliging the Appellate Body to respect a standard of review.

This omission is of hardly any importance, though, for even if the Art. 11 DSU-equivalent were foreseen in the DSU and imposed on the Appellate Body, the question to ask would be what does objective assessment actually amount to and which body will judge whether the Appellate Body has adhered to this standard?

The Appellate Body has already developed a noteworthy jurisprudence in the context of Art. 11 DSU. Referring to the dispute between the European Community and the United States on *Wheat Gluten,* the Appellate Body for the first time found that a Panel had not respected the Art. 11 DSU standard: in the case at hand, the Panel had erroneously accepted that a declaration by a U.S. attorney before the Panel amounted to a finding by the U.S. government authority which was attacked before the Panel.

Who would judge the Appellate Body, though? There is nothing like a formal multilateral control of its performance. There is, however, an informal control. Evidence of this is provided by the upheaval in Geneva following the Appellate Body's initiative to invite *amicus curiae* briefs in the context of the *Asbestos* litigation. The overwhelming majority of the WTO Membership put into question the well-foundedness of the Appellate Body's initiative arguing that the frontier between the judiciary and the legislative function had, as a result, been blurred. This was perhaps the most polite way to formulate a series of interventions the crux of which was a message that the Appellate Body had trespassed its authority.

This is neither the time nor the place to pronounce on this issue. It is clear, however, that from a strictly legal perspective, it is the Membership which through its appointments will *ex ante* ensure that the quality of Appellate Body reports will be preserved.

Ex post, the civic community discusses the activities of the WTO adjudicating bodies and through its writings gives or denies its vote of confidence.

The participants of the Forum this year were requested to tackle the role of the judge in international trade regulation. To this effect a simulation case (see Appendix) was designed to serve as the benchmark. The reasons why such a benchmark was preferred to the actual panel and Appellate Body's case law could be synopsized as follows: it was felt that by using a simulation case, the case law of Panels and the Appellate Body could in any way serve as the basis for the various reactions; the question of the standard of review is more relevant in cases where trade is obstructed for non-economic motives (health, environment, etc.). In such cases, where the stakes are really high, it is important to see whether the international trade judge adopts a more deferential attitude or whether the standard of review applied is the same as in any other case brought before the WTO: The simulation case, accordingly, focused on a health-based trade-obstructing measure. Moreover, this is the area where most of the criticism against the WTO comes from: the jurisprudence in the field of trade and health and/or trade and environment.

The problem, of course, is what is the appropriate benchmark according to which we should assess whether the WTO judge (Panelist or member of the Appellate Body) has honored his/her commitment. And this in itself is a crucial issue: Should we pay more attention to the reactions of the addressees? To the reactions of the civic community? To the intellectual integrity of the argument put forward by the judge independently of the reactions?

The Forum tried to respond to all of the above questions. To do that, the first category of papers placed the simulation case before a different level of integration and each time requested responses according to the applicable positive law: the federal level (the United States), the quasi-federal level (the European Union) and the international level (the WTO). Then, the second category of papers asked the question whether the different level of integration in itself argues in favor of a different standard of review to be followed by the judge depending on whether he/she is sitting on the bench of a national or an international court.

In the first category of papers, *in concreto,* Robert Howse and William Davey aimed, through their papers, at responding to the question whether, in all cases submitted to the WTO since January 1, 1995, the WTO judge has exceeded his/her authority. The first paper focused more on the Appellate Body case law, the second on the Panels' record. They both reached the same conclusion, namely that the WTO judge has operated within the limits imposed by Art. 3.2 DSU: judges are agents who have to respect the legislative mandate as defined by the principals, the WTO Members. Howse argued that the debate should rather focus on the conception of the judicial process and its relationship with the interpretation of WTO law. For Davey, the WTO dispute settlement system could make a greater use of what he termed "issue-avoidance" techniques to dispose of certain specific cases, provided that clear standards be used in order to avoid inequalities of treatment among members.

In his comments to the paper, Ernst-Ulrich Petersmann, on the one hand shared the conclusions reached by Davey, but on the other urged the WTO judge to adopt a more human rights-oriented and inspired attitude. In his mind, it is crucial for the legitimacy of the WTO adjudicating bodies as such to recognize the increasing role that the civic society is playing. Frieder Roessler's oral comments revolved around the institutional equilibrium that was struck by the Uruguay round agreements and put into question by the recent case law of the Appellate Body in the *India - Balance-of-payments* and *Turkey - Textiles* cases. On both occasions, the Appellate Body affirmed the competence of WTO adjudicating bodies to adjudicated disputes that were also pending before WTO Committees. In Roessler's mind, such judicial activism can put into question the function of the whole WTO edifice since the judiciary requests a share larger than forecasted in the Uruguay Round Agreements.

We then moved to papers that examined the simulation case under the prism of a particular body of law. The first set of papers was the U.S. response to the simulation case. Donald Regan advanced the point that, independently of the eventual formulation of a U.S. court's decision, the U.S. judge will invariably ask the question whether the intention of the competent authority was indeed to promote a health goal or conversely, whether the intent was to simply protect the local producer. He took the stand that in whatever context, national or international, the judicial review should concentrate on purpose, and not on balancing. Diane Wood took a more nuanced approach. In her view, the U.S. judge will focus on the effects of a particular measure and work with procedural requirements. She thought that the WTO would be well-inspired to emulate with the best of member-states judicial systems, particularly on procedural issues.

Gary Horlick, in his comments, stated that the questions of deference would be linked to the legitimacy of the WTO itself. He also asked the question how it is possible to detect intentions especially since preparatory work of legislation is often impenetrable or difficult to clarify. Joel Trachtman added to this problematic by arguing that it is frequently the case that multiple objectives are sought through the very same piece of legislation. Contrarily to Professor Regan's opinion, he defended judicial balancing as a possibly efficient solution in the U.S. federal, European Union, or WTO context.

Piet Eeckhout provided the response by the EC judge to the simulation case. His main points focused on the proportionality-test as applied by the EC courts. In his view, albeit with minor exceptions, the EC judge will apply a necessity-test, that is, he/she will ask whether a less restrictive measure exists which can reach the objective sought, and not a *stricto sensu* proportionality-test, that is, he/she will not strike down the least restrictive measure in light of the fact that other objectives will be negatively influenced as a result. In Michel Waelbroeck's view, the authority of the EC judge as accurately described by Eeckhout is the direct consequence of the quasi-federal structure of the European Community. Jacques Bourgeois' oral comment added that the EC judge's powers evolve indeed as the European Community itself evolves. In his mind, there is an undeniable dynamic aspect in this discussion, in the sense that as the European Community progresses towards more integration so will the EC judge's powers increase.

Two papers examined the response to the simulation case in light of the current WTO law. Joost Pauwelyn first acknowledged the fact that, contrary to the WTO Antidumping Agreement, where a deferential standard of review was explicitly inserted in the Agreement (Art. 17.6), the WTO SPS Agreement knows of no explicit standard of review. Hence, the judge had to create a standard for health cases, and Article 5.5 SPS is where the focus should be, as some of its elements need clarification. Mitsuo Matsushita, a former member of the Appellate Body himself, focused on the fact that the Appellate Body is mindful of the specificities of health cases. This, the absence of an explicit deferential standard notwithstanding, led it to adopt a *in dubio pro mitius* standard, although its *Hormones* decision, for example, was criticized for being too deferential.

Steve Charnovitz offered comments to the effect that the Appellate Body, through its recent case law, has corrected the approach that Panels used to take in the first trade and environment cases. In his mind, regulatory diversity obliges that the right of individual WTO Members to protect environment or health should not as such be put into question as long as the letter of the WTO Agreement is observed. David Palmeter insisted on the fact, already mentioned by Pauwelyn, that WTO negotiators showed considerable deference towards antidumping and not towards health. While not putting into question the fact that health issues deserve a more cautious approach by the judge, he expressed his uneasiness with a series of imprecise responses provided by the Appellate Body in its case law.

Natalie McNelis provided a comparative analysis of all papers presented above. She first examined in her paper whether there is an overlap in the legislative mandate in the U.S.-, the EC-, and the WTO-legal order. She then asked the question whether the judicial review standard adopted in each of the three legal standards is the same or not. And she finally responded to the question how the different standards of review influence the outcome of each legal order. Three commentators reacted to her paper. Merit Janow focused on the comparison between the U.S. and the WTO law. In her view, the different levels of integration *per se* legitimize the variance in the response. A very similar response was provided by George Bermann, who focused on the comparison between the EC and the WTO law. Without assimilating the European Community to a full-fledged federal state, Bermann still made the point that the Community is an ever-integrating process and insisted on the political willingness widespread among EC Member states' governments to continue the process. André Sapir (oral comment) offered a similar perspective. In his view, the level of integration should be reflected in the attitude of the judge. Other concerns, however, count as well: the expertise of the judge, the role of expert witnesses, etc.

Henrik Horn and Petros C. Mavroidis had a different task: to provide an overview of the panel and Appellate Body case law in the field of the SPS Agreement and then give their assessment as to its well-foundedness. In their view, all breakthroughs in modern economic analysis relating to detecting intentions are heavily influenced if the assumptions on which outcomes are based change. Hence, in the absence of a generic standard to be employed in all health cases, a certain amount of political protectionism is needed for the institution as such to avoid moving into unwarranted adventures. For them, the Appellate Body case law with respect to Art. 5.5 SPS for example, is too daring. Richard Baldwin, orally commenting on the paper, felt more confident about the insights of economic theory in this respect and requested a more daring approach. In his view, modern economic theory can offer solutions even to a thorny issue like trade and health.

Thomas Cottier and Matthias Oesch addressed what they called the paradox of judicial review. They detected standards of deference in national or regional courts in administrative, but not civil, matters relating to external economic relations, while the WTO Panels and the Appellate Body are called upon for fully and *de novo* legal assessment under the rules of the Vienna Convention on the Law of Treaties. This can be explained by structural differences between national, regional, and international law, and the absence of a constitutional doctrine on the international level. Separation of powers, allocating appropriate functions of the judiciary, need to be discussed in a comprehensive manner, including the international and global level. This will entail a process of constitutionalization of WTO law and jurisprudence, allowing to determine in a more nuanced manner the proper role and province of the judicial branch. The authors argued that the current WTO architecture suffers from the fact that it scarcely resembles a constitution. In their view, a constitutional approach is warranted. This would imply not only changes in substantive law, in terms of a new enlarged WTO mandate, but also in the procedural aspects as to who participates in the meetings, etc.

Robert Howse and Kalypso Nicolaidis discussed the optimal standard of review for trade and health cases. Their papers were a look into the future, unconstrained by the existing legislative mandate given to the judge. They asked the question of the political legitimacy of the WTO. In their view, the WTO is a mere intergovernmental contract aiming to promote trade liberalization. Hence, the treaty should not be light-heartedly putting into question democratic choices reached at the domestic level.

Marco Bronckers, in his oral comments, insisted on the fact that a more enlarged WTO mandate requires a more serious discussion on the criteria under which new items should be brought under the WTO auspices. He cast doubt, however, as to the validity of the proposition that an enlarged mandate *ipso facto* leads to increased legitimacy of the institution. Joseph Weiler, orally commenting, compared the EC with the WTO process. He noted the absence of equivalence in the WTO of judicial restraint (in the form of *Keck and Mithouard* as we know it from ECJ case law) notwithstanding the fact that the WTO is, as expressly acknowledged in its mandate, a much less ambitious process. He sided with those who recommended caution, a first do-no-harm approach, to the WTO judge when tackling trade and health issues and argued in favor of the thesis that the judge cannot see his/her mandate independently of the context within which she operates.

Part I: Does the WTO Judge Trespass His Mandate?

CHAPTER 1

The Most Dangerous Branch? WTO Appellate Body Jurisprudence on the Nature and Limits of the Judicial Power

Robert Howse

The creation of a judicial power at the World Trade Organization is now widely understood to be among the most fundamental and perhaps fateful innovations of the Uruguay Round of multilateral trade negotiations. Under the GATT, decisions of panels (increasingly) bore some of the marks of adjudication, but they remained, in the end, diplomacy by other means. The decisions were the product of *ad hoc* panels, mostly staffed by officials or retired officials of national governments, who, to some important extent, were guided in their rulings by an expert staff of international civil servants, the bureaucratic power of the GATT. Moreover, to have legal effect, of course, these rulings needed to be adopted by the membership of the GATT, and the practice was that such adoption must occur by consensus.

With the WTO Dispute Settlement Understanding, the role of the panels remained much as it had evolved in GATT practice—but superimposed on that process was a new judicial power, that of the Appellate Body, a standing corpus of expert jurists, operating with a supporting professional staff, but clearly independent of the WTO political organs and the secretariat.[1] Moreover, reports of panels (to the extent not reversed or modified on appeal) and of the Appellate Body were to be adopted as a legal binding settlement of the dispute, unless a negative consensus existed *against* adoption (effective automaticity). Thus, with respect to the interpretation of the law in any particular dispute, the last word would now, normally, be that of the Appellate Body, an independent judicial tribunal, operating, however, in a world whose official culture remained dominated by the values of bureaucracy and diplomacy, not those of the law.[2] Even strong proponents of the juridification of the multilateral trading system, such as John Jackson, had never gone so far as to advocate relinquishing altogether political or diplomatic control over the results of dispute settlement.[3]

Acknowledgements: As usual, my greatest debt is to Petros Mavroidis, for our many exchanges about some of these cases, and the underlying issues, from which I have learned enormously. I have also learnt much of relevance from Arthur Appleton, Bill Davey, Yvo De Vries, Jyoti Larke, Kalypso Nicolaidis, and Werner Zdouc.
Email: rhowse@umich.edu.

As someone who came to the law after a first career in diplomacy and foreign policy-making, it has been fascinating for me to observe the clash of values that has manifested itself in the reactions of the official WTO culture to the first five years of WTO appellate jurisprudence. It has been equally fascinating to see the minds of practiced jurists on the AB puzzle over, and sometimes be manifestly exacerbated by, the way legal rules have been understood and employed within a bureaucratic and diplomatic culture.

One kind of criticism that has been made of the Appellate Body within, or by those close to, official WTO culture is that, in certain cases, the Appellate Body has exceeded its authority, or its grant of power under the DSU. The notion that an adjudicative body has exceeded its authority or jurisdiction finds its place in the international law of arbitration (it is often one of the grounds on which an arbitral award may be challenged by appeal either to a domestic or an international tribunal[4]) and is present also in the municipal administrative law of some states. In practice, such a notion usually amounts to reconsideration of the substantive legal interpretations of the original adjudicator although it is purportedly a much more deferential standard than review for error of law. At the same time, since a finding of lack of jurisdiction essentially vitiates the *bona fides* of the original judgment altogether, it can lead to harsh and sometimes unfair consequences.[5] Since, as will be discussed in the first section of the paper below, it is very unclear to whom one could take a complaint about excess of Appellate Body jurisdiction, given that the AB is a tribunal of last resort, one can question whether this notion can have any real legal meaning in the WTO system.

From my own perspective as legal academic, given the kind of moral and intellectual ground from which I aspire to engage with the jurisprudence, the notion of excess of authority or jurisdiction is a troubling way of articulating disagreement with legal interpretations of the AB, including interpretations of the judicial function itself, for this idea buys into a highly positivistic, and quite problematic and contestable, view of the relationship between law and legitimacy. Judges have often acted abominably when they have viewed themselves, or justified themselves, in those terms (South Africa under Apartheid and antebellum America are examples explored in recent literature[6]). Conversely, judges have often behaved admirably when they have pushed the formal limits of their authority as established in positive law. Indeed, there is a strong case that judicial review of government action against constitutional norms—a practice that is increasingly accepted as a requirement of liberal democracy—had its origins in a judicial self-assumption of power or authority with a weak foundation in pre-existing positive law.[7]

And it is far too simplistic to claim that, with its insistence on fidelity to the treaty texts, the AB has brought on itself criticism on the standards of narrow formalism or positivism. For, as I have argued elsewhere,[8] from the very start, the AB balanced its emphasis on taking seriously the ordinary meaning of the exact words of the treaty with an equal emphasis on the interpretation of those words in light of context, object and purpose.[9]

In this paper, I argue that, in all of the prominent instances where the AB has been accused of exceeding its authority, it has based itself upon a defensible interpretation of WTO law, consistent with the interpretive rules and principles in the Vienna Convention on the Law of Treaties. However, in making its own legitimate interpretive choices, the AB has necessarily been influenced by a conception of the judicial process, and its place within the WTO system as a whole; the real debate ought to focus on this conception and its interrelationship with the interpretation of WTO law. The cases I consider are: *Periodicals,*[10] *Turtles,*[11] *Steel*[12] (the amicus issue solely), *India Balance of Payments,*[13] and *Turkish Textiles.*[14]

1. The Authority of the Appellate Body and Its Basis in the WTO Treaties

There is no single provision of the WTO treaties which establishes the legal status or authority of the Appellate Body. We can only understand that status or authority once we examine, and *interpret,* a range of treaty provisions, and not only those contained in the Dispute Settlement Understanding. Most obviously relevant to the authority of the Appellate Body are three kinds of provisions in the DSU: 1) those that state what the Appellate Body *may* do; 2) those that state what it *must* do; and 3) those that state what it *may not* do. Anything within 1 and 2, will be within the AB's authority. Anything in 3, will be outside it. Art. 17.13 of the DSU states that the "[t]he Appellate Body may uphold, modify or reverse the legal findings and conclusions of the panel." Art. 19.1 provides that the AB may, in addition to recommending that a Member bring its measures into conformity, when the Appellate Body concludes that a measure is inconsistent with a covered agreement, "suggest ways in which the Member concerned could implement the recommendations." As for things that the Appellate Body must do, these include: staying "abreast of dispute settlement activities and other relevant activities of the WTO" (Art. 17.3); drawing up its own working procedures in consultation with the Chairman of the DSB and the Director-General; addressing each of the issues of law covered in the panel report or any legal interpretations of the panel that has been raised in the appellate proceeding (Arts. 17.6 and 17.12); recommending that a Member bring its measure into conformity when that measure has been found inconsistent with a covered agreement; keeping confidential submissions from parties and third parties (18.2); providing an opportunity for third parties to make written and oral submissions. Now, as for 3, the things that the Appellate Body, or its Members, shall *not* do, these include: entertaining *ex parte* communications concerning matters under its consideration; adding to or diminishing the rights and obligations provided in the covered agreements (19.2); sitting on cases that would create "a direct or indirect conflict of interest"; entertaining requests by the appellant for a review of findings of fact, unless directly connected to, or inseparable from, "issues of law covered in the panel report and legal interpretations developed by the panel," inasmuch as Art. 17.6 states that "[a]n appeal shall be limited" to those matters.

This is not a comprehensive list, but several important features of the manner in which the AB authority is articulated in the DSU are already evident. First of all, the drafters clearly did not choose to delimit the AB's authority by simply specifying what it *could* or *must* do, on the principle that what was not specified could be *assumed* to be outside the AB's authority and *im*permissible. Hence, a host of provisions that effectively say what the AB *cannot* do. Secondly, and consistent with this first observation, there are many things that the AB can and arguably must do, based upon what is implicit in the nature of the role of an appellate court, that are not specified at all in the DSU. Take, for instance, consideration of written and oral submissions by the appellant and the appellee. While, as noted, the DSU provides for rights of third party intervention, it says nothing about representations by the parties themselves before the Appellate Body! The DSU would thus appear to give more rights to third parties than to parties. But, of course, that is nonsense. The right of third parties to intervenor standing in a proceeding is not obvious and uncontroversial in international law generally.[15] Thus, while appellate jurisdiction might logically and obviously imply an obligation to hear the parties, and perhaps a discretion to hear third parties, it is understandable that the *right* of third parties to be heard might need to be specified in the treaty. The broad power of the Appellate Body to define its own authority, within the general parameters of the DSU, established by Art. 17.9—which makes the judges masters and mistresses of their own procedure—is thus crucial to the effective operation of appellate review, as so many of the particulars of the judicial role are left un- or underspecified in the DSU itself.

Nevertheless, there is a range of provisions of the DSU which arguably can and should guide the AB in this exercise of self-definition. First of all, there are provisions that go to the purposes of the dispute settlement system as a whole. Art. 3.2 states that there is, among the functions of the system, one to clarify the existing WTO law "in accordance with customary rules of interpretation of public international law." The AB has interpreted this provision as incorporating the obligations on treaty interpreters that are imposed in Art. 31 of the *Vienna Convention on the Law of Treaties.*[16] DSU Art. 3.3 states that a "prompt settlement" of disputes is "essential to the effective functioning of the WTO." DSU Art. 3.10 states that "[i]t is understood that . . . the use of dispute settlement procedures should not be intended or considered as contentious acts and that, if a dispute arises all Members will engage in these procedures in good faith and in an effort to resolve the dispute." As already noted, the DSU specifically prohibits rulings of the dispute settlement organs from spilling over into the making of new law (19.2). The drafting here might seem to reflect crude or naïve positivistic assumptions about a clear identifiable line between interpretation and development of the law. However, if we did refer back from this limitation on the AB to the original use of the formula about not diminishing or adding to existing rights and obligations in DSU—this occurs in the same paragraph (3.2) that refers to the customary rules of interpretation of public international law. These rules, especially as reflected in *Vienna Convention* Art. 31, give a dynamic or evolutionary dimension to the interpretation of *existing* rights and obligations, with subsequent agreements and practice between the parties, as well as other rules of international law (including rules that arise subsequent to the original obligations) to be taken into account.[17] It is really these customary rules of interpretation that allow the line to be drawn between interpretation and (impermissible) lawmaking in a manner consistent with the needs of the international system—when the AB is interpreting existing provisions in accordance with the customary rules (including their dynamic dimension) it is not, impermissibly, adding or diminishing to existing obligations.

Of considerable and unappreciated significance, however, in understanding the scope of the authority of the Appellate Body is the non-finality of its rulings as interpretations of WTO law. Art. IX:2 of the WTO Agreement (Marrakesh Protocol) states that "[t]he Ministerial Conference and the General Council shall have exclusive authority to adopt interpretations of this Agreement and the Multilateral Trade Agreement." Thus, any interpretation of WTO law invoked by the AB in the settlement of a particular dispute may be superseded by a definitive interpretation by the political organs of the WTO. Such an interpretation may be adopted by a three-fourths majority of the membership. While there is effective automaticity with respect to AB rulings as settlements of the particular dispute, this is balanced by ultimate political control of the legal interpretations that the AB makes. However, while a three-fourths vote is always possible, the WTO Agreement reaffirms the general pre-existing GATT practice of decision by consensus. Thus, the AB finds itself in a very special situation—because of the problems of decision-making in the political bodies of the WTO, its decisions are likely to have a kind of *de facto* finality as interpretations of the law, even if they lack *de jure* finality.

This leads us to reflect on what would be the legal consequences or remedies, in a situation where the AB was claimed to have exceeded its authority. Along the lines just discussed, subject to obtaining the requisite three-fourths majority, the membership could clarify the extent of that authority through an authoritative interpretation of the relevant DSU provisions. However, as we have already noted in the arbitration context, where a tribunal acts outside of its jurisdiction, its ruling should normally be a nullity. Because of effective automaticity in adoption by the DSU, there is little scope for control of this kind over excess of authority. Moreover, in the absence of negative consensus, the report must be "unconditionally accepted" by the parties to the dispute. Perhaps, however, a waiver might be available—the "unconditionally accepted" language arguably cannot prevent an affected party from applying for a waiver under the WTO Agreement, because in the event of a conflict between the WTO Agreement and, *inter alia,* the DSU, the relevant provision of the WTO Agreement prevails (XVI:3). However, as Davey and Zdouc observe, the jurisprudence suggests a very narrow conception of the notion of conflict between agreements, tending to limit a situation of conflict to one where it is impossible to comply with the obligations in both agreements[18] (the waiver would probably have to be phrased in terms of a waiver from the obligation to implement the adopted ruling). The voting rule for waivers is three-fourths, but again here the WTO Agreement supports the GATT practice of attempting to resolve such matters by consensus.

What about the possibility of review of the AB's exercise of jurisdiction by the International Court of Justice? Because the WTO is not a specialized agency of the United Nations, the advisory jurisdiction of the ICJ does not apply; if the WTO were to have such status, it could be authorized by the General Assembly of the UN to seek advisory opinions from the ICJ, and the issue of Appellate Body jurisdiction would be the kind of matter that would be appropriate, arguably, for the ICJ to hear in its advisory capacity.[19] What about a contentious ICJ proceeding pursuant to the ICJ's Art. 36(1) jurisdiction? Here, the WTO Member who seeks such review would run up against the obstacle to be found in the DSU provision that, absent negative consensus, the parties shall unconditionally accept AB rulings. However, it would be an interesting question as to whether, in a context where a party was contending that the AB was acting beyond its legal powers, the ICJ would accept such a provision as an effective ouster of its jurisdiction. In this context, it should be noted that the ICJ Statute 34(3) provides that "[w]henever the construction of the constituent instrument of a public international organization or of an international convention adopted thereunder is in question in a case before the Court, the Registrar shall so notify the public international organization concerned and shall communicate to it copies of all the written proceedings." This provision clearly supposes that, in appropriate cases, the ICJ will be construing constitutive instruments of public international organizations, not limited to organs and the specialized agencies of the United Nations.

In light of this general discussion of the authority of the AB, I now proceed to discuss those instances where it has been most susceptible to accusations of exceeding its authority.

2. The Fact/Law Distinction and "Completing the Analysis": *Periodicals* and *Turtles*

It will be recalled that "appeals" are limited to issues of law in the panel report and other legal interpretations developed by the panel. The choices explicitly available to the AB in disposing of the appeal are to uphold, reverse, or "modify" the findings or legal interpretations of the panel. From early on, beginning with *Reformulated Gasoline,* the Appellate Body engaged, selectively, in a practice that it called, and is now widely known as, "completing the analysis." That is, where the panel has made an error of law in finding a violation of a covered agreement, the AB, instead of simply reversing the finding, has instead proceeded to apply a correct interpretation of the law to the factual record. This means that, even though the appellant has won the appeal on the error of law claimed in their factum, they can nevertheless be found to be in violation of a provision of the covered agreements. The AB will, generally, only complete the analysis where the existing factual record is adequate to allow it to do so (*Salmon*). However, in the *Turtles* case, the AB itself engaged in fact-finding with a view to completing the analysis. It is useful to consider both separately and tandem "completing the analysis" on the existing adequate factual record and fact-finding by the AB, as possible excesses of the AB's authority. Further, in *Periodicals, Gasoline* and *Turtles,* the AB's completion of the analysis involved the application of particular treaty provisions or language not applied by the panel. This is in itself a discrete aspect of the issue of whether completing the analysis is within the AB's authority. Having disaggregated some of the issues raised by completing the analysis, let us begin our examination by considering the AB's own justification for this practice.

In *Periodicals,* the Canadian appellant challenged *one aspect* of the jurisdiction of the Appellate Body to complete the analysis, namely the application to the facts of a specific clause or provision not the subject of the appeal or cross-appeal. In that case, the Appellate Body had reversed the panel's finding of a violation of the first sentence of Art. III:2 of the GATT, based upon mixed considerations of law and fact—the factual underpinnings of the legal analysis by the panel were sufficiently flawed as to taint the legal analysis itself. As the AB noted, for this very reason, there was not an adequate factual record to which the AB could then apply the law. So instead, the AB went on to apply the second sentence of Art. III:2, which had not been applied by the panel for reasons of judicial economy, a violation of the first sentence having been found. Canada argued that since Art. III:2 was not appealed either by the appellant or in cross-appeal by the appellee, the AB had no jurisdiction to complete the analysis with respect to the second sentence of Art. III:2. The AB responded as follows: "[W]e believe the Appellate Body can, and should, complete the analysis . . . in this case by examining the measure with reference to its consistency with the second sentence of Art. III:2, provided that there is a sufficient basis in the Panel Report to allow us to do so. . . . As the legal obligations in the first and second sentences are two closely-linked steps in determining the consistency of an internal tax measure with the national treatment obligations of Article III:2, the Appellate Body would be remiss in not completing the analysis of Article III:2." (p. 26) The AB also emphasized that the beginning point for completing the analysis is a reversal of a finding of law by the panel.

In my view, there is a range of textual provisions in the DSU that supports the practice of completing the analysis thus circumscribed by the AB. First of all, there is 3.3 of the DSU which refers to prompt settlement of disputes. As has been frequently noted by commentators, especially since there is no remand power in the DSU, the implication of not completing the analysis is that, even though the original complainant turns out to have a valid legal claim, they must commence a new dispute action in order to get that claim heard. Secondly, the DSU permits the AB not only to uphold or to reverse, but also to "modify" the findings of the panel. Thirdly, in providing that appeals should be confined to issues of law and legal interpretations developed by the panel, the DSU requires the Appellate Body to interpret the scope of an "issue of law." If "issues of law" were interpreted too narrowly, not only would the objective of prompt settlement of disputes be undermined but so would other objectives of the dispute settlement system. While the satisfactory resolution of disputes *inter partes* is a fundamental objective of the dispute settlement system, the system is also intended to provide "security and predictability" in the trading system to clarify the law (DSU 3.2). These goals may militate in favor of the Appellate Body not refraining from clarifying fully an "issue of law" raised in an appeal just because it has reversed a legal finding of the panel on narrower grounds. Where provisions of a single treaty article are closely related, as the AB considered to be the case with respect to the first and second sentences of Art. III, it hardly seems unreasonable for the AB to consider as an "issue" in the appeal the application of the article as a whole to the dispute in question.

Perhaps, then, the more pertinent question is what values and interests protected by the DSU would be undermined by so doing. In classic public international law, the jurisdiction of an arbitral tribunal is established by *compromis,* or agreement between the parties—the parties decide on exactly which questions they will submit themselves to the authority of the tribunal, and failure to decide the case exactly within the parameters of the *compromis* may result in the award being invalidated.[20] However, in the case of the

"Standing" Appellate Body, jurisdiction over the parties is not established by an agreement between them or *compromis*—the Appellant's notice of appeal along with the Appellee's response are *not* a *compromis.* The appellee is compelled to accept the jurisdiction of the AB by virtue of adhesion to the WTO covered agreements, provided that the notice of appeal has been correctly filed. In the case of *panel* jurisdiction, it should be noted, something of the tradition of the *compromis* is preserved, even under a system of compulsory jurisdiction. Thus, the parties can agree on the terms of reference for the panel, and the panel is prohibited from considering legal claims that fall outside those terms of reference, a limitation that the AB has interpreted quite strictly.[21] But the *default*—should the parties not agree—is standard terms of reference that allow the panel to address all relevant provisions. Perhaps then completing the analysis by the AB should be limited to those cases where the particular legal provision that the AB is applying in completing the analysis was encompassed within the terms of reference for the panel. In all of the cases discussed in this paper, the provisions that the AB went on to apply in completing the analysis were extensively canvassed in the panel proceedings, and discussed in the parties' submissions. This addresses concerns of predictability and uncertainty—if Members wish to have a legal provision excluded from the scope of an adjudication, they retain a secure means of doing so, which is to exclude that provision from the panel's terms of reference. At the same time, it has already been suggested that the right to make submissions, written and oral, is arguably implicit in the very notion of appellate review. Completing the analysis arguably undermines this right, in that the parties cannot rely on the notice of appeal in determining on which matters they need to make submissions. For these reasons, it would seem appropriate, where the AB is intending to complete the analysis, to provide parties, and perhaps indeed third parties, with notice that it so intends, so that parties and third parties are afforded the opportunity to be heard on the provisions in question, and indeed on the preliminary question of whether the necessary preconditions are present for completing the analysis, particularly the existence of an adequate factual record.

The classic argument in municipal legal systems for leaving to the trial adjudicator the task of applying the law as corrected by the appellate court to the facts sounds reasonable in a conception of institutional competence.[22] However, WTO panelists, unlike trial judges, could hardly be described as expert fact finders. Where the factual record established at trial is not itself defective, the AB does not have any particular disadvantage in relation to a panel; in fact, given the respective professional backgrounds of the AB members in comparison to those of most panelists, they may have an advantage at both. In municipal systems where remands exist, another advantage of leaving the application of the corrected law to the level of trial adjudication is that one can refer the matter back, i.e., remand it, to the original panel. Under the DSU the sole such remand mechanism is with respect to article 21.5 implementation issues.[23]

David Palmeter suggests a further reason why, if it were available, remand to the original panel would be superior to completing the analysis: "[W]hy is the Appellate Body's 'completing the analysis' a problem? It is a problem because it is the equivalent of *de novo* review, and *de novo* decisions of the Appellate Body do not themselves benefit from appeal. *De novo* decisions of the Appellate Body lack the primary benefit of appellate review which is a second, more focused look at a contentious issue by a group of individuals other than those who made the initial decision."[24] This is a strong point. However, the existence of contentious findings of law in a panel report does not guarantee appeal—for various reasons the parties may choose, strategically, not to risk an appeal, thereby allowing the panel report to be adopted with the findings in question not subject to a second look. There were lots of contentious findings, indeed findings of first impression, in the *Canadian Generic Medicines* ruling, yet because both parties were able to live with the *result,* it was not appealed.

One should also bear in mind Elihu Lauterpacht's observation that the relationship between an adjudicator of first instance and an appellate tribunal is vertical, as Lauterpacht reminds us: "the concept of appeal also reflects another assumption [besides that of the fallibility of judges] that those to whom appeal lies are as judges in some way better than, or superior to, those whose judgment is being reviewed."[25] A remand may simply result in a new appeal to the higher tribunal, which will likely end up making a final legal interpretation of the kind that it would have made anyhow had it completed the analysis. A final consideration is that, particularly on issues that have not been long settled in the jurisprudence, and even more particularly where the legal analysis is context- or fact-intensive (as the AB has interpreted Art. III analysis to be), an appellate tribunal may be able to give more adequate guidance to the lower tribunals, by illustrating the manner in which its legal interpretation is actually to be applied to the facts in context. To my mind, these various considerations suggest that, even if the DSU were amended to allow for remands, there would still be a role for "completing the analysis" in appropriate cases. But what if "completing the analysis" requires the AB to make finding of facts on its own? As already noted, the AB has stated that there may be situations where the factual record is so defective or inadequate that completing the analysis will be impossible. It refused to do so on such grounds, for example, in respect of the first sentence of III:2 *in Periodicals* as well as later in the *Salmon* case. But there may be other situations where the Appellate Body would be able to complete the analysis by doing some supplementary fact-finding of its own, i.e., where the failure of the trial adjudicator to make certain finding of facts is not *fatal* to completing the analysis. In *Periodicals* itself, the AB made findings of facts concerning the protective design of the Canadian measures at issue, based upon an official report of a public taskforce in Canada and the government of the day's response to that task force report. The documents in question presumably formed part of the factual *record* at trial, but the finding that the report and related statements of the government revealed a protectionist design or intent was, strictly speaking, a finding of the Appellate Body itself. In the *Turtles* case, however, according to one of the lawyers for the appellees, the AB went even further, in making findings of fact from evidence other than that already in the factual record at the panel level.[26] Here, Dr. Appleton would appear to be referring to facts that AB found about the operation of the U.S. scheme at issue through questioning of counsel for the U.S. at the oral hearing (paras. 177–91 and footnotes). There is the threshold issue of whether Dr. Appleton is correct to characterize such findings as findings of fact *simpliciter*. Does the characterization of a Member's legal and administrative practice for purposes of determining whether it conforms to WTO law constitute, in all instances, a finding of fact? In the *India Patents* case, the AB apparently took the view that a panel's interpretation of a Member's municipal law is reviewable by the AB as a finding of law.[27] However, the more recent, adopted *S. 301* panel ruling, held that it was called upon to "establish the meaning of Sections 301-310 [of the Trade Act of 1974] as factual elements and to check whether these factual elements constitute conduct by the U.S. contrary to its WTO obligations. The rules on burden of proof for the establishment of facts . . . also apply in this respect [footnote omitted]."[28] At the same time, the *S. 301* panel cited a decision of the ICJ which, even if it supposed that municipal law is a question of fact before an international tribunal, supposed equally that these kinds of findings of fact could be made through the adjudicator's own interpretation of the decisions of municipal tribunals.[29] The panel went on to note that its findings of fact had not only "evidence" submitted to the panel as their basis, but "examination of the text itself" and the "arguments submitted to us" (para. 7.31).

Thus, either findings concerning a Member's law, which in the broadest sense includes non-statutory elements of an administrative or institutional nature,[30] are findings of fact of a sort that need not be based on "evidence" placed into the record by the parties, or alternately they might be findings of law. In either case, they do not appear to be the kind of findings that it would be inappropriate, in principle, for an appellate tribunal to make. From the institutional competence perspective, an appellate judge may be more capable of interpreting legal and administrative practice than a trial adjudicator—especially if the trial adjudicator is a non-lawyer, and not a professional adjudicator, as is often the case for WTO panels.

The DSU requires, as already noted, that appeals be limited to issues of law in the panel report and other legal interpretations developed by a panel. But this simply means that appeal is not available against findings of fact by the panel—it does not prohibit the AB from finding facts where that is necessary and incidental to its role in correcting errors of law. So if that latter role can legitimately include completing the analysis in certain cases, it may also include on some occasions making findings of fact. But, as already noted, there are institutional limits on the ability of an appellate tribunal legitimately to engage in fact-finding, and so where completing the analysis requires that those limits be pushed too far, the AB will refrain from doing so.[31]

Apart from the notion that findings of fact concerning municipal law and its operation might fall within the institutional limits, how might those limits be drawn more generally? One issue is clearly resources—the extremely tight time frame for AB decision-making, and the staff resources assigned to it, would not support fact-finding, such as extensive *vive voce* testimony, consideration of detailed technical or scientific material, and so forth. The AB must decide whether it can legitimately make factual findings without the need to adduce new evidence of a kind that cannot be appropriately brought forward in an appellate hearing, given resources and the structure of appellate litigation, too. But we should remember that municipal appellate tribunals do find facts in certain instances and some of them not infrequently,[32] and one also should not exaggerate the resources and structural mechanisms available for more adequate fact-finding at the panel level. As the AB noted in *India Patents,* there is no discovery mechanism available for sifting of evidence in WTO panel procedure. Further, the resources available for extensive evidentiary hearings at the panel level at the WTO are far less than is the case for comparably complex municipal public law matters in states such as the U.S.[33]

This is far from an exhaustive or adequate statement about the institutional limits of appellate fact-finding at the WTO. But it is perhaps enough to show that the AB has, so far, operated well within those limits—confining its fact-finding to interpretation of government documents and of legal and administrative practices as described by counsel for the jurisdiction in question.[34]

3. *Amicus Curiae: Turtles* and *Steel*

In *Turtles,* the Appellate Body reversed a finding of the panel below that it did not have the authority to accept *amicus* submissions from non-governmental entities. The panel had considered that, since it had a right to "seek" information from any person pursuant to Art. 13 of the DSU, it was thereby prohibited from considering non-requested information. The AB held that the reading of the word "seek" as a prohibition of this kind ignored the context, which was a very broad grant of fact-finding authority to the panel, in order that the panel may discharge its Art. 11 obligation to make an "objective assessment of the facts" (paras. 107, 108). As well, the AB noted the semantic difficulties that would arise, were the term "seek" to be interpreted in the manner suggested by the panel. Since the panel is only legally *required* to consider information submitted by parties and third parties, the consideration of information from any other source entails a positive decision on the part of the panel to so exercise its discretionary authority, i.e., arguably to *seek* the information. In light of some commentary on the decision, it is important to note that the AB did *not* base the authority to accept *amicus* briefs on the right to "seek" information from any individual or body in Art. 13—it reversed an interpretation of the panel that the word "seek" in Art. 13 implies a *prohibition* on the acceptance of such briefs.[35] Instead, the AB held that the breadth of Art. 12 which allows a panel to create its own procedures, deviating from the default procedures in Annex 3 of the DSU, and Art. 13 enable in particular ways the panel to discharge its DSU Art. XI duty "to make an objective assessment of the matter before it, including an *objective assessment of the facts of the case and conformity with the relevant covered agreements* . . ." (para. 106 emphasis added by AB). In other words, subject to any explicitly limiting or prohibitive provisions in the DSU, the real scope of the panel's authority is defined by what is "indispensably necessary" to perform its functions under Art. XI. This is good sense, for—even taken together with the working procedures in Annex 3—the provisions of the DSU hardly amount to a comprehensive *code* of civil procedure or evidence.[36]

It is by appreciating the exact nature of the ruling in *Turtles* concerning the powers of *panels* to consider unsolicited *amicus* submissions, that we can understand its approach to the AB's own authority to consider such submissions. In *Turtles,* in preliminary rulings not reproduced in full in the AB final report, the AB accepted at least one *amicus* submission that was made directly to the Appellate Body, and not attached to a Member's submissions. Three other submissions were accepted as attachments to the U.S. brief—the appellees had challenged the right of the U.S. to attach material that was not an integral part of its brief. The AB admitted these submissions with the caveat that "considering that the United States has itself accepted the briefs in a tentative and qualified manner only, we focus in the succeeding sections below on the legal arguments in the main U.S. appellant's submission." (para. 91)

According to Dr. Appleton, the fact that the AB, in *Turtles,* did not give any basis for accepting the brief unattached to any Member's submission, suggests that it somehow retreated, given the challenge to its authority by the appellees, from its preliminary ruling accepting the unsolicited brief. Dr. Appleton opines: "Other than Article 16.1 of the Working Procedures, there would not appear to be a legal basis in either the Working Procedures or the DSU that would support the direct acceptance of such submissions. Unlike

Panels which are specifically granted the power to 'seek' information. In fact, its authority would seem to be constrained by DSU Article 17.6 which limits it, perhaps unrealistically, 'to issues covered in the panel report and legal interpretations developed by the panel.' "[37]

More recently, in the *Steel* case, the AB has affirmed explicitly its authority to consider unsolicited *amicus* briefs, thus seemingly disproving Dr. Appleton's theory of a retreat. The AB held: "[I]n considering this matter, we first note that nothing in the DSU or the *Working Procedures* specifically provides that the Appellate Body may accept and consider submissions or briefs from sources other than the participants and third participants in the appeal. On the other hand, neither the DSU nor the *Working Procedures* explicitly prohibit acceptance or consideration of such briefs. However, Article 17.9 of the DSU provides [that working procedures are to be drawn up by the Appellate Body]. This provision makes clear that the Appellate Body has broad authority to adopt procedural rules which do not conflict with any rules and procedures in the DSU or the covered agreements [footnote omitted]." (para. 39) In the footnote, the AB referred to 16(1) of the *Working Procedures* which allows a division to develop an appropriate procedure where a procedural question is not covered by existing rules of procedure.

I cannot see any flaw in this reasoning. However, it is useful to respond to a number of objections. Perhaps the silliest kind of objection is that the AB's authority is limited to what the DSU, along with the *Working Procedures,* explicitly specifies it can do. This is silly, because as discussed in the first section of this paper, if that were true, the AB would be paralyzed in the exercise of normal functions of appellate review—the DSU does not, as we discussed, even provide explicitly the AB with the power to hear the parties. A second, related but less silly, objection—actually argued by the EU in this case in opposing the AB's authority to accept *amicus* submissions—is that since in the case of panels, the authority to receive *amicus* briefs is grounded in an explicit right to seek information from any individual or body, this is the kind of authority that would have been granted explicitly by the DSU, if the AB were supposed to have it. This objection reposes in a misreading of the decision in *Turtles* with respect to the source of the panel's authority to consider *amicus* submissions—as we have noted above, while correcting the panel's view that Art. 13 did not prohibit a panel from considering unsolicited information, the AB found the authority to accept such information to be based on Arts. 12 and 13 of the DSU taken together, and read in light of the panel's duty to make an objective assessment of the matter, and the scope of authority implicit in that duty. This disposes of a further, and very closely related, objection raised by the EU in *Steel* and adumbrated in Dr. Appleton's interpretation of *Turtles:* the panel's authority to receive *amicus* submissions reposes on its authority with respect to fact-finding; the AB is prohibited from fact finding, therefore it cannot possibly have the authority to accept *amicus* briefs. The first premise of this pseudo-syllogism is incorrect, because the AB stated the scope of the authority of the panel in terms of *both* aspects of making an objective assessment of the matter—the duty to make an objective assessment of the facts *and* the applicability and conformity with the relevant agreements. Indeed, it would seem that the AB wanted to forestall the mistake in the first premise of the Appleton syllogism, for in the relevant passage, as cited above, the AB actually put both aspects of the duty of objective assessment of the matter—fact and law—in italics. As for the second premise of Dr. Appleton's syllogism, we have disposed of it at length in the previous section of the paper on the fact/law distinction.

A different objection, also made by the EU, is that the *discretion* to receive *amicus* submissions is inconsistent with the limitation of participatory *rights* to parties and third parties (i.e., to WTO Members). At one level, this objection is a *non sequitur*. It in no way follows that because x does not have a right to something, I do not have the authority to grant x that thing. At another level, much more sophisticated, the claim is that acceptance of unsolicited information by non-WTO Members is systemically incompatible with a mechanism that limits rights of participation to parties and third parties.

In the *S. 301* case (no aspect of which did the EU choose to appeal), the panel made the important observation that, even if the WTO system does not provide direct rights to non-Members but only to Member states, the fact that the rights and obligations in the WTO treaties, in many instances, affect the interests of non-state actors, may still be relevant to the interpretation of those rights and obligations: "[T]he GATT/WTO did *not* create a new legal order the subjects of which comprise both contracting parties or Members and their nationals. However, it would be entirely wrong to consider that the position of individuals is of no relevance to the GATT/WTO legal matrix . . . The very first preamble to the WTO Agreement states that Members recognize 'that their relations in the field of trade and economic endeavor should be conducted with a view to raising standards of living, ensuring full employment and a large and steadily growing volume of real income and effective demand, and expanding the production of and trade in goods and services.' "(paras 7.73-7.75)[38] Given the context of the *301* case, the panel necessarily focused on the indirect protection of the rights of traders afforded by the system, but many other interests of individuals are protected as well—for example, by the exceptions in Art. XX that permit otherwise GATT-inconsistent action that is necessary to protect various environmental or health interests of citizens.

Indirect access to dispute settlement proceedings through *amicus* submissions recognizes these realities, without thereby changing the nature of the system as one which grants or recognizes rights only among states parties to the treaties.

Yet another objection raised by the EU is that the DSU provides for confidentiality of AB proceedings, and that this is somehow incompatible with discretionary acceptance of *amicus* submissions. Confidentiality as a general rule, of course, differs from normal judicial process in liberal democracies throughout the world. The irony in the EU's objection is that the confidentiality constraint suggests that where the DSU wishes to place restrictions on the AB's authority that are inconsistent with normal judicial practice, it does so explicitly. But, in any case, there is no logical or structural incompatibility with the acceptance of written briefs from *amici* and confidential proceedings.

It should also be borne in mind that, while one basic purpose of dispute settlement is to settle disputes to the satisfaction of parties and perhaps of third parties with legal interests in the particular dispute, the DSU confers on the dispute settlement organs the broader role of clarifying the law (DSU 3.2). The dispute settlement organs, including the AB, must take into account both the objective of satisfactory settlement of disputes *inter partes* and the objective of clarification of the law. One might dare say that this latter objective is of particular importance in appellate review. Parties to a dispute may have many strategic reasons for making legal arguments in a particular way or avoiding other legal arguments altogether—complete party control over the scope of appellate legal interpretation may not serve the interests of clarification of the law. One response has been for the AB to take a very broad view of who may be a party or third party to a proceeding (see *Bananas*). Another response, articulated in *Hormones,* has been to balance party control of the legal claims to be considered by panels, and ultimately the AB, with the ability to consider legal *arguments* other than those raised by the parties (*Hormones,* para. 156). Likewise, the discretion to accept *amicus* briefs may be considered to be related to the AB's broader institutional role in clarifying the law.[39]

This does not exhaust the range of legal sources that suggest the appropriateness of an implicit authority to accept unsolicited *amicus* submissions. Art. 17.3 requires that AB Members "stay abreast" of dispute settlement activities of the WTO. *Opinio juris* is a source of international law, recognized in the ICJ Statute as such, and potentially to be drawn upon in WTO dispute settlement.[40] Appellate Body members have on at least one occasion been addressed by an independent academic on general legal issues (not albeit on a specific case under judicial consideration), according to some sources. They can be presumed to read law review articles, and perhaps in some cases draft manuscripts by publicists. And, of course, they are also briefed by their clerks. In all these respects, AB members receive advice about the law that is not controlled by the parties, or third parties to the proceeding, and of which parties and third parties may not even be aware.[41] The sources of information and advice may be broadened out by unsolicited briefs, and indeed *amicus* submissions may counter the danger that a court develops unconscious biases and blinkers with respect to what it reads, or seeks its legal ideas from.[42]

Another source of law (as provided in the ICJ statute) is judicial decisions. At the international level this includes not only the ICJ but also tribunals established to deal with specific kinds of disputes as well as the ECJ, the European Court of Human Rights, and the Inter-American Court of Human Rights. "Governments and tribunals refer to such decisions as persuasive evidence of law."[43] Moreover, the decisions of municipal courts and tribunals may also be relevant: "[D]ecisions of the United States Supreme Court have been relied on by arbitral bodies and have been cited by states in support of their claims."[44] These sources of law support the AB's interpretation of its scope of authority under the DSU. The European Court of Human Rights, pursuant to Article 55 of the European Convention on Human Rights, which, like 17.9 of the DSU, empowers the court to make its own rules and determine its own procedure, has permitted by its own rules the granting of an invitation or leave to "any person concerned" to "submit written comments within a time-limit and on issues which he shall specify."(Revised Rule 37.1) Even prior to these rules, the Court had exercised on occasion its general discretion to accept such submissions,[45] even though only Contracting States and the Commission could be Parties to such proceedings. In the case of the Inter-American Court of Human Rights, the Court has apparently received, and indeed formally noted, receipt of *amicus* submissions in numerous cases, while the Convention, the Statute of the Court and its Rules of Procedure are all apparently silent on the matter.[46] The Inter-American court practice may be of particular significance, since one sometimes hears it asserted that the practice of *amicus* submissions is somehow alien to non-Anglo-American, or developing country legal traditions. The U.S. Supreme Court accepted *amicus* briefs, even before *amicus* practice was codified in the rules. In municipal practice, the *amicus* as an institution has been more prominent in common law rather than civil law jurisdictions, which can be explained by the fact that, in the civilian context, there has not been the traditional assumption of party control of proceedings and therefore less of a need to create a special practice in order for the adjudicator to consider arguments or information outside the four corners of the parties submissions and the evidence that they adduce.[47]

While there are many interesting issues concerning the exact manner in which the AB should exercise its discretion to accept unsolicited *amicus* submissions, such as time limits, rights of response by parties or third parties, and so forth, those can be left to another day. My concern here has been simply to show that the AB acts within its legal authority in exercising discretion to accept such submissions.

4. AB Jurisdiction and the Interpretive Authority of the Political Organs of the WTO: *India Balance of Payments* and *Turkish Textiles*

As was noted in the first section of this paper, pursuant to the WTO Agreement, Art. IX:2, final interpretive authority with respect to the WTO treaties rests with the Ministerial Conference and the General Council of the WTO, who have the "exclusive authority" to adopt interpretations of the treaties that are legally binding on Members. It may be, however, that in certain cases, interpretation and application of particular treaty provisions by panels and the Appellate Body is actually prohibited, even in the course of adjudicating contentious cases, and conferred exclusively on some political body of the WTO.

This issue arose in the *India Balance of Payments* case, where the United States claimed that India was maintaining trade restrictions purportedly to protect its balance of payments, in contravention of the criteria for maintaining such restrictions, as set forth in Arts. XI and XVIII of the GATT. India argued that solely the Balance of Payments Committee and General Council of the GATT had the competence to review India's justification of its balance of payments restrictions under XVIII:B of the GATT 1994. The panel below found that the competence of the Balance of Payments Committee and that of the panel were not mutually exclusive in these matters. India appealed this finding. The AB first observed, in disposing of this appeal, that according to Article 1.1 of the DSU, the dispute settlement procedures in the DSU apply generally to disputes brought under the dispute settlement provisions of the covered agreements (in this case Art. XXIII of the 1994 GATT), and that furthermore the DSU rules and procedures are subject only to special or additional rules identified in agreements as listed in Appendix 2 of the DSU. The AB noted that "Appendix 2 does not identify any special or additional rules or procedures relating to balance of payments restrictions" (para. 86). In particular, it did not mention Art. XVIII:B of the GATT, which calls for review by the CONTRACTING PARTIES of balance-of-payments restrictions maintained on the basis of developmental considerations set out in XVIII:B. Thus, one could not infer any limitation on the rights of access to dispute settlement under the DSU, or on the competence of panels to interpret and apply the balance-of-payments provisions of the GATT, from the grant of competence to review XVIII:B justifications for such restrictions to the CONTRACTING PARTIES.

India, however, also argued that GATT practice with respect to Art. XXIII precluded access to dispute settlement for balance-of-payments purposes. Since Art. XXIII is the very basis on which DSU procedures may be invoked in the case of the GATT, practice with respect to Art. XXIII of the GATT *is* relevant to the ultimate scope and limits of authority of panels and the Appellate Body when they are applying the GATT. Here, however, whatever pre-existing GATT practice existed in this matter was codified and perhaps also modified by the *Balance of Payments Understanding* negotiated in the Uruguay Round. The second sentence of footnote 1 to the *BOP Understanding* reads: "[T]he provisions of Art. XXII and XXIII of GATT 1994 as elaborated and applied by the Dispute Settlement Understanding may be invoked with respect to any matters arising from the application of restrictive import measures taken for balance-of-payments purposes." Here, India argued that the expression "application" somehow limited the competence of the dispute settlement organs in balance-of-payments disputes, in favor of that of the membership, sitting as the Balance of Payments Committee. The distinction that India drew was between disputes about the "application" of Balance of Payments measures and those that concerned the substantive justification of the measures. The AB, however, held that the use of the word "application" merely reflected "traditional GATT doctrine that, with the exception of mandatory rules, only measures that are effectively applied can be the subject of dispute settlement proceedings" (para. 93).

But, at first glance, this very interpretation would seem to risk reducing the word to complete inutility—as *that* much, the AB is saying, has already been established by GATT practice. However, the *BOP Understanding* is intended to "clarify" Arts. XII and XVIII:B of the GATT. Such clarifications provide greater legal certainty and security, but will amount in large measure to restatements of what a sound treaty interpreter would already find to exist in the *status quo.* The assumption in treaty interpretation developed in *Reformulated Gasoline* and subsequent cases that each treaty provision should be assumed to have a discrete, non-redundant legal meaning may have to be modified in cases where the text being interpreted is an understanding that clarifies and largely affirms other, existing legal provisions.

The problem with the AB's reading is, however, with the semantic structure of the footnote. The footnote first asserts that "[n]othing in this Understanding is intended to modify the rights and obligations of Members under Articles XII or XVIII:B of GATT 1994." Then, the footnote goes on to express the situation with respect to XX and XXIII of the GATT in terms of the right to invoke these procedures in matters arising from application of BOP measures. Now if, as the AB suggests, the effect is simply to confirm existing rights under XXIII, then why was Art. XXIII not added to the list of GATT provisions containing rights and obligations that the *BOP Understanding* is not intended to modify?

The AB's interpretation of the word "application" is also undermined by the structure of Art. XVIII:B of the GATT itself. XVIII:B (9) contains the criteria for justification of BOP measures under XVIII:B, while XVIII:B (10) states certain conditions that a Member must adhere to in the application of its BOP measures, even if they are justified under XVIII:B (9). Thus, the relationship between XVIII:B (9) and XVIII:B (10) is not dissimilar to the relationship between the various lettered paragraphs of Art. XX and the *chapeau.* Thus, the most obvious interpretation of "application" in the footnote is that the *BOP Understanding* modifies rights and obligations under Art. XXIII of the GATT to the extent that it limits dispute settlement action under XXIII to claims that the *application* of BOP measures is inconsistent for the criteria for such application contained in XVIII:B (10), which would be consistent with exclusive competence for the BOP Committee with respect to review of justification of such measures under XVIII:B (9).

Despite all this, I believe that there are good legal reasons why the AB came to the conclusion that footnote 1, second sentence of the *BOP Understanding,* does not oust the jurisdiction of the dispute settlement organs to consider complaints related to the justification of BOP measures under XVIII:B (9). As the Appellate Body noted, the DSU itself purports to provide transparency with respect to any special procedures that might apply so as to modify or supplement DSU procedures in the case of particular covered agreements, and the *BOP Agreement* is not on the list. Art. 3.2 of the DSU provides, in part, that "[t]he dispute settlement system of the WTO is a central element in providing security and predictability to the multilateral trading system." Art. 23.1 of the DSU provides that redress of a violation of obligations or other nullification and impairment of benefits, *must* be had through DSU procedures. Whatever the best ordinary language interpretation of the word "application" in the context of Art. XVIII, there is a certain overall implausibility to the notion that, in the absence of any explicitly *restrictive* language, a footnote in an *Understanding* interpreting Art. XVIII of the GATT could alter another, more fundamental and general provision of the GATT, so as to qualify such basic provisions of the DSU as Art. 23.1. Thus, the *broader* interpretive context supports the reading of the Appellate Body.

India, however, made a further argument that the "institutional balance" in the WTO would be undermined if the dispute settlement organs were not to defer to the competence of the BOP Committee with respect to the justification of balance-of-payments measures. The AB's rejection of this argument has been criticized *in extenso* by Dr. Frieder Roessler.[48] Dr. Roessler concedes that the AB may be right that access to dispute settlement to adjudicate the justification of BOP measures does not, formally, undermine the competence of the BOP Committee to examine the justification of such measures. Nevertheless, "the legal alternatives formally available in one forum can be curtailed, or even reduced to inutility, by the creation of new legal opportunities in another. It is obvious that the process of reaching a consensus in the BOP Committee, as in any other WTO body, takes place in the shadow of the procedural alternatives available in the absence of a consensus and that these alternatives can effectively dictate the outcome of the process."[49] True enough, but this just begs the question about the correct balance. Under consensus decision-making in the BOP Committee, a single WTO Member can block a decision concerning the interpretation and application of Art. XVIII of the GATT. In the presence of such blockage, it would indeed seem to undermine institutional balance in the WTO to prevent the dispute settlement organs from acting to apply and interpret the law. The implication of Professor Roessler's suggestion that the dispute settlement organs desist, in the presence of inaction by the BOP, amounts to a single Member of the WTO impeding the application of the law altogether. The automaticity of adoption of panel reports, as well as the clear statement of rights to dispute settlement, in the WTO DSU testify to the increasing unacceptability of such a situation under the older GATT system, and to the resolve to create a very different kind of institutional balance in new WTO system.[50]

Where the BOP Committee has *acted* by consensus, that is another matter—here Dr. Roessler is surely right that there would be a strong case for the panels and the AB to be deferential to its views. But these views would likely amount to "subsequent practice" among the parties, within the meaning of Vienna Convention 31, and so the requisite institutional balance can be achieved through the dispute settlement organs simply applying the treaties in accordance with the customary rules of interpretation of international law. No special doctrine of restraint or deference is necessary. Moreover, Dr. Roessler's view of institutional balance is influenced by his assumption that "the rulings of the DSB emerge from a proceeding in which only the facts and claims submitted by the parties to the dispute are considered and the results of which are binding only on the parties to the dispute."[51] As we have seen, in our discussion of the *amicus* issue, the first part of this statement is not strictly true. There is no difficulty, through the *amicus* procedure, with the panels or Appellate Body considering information from or views of the IMF, nor—as might in some situations be even more appropriate—of various UN entities or organizations such as UNCTAD.

But there is a *sort* of *Kompetenz-Kompetenz* question buried in *India Balance of Payments* case, which Roessler almost—but not quite—reaches by his reference to the international law principle that a body has the right "in the first place" to determine the extent of its jurisdiction.[52] Of course, a true *Kompetenz-Kompetenz* question is really that of who, in the *last* resort, gets to decide or determine competences within a legal system.[53] While India argued that the panel did not have competence in the dispute, India did not argue that the panel did not have the power to determine, in the first instance, its competence in relation to that of the BOP Committee, and neither India nor the United States questioned the competence of the AB to make determinations on the extent and limits of the competence of the BOP Committee relative to that of the panels and itself, in the course of deciding an appeal. To my mind, this is important, and does solidify a certain shift in institutional balance between the old GATT system and the WTO. By virtue of effective automaticity, such determinations will be binding with respect to the specific dispute in question. Now, of course, true finality, strict *Kompetenz-Kompetenz*, rests with the membership as a whole, which can adopt by three-fourths vote an interpretation of a WTO treaty, and which has the exclusive authority to do so. However, since the general practice is not to adopt such interpretations save by consensus, in practice a very large role for the determination of competences now lies with the dispute settlement organs. This is broadly consistent with the evolving institutional role and logic of tribunals within international organizations and regimes.[54]

A similar issue of institutional balance arose in the *Turkish Textiles* case. In that case, Turkey purported to justify certain import restrictions as necessary to the implementation of a customs union with the EU, pursuant to Art. XXIV of the GATT. Art. XXIV allows the formation of customs unions and free trade areas among GATT Contracting Parties, subject to certain criteria being met. Art. XXIV does *not*—as is often assumed, or was before this case—provide a "carve out" from GATT obligations for members of a customs union or free trade area. However, there are certain GATT obligations that would simply render it impossible by definition to have a customs union or free trade area—in particular, Art. I, which would seem to exclude preferentiality, i.e., the application of a more favorable commercial policy as between members of the customs union or free trade area and other GATT Contracting Parties who are non-members of that area. Thus, Art. XXIV, in stating that the provisions of the GATT shall not *prevent* the *formation* of a customs union, provides relief for members of such a union from GATT obligations only to the extent that those obligations are inconsistent with the *very existence* of a customs union or free trade area. Article XXIV:7 provides that the CONTRACTING PARTIES are to review and make recommendations on whether a proposal for a customs union or free trade area is consistent with the various criteria in Art. XXIV. However, the CONTRACTING PARTIES may by two-thirds majority vote nevertheless approve proposals that do not strictly comply with the criteria, provided they "lead to the formation of a customs union or free trade area in the sense of this Article" (XXIV:10). The *Understanding on Article XXIV* negotiated in the Uruguay Round affirmed that "[c]ustoms unions, free-trade areas, and interim agreements leading to the formation of a customs union or free-trade area, to be consistent with Article XXIV, must satisfy, *inter alia,* the provisions of paragraphs 5, 6, 7 and 8." While also affirming the role of the membership, through the Council for Trade in Goods, in reviewing the consistency of customs unions and free trade agreements with Art. XXIV, the *Understanding* also provides that the dispute settlement provisions of Arts. XXII and XXIII of the GATT apply with respect to application of provisions of Art. XXIV relating to customs unions, free trade areas, and interim agreements. Clearly, this language parallels that in the *BOP Understanding.*

In the *Turkish Textiles* case, the panel did not have to decide the issue of whether the customs union in question actually conformed to the Art. XXIV criteria for the formation of a customs union or free trade area, since it was able to come to the conclusion that in any case the specific measures challenged were not needed to maintain a customs union, and thus could not be justified if otherwise inconsistent with the GATT. The panel, however, expressed some uncertainty as to whether it would have the competence to decide such a question, given the role of the membership, through the Council for Trade in Goods and its Committee on Regional Trade Arrangements, in deciding whether customs areas or free trade areas conform to the criteria in Art. XXIV. On appeal, in *dicta,* the AB suggested that on this issue reference should be had to its reasons in *India Balance of Payments* (para. 60). Moreover, the AB suggested that in some cases the judicial economy exercised by the panel appropriately in this case would not be possible—one might not always be able to come to conclusion about whether a measure is necessary for the maintenance of a customs union, without first ascertaining whether "the measure is introduced upon formation of a customs union that fully meets the requirements of sub-paragraphs 8(a) and 5(a) of Article XXIV" (para. 58).

Here again, Dr. Roessler appears to believe that the AB has undermined the institutional balance in the WTO system. I believe that a more careful examination of the matter will reveal that this is not so. Where a Member challenges a possibly otherwise GATT-inconsistent measure under the chapeau of XXIV:5, there are three possibilities: 1) the customs union or free trade area has been approved by the membership, either unconditionally or subject to certain conditions or recommendations being followed; 2) the customs union fails to meet approval after examination by the membership; 3) as in the *Turkish Textiles* case, the customs union or free trade area has been notified to the membership but no determination has been made as to its conformity with the criteria in Art. XXIV. Should 1) or 2) be the case, I find it hard to imagine that the panel or the Appellate Body would not defer to the judgement of the membership. Such deference would not result from lack of competence or jurisdiction of the dispute settlement organs—it would result from taking into account the decision of the membership as a subsequent agreement or subsequent practice of the parties within the meaning of Art. 31 of the Vienna Convention. The third case, however, is rather different. If the dispute settlement organs are called upon to decide, in the absence of action by the membership, whether—for purposes of justifying otherwise GATT-inconsistent measures—a customs union or free trade area is in conformity with Art. XXIV, what does deference or judicial restraint mean? Does it mean that the dispute settlement organs are to *assume* conformity? If so, then we would have the anomalous result that, through delay or disagreement, the Council on Trade in Goods and/or its Committee on Regional Trade Arrangements could produce a situation whereby the defendant could maintain GATT-inconsistent measures without having to prove one of the essential ingredients of the defense of such measures. The political organs of the GATT could thus frustrate the existing rights of the complaining Member under the treaty. This *would* disturb the institutional balance in the WTO. What of the converse? Suppose in the presence of inaction, the dispute settlement organs "defer" by simply saying that they have no competence to make an affirmative determination that the conditions of Art. XXIV have been met? Then, in that case, the defendant's treaty right to maintain the measures, provided they are required for a customs area or free trade area, could be undermined. This also would result in institutional imbalance. Thus, the clear solution, which undermines the rights of neither the complainant or the defendant, is for the dispute settlement organs to exercise competence to determine conformity with Art. XXIV, where the Council on Trade in Goods has failed to act. Since it is only binding with respect to the particular dispute in question, such a ruling, one way or another, would not preclude or foreclose or prejudice a future, opposite decision of the political organs. Such a future, opposite decision would change the legal landscape. Thus, it would allow the complainant or defendant, as the case may be, to reopen the matter. If the dispute settlement organs were to find otherwise GATT-inconsistent measures to be justified, in part because of a holding that the customs union or free trade area conformed with Art. XXIV, and the political organs were eventually to make the reverse finding, the complainant could surely commence new proceedings in these circumstances. Conversely, if the dispute settlement organs were to find that measures were not justified by reason of the customs union or free trade area not being in conformity with Art. XXIV, and a subsequent decision of the political organs were to determine the opposite, it would surely be open to the losing party in dispute settlement to now reinstate its measures. The party that won the original action, the complainant, could commence a new action, but—as I have suggested—the dispute settlement organs, in this new action, would almost certainly defer to the political determination of conformity.

5. Conclusion or Postscript: Is Judicial "Activism" the Real Issue?

When examined carefully, the main criticisms that the Appellate Body has extended beyond its mandate prove to be without good foundation. However, such complaints need also to be considered in the broader context of increased anxiety by the traditional trade policy elites concerning "judicial activism" by the Appellate Body. While framing the point more in terms of a demand for self-restraint on the part of Members considering whether to bring actions to the dispute settlement system, a recent communication by three former Directors-General of the GATT/WTO suggests that dispute settlement is not the appropriate place to "fill gaps" or resolve "differences of interpretation" in WTO rules.[55] With respect to trade and environment, Jagdish Bhagwati has argued, in a recent paper, that the AB body, engaging in activism under political pressure, has altered established GATT jurisprudence in the *Turtles* case, presumably by holding that there is no intrinsic limit on the ability of a Member to invoke Art. XX defenses with respect to measures targeted at other Members' policies.[56]

Any adequate understanding of the meaning of judicial activism, or judicial restraint, in international law should begin with a consideration of the *Lotus* case: this ruling stands for the fundamental principle that states have complete freedom of action, in the absence of any specific rule or norm of international law that constrains their conduct.[57] From this perspective, judicial activism would be a tendency to impose on states legal limits or constraints not justified by the strict rule of international law. Judicial restraint, by contrast, would reflect a hesitation to constrain state conduct, in the absence of clear and well-defined rules of law. Thus, judicial restraint cashes out, as a principle of treaty interpretation, into the idea, invoked by the AB in *Hormones,* of *in dubio mitius*—in the presence of two possible or plausible readings of a treaty provision, the interpretation that legally constrains sovereignty the *least* ought to be preferred.[58]

It will clearly be seen, once we have properly defined judicial activism and restraint as they are to be understood in the context of the structure of international law, that the AB has, in *Turtles,* taken an approach of judicial restraint to the trade and environment issue, in contrast to the extreme activism of the *Tuna/Dolphin* panels and the panel level ruling in *Turtles.* That activism was extreme, because those panels invented limitations on the sovereign rights of Members under Art. XX, which had no foundation in the treaty text, and no general basis in international law.[59] Moreover, each of these panels contradicted the other as to the nature of those limitations—not surprisingly, since there was no legal anchor in the treaty for any such limitation whatever.[60] Thus, when deciding the appeal in *Turtles* the AB (contrary to Bhagwati's suggestion) was not faced with an established, consistent jurisprudence ruling out trade measures to protect the global environment. It was faced with three panel reports, two of which were unadopted and the third of which was the very ruling under appeal, comprising three conflicting efforts to find a legal hook on which to hang the trade policy elite's visceral hostility to trade measures to protect the global environment. Such visceral hostility, or intuitive rejection, does not make a jurisprudential *acquis*, much less does it satisfy the Vienna Convention notion of subsequent practice in the application of the treaty which establishes agreement of the parties concerning its interpretation of Art. 31.3 (b). Even if one ignores the fact of non-adoption (itself a strong indicator of absence of agreement of the parties), there is no *treaty interpretation* common to the three rulings—only an arrogantly self-certain intuition that the GATT "must not" allow trade measures for protection of the global environmental commons.

Of course, "activism" and "restraint" as categories tell us little in and of themselves about judicial interpretive style and approach. As suggested in the introduction, sometimes "activism" may be the most appropriate or justified approach—international judicial activism in the presence of unprecedented acts of genocide might well be legitimate, whereas judicial activism to shut down trade measures to protect the environment might well not be. But that raises much broader issues of institutional legitimacy, which Professor Nicolaidis and I address in another contribution to this volume (see p. 307). My concern here is only to counter the polemical abuse of the concept of judicial activism by certain critics of the Appellate Body.

NOTES

1. One forceful expression of this independence is the provision in the AB's own Working Procedures for Appellate Review that a "Member shall exercise his/her office without accepting or seeking instructions from any international, governmental, or non-governmental organization or any private source." "Any" obviously includes the WTO itself. Some observers have suggested that, in fact, under older GATT practice the involvement of the Secretariat in panel proceedings often amounted to "instruction" of the panelists on how the case should be decided.

2. I have elaborated on some of the differences in values and legitimating principles as among the diplomatic, bureaucratic and judicial branches of the WTO in R. Howse, The Legitimacy of the World Trade Organization, in Heisekanen, et al., eds., *The Legitimacy of International Institutions* (United Nations University Press, 2000).

3. J. H. Jackson, Restructuring the GATT System; see also R. Howse, Restructuring the GATT System: The House that Jackson Built, 20 *Mich.J.Intl.L.* 107 (1999).

4. See E. Lauterpacht, Appeals, in *Aspects of the Administration of International Justice* (Cambridge: Grotius, 1991), pp. 101-103. See also Feldman, The Annulment Proceedings and the Finality of ICSID Arbitral Awards (1987), 2 *ICSID Review* 85 (1987).

5. For criticism along these lines, see Lauterpacht, ibid., p. 103.

6. David Dyzenhaus, *Judging the Judges, Judging Ourselves: Truth, Reconciliation and the Apartheid Legal Order* (Oxford: Hart Publishing, 1998); Robert Cover, *Justice Accused: Antislavery and the Judicial Process* (New Haven: Yale University Press 1975).

7. See Alexander Bickel's classic discussion of *Marbury* v. *Madison,* in Bickel, *The Least Dangerous Branch: The Supreme Court at the Bar of Politics*, New Haven: Yale UP, 1986.

8. "Adjudicative Legitimacy and Treaty Interpretation in International Trade Law: The Early Years of WTO Jurisprudence," in J. H. H. Weiler, ed., *The EU, the WTO, and the NAFTA: Towards a Common Law of International Trade?* (Oxford/NY: OUP, 2000), 35-70.

9. See *S. 301* panel, adopted, para. 7.22, citing the Appellate Body in *Japanese Alcohol,* pp. 11-12. While the text is the foundation for the interpretive process, the provisions of the text have to be given their ordinary meaning in their context. The object and purpose of the treaty are also to be taken into account in *determining* the meaning of the provisions." (my emphasis).

10. *Canada-Certain Measures Concerning Periodicals,* WT/DS31/AB/R (1997) [hereinafter, *Periodicals*]

11. *United States-Import Prohibition of Certain Shrimp and Shrimp Products,* WT/DS58/AB/R (1998) [hereinafter, *Turtles*].

12. *United States-Imposition of Countervailing Duties on Certain Hot-Rolled Lead and Bismuth Carbon Steel Products Originating in the United Kingdom,* WT/DS138/AB/R (2000) [hereinafter, *Steel*].

13. *India-Quantitative Restrictions on Imports of Agricultural, Textile, and Industrial Products,* WT/DS90/AB/R (1999) [hereinafter, *India Balance of Payments*].

14. *Turkey-Restrictions on Imports of Textile and Clothing Products,* WT/DS34/AB/R, 1999 [hereinafter, *Turkish Textiles*].

15. See Christine Chinkin, *Third Parties in International Law*, Oxford 1993.

16. *United States-Standards for Reformulated and Conventional Gasoline*, Report of the Appellate Body, adopted 20 May 1996, WT/DS2/AB/R; *Japan-Taxes on Alcoholic Beverages,* Report of the Appellate Body, WT/DS8, 10-1/AB/R, 4 October 1996.

17. An arbitral panel under the North American Free Trade Agreement, chaired by Professor Elihu Lauterpacht, was required to interpret a provision of the predecessor treaty to NAFTA, Art. 710 of the Canada U.S. FTA, which stated that the parties "retained their rights under GATT." The panel held that, despite the use of the word "retain," because the multilateral trading order was, *inherently,* an evolving legal system, the rights in question had to be understood in light of subsequent agreements and practice (paras. 134, 139), *In the Matter of Tariffs Applied by Canada to Certain U.S.-Origin Agricultural Products,* Secretariat File No. CDA-95-2008-01, Final Report of the Panel, 2 December 1996. The panel also noted that drafters of the FTA had, in one case, purported to impose a temporal "freeze" on interpretation; thus Art. 501.2 provided that national treatment in the FTA was to be applied "in accordance with existing interpretations adopted by the Contracting Parties to GATT." The drafters of the DSU might have similarly entrenched the GATT interpretive *acquis,* but, instead, chose to refer to the clarification of "existing *provisions*" in accordance with the (dynamic) customary international law rules of interpretation, para. 137.

18. William J. Davey and Werner Zdouc, The Triangle of TRIPs, GATT and GATS, *The World Trade Forum, Volume 3: Intellectual Property: Trade, Competition and Sustainable Development* (Ann Arbor: University of Michigan Press 2003), pp. 53-84.

19. See *Judgments of the Administrative Tribunal of the ILO upon Complaints made against UNESCO,* ICJ Reports 1956, 23 *ILR* 517.

20. See, for instance, *In the Matter of the International Title to the Chamizal Tract,* Award of the International Boundary Commission, 1911. For-Rel U.S. 573.

21. See *India-Patent Protection for Pharmaceutical and Agricultural Chemical Products,* Report of the Appellate Body, WT/DS50/AB/R, 19 December 1997, para. 92.

22. Stuart Minor Benjamin, Stepping into the Same River Twice: Rapidly Changing Facts and the Appellate Process, *Texas Law Review* Vol. 78 (1999), pp. 327ff. See *Anderson* v. *Bessemer City,* 470 U.S. 564, 575 (1985) ("The trial judges' major role is the determination of fact, and with experience in fulfilling that role comes expertise.").

23. Yet one should not be too influenced by a lack of explicit remand authority as a justification for completing the analysis. This justification can be overdone. If the AB were simply to leave matters at reversing the panel's findings of law, and thereby in effect forcing the complainant to begin litigation again, it could be argued that: 1) the consultations requirement had already been satisfied, when interpreted appropriately; 2) that the Secretariat, where possible, should propose the same or an overlapping group of panelists, given that familiarity with the record is certainly part of what it means to be "well-qualified;" 3) that because the complainant has had to go back to the panel stage in order to get their claim fully resolved, this is an appropriate case for "urgency" within the meaning of DSU 12.8-9.

24. David Palmeter, The WTO Appellate Body Needs Remand Authority, *Journal of World Trade* Vol. 32 (1998), No. 1, p. 43.

25. Lauterpacht, supra n. 4, p. 111.

26. Arthur Appleton, *Shrimp/Turtle:* Untangling the Nets, *Journal of International Economic Law* Vol. 2 (1999), No. 3, pp. 480-481.

27. *India-Patent Protection for Pharmaceutical and Agricultural Chemical Products,* supra n. 21, para. 68).

28. *United States-Sections 301-310 of the Trade Act of 1974,* Report of the Panel, WT/DS152/R (1999), adopted January 2000, paras. 7.18, 7.19.

29. *S. 301,* ibid., fn. 635.

30. Ibid., fn. 641.

31. Thus, we should not rush to accept the intriguing hypothesis of Dr. Appleton that there may be disagreement among different members of the AB, since one division in *Salmon* declined to complete the analysis because of an inadequate factual record at the panel level, while another in *Turtles* found facts itself in order to be able to complete the analysis. Appleton, supra n. 26, p. 480.

32. Benjamin, supra n. 22, pp. 345-350, gives numerous examples of important cases in which the Supreme Court of the United States has made findings of fact that were crucial to its legal rulings.

33. See J. H. Jackson, *The World Trade Organization: Constitution and Jurisprudence* (London: Royal Institute of International Affairs/Pinter, 1998), p. 92.

34. This does not mean that appellate fact-finding cannot be irresponsible in these aspects as well—for instance, without a strong evidentiary record at the panel level it would be

irresponsible, or at least insensitive for the AB, say, to conclude as a fact that a Member's customs service was notoriously corrupt and inefficient based on newspaper or magazine articles. But the point is that these are not matters which can be addressed through codified control of an appellate tribunal's jurisdiction—they go to professional ethics and responsibility, and a sense of what is proper and fair in appellate proceedings. It is not for nothing that the DSU requires that AB shall be compromised of "persons of recognized authority" with expertise in "law," not just international trade or the content of the WTO treaties. And it is, again, to these "persons of recognized authority" that the DSU entrusts the establishment of procedures for appellate review.

35. See for example Edwin Vermulst, Petros C. Mavroidis, and Paul Waer, The Functioning of the Appellate Body After Four Years—Towards Rule Integrity, *Journal of World Trade* Vol. 33 (1999), No. 2, p. 3. The authors are wrong in any case about the ordinary language meaning of the word "seek." Consider an example from the bad old days when only the men were supposed to do the asking—Ms. X lets me know that she would be favorably disposed if I were to ask her out. But I still have to ask. There is nothing that stretches the ordinary language meaning of "seek," for me to say that I am "seeking" a date with Ms. X—even though this possibility has been brought to my attention unsolicited. Or let's say I am offered some kind of official position. I think about it for a couple of weeks and come back to the offerer and say, "I'm now seeking that position you mentioned." Again, this seems a natural and unproblematic use of the word "seek" even if the context discloses that what is being sought has been brought to my attention, or frame of interest and knowledge, without prior effort of my own.

36. See also the ICJ decision *Reparation for Injuries Suffered in the Service of the United Nations,* 1949 I.C.J. 174, which held that an international organization should be considered to possess those powers not explicitly granted in its constitutive treaty instrument that are necessary for the performance of its duties.

37. Appleton, *supra* n. 26, p. 487. Trebilcock and myself explained the silent acceptance of the fourth, unattached brief in a different way: "Perhaps the AB quite reasonably considered the ability to accept such material as implicit in the very notion of appellate jurisdiction, which would be consistent with general appellate court practice." Michael J. Trebilcock and Robert Howse, *The Regulation of International Trade, Second edition* (London and New York: Routledge, 1999), p. 66.

38. See also Petersmann's contribution to WTF last year, on the character of intellectual property rights as indirectly protected private rights in WTO system.

39. In suggesting that the ICJ should actively use the discretion afforded to it to accept submissions from international organizations (including non-governmental organizations, by implication) in its grant of advisory jurisdiction, Shelton notes: "The long-term institutional interests of the Court may be best served by ensuring its opinions are based upon the fullest available information and reflect consideration of the public interest, as well as the desires and concerns of the litigating parties." D. Shelton, The Participation of Non-Governmental Organizations in International Judicial Proceedings 88 *A.J.I.L.* 611, p. 625.

40. David Palmeter and Petros C. Mavroidis, *Dispute Settlement in the World Trade Organization: Practice and Procedure* (The Hague, London, Boston: Kluwer, 1999), pp. 35-36.

41. See also Petros C. Mavroidis, *Amicus Curiae* Briefs Before the WTO: Much Ado About Nothing, *European Integration and International Co-operation. Studies in Transnational Economic Law in Honour of Claus-Dieter Ehlermann*, The Hague, London, New York: Kluwer, 2002, pp. 317-329. It can be argued, of course, that these sorts of materials are distinguished from *amicus* submissions in that the latter constitute advocacy in a particular case under

adjudication. However, U.S. Supreme Court practice indicates that, to the extent that they constitute mere advocacy or preaching of one party or the other's side of the case, *amicus* submissions are likely to be ignored.

42. This point is emphasized particularly well by Trocker, in commenting on *amicus* practice at the European Court of Human Rights. Niccolo Trocker, L'"Amicus Curiae" nel giudizio davanti alla Corte Europea dei Diritti Dell'Uomo 35 *Rivista di Diritto Civile* 119 (1989), p. 124.

43. Henkin, Pugh, Schacter, and Smit, *International Law Cases and Materials, Third Edition* (St. Paul, MN: West, 1993), p. 122.

44. Ibid., p. 12.

45. The most comprehensive examination of international and transnational practice is in an article by G. Marceau and M. Stilwell, "Practical Suggestions for *Amicus Curiae* Briefs before WTO Adjudicating Bodies," *Journal of International Economic Law* Vol. 4 (2002), No. 1, pp.155-187. This excellent article went to press, however, too soon to include a consideration of the important ruling of an investor-state arbitral panel under the North American Free Trade Agreement, which held that it had discretion to consider *amicus* briefs and exercised that discretion in favor of consideration in the case at bar, *Methanex Corporation* v. *United States of America, Decision of the Tribunal on Petitions from Third Persons to Intervene as "Amici Curiae,"* January 15, 2001. This ruling examines the due process issues surrounding *amicus* practice, including confidentiality, in greater detail than the AB has done so far. See also A. Lester, Amici Curiae: Third-Party Interventions Before the European Court of Human Rights, in *Protecting Human Rights: The European Dimension, Studies in Honour of Gerard J. Wiarda,* ed. F. Matscher (Cologne: Carl Heymann, 1988), 341-51, pp. 341-42. In what follows I have been greatly aided by an excellent research paper by Mr. Yvo DeVries, an LLM student at the University of Michigan Law School, 1998-1999, comparing *amicus* practice at the WTO with that of other international and municipal tribunals. My hope and expectation is that Mr. DeVries will soon publish this research.

46. Lester, ibid., p. 344.

47. I owe this point to Mr. Yvo De Vries. But this does *not* mean that the practice of considering unsolicited non-party submissions is unknown to civilian jurisdictions. See Y. Laurin, L'amicus curiae, *La semaine juridique: doctrine, jurisprudences, textes* 345 (1992), pp. 345-48.

48. The Institutional Balance Between the Judicial and Political Organs of the WTO, paper presented at the Kennedy School of Government, Harvard University, June 1, 2000, Conference on Efficiency, Equity and Legitimacy: The Multilateral Trading System at the Millenium (honouring Ray Vernon). In reflecting on what follows, I benefited from hearing the exchange between Dr. Roessler and Professor William Davey, a commentator on the paper, at that conference.

49. Ibid., p. 21.

50. See Howse, The Legitimacy of the World Trade Organization, supra n. 2 See also Howse, Restructuring the GATT System: The House that Jackson Built, supra n. 3.

51. Roessler, supra n. 49.

52. Roessler, supra n 49, citing *Greco-Turkish Agreement of December 1st, 1926,* PCIJ Rep. 1928, Series B No. 16 and the *Certain Expenses* case, ICJ Rep. 1962, p. 168.

53. See, in the EU context, Joseph H. H. Weiler, The Autonomy of the Community Legal Order: Through the Looking Glass, in The Constitution of Europe (Cambridge: Cambridge University Press, 1999), p. 288ff (originally co-authored with Ulrich Haltern).

54. See Weiler, ibid., pp. 299-304.

55. A. Dunkel, P. Sutherland, R. Ruggiero, Davos Statement-Third Draft, 1 February 2001.

56. Paper presented at Conference on Equity, Efficiency and Legitimacy, Kennedy School of Government, Harvard University, June 1, 2000.

57. *France v. Turkey,* P.C.I.J. Reports, Series A, No. 10 (1927).

58. *EC-Measures Concerning Meat and Meat Products (Hormones),* Report of the Appellate Body, WT/DS26/AB/R, 16 January 1998, para. 165.

59. See R. Howse, The Turtles Panel: Another Environmental Disaster in Geneva, *Journal of World Trade* Vol. 32 (1998), No. 5, October, pp.73-100.

60. The *Tuna/Dolphin I* panel dreamed up the notion that Art. XX (b) and (g) of the GATT could only be used to justify measures to protect the environment in one's own territory. The *Tuna/Dolphin II* panel actually exposed the groundlessness of that limitation, but invented its own—to be justified under these provisions of Art. XX, a measure must have environmental-protection effects even if it does not succeed in inducing any other country to change its policies. In addition to lacking a basis in the treaty, this was economically illogical, since **any** embargo of dolphin-unfriendly tuna or turtle-unfriendly shrimp, especially on the part of a country that constitutes a large market for the product, will always have positive environmental protection effects—assuming that the producers are selling before the embargo where marginal revenue equals marginal cost, and elasticities are in the normal range, the embargo reduces the quantity demanded of dolphin-unfriendly tuna or turtle-unfriendly shrimp, leading to less such tuna or shrimp being produced, and therefore reduced dolphin and shrimp mortality, regardless of any country changing its policies. Finally, the panel in *Turtles* went off on yet another direction, reading into the *chapeau* of Art. XX a notion that measures that condition import access on adoption of certain laws or policies by the country of origin cannot ever be justified under Art. XX (whether or not discriminatory on any normal meaning of that word). See Howse, ibid.

CHAPTER 2

Has the WTO Dispute Settlement System Exceeded Its Authority? A Consideration of Deference Shown by the System to Member Government Decisions and Its Use of Issue-Avoidance Techniques

William J. Davey

Since its inception in 1995, the World Trade Organization's dispute settlement system has attracted a great deal of attention—from WTO Members, who have made extensive use of it and who have frequently insisted that it rule on quite difficult and controversial disputes—to the public at large, who may know little details about its operation or decisions, but who have (or are told by various sources that they should have) serious concerns about its threat to national sovereignty or their preferred environmental policies. Among academics—both legal and economic—who have followed the evolution of the GATT into the WTO, there is sometimes concern expressed that some controversial decisions emanating from the WTO dispute settlement mechanism may undermine popular, and ultimately governmental, support for the multilateral trading system to the detriment of world at large. In light of these concerns, it is appropriate to consider whether the WTO Appellate Body and dispute settlement Panels have overreached by exceeding their authority—either (i) by failing to accord sufficient deference to legitimate policy decisions made by WTO Member governments or (ii) by ruling on cases or issues where they should have used traditional judicial doctrines to avoid rulings.

This paper consists of two parts. The first part considers the extent to which the Appellate Body and Panels have appropriately deferred to legislative and regulatory actions of WTO Member governments. The second part evaluates the extent to which Panels and the Appellate Body have considered or used issue-avoidance techniques and whether such techniques should be used more frequently. It is not possible to analyze in detail the myriad issues discussed in the thousands of pages of findings contained in the 38 Panel and the 28 Appellate Body reports adopted by the WTO's Dispute Settlement Body (DSB) through September 25, 2000. I have tried to focus

---

When Director of the WTO, the author was responsible for supervising legal advice given to almost all of the 38 Panels whose reports had been adopted as of September 25, 2000.

attention on the final substantive outcome only and consider (i) whether that outcome was at all unexpected (e.g., was in line with relevant past precedents or based on the [relatively] clear wording of the agreements) and (ii) whether the result significantly constrained government policy-makers in achieving desired policy goals. In this regard, it is important to remember that one of the stated purposes of the dispute settlement system is to clarify the meaning of the WTO agreements, but the system must not impose new obligations in doing so. Given space constraints, I paint with a *very* broad brush, but I think that the exercise is a useful one.

1. The Exercise of Deference by the Appellate Body and Panels

The exercise of deference by the Appellate Body and Panels can usefully be evaluated in two different situations: first, in review of governmental measures generally; second, in review of actions by administrative agencies in the trade remedies field. While this distinction is somewhat arbitrary, it is useful, *inter alia*, because a specific standard of review is required in some trade remedy cases (i.e., antidumping and arguably countervail cases) and inevitably affects the treatment of similar issues in other such cases.

As was the case under GATT, complainants in the WTO are usually successful, at least in part. Of the 38 Panel reports that had been adopted as of September 25, 2000,[1] the complaining party lost in only six cases (16%).[2] Since the government measures challenged in these cases were upheld, there was arguably no overreaching by Panels or the Appellate Body in these cases. Two comments should be made, however. First, in two of the cases, the Panels may have expanded the type of measure that could be challenged in WTO dispute settlement. To be specific, in *Film,*[3] the Panel took a rather broad view of when technically private acts might be attributed to a government; and in *Section 301,* the Panel arguably broadened the circumstances in which a discretionary, not-yet-applied, government measure might be challenged in dispute settlement. Since neither case was appealed, it is not clear whether these expansive views will ultimately be accepted by the Appellate Body. Second, and going in the direction of increased Member autonomy, in two of these cases, *LAN Equipment* and *Korea Procurement,*[4] Members were accorded considerable discretion in how they interpret and implement their scheduled tariff and other commitments.

Of the 32 cases where the complaining party prevailed, I have categorized 25 as general cases and seven as trade remedy cases. In considering the extent of deference afforded by WTO dispute settlement system, I have not considered Panel reports to the extent that they were modified by the Appellate Body. In this regard, it should be noted that in some significant cases, the Appellate Body clearly afforded more discretion to governments than the Panel had (e.g., *Gasoline, Hormones, Shrimp, LAN*

Equipment). In some cases, it has gone in the opposite direction (e.g., *Salmon*, safeguard cases).

General Cases

For analytical purposes, it is convenient to place the 25 general cases in ten subdivisions: (i) Article III:2 cases – *Japan, Korea* and *Chile Taxes* and *Periodicals;* (ii) Article III:4 cases – *Gasoline, Periodicals, Bananas, Indonesia Autos, Canada Autos;* (iii) MFN cases – *Bananas, Poultry, Indonesia Autos, Canada Autos;* (iv) other GATT and "goods" cases – *Argentina Textiles, Poultry;* (v) GATT political balance cases – *India QR, Turkey Textiles;* (vi) GATT Article XX cases – *Gasoline, Shrimp;* (vii) subsidy cases – *Australia Leather, Canada Dairy, Brazil Aircraft, Canada Aircraft, FSC;* (viii) SPS cases – *Hormones, Salmon, Japan;* (ix) TRIPs cases – *India Patents I & II, Canada Pharmaceutical Patents, U.S. Copyright;* and (x) GATS cases – *Bananas, Canada Autos.* Some cases (e.g., *Bananas*) fall within more than one subdivision.

Article III:2 Cases –
Japan, Korea and *Chile Taxes* and *Periodicals*

In the three cases dealing with allegations of discriminatory internal taxes favoring local alcoholic beverages, Panels and the Appellate Body upheld the claims of discrimination. Given past GATT precedents (especially the prior Japan case[5]), the results of these cases were unexceptional. They turned on the application of the term "directly competitive or substitutable products" in a specific factual situation,[6] and while one may disagree over the precise nature and extent of the evidence needed to establish such a relationship or over what range of alcoholic drinks is truly competitive, the decisions do not seem to be particularly intrusive into the ability of governments to implement tax policies.

In *Periodicals,* the Appellate Body reversed a Panel finding that like products were involved because of deficiencies in the Panel's reasoning. It then determined itself on the basis of material in the record that there were directly competitive or substitutable products at issue, that they were not similarly taxed and that the taxes were applied so as to afford protection to the Canadian products (thereby establishing the prerequisites for finding a violation of Article III:2, second sentence). While some have criticized the Appellate Body for exceeding the proper scope of appellate review by making those determinations itself, as opposed to leaving it to a Panel decision (presumably by a new Panel), there was considerable material in the record to support its factual conclusions that competitive domestic and imported products existed, were taxed differently and that the scheme was designed to protect Canadian periodicals from U.S. competition.

Thus, while Panels and the Appellate Body did not defer to the governmental tax policy choices in these cases, the lack of deference seems appropriate, especially in light of the wording of Article III:2 and past GATT practice. In the end, the only limitation on government discretion is that taxation must not discriminate against foreign products. No constraints are placed on the levels of nondiscriminatory taxes that may be imposed, nor on the discretion to tax different classes of (non-competing) products differently.

One additional comment. While these cases were unexceptional, it is noteworthy that the Appellate Body in *Japan Taxes* rejected the so-called "aim and effect" test for determining the likeness of products under Article III. This test had been used (mainly in connection with Article III:4 cases) to afford greater deference to government regulatory actions by focusing on whether the regulation at issue had a protectionist aim or effect.[7] The rejection of this test is not of great importance for the interpretation of Article III:2, since most cases under that article will arise under its second sentence, which requires a demonstration that the tax difference is applied "so as to afford protection." However, the Appellate Body held explicitly in *Bananas* that there is no such requirement under Article III:4. Thus, it is possible that in future Article III:4 cases, regulations that would have been upheld under the "aim and effect" test will be found to violate Article III:4. To date, that has not happened.

Article III:4 Cases –
Gasoline, Periodicals, Bananas, Indonesia Autos, Canada Autos

In each of these cases, there was no question but that there was discrimination against imported products. While technical arguments could be made as to whether all of the required conditions of Article III:4 had been met, the fact of discrimination was incontrovertible. Indeed, the U.S. did not appeal the finding of an Article III:4 violation in *Gasoline;* nor did Canada appeal the finding of an Article III:4 violation in *Periodicals.* Indonesia did not appeal at all and in *Canada Autos,* Canada did not appeal the finding of an Article III:4 violation. In *Bananas,* the principal EC argument was not that its licensing scheme did not discriminate, but rather that the distribution of import licenses was a border measure not subject to Article III:4's constraints on the use of discriminatory internal measures. Thus, to a large extent, these violations were virtually admitted by the Members concerned.

As to whether the decisions inappropriately failed to defer to government policy choices, it is important to recall that WTO rules allow certain mechanisms to be used to afford protection to domestic industry (e.g., certain direct subsidies to producers; safeguards), but not the use of discriminatory internal regulations. Given that WTO Members have long agreed on this approach, it is difficult to argue that these cases inappropriately limited Member government policy options.

MFN Cases –
Bananas, Poultry, Indonesia Autos, Canada Autos

There have been a number of cases where violations of GATT most-favored-nation (MFN) requirements have been found. In *Bananas,* a number of aspects of the EC's licensing system were found to violate GATT Article I because they accorded advantages to goods of certain Members that were not given to others. The key issue in the case turned on whether the differences in treatment amounted to an advantage in terms of Article I, as there was no question but that there was different treatment given to imports depending on the country of origin. Given the fundamental place of the MFN clause in GATT and the traditionally broad scope given to the term "advantage,"[8] I do not think that finding the EC banana regulation in violation of Article I amounted to overreaching or inadequate deference by the Panel and Appellate Body. Also in *Bananas,* the use of completely separate and distinct regimes for allocating banana import quota shares based on country of origin was found to violate GATT Article XIII:1. I think that result was appropriate also in that acceptance of the EC argument that its separate regimes should not be compared for MFN purposes would have gutted the MFN requirement.

In *Poultry,* the Panel and Appellate Body found that Article XXVIII compensation agreements should be applied on an MFN basis, contrary to Brazil's position. I think that result was clear and unexceptional in light of the terms of Article XXVIII and its drafting history.

In *Indonesia Autos* (which was not appealed), the Panel interpreted the term "unconditionally" in Article I rather broadly, by finding that if any product from any country receives favorable tariff treatment then like products from all countries are entitled to that treatment. This approach, which might in some cases call into question tariff differences based on various regulatory distinctions, was not followed by the Panel in *Canada Autos.* That Panel rather relied on the fact that there was *de facto* discrimination by Canada in favor of products of certain origin (a conclusion which could have been found following a similar analysis in the *Indonesia* case as well). On appeal, the Appellate Body upheld the Panel's *de facto* finding of discrimination, but did so using language which was not inconsistent with the broader approach taken by the *Indonesia Autos* Panel. Given the facts of the two cases, the results seem appropriate to me. It is necessary to be on guard, however, so as not to find *de facto* discrimination simply on the basis of the result of competitive market forces. Moreover, if the broader rule of *Indonesia Autos* is applied in the future, it might lead to intrusion into government policy-making. For the moment, however, that is simply speculation.

Overall, these decisions seem to me to be in line with past GATT practice. Moreover, they are completely appropriate given that Article I's ban on origin-based discrimination is often described as *the* fundamental GATT principle. As such, I see no problems in the way in which these cases curtail a Member's discretion to discriminate among other Members.

Other GATT and "Goods" Cases –
Argentina Textiles, Poultry

The Argentina Textiles case involved a clear violation of two GATT rules. There were specific examples of where Argentina had imposed tariffs in excess of its Article II tariff bindings and there was no serious argument that its 3% statistical tax covered only the cost of statistical analysis as required by Article VIII. The Appellate Body modification of the Panel report clearly allows a Member to do what Argentina did in respect of tariffs (i.e., change from *ad valorem* to specific tariffs), but only so long as there is a mechanism to ensure that tariffs in excess of bound rates are not imposed. As such, Member discretion is not inappropriately limited. With one exception, all of Brazil's numerous attacks on EC import licensing procedures for poultry were rejected in the Poultry case. The only violation found was under the Agriculture Agreement in respect of one aspect of the EC's rules for application of special safeguard measures permitted under that agreement. Since the Panel had not considered the issue, the Appellate Body may be criticized for ruling upon it. However, the finding of violation was a relatively straightforward application of the wording of the Agriculture Agreement and certainly did not significantly limit Member discretion to make use of the special safeguards provided for in that agreement. Indeed, the EC argued that its rules were actually more beneficial for exporters to the EC than the rule adopted by the Appellate Body.

GATT Political Balance Cases –
India QR, Turkey Textiles

The *India QR* and *Turkey Textiles* cases present more difficult issues than the foregoing ones. They raise the issue of whether it is appropriate for Panels and the Appellate Body to review the justification of balance of payments measures taken under GATT Articles XII or XVIII:B or to review whether a claimed free-trade area or customs union in fact meets the criteria of GATT Article XXIV. In GATT, in respect of Article XXIV, there were a number of unadopted Panel reports in which this issue was discussed. In one (*Citrus*), the Panel explicitly declined to rule on whether the terms of Article XXIV had been met, viewing it as a matter for the Contracting Parties alone.[9] In later cases (*Bananas I* and *II*), Panels indicated that they could examine at least the facial validity (and probably more) of a defense that a measure was part of a legitimate free-trade area.[10] Under Article XVIII:B, one adopted Panel report considered the legitimacy of Korean balance-of-payments measures.[11] It did so, however, subsequent to a decision by the GATT Balance-of-Payments Committee that they were not necessary.

The Panel in the *India QR* case carefully considered if WTO dispute settlement Panels should determine whether balance-of-payments restrictions in a specific case are justified in the absence of decision on that issue by the WTO Committee on Balance-of-Payments Restrictions. In light of standard principles of treaty interpretation, the Panel concluded that it should do so and the Appellate Body upheld that decision. In connection with the decision, four specific points should be noted.[12]

First, the proper basis for interpreting treaty text is the ordinary meaning of the text. The specific WTO rules that deal with the issue of dispute settlement in cases arising under the GATT balance-of-payments and regional trading exceptions are similar and worded quite broadly. One text authorizes consideration under WTO dispute settlement procedures of "*any matters* arising from the application of restrictive import measures taken for balance-of-payments purposes" and the other authorizes consideration of "*any matters* arising from the application of those *provisions of Article XXIV* relating to customs unions. . ."[13] The ordinary meaning of the emphasized text (especially that referring to Article XXIV) clearly demonstrates that there is a broad grant of authority to dispute settlement Panels to consider issues related to the underlying basis for invocation of the two exceptions.[14]

Second, to me it is clear that the understandings adopted in the Uruguay Round were not intended to restrict the power of Panels as compared to GATT practice. In that regard, it is noteworthy that while the 1989 *Korea* Panel took into account past action by the GATT BOP Committee, it also made its own independent determination of Korea's balance-of-payments situation as of the time of the Panel proceeding.[15] In addition, it explained how review by the Committee and a dispute settlement Panel were not mutually exclusive.[16]

Third, and more importantly, consideration in dispute settlement proceedings of such issues as the justification of balance-of-payments restrictions does not upset the political-judicial balance within the WTO. To the contrary, in the absence of the possibility of consideration of such issues by the dispute settlement system, there is a much greater possibility that the balance of WTO Members' rights and obligations will be unfairly and inappropriately tilted. Without the possibility of review in dispute settlement of the justification of balance-of-payments measures, the consensus decision-making practices of the WTO would mean that the Member applying those measures would have free rein to decide when and for how long to keep such measures in place, with no possibility of review. With the possibility of dispute settlement review, the complaining party only is given the right to ask an independent three-person Panel to consider the justification issue, with the advice of the IMF and subject to appeal. Moreover, consideration of the justification of BOP measures is not done without any normative framework. The key issue under GATT Article XVIII:B is the adequacy of a Member's reserves. The Panel may ask the IMF, as it did in the *India QR* case, to opine on the adequacy of India's reserves, in light of the IMF's normal standards. Having this issue considered in dispute settlement cannot be said to upset the political-judicial balance nor the balance of Members' rights and obligations. Rather, it is a way to ensure that these balances are appropriately maintained in light of Members' procedural (the Uruguay Round understandings) and substantive (the justification issue) agreements.

Finally, and turning to the specific facts of the *India QR* case, it was a relatively straightforward case in that India had reserves significantly in excess of what the IMF calculated was necessary. Indeed, India's reserve situation today is even more favorable. Thus, the conclusion that there was no justification for BOP measures seems appropriate in light of the facts of the specific case at issue. One can be legitimately concerned, however, that there may be close cases where it would be inappropriate for a Panel to second-guess the decisions of a Member government to apply BOP restrictions. I would expect that Panels would typically accord a fair degree of discretion to governments in such cases. However, I believe it is appropriate for BOP justification issues to be considered by Panels and do not believe that there was any overreaching or inadequate deference shown in the *India QR* case.

The same analysis applies to the Article XXIV issue, with two important caveats: (i) the issue of whether a regional trading agreement complies with Article XXIV is more complex than the question of reserve adequacy under the balance-of-payment rules and there is no international body for Panels to turn to for expert advice and (ii) the Appellate Body suggested in *Turkey Textiles* that Panels should always first consider the compatibility of a regional trading agreement with the requirements of Article XXIV. Given the complexity of this issue, in my opinion it would be preferable for Panels to avoid that issue where possible. That was the approach taken in the *Turkey Textiles* Panel report, which suggested that in general Panels should leave that issue to the appropriate WTO committee. I do not view that Panel report as saying that Panels cannot consider such issues, only that they should try to avoid them. In the context of the *Turkey Textiles* case, the value of that approach is apparent. It might have been quite complicated and controversial for a Panel to decide if the Turkey-EU arrangement is a proper customs union in accordance with Article XXIV. Yet, the basic issue in the case was much simpler and was appropriately resolved in my view without considering the larger issue.

In conclusion, while these two cases involve difficult issues, the two cases in which they arose were not that complicated and were appropriately decided without unduly limiting the discretion of the governments involved.

GATT Article XX Cases –
Gasoline, Shrimp
Two of the more controversial cases to date under WTO dispute settlement were the *Gasoline* case and, particularly, the *Shrimp* case. In both cases, the key issue (indeed, the only issue on appeal) was the applicability of the exception contained in Article XX(g) for measures related to the conservation of exhaustible natural resources. To invoke the exception successfully, a respondent must demonstrate that the challenged measure falls within the scope of Article XX(g) and that it is consistent with the requirements of the chapeau of Article XX (i.e., the measure must not discriminate between Members unjustifiably or arbitrarily and must not be a disguised restriction on trade).

While the U.S. lost in both cases, the way in which it lost limited the effect of the decisions on the ability of the U.S. and other Members to take conservation measures in the future. In both cases, the Appellate Body found that the U.S. measure fell within the scope of Article XX(g), and did so in a way that expanded the availability of that exception. As to the chapeau, the Appellate Body found in both cases that the U.S. measure was discriminatory because of the way it had been applied. While the full meaning of the *Shrimp* case's extensive discussion of the chapeau awaits fuller development by the Appellate Body, it is certainly arguable that the *Shrimp* case affords considerable discretion to Member governments to implement conservation measures, so long as they follow certain steps—such as at least attempting to negotiate agreements where the problem is international and treating similarly situated countries the same.

Subsidy Cases –
Australia Leather, Canada Dairy, Brazil Aircraft, Canada Aircraft, FSC
There have been five subsidy cases to date—one arising under the Agriculture Agreement (*Canada Dairy*) and four arising under the Agreement on Subsidies and Countervailing Measures (SCM Agreement).

As to *Canada Dairy,* there were difficult definitional issues as to whether the Canadian scheme at issue constituted subsidization covered by the Agriculture Agreement. In my view, the conclusion that it did was a reasonable one. Certainly, the conclusion that the word "payment" encompasses a "payment-in-kind" is easily supportable. A broad definition was also given to what constitutes financing by government action, but it, too, was supportable given the wide involvement of Canadian governmental entities in the management of the supply of milk. A closer question may have been presented as to whether the provincial marketing boards were properly viewed as governmental entities, but in view of the broad powers delegated to them by governments and their role in performing typical governmental regulatory functions, the decision seems reasonable and basically just follows similar approaches taken in cases involving Japan (in the *Film* case and GATT cases cited therein). To decide otherwise would seem to risk undermining considerably the disciplines intended to be put in place by the Agriculture Agreement.

In *Australia Leather* (not appealed) and *Canada Aircraft,* the difficult issue was whether the subsidies at issue, which were not *de jure* contingent on export, were in fact contingent on export. While the answer to this question was not crystal clear, I think that the conclusions of the Panels and the Appellate Body were reasonable and not too limiting of governmental discretion. There is general agreement in the WTO that export subsidization should not be permitted for industrial products, but it will remain difficult to implement that agreement, given the desire of government to promote exports and the lack of clarity of when a subsidy is a *de facto* export subsidy.[17]

In *Brazil Aircraft,* it was conceded that export subsidies had been granted. The issue was whether they were permitted because of an exception, either the exception for developing countries or one implied from the illustrative list of export subsidies attached to the SCM Agreement. The developing country exception clearly did not apply because Brazil had increased its level of export subsidies. The interpretation of the illustrative list presents a more difficult issue. While the Appellate Body seems willing to accept Brazil's argument that certain subsidies not meeting the criteria of the list should be presumed not to be export subsides, Brazil was found not to have established that its subsidies did not fall within the criteria as a factual matter. As such, I do not find the results of this case too intrusive into government policy-making, although there is a fairness question lurking here in that Brazil claims that it is only doing what Canada is permitted to do by the OECD understanding on export credits.

Finally, with respect to the *FSC* case, I think that the result was expected. Although there may have been some sort of tacit understanding that the EC was not going to challenge the system (or so the U.S. has suggested), there has long been doubt about whether the FSC system was GATT- or WTO-compatible.

All in all, these five cases enforce rather strictly the WTO's export subsidy rules. It would have been possible, given the wording of the agreements, to take a narrower view of what constitutes an export subsidy—generally under the Agriculture Agreement in the *Canada Dairy* case and in the two *de facto* cases (*Australia Leather* and *Canada Aircraft*). However, given that the Agriculture Agreement and the SCM Agreement were clearly intended and designed to tighten multilateral controls on the use of such subsidies, the restrictions on government discretion resulting from these decisions seem appropriate. One caveat should be mentioned: the SCM Agreement does not prohibit domestic subsidies and care must be taken to ensure that the concept of *de facto* export subsidies is not read so broadly as to prohibit domestic subsidies to industries which export.

SPS Cases –
Hormones, Salmon, Japan

The cases arising under the Agreement on Sanitary and Phytosanitary Measures (the SPS Agreement) have been among the most controversial WTO matters. As interpreted by the Appellate Body, essentially two types of violations of the SPS Agreement have been upheld on appeal. First, either a failure to conduct a risk assessment or a failure to base the challenged SPS measure on the risk assessment; second, a violation of Article 5.5 of the SPS Agreement.[18]

In respect of risk assessments, I think that the Appellate Body's decisions have been reasonable and not too restrictive of Member government discretion. Requiring a reasonable relationship between an SPS measure and the relevant risk assessment seems a faithful interpretation of the requirement that SPS measures be "based on" a risk assessment. The EC measure in *Hormones* was clearly not based on the risk assessments presented by the EC; the same was true of the second Australian measure on salmon. For me, the risk assessment requirement is largely a procedural one. Since the process of risk assessment is under the control of Members and a Member is permitted to follow a non-majority scientific opinion and choose a zero-risk strategy, any Member should be able to accomplish any reasonable SPS goal if it takes care in respect of procedures. Thus, I do not see the WTO's SPS decisions as particularly limiting government discretion in that regard.

The other major issue that has arisen in the SPS cases concerns the interpretation of Article 5.5 of the SPS Agreement, which requires Members to avoid arbitrary or unjustifiable distinctions in levels of health protection provided by sanitary measures if they result in discrimination or disguised restrictions on trade. There has been some difficulty in applying the last component of Article 5.5 – the need to show that the arbitrary or unjustifiable distinction results in discrimination or a disguised restriction on trade. In fact, this component seems to have been interpreted somewhat loosely. That is, if it is found that there is an unjustifiable or arbitrary distinction between comparable situations, there seems to be a willingness to find discrimination or a disguised restriction.[19]

In the *Salmon* case, the Panel looked at three warning signals (the arbitrariness and unjustifiability of the distinctions in the level of protection provided by different, but comparable, Australian SPS measures; the substantial size of those distinctions; the inconsistency of the Australian measure with SPS Articles 5.1 and 2.2) and three additional factors (the substantial difference in the SPS measures applied by Australia in comparable situations; the change in the conclusions between the draft risk assessment and the final risk assessment; and the absence of measures controlling internal fish movements within Australia) that it cumulated to find discrimination or a disguised restriction.[20] The Panel's analysis was upheld by the Appellate Body, although it found that the first additional factor was equivalent to the first warning signal.[21] The compliance Panel, in examining the new Australian measure implemented in response to the Panel/Appellate Body reports, found that there was no longer an unjustifiable or arbitrary distinction between comparable situations. It also noted the absence of two of the three warning signals and of all of the additional factors noted in the original case. Accordingly, no violation of Article 5.5 was found.[22]

The use of "warning signals" and "additional factors" to determine whether Article 5.5 has been violated is not very satisfactory. Perhaps it is only a matter of language, but there is a suggestion by using those two categories that there is a missing third category—"factors establishing a violation." In other words, the warning signals cause you to be suspicious that there might be a violation (but by definition cannot establish it) and the additional factors support your finding that there is a violation, but do not themselves establish the violation. In the future, more precise standards for the application of Article 5.5 need to be established with respect to this third factor. In doing so, it needs to be considered what, if anything, Article 5.5 adds to what is already covered by Article 2.3.

Thus, I think that the interpretation of Article 5.5 to date may limit Member discretion inappropriately, but so far that has not been the major issue in the SPS cases, although it was a factor in the *Salmon* case in that Australia has had to try to harmonize its policies with respect to fish sanitary measures, as well as deal with risk assessment issues for salmon. Rather, the major issue in SPS cases so far has been a failure to conduct a risk assessment or base a measure on the assessment and the WTO rules, as interpreted by the Appellate Body, are reasonably deferential.

TRIPs Cases –
India Patents I & II, Canada Pharmaceutical Patents, U.S. Copyright

In the *Canada Pharmaceutical Patents* case, the Panel rejected the main EC argument by finding that the basic provision of the challenged Canadian statute, which allowed generic pharmaceutical makers to "use" a patented product without permission to obtain marketing approval prior to the expiration of the patent term, fell within a general exception to the TRIPs patent protection obligations. As such, this case, if anything, demonstrates Panel deference to governmental decisions in the social field, since the measure was designed to lower prescription drug prices. The Panel decision was not appealed.

In the *U.S. Copyright* case, the Panel found the principal feature of the U.S. measure that was challenged to be inconsistent with U.S. obligations under the TRIPs Agreement. That decision was expected in my view (from the time when the measure had been enacted) and the U.S. did not appeal. As such, I do not think that this decision can be viewed as too intrusive.

The *India Patents* cases present more difficult issues. In these cases, there was no question as to what the Indian government was supposed to do, but only whether its "measure" had succeeded in accomplishing what was required. To a significant extent, determining that issue required speculation as to whether the Indian judicial system would give effect to government action that was arguably inconsistent with existing statutory law. India argued that it would in this case, but the Panel and the Appellate Body ultimately concluded that the Indian measure did not provide a sound legal basis under Indian law for achieving what was required by the TRIPs Agreement. The decision can be defended on the grounds that legal certainty is required in this area and that the Indian measure did not provide that certainty. Moreover, given the controversy over the TRIPs Agreement in India, it can be argued that providing such certainty was particularly important. However, the Panels and the Appellate Body did effectively reject the Indian government view of its powers and the likely reaction of Indian courts to its actions. One can argue that given the uncertainty over what Indian courts might do, greater deference to the government's view would have been appropriate.

GATS Cases –
Bananas, Canada Autos

The two GATS cases to date are unusual in that they are not really "services" cases but are largely appendages to "goods" cases. In both, the service sector at issue was the distribution services sector. I do not think that the legal interpretations of GATS reached by the Panels and the Appellate Body threatens Member government discretion. The key issue in both cases was whether there was *de facto* discrimination against foreign services or service suppliers. As such, the two cases largely turn on facts. In *Bananas,* the Appellate Body declined to review the facts found by the Panel; in *Canada Autos,* the Appellate Body found that the Panel's factual analysis was not adequate and it reversed its findings. In *Bananas,* the GATS violations found concerned the same measures found to have violated GATT rules. In the compliance Panel proceeding, there were GATS violations found that did not duplicate GATT violations, but the GATS violations were a result of the carry-over effect of the prior GATS (and GATT) violations. In short, it is too early to draw conclusions on the way in which GATS may be interpreted, given the unusual nature of these two cases.

Trade Remedy Cases

By trade remedy laws, I mean such laws as those authorizing the imposition of antidumping or countervailing duties or of safeguard measures. What distinguishes cases arising under these laws from others is that the challenge is typically to the decision of an administrative agency that is charged with determining whether certain facts exist (e.g., dumping, subsidization or injury to a specified industry). The distinction between these cases and other dispute settlement matters is recognized in the WTO Antidumping Agreement, which provides in its Article 17.6 that

> (i) in its assessment of the fact of the matter, the Panel shall determine whether the authorities' establishment of the facts was proper and whether their evaluation of those facts was unbiased and objective. If the establishment of the facts was proper and the evaluation was unbiased and objective, even though the Panel might have reached a different conclusion, the evaluation shall not be overturned;
>
> (ii) the Panel shall interpret the relevant provisions of the Agreement in accordance with the customary rules of interpretation of public international law. Where the Panel finds that a relevant provision of the Agreement admits of more than one permissible interpretation, the Panel shall find the authorities' measure to be in conformity with the Agreement if it rests upon one of those permissible interpretations.

Although this provision is unique to the Antidumping Agreement, there is a Ministerial Declaration adopted at Marrakesh that recognizes "the need for the consistent resolution of disputes arising from antidumping and countervailing duty measures." It has been suggested that this declaration effectively extends Article 17.6 to cover the countervailing duty provisions of the SCM Agreement.

The meaning of Article 17.6 has been the subject of some dispute. As to paragraph (i), it had been the practice of GATT Panels not to engage in so-called *de novo* review in antidumping and countervailing duty cases. Thus, it is unclear that paragraph (i) changed past practice at all. While Panels are now required by Article 11 of the DSU to make "an objective assessment of the matter," they have interpreted this in practice in line with the GATT Panels. Paragraph (ii) in its first phrase simply restates the obligation that Panels are under pursuant to Article 3.2 of the DSU to follow the customary rules of interpretation of public international law. There is some controversy, however, whether the rest of paragraph (ii) adds much, as it could be questioned whether the relevant interpretative rules would permit multiple interpretations of the agreement. However, it is certainly the case that there could be a number of ways of implementing some of the requirements of the agreement where a minimum standard is expressed.

As of September 25, 2000, 9 of the 38 reports that had been adopted involved trade-remedy cases where administrative authorities had imposed import restrictions following an investigation of injury. Three of the cases arose under the Antidumping Agreement and two each under the SCM, Textiles and Safeguard Agreements. In two of the antidumping cases (*Coconuts* and *Cement*), the complainants lost.

The two cases under the Textiles Agreement involved challenges to U.S. safeguards imposed on Costa Rica (*Underwear*) and India (*Wool Shirts*). In each case, the underlying U.S. investigation was found to have been inadequate in light of the requirements of the Textiles Agreement. I think that most observers would agree that the U.S. procedures, which had not been updated after the Uruguay Round, were deficient. Indeed, a contemporaneous internal U.S. government study was somewhat critical of U.S. investigation procedures in this area and the U.S. did not appeal either case.[23]

The two antidumping cases (*DRAMS* and *HFCS*) were not appealed either. Both of them concerned relatively narrow issues and, in my mind, were not that controversial. Somewhat similarly, the result in the one countervailing duty case (*Lead and Bismuth Steel*) was not that unexpected, although the U.S. appealed the Panel report. That may be explained by the fact that the case involved the steel industry, which is one of the stronger supporters of strictly enforced U.S. AD/CVD laws. Interestingly, and the main reason I view this case as not all that intrusive, U.S. courts have reached a result similar to the WTO reports on the underlying issue in this case—which involves the countervailability of subsidies following the sale of the subsidized company to new owners at a market price. Obviously, the WTO decision is potentially more far-reaching in that the U.S. court decisions could be overridden by legislative action, whereas the U.S. by itself cannot change the WTO rules. Moreover, the U.S. court case was remanded, involved somewhat different facts and the U.S. agency may yet find a way to conclude that a subsidy was provided.

The remaining two trade remedy cases involve the Safeguards Agreement—in both cases the challenger was the EC. One case involved a Korean safeguard on certain dairy products; the other an Argentine safeguard on footwear. In these cases, the Appellate Body decisions were more limiting of government discretion than were the Panel decisions. While the WTO decisions in the AD/CVD and Textile cases could be viewed as relatively limited in impact, the Appellate Body decisions in the safeguards cases arguably place more constraints than some might have predicted on Member ability to use safeguards. First, the Appellate Body found that the GATT Article XIX requirement that safeguards may be imposed only in unforeseen circumstances remains in effect. This requirement had been viewed by some to have been eliminated given its absence from the new Safeguards Agreement. Second, the Appellate Body interpreted the agreement to require a recent and sudden increase in imports, unlike the common practice, at least in the U.S., of considering whether imports have increased over a five year period. Since these two requirements will impact every safeguards case, they are potentially much more important than the other trade-remedy decisions.

In a recent safeguards case that was appealed (*Wheat Gluten*), a Panel gave considerable deference to the way in which the U.S. authorities analyzed various injury criteria, but found that the U.S. authorities had used an improper standard (which is largely specified in the U.S. statute) to determine the existence of causation between the increased imports and significant injury.

Thus, in the trade-remedy area, it would appear that there has been reasonable deference to governments under the Antidumping, SCM and Textile Agreements, but that Panels and the Appellate Body may be less deferential and more intrusive in the safeguards area.

Summary

To date, I do not believe that the results of WTO dispute settlement evidence to any substantial degree overreaching by the Appellate Body or Panels so as to impose new obligations on Members or to limit inappropriately the discretion of Member government policy-making. The only possible exceptions to this statement concern the analysis of Article 5.5 in SPS cases, and perhaps the safeguards cases and, in respect of interpretation of national law, *India Patents I.*

2. Issue-Avoidance Techniques in WTO Dispute Settlement

The foregoing suggests that WTO Panels and the Appellate Body have not been all that intrusive. However, I have also noted a few examples (and there are more) where language in a specific case is capable of broad interpretation in the future. Thus, to the extent that the WTO system is believed to have been too intrusive or might be in the future, it is appropriate to consider whether the WTO dispute settlement system should make greater use of what I term "issue-avoidance" techniques.[24] Over time, courts have developed a variety of such techniques to dispose of cases or issues within cases where a decision seems unnecessary, inappropriate or perhaps simply too controversial. Among the techniques used are:

- limitations on the parties who may bring an action (e.g., "standing" or legal interest requirements);

- restrictions limiting the time at which an action may be brought (e.g., categorizing actions as too late [mootness] or too early [ripeness or failure to exhaust other remedies]);
- categorization of actions as inappropriate for judicial consideration (e.g., political questions, *non liquet*); and
- exercise of judicial economy so as avoid considering issues (e.g., strict interpretation of terms of reference; resolution of only necessary issues).

Readers familiar with WTO/GATT dispute settlement case law will recognize that Panels and the Appellate Body have considered all of these issues: (i) standing – *Bananas;* (ii) mootness – *Indonesia Autos;* (iii) ripeness – *Section 301;* (iv) exhaustion – *U.S. Salmon* (GATT Antidumping Code); (v) political-judicial balance – *India QR;* (vi) non liquet – *Coconuts, EEC Wheat Flour Export Subsidies* (Tokyo Round Subsidies Code); (vii) terms of reference – *Bananas, India Patents I, Korea Dairy;* and (viii) judicial economy – *Wool Shirts, Salmon.* In this section, I will consider the U.S. and international law rules in respect of these techniques and then consider whether the right balance has been struck by the WTO dispute settlement system in using them in the mentioned and other similar cases.

Standing or Legal Interest

The issue considered under the heading of "standing" is whether the complaining party is entitled to have the court decide the merits of the dispute.[25] Or, put another way, whether the complainant has a legal interest that a court will protect.

In U.S. constitutional law, the Supreme Court's constitutionally based standing requirements have been summarized as follows: the complainant must allege (i) injury (actual or imminent) that is (ii) caused by the defendant (iii) in a manner redressable by the court.[26] In addition, the Court has imposed three additional requirements based upon prudent judicial administration.[27] First, a party may assert only its own rights (i.e., no third-party standing). Second, a plaintiff may not sue simply as a taxpayer or citizen on the basis of an interest shared with all other taxpayers (i.e., no generalized grievances). Third, a plaintiff must be within the zone of interests protected by a statute. There are, of course, various exceptions to these rules, but the foregoing gives their general contours. The Court has at times identified a variety of values that are served by limiting standing.[28] Standing requirements are said to promote the separation of powers by limiting judicial review, to serve judicial efficiency by preventing a flood of lawsuits, to improve the quality of judicial decision-making by ensuring the existence of a specific factual dispute and to ensure fairness by preventing intermeddling.

The International Court of Justice has also applied a standing or legal interest requirement. For example, in *Barcelona Traction,* the Court ruled that Belgium did not have standing to sue Spain on behalf of Belgian shareholders of a Canadian company.[29] In *Southwest Africa,* it ruled that two African nations did not have standing to challenge whether South Africa had properly exercised the mandate it had been given by the League of Nations in respect of Southwest Africa.[30]

In WTO dispute settlement, the issue of standing or legal interest was presented in the *Bananas* case. The EC argued that the Panel should reject the U.S. claims made in respect of GATT 1994 because the U.S. did not export bananas and thus had no legal interest in claims related to trade in bananas as goods. The Panel noted that there is no explicit requirement in the DSU that a complaining party must have a legal interest in order to bring a case. It also noted that GATT rules were concerned with competitive opportunities and that the U.S. did produce bananas. Moreover, the U.S. market was affected indirectly by the EC import regime for bananas. In the Panel's view, a potential trading interest and a Member's interest in a determination of rights and obligations under the various WTO agreements were each sufficient.

On appeal, the Appellate Body noted that the case law of the International Court of Justice did not indicate that there was a general international law rule that a party must have a legal interest to bring a case. In turning to the wording of GATT Article XXIII, the Appellate Body stressed that it provided that "[i]f any *Member should consider* that any benefit accruing to it is being nullified or impaired. . ." the Member is permitted to initiate consultations and thereafter dispute settlement proceedings. It also noted the language of DSU Article 3.7, which requires Members to exercise judgment in deciding whether to bring cases. For the Appellate Body, these provisions suggest that it is largely up to the WTO Member concerned to decide for itself whether it wishes to start an action and whether it will be fruitful.

In addition, the Appellate Body noted that the U.S. did in fact have a potential export interest in bananas as a producer and that the internal market of the United States could be affected by the EC regime. It noted its agreement with the Panel that

> with increased interdependence of the global economy . . . Members have a greater stake in enforcing WTO rules than in the past since any deviation from the negotiated balance of rights and obligations is more likely than ever to affect them, directly or indirectly.[31]

Finally, it noted that the GATT claims were closely related to the GATS claims and that there was no question that the U.S. had a right to bring the GATS claims.

From the foregoing, it would appear that a standing or legal interest requirement does not exist under the DSU. However, the Appellate Body concluded its discussion of standing in *Bananas III* by stating that while the above-mentioned factors taken together were enough to give the U.S. the right to bring claims under GATT in that case, that did not mean that "one or more of the factors we noted in this case would necessarily be dispositive in another case."[32] There have been no other cases to date, so the meaning of the Appellate Body's remark remains uncertain.

It is instructive to consider whether the factors cited as supporting the doctrine of standing in the U.S. are relevant for WTO dispute settlement. The requirements under U.S. law of redressable injury caused by the respondent arise from the U.S. constitutional limitation of federal court jurisdiction to "cases" and "controversies." These requirements are not relevant to WTO dispute settlement since the DSU does not require injury to be shown (nullification or impairment is presumed if a rule violation is established) and redress in the form of a recommendation to bring a measure into conformity with WTO rules is always available. The other three factors, based on prudential concerns, do not seem relevant to WTO dispute settlement either. The rights asserted in WTO dispute settlement are by their nature the rights of a Member. Thus, the rules against third-party standing and generalized grievances seem inappropriate and the requirement that a plaintiff must be within the zone of interests protected by a statute is always met. Moreover, to the extent that the WTO Agreement represents a balance struck by all Members, the general concern about intermeddling does not seem applicable to the WTO. Thus, in my view, there does not seem to be a need to have a standing requirement in WTO dispute settlement proceedings.[33]

Mootness

The issue of mootness arises when an event occurs after the commencement of a case that effectively resolves the dispute. For example, a challenge to a statute may be viewed as moot if the statute is repealed.

Under Article III of the U.S. Constitution, the federal judicial power extends to defined "cases" and "controversies." This specification has been interpreted to preclude issuance by federal courts of so-called advisory opinions. Consequently, if a case is resolved before a decision is issued, no case or controversy continues to exist and a federal court should decline to rule thereon.[34] There are non-constitutional justifications for the mootness doctrine as well, such as judicial economy and the need to have a real controversy in order to ensure a good record for deciding a case.[35] Despite the constitutional underpinnings of the mootness doctrine, the Supreme Court has carved out a number of exceptions, some potentially far-reaching. For example, mootness may not be found if the issue is viewed as one capable of repetition but evading review (e.g., measures that are implemented periodically but only for short periods of time) or, somewhat similarly, if the challenged party has voluntarily stopped the challenged practice but remains free to resume it.[36]

The ICJ has also recognized the concept of mootness. In the *Lockerbie* case in 1998, it noted:

> The [ICJ] has already acknowledged, on several occasions in the past, that events subsequent to the filing of an application may "render an application without object" (Border and Transborder Armed Actions [Nicaragua v. Honduras], Jurisdiction and Admissibility, Judgment, I.C.J. Reports 1998, p. 95, para. 66) and "therefore the Court is not called upon to give a decision thereon" (Nuclear Tests [Australia v. France], Judgment, I.C.J. Reports 1974, p. 272, para. 62) (cf. Northern Cameroons, Judgment, I.C.J. Reports 1963, p. 38).[37]

In *Lockerbie,* the ICJ rejected a U.S. preliminary objection to jurisdiction based on the argument that Libya's claims had become moot because certain United Nations Security Council resolutions had rendered them without object. In the ICJ's view, a ruling on the U.S. objection involved a ruling on the merits and it deferred consideration of the issue. In the *Nuclear Tests* case, Australia was seeking to stop further French atmospheric nuclear tests in the South Pacific. During the action, the French Government (including the French President and senior ministers) announced that its 1974 series of atmospheric tests would be the last. In consequence, the ICJ found that the Australian claim no longer had any object and that it was therefore not called upon to give a decision thereon.

In WTO practice, the concept of mootness has been treated somewhat inconsistently. In the first WTO case *(Gasoline),* the Panel declined to consider a claim by Brazil and Venezuela on the grounds that the challenged statutory provision had not been used within a specified time-limit and therefore could never be used. However, in a later case *(Wool Shirts)* involving an Indian challenge to a U.S. textile safeguard measure, the Panel issued its final report even though the U.S. had withdrawn the measure two weeks earlier. In that case, however, neither side requested that the Panel not issue its report. Subsequently, in *Indonesia Autos,* Indonesia asked the Panel not to rule on claims involving a measure that it claimed it had withdrawn. Its request was opposed by the complainants in the case, who contested the assertion that the measure had effectively been withdrawn. The Panel decided to rule on the measures.[38] In so doing, it noted that (i) many other (particularly GATT) Panels had followed that practice[39] and (ii) the Appellate Body had ruled on an Argentine statistical tax that had been reduced from 3% to 0.5%, arguably bringing it into compliance with GATT rules, between the issuance of the Panel report and the Appellate Body report. The Appellate Body had done so without discussing the mootness issue.

I think that as the WTO dispute settlement system matures, it could usefully adopt stricter rules on mootness. While it will sometimes seem a waste of resources to dismiss a case right before the end of the process without a definitive result, the ultimate goal of dispute is to ensure that Members comply with their obligations and withdrawal of the challenged measure does that. As the Appellate Body noted in *Wool Shirts,* the purpose of dispute settlement is not to make law but to resolve disputes. The problem, of course, is that there would have to be exceptions to such a rule. Primarily, the exceptions would concern measures that by their nature are short-term and therefore likely to always evade review in dispute settlement. Such an exception is a common one in some national systems and could be applied in WTO dispute settlement. There would also have to be a catch-all exception to avoid potential abuses.

There is even a stronger argument for the Appellate Body to dismiss appeals as moot if the measure is withdrawn before the appeal is heard or before the report is issued. Dismissing an appeal as moot would lend no particular standing to the Panel report. The issues would clearly remain open for future appellate consideration, even if the Panel report were adopted. It would, however, conserve what seem to be somewhat overstretched Appellate Body resources.

Ripeness (Mandatory vs. Discretionary Measures)

The doctrine of ripeness is concerned with ensuring that cases presented to a court are ready for review in the sense that they are not too speculative. It is designed both to avoid cases about injury that may never occur and to ensure that a proper record exists on which a decision can be based. There is an obvious overlap with standing requirements, insofar as they require a plaintiff to show injury, but ripeness focuses on whether there has been injury as opposed to who has been injured.

In U.S. constitutional law, the "case or controversy" requirement has been interpreted to require the existence of injury. As such, the absence of injury (lack of ripeness) is a ground for a federal court to decline to exercise jurisdiction.[40] However, it has been recognized that this rule may cause significant hardship. For example, must one violate a statute and run the attendant risks in order to challenge its constitutionality? If so, people may feel compelled to acquiesce to a statute that they are convinced is unconstitutional because they cannot afford to run the risk of violating the statute and losing on their constitutional claim. To address this problem, the Supreme Court has allowed pre-enforcement challenges to legislation when there would be hardship if review is denied, provided that the issue is ripe for judicial consideration (e.g., whether there is an adequate factual record to review). If these factors are present, the injury requirement is viewed as satisfied. However, since these factors are rather nebulous, U.S. federal courts have considerable discretion in deciding whether a case is ripe and their exercise of discretion is not always done in a consistent manner.[41]

Concerns about ripeness also exist at the ICJ. While the ICJ is permitted to, and has often issued, advisory opinions, these may only be requested by an international organization. Individual states may not request advisory opinions. In contentious proceedings between states, the ICJ's function is said to be "to decide in accordance with international law such disputes as are submitted to it."[42] What is a "dispute"? The ICJ has indicated:

> The Court, as a judicial organ, is however only concerned to establish, first that the dispute before it is a legal dispute, in the sense of a dispute capable of being settled by the application of principles and rules of international law, and second, that the Court has jurisdiction to deal with it . . .[43]

The Court has generally not interpreted this requirement that strictly, having stated, *inter alia*, that "a dispute is a disagreement on a point of law or fact, a conflict of legal views or interests between parties." However, in more general terms, it is noted in *Northern Cameroons* that:

> The function of the Court is to state the law, but it may pronounce judgment only in connection with concrete cases where there exists at the time of the adjudication an actual controversy involving a conflict of legal interests between the parties. The Court's judgment must have some practical consequence in the sense that it can affect existing legal rights or obligations of the parties, thus removing uncertainty from their legal relations. No judgment on the merits in this case could satisfy these essentials of the judicial function.[44]

In that case, the agreement invoked by Cameroon had expired and it asked for no reparations or other relief (e.g., the detachment of the Northern Cameroons from Nigeria). In the *Northern Cameroons* case, however, it was noted that a determination of a legal issue under an extant treaty "necessarily operates as a finding about the correct interpretation or application of the treaty, and therefore serves a useful and effective legal purpose during the life-time of the treaty."[45]

In the WTO and GATT before it, much has been made of the ripeness issue. As a general rule, it has been said that under GATT dispute settlement precedents, if a measure is mandatory, i.e., if certain circumstances occur, the government does not have discretion as to whether or not to apply the measure, then it is challengeable in GATT dispute settlement proceedings even if it has not been applied and even if it has not yet come into effect. However, a discretionary measure is not challengeable.[46] The principal case involving this issue in the WTO is the *Section 301* case. The U.S. and the EC devoted the lion's share of their arguments to exploring this distinction. The Panel concluded that the issue had to be decided on a case-by-case basis by examining WTO provisions at issue. In that case, it found essentially that a discretionary statute could be challenged under certain WTO rules because of the nature of the obligations contained in those rules.

The *Section 301* report seemed to expand significantly the type of measures subject to challenge in WTO dispute settlement. While the report stressed that the issue had to be decided on a case-by-case basis in light of the relevant WTO provisions, its reasoning could be used to justify examination of many measures formerly thought to be discretionary, at least so long as they may raise questions as to the certainty that a Member will use only WTO-consistent measures to govern trading relationships. In the *Section 301* case, after having broadened the scope of challenge measures and found on a preliminary basis that the U.S. measure violated DSU Article 23, the report then found that other factors (official government statements) effectively cured the violation. It is not clear that such "cures" will often be available.

In the end, the clearest justification for allowing a WTO challenge to discretionary legislation is that such legislation may have an impact on trade, even if it has not (yet) been applied. Indeed, Panels in the past have refused to consider that the long-time and consistent non-enforcement of mandatory legislation renders it immune from challenge.[47] Given the focus of WTO rules on competitive opportunities, this would argue for not strictly applying the discretionary/mandatory legislation rule. I tend to think, however, that Panels and the Appellate Body should exercise some restraint in this area. I can imagine laws that do affect trade even though they are not applied, while others would likely not. It would probably be prudent to avoid rulings in the latter cases. Indeed, one can imagine cases where a Member believes that it is politically necessary for it to have certain measures on the statute books that may be of questionable WTO-consistency, but not politically necessary for that Member to take action under such measures.

Exhaustion of Available Remedies/Abstention

The requirement that a plaintiff exhaust available remedies (i.e., more appropriate remedies available in another forum) is a device to provide for orderly consideration of issues. It is designed in part to ensure the use of the more appropriate tribunal to decide cases.

In the United States, there is a requirement commonly applied for persons challenging administrative actions to exhaust their administrative remedies before turning to the courts. Somewhat similarly, federal courts may abstain from deciding cases which can be resolved in state courts on state legal grounds or to avoid interference in state court proceedings.[48]

Somewhat analogously, the ICJ typically requires complaining countries to have exhausted local remedies before invoking its jurisdiction.[49]

In GATT/WTO jurisprudence, no such rule has been applied. In a GATT antidumping case (*U.S. Salmon*),[50] the Panel rejected the argument by the U.S. that a party could not raise before a Panel an argument that it had not raised before an administrative agency. Typically, GATT/WTO Panels have considered trade remedy cases where resort to national courts was still possible. Indeed, given procedures in some Members, such as the U.S., a requirement that all national appeals be exhausted could make it difficult to obtain WTO review of trade remedy actions as it is often many years before all judicial review is exhausted. The Panel in the *Argentina Textiles* case rejected a related argument by Argentina, i.e., that since Argentine courts must follow international law, there was no WTO violation because an adequate remedy was available to correct any WTO violation before a national court.

A requirement to exhaust national remedies would too often be tantamount to denying effective enforcement of WTO obligations for too long a period of time and would not seem to be an appropriate mechanism for avoiding difficult issues.

Political-Judicial Balance

In the United States, the U.S. Supreme Court has developed the so-called political question doctrine, which it invokes to avoid decisions in certain cases that have political ramifications. Of course, any court decision may have such ramifications, but the political question doctrine is designed to avoid decision by the Court that would bring it into conflict with politics. As expressed in *Baker v. Carr:*

> Prominent on the surface of any case held to involve a political question is found a textually demonstrable commitment of the issue to a coordinate political department; or a lack of judicially discoverable and manageable standards for resolving it; or the impossibility of deciding without an initial policy determination of a kind clearly for nonjudicial discretion; or the impossibility of a court's undertaking independent resolution without expressing lack of respect due coordinate branches of government; or an unusual need for unquestioning adherence to a

> political decision already made; or the potentiality of embarrassment from multifarious departments on one question.[51]

While commentators have viewed these criteria of limited use, the Court has often quoted this language. In practical terms, the Court has declined to rule, *inter alia*, on whether a state has a republican form of government as required by Article IV(4) of the U.S. Constitution, on matters related to congressional governance, on the process for ratifying constitutional amendments and on some matters related to foreign policy. Its decisions are not that consistent, however, and counter-examples in the above categories may be found.[52]

The ICJ has generally not accepted arguments that it should decline to rule on an issue because it is a political question. Rather, it has noted that many disputes have political ramifications, but that is not an excuse not to examine the legal issues presented.[53]

As noted in Part I of this paper, in the GATT/WTO context, a political-question type issue has arisen in respect of whether certain matters arising under the balance-of-payments exceptions in GATT Articles XII and XVIII:B and under the regional trade rules of Article XXIV should be subject to review by Panels and the Appellate Body. Generally, I conclude above that in considering the issue of balance within the WTO system, it is important that Panels and the Appellate Body do not create rules that cause them to reject cases on *a priori* grounds. To do so risks upsetting the balance of rights and obligations among Members. The fundamental purpose of the dispute settlement system is to provide security and predictability to the multilateral trading system. It cannot do that if certain obligations are viewed as too political to be reviewed in dispute settlement. It may well be that Panels and the Appellate Body should defer to a Member's decision in a specific case (e.g., where the issue of whether a measure meets the terms of an exception is a close one), but that does not mean that the dispute settlement system should not consider the claims in the first instance.

I would take this position even in cases where the respondent invokes GATT Article XXI – the national security exception. Of course, given the wording of Article XXI ("any action which it considers necessary"), I would expect Panels and the Appellate Body to afford considerable discretion to the Member invoking that exception. Nonetheless, the possibility of dispute settlement review to prevent abusive invocations is appropriate.

Non Liquet

A *non liquet* occurs when a judicial body decides not to rule on a case because the law is not clear or, put another way, there is a gap in the law. As so formulated, it is not an issue-avoidance technique found in U.S.

constitutional law, although it is not all that dissimilar to certain techniques discussed herein. The authorization to the ICJ to use general principles of international law as a source of law[54] has been viewed as an attempt to prevent the use of *non liquet* by the ICJ.[55]

The prime example of *non liquet* in GATT dispute settlement was the unadopted Panel report in *EEC Wheat Flour Export Subsidies* where, in a somewhat confusing Panel report, the Panel, *inter alia*, noted an absence of legal certainty as to the meaning of the Tokyo Round Subsidies Code. That Panel report is generally viewed as unsatisfactory. In WTO jurisprudence, the *Coconuts* case has been viewed as a *non liquet.*[56] In that case, the complainant was essentially denied WTO relief, but in circumstances where it could have pursued a claim under the Tokyo Round Anti-dumping Agreement.

Generally speaking, I think that *non liquet* is and should be a disfavored judicial technique. The WTO dispute settlement system is typically asked if a measure violates one or more of the covered agreements. Normally, the Appellate Body and Panels should be able to answer that question using standard treaty interpretation methods. If a complainant is unable to establish a violation of an agreement, it will simply lose for that reason. Thus, I think that *non liquet* is not a technique that WTO dispute settlement should embrace.

Terms of Reference

One way to avoid or at least delay decisions in a dispute is to adopt and to apply strictly various pleading requirements so as to increase the possibility of rejecting disputes because of a pleading irregularity.

In the U.S., modern codes and rules of civil procedure have largely adopted the opposite approach. While pre-trial motion practice is extensive, a non-substantive reason for dismissing a claim is usually not fatal in that the claimant is permitted to amend its complaint within a specified period to correct the irregularity. It is my impression that the ICJ does not follow an overly technical approach to such matters of procedure.

To date, Panels and the AB have been relatively unsympathetic to arguments concerning procedural irregularities. The arguments have, however, been regularly made. For the most part, these arguments have been of two sorts. First, that the request to establish the Panel included matters that were not the subject of consultations; second, that the request for the Panel failed to meet the terms of DSU Article 6.2 by failing to give a brief summary of the case.[57]

In respect of the arguments concerning the relationship of the request for consultations and the Panel request, it should be noted that the only prerequisite in the DSU for requesting a Panel is that consultations have failed to resolve the *"dispute."* While it should be open to argue that a Panel has been requested in respect of a different "dispute" than that on which consultations were held, to find that the disputes are different should require a determination of a serious difference. A requirement of identity between the consultation and Panel requests serves no useful purpose. Third parties will be able to discern any change between the consultation and Panel requests. It cannot be argued persuasively that a requirement of additional consultations on the dispute would likely resolve it. In fact, the argument that there should be identity and that the lack of such identity requires supplemental consultations is typically a ploy raised by respondents to gain time since a new consultation request would put back the process by a minimum of five or six months (three months for the consultations and re-establishment of the Panel, plus a month or more to select the Panel and to re-file submissions). Since WTO Members have committed to bring all of their WTO-related disputes to the WTO, the identity issue does not raise a serious jurisdictional issue, as the claims at issue can clearly be brought to the WTO dispute settlement system.

There are clear disadvantages for the system in imposing such a requirement of identity between the consultation and Panel requests. First, it could lead to the splitting of cases into two parts and the creation of two Panels to consider what is essentially one case. Second, it would place a premium on the involvement of lawyers before the consultations are requested. This is unlikely to promote settlement and may be to the disadvantage of developing country Members. Third, its principal impact would be to promote procedural wrangling over a non-outcome-determinative subsidiary issue, thereby delaying the resolution of the dispute. Given that one of the hallmarks of the GATT/WTO system has been its prompt treatment of disputes, this would be particularly unfortunate.

Thus, so long as there is control for abuse so that an SPS case does not become a TRIPs case between the consultation and Panel stages, the requirement of prior consultations should be construed liberally. Fortunately, thus far, Panels have rejected the argument that there must be an identity between the consultation request and the Panel request.[58] In the *Brazil Aircraft* case, the Panel noted that one function of the consultation process is to clarify the issues in a dispute, which suggests that there should not be an identity between the two requests. On appeal, the Appellate Body stated that it did not believe that the DSU required "a *precise and exact identity* between the specific measures that were the subject of consultations and the specific measures identified in the request for the establishment of a Panel."[59] It is not clear how much deviation from "precise and exact" identity the Appellate Body would accept. Hopefully, it will adopt the approach suggested above.

The same considerations apply to the requirement in Article 6.2 that there be a summary of the legal claim. In *Bananas,* that summary consisted of a list of provisions of WTO agreements alleged to have been violated. While the Panel and the Appellate Body characterized a simple listing of provisions as the minimum possible, they did accept it as complying with the requirements of Article 6.2. In a subsequent case, the Appellate Body suggested that Panels should be more rigorous in enforcing this requirement, and it backed away from accepting a mere listing of provisions. It went on to rule, however, that the respondent had not shown that it was prejudiced and so rejected its claim.[60] This result will probably not discourage, and may even encourage, this type of argument, which is unfortunate. Considerable time will be spent trying to decide whether the summary is adequate, after which a finding of no prejudice will typically be made. Unfortunately, one may anticipate confusing and conflicting decisions on the adequacy issue.

Thus, while an unnecessarily strict reading of procedural rules could avoid dealing with certain issues or cases in the short run, it seems an inappropriate approach for WTO dispute settlement.

Judicial Economy

GATT and WTO Panels have traditionally ruled only on those claims of a party that must be addressed in order to resolve the matter at issue. Thus, if an aspect of a measure has been found to violate one GATT provision, Panels have typically not considered whether it violates another provision as well. This practice, referred to as judicial economy, has been approved by the Appellate Body,[61] although it has not always been followed.

There are essentially two pressures that have caused Panels not to exercise as much judicial economy as they could. First, the advent of intensive appellate review has caused some Panels to consider additional issues so as to provide alternative bases for findings that will increase the chance that their basic decision will be upheld or so as to enable the Appellate Body to have more of a record of factual determinations in the event it decides to "complete the analysis" in respect of an issue not dealt with by the Panel.

Second, the Appellate Body has stated that Panels should not exercise judicial economy to the extent that only a partial resolution of the matter results. In its words:

> A Panel has to address those claims on which a finding is necessary in order to enable the DSB to make sufficiently precise recommendations and rulings so as allow for prompt compliance by a Member with those recommendations and rulings "in order to ensure effective resolution of dispute to the benefit of all Members" (quoting DSU Article 21.1).
>
> In this case, for the Panel to make findings concerning violation of Article 5.1 with respect to other Canadian [i.e., other than ocean-caught

> wild Pacific] salmon, without also making findings under Articles 5.5 and 5.6, would not enable the DSB to make sufficiently precise recommendations and rulings so as to allow for compliance by Australia with its obligations under the *SPS Agreement,* in order to ensure the effective resolution of this dispute with Canada. An SPS measure, which is brought into consistency with Article 5.1, may still be inconsistent with either Article 5.5 or Article 5.6, or with both.[62]

It is unclear how this guidance should be interpreted. It could be read to reject the very notion of judicial economy since more information about what would comply with an agreement would always be useful for implementation purposes.

As a general matter, I think that judicial economy is an appropriate technique for Panels to use to avoid controversial issues. If a measure can be found to be inconsistent with WTO rules without addressing a difficult issue in the case, Panels should not hesitate to avoid the difficult issue. Perhaps the issue will arise again, but perhaps it will not.

It should be noted that it is evident from the discussion of the exercise of judicial economy—in the argument sections of Panel reports, in the interim review process and in the Appellate Body—that parties are often frustrated by the exercise of judicial economy. This is understandable, as a party may have devoted considerable time and effort to make a whole range of arguments and feel quite frustrated if many of them are not even considered. In my view, however, if the Panel accepts one of a party's theories as to why a measure is WTO-inconsistent, that should be sufficient, particularly where the additional arguments may be difficult or controversial. For me, if anything, Panels should probably be more willing to exercise judicial economy than they seem to be nowadays.

Scope of Appellate Review and Appellate Judicial Economy

The Appellate Body has never articulated a standard of review to apply to its consideration of appeals. While DSU Article 17.12 provides that the AB shall "address each of the issues raised," it would seem that the AB has the flexibility of exercising judicial economy as well. It can simply say that having addressed certain issues, the remaining issues do not need to be considered separately. That statement, in itself, "addresses" the remaining issues.

To date, the Appellate Body does not seem to have exercised much judicial economy, except when it has declared that appealed issues are factual in nature and therefore beyond its purview. Indeed, in a recent decision, it went to the other extreme and announced, without any accompanying reasoning, that it would not rule as the Panel had done on an issue that the

Appellate Body had itself described as moot.[63] For me, the Appellate Body could appropriately deal with more issues on the basis of judicial economy.

3. Conclusion

In general, I do not believe that the Appellate Body and Panels have overreached in the various reports adopted through September 25, 2000, in the WTO dispute settlement system, except perhaps in the few, relatively minor, matters mentioned at the end of Part I. In respect of issue-avoidance techniques, I think that over time the WTO system could profitably make more use of such techniques in respect of the timing of consideration of issues (mootness and ripeness) and the exercise of judicial economy. This is particularly true in the case of the Appellate Body in respect of mootness and judicial economy. The one caveat has been noted in connection with the discussion of judicial economy—it is necessary to have clear standards as to when these techniques will be used, so as to avoid having some Members believe that they have been unfairly treated differently than other Members.

APPENDIX

LIST OF WTO APPELLATE BODY AND PANEL REPORTS

Note: Appellate Body Reports are numbered WT/DS##/AB/R;
Panel Reports are numbered WT/DS##/R

SHORT NAME	FULL CITATION INFORMATION
Argentina Footwear	Argentina – Safeguard Measures on Imports of Footwear, WT/DS121, Appellate Body Report modifying Panel Report, adopted January 12, 2000
Argentina Textiles	Argentina – Certain Measures Affecting Imports of Footwear, Textiles, Apparel and Other Items, WT/DS56, Appellate Body Report modifying Panel Report, adopted April 22, 1998
Australia Leather	Australia – Subsidies Provided to Producers and Exporters of Automotive Leather, WT/DS126, Panel Report, adopted June 16, 1999
Bananas	European Communities – Regime for the Importation, Sale and Distribution of Bananas, WT/DS27, Appellate Body Report modifying Panel Report, adopted September 25, 1997
Brazil Aircraft	Brazil – Export Financing Program for Aircraft, WT/DS46, Appellate Body Report modifying

	Panel Report, adopted August 20, 1999
Canada Aircraft	Canada – Measures Affecting the Export of Civilian Aircraft, WT/DS70, Appellate Body Report upholding Panel Report, adopted August 20, 1999
Canada Autos	Canada – Certain Measures Affecting the Automotive Industry, WT/DS139 & 142, Appellate Body Report modifying Panel Report, adopted June 19, 2000
Canada Dairy	Canada – Measures Affecting Dairy Products, WT/DS103 & 113, Appellate Body Report modifying Panel Report, adopted, October 27, 1999
Canada Pharm. Patents	Canada – Patent Protection of Pharmaceutical Products, WT/DS114, Panel Report, adopted April 7, 2000
Cement	Guatemala – Anti-Dumping Investigation Regarding Imports of Portland Cement from Mexico, WT/DS60, Appellate Body Report reversing Panel Report, adopted November 25, 1998
Chile Taxes	Chile – Taxes on Alcoholic Beverages, WT/DS110, Appellate Body Report modifying Panel Report, adopted January 12, 2000
Coconuts	Brazil – Measures Affecting Desiccated Coconut, WT/DS22, Appellate Body Report upholding Panel Report, adopted March 20, 1997, DSR 1997:I, page 167
DRAMS	United States – Anti-Dumping Duty on Dynamic Random Access Memory Semiconductors (DRAMS) of One Megabit or Above from Korea, WT/DS99, Panel Report, adopted March 19, 2000
Film	Japan – Measures Affecting Consumer Photographic Film and Paper, WT/DS44, Panel Report, adopted April 22, 1998
FSC	United States – Tax Treatment for "Foreign Sales Corporations," WT/DS108, Appellate Body Report modifying Panel Report, adopted March 20, 2000
Gasoline	United States – Standards for Reformulated and Conventional Gasoline, WT/DS2 & 4, Appellate Body Report modifying Panel Report, adopted May 20, 1996, DSR 1996:I, page 3
HFCS	Mexico – Anti-Dumping Investigation of High-

	Fructose Corn Syrup (HFCS) from the United States, WT/DS132, Panel Report, adopted February 24, 2000
Hormones	European Communities – Measures Affecting Livestock and Meat (Hormones), WT/DS26 & 48, Appellate Body Report modifying Panel Report, adopted February 13, 1998
India Patents I	India – Patent Protection for Pharmaceutical and Agricultural Chemical Patents (complaint by the United States), WT/DS50, Appellate Body Report modifying Panel Report, adopted January 16, 1998
India Patents II	India – Patent Protection for Pharmaceutical and Agricultural Chemical Patents (complaint by European Communities), WT/DS79, Panel Report, adopted September 2, 1998
India QR	India – Quantitative Restrictions on Imports of Agricultural, Textile and Industrial Products, WT/DS90, Appellate Body Report upholding Panel Report, adopted September 22, 1999
Indonesia Autos	Indonesia – Certain Measures Affecting the Automobile Industry, WT/DS54, 55, 59 & 64, Panel Report, adopted July 23, 1998
Japan Apples	Japan – Measures Affecting Agricultural Products, WT/DS76, Appellate Body Report modifying Panel Report, adopted March 19, 1999
Japan Taxes	Japan – Taxes on Alcoholic Beverages, WT/DS8, 10 & 11, Appellate Body Report modifying Panel Report, adopted November 1, 1996, DSR 1996:I, page 97
Korea Beef	Korea – Measures Affecting Imports of Fresh, Chilled and Frozen Beef, WT/DS161, Panel Report, appealed September 11, 2000
Korea Dairy	Korea – Definitive Safeguard Measure on Imports of Certain Dairy Products, WT/DS98, Appellate Body Report modifying Panel Report, adopted January 12, 2000
Korea Procurement	Korea – Measures Affecting Government Procurement, WT/DS163, Panel Report, adopted June 19, 2000
Korea Taxes	Korea – Taxes on Alcoholic Beverages, WT/DS75 & 84, Appellate Body Report upholding Panel Report, adopted February 17, 1999
LAN Equipment	European Communities – Customs Classification

	of Certain Computer Equipment, WT/DS62, 67 & 68, Appellate Body Report modifying Panel Report, adopted June 22, 1998
Lead & Bismuth Steel	United States – Imposition of Countervailing Duties on Certain Hot-Rolled Lead and Bismuth Carbon Steel Products Originating in the United Kingdom, WT/DS138, Appellate Body Report upholding Panel Report, adopted June 7, 2000
Periodicals	Canada – Certain Measures Concerning Periodicals, WT/DS31, Appellate Body Report modifying Panel Report, adopted July 30, 1997, DSR 1997:I, page 449
Poultry	European Communities – Measures Affecting Importation of Certain Poultry Products, WT/DS69, Appellate Body Report modifying Panel Report, adopted July 23, 1998
Salmon	Australia – Measures Affecting the Importation of Salmon, WT/DS18, Appellate Body Report modifying Panel Report, adopted November 6, 1998; Compliance Panel Report, adopted March 20, 2000
Section 301	United States – Sections 301–310 of the Trade Act of 1974, WT/DS152, Panel Report, adopted January 27, 2000
Shrimp	United States – Import Prohibition of Certain Shrimp and Shrimp Products, WT/DS58, Appellate Body Report modifying Panel Report, adopted November 6, 1998
Turkey Textiles	Turkey – Restrictions on Imports of Textiles and Clothing Products, WT/DS34, Appellate Body Report modifying Panel Report, adopted November 19, 1999
Underwear	United States – Restrictions on Imports of Cotton and Man-Made Fibre Underwear, WT/DS24, Appellate Body Report modifying Panel Report, adopted February 25, 1997, DSR 1997:I, page 11
U.S. Copyright	United States – Section 110(5) of the U.S. Copyright Act, WT/DS160, Panel Report, adopted June 19, 2000
Wheat Gluten	United States – Definitive Safeguard Measures on Imports of Wheat Gluten from the European Communities, WT/DS166, Panel Report, appealed September 26, 2000

Wool Shirts	United States – Measures Affecting Imports of Woven Wool Shirts and Blouses, WT/DS33, Appellate Body Report upholding Panel Report, adopted May 23, 1997, DSR 1997:I, page 323

NOTES

1. I have not counted in these statistics Panel and Appellate Body reports issued pursuant to DSU Article 21.5 (so-called compliance reports), although I do refer to them where relevant to specific substantive issues.

2. The six cases where complainants lost included some of the more controversial ones, such as *Film* and *Section 301,* neither of which was appealed. The other four cases were *Coconuts* (loss upheld on appeal), *LAN Equipment* and *Cement* (victories at Panel level for complainants effectively reversed on appeal), and *Korea Procurement* (loss not appealed).

3. Full citations to the 38 WTO cases considered are contained in Annex I.

4. For similar results, see *Canada Dairy* (re Article II) and *Korea Beef* (not yet adopted, on appeal).

5. Panel Report on Japan – Customs Duties, Taxes and Labeling Practices on Imported Wines and Alcoholic Beverages, adopted on November 10, 1987, BISD 34S/83.

6. The Japan case also involved two products found to be like – vodka and shochu.

7. Panel Report on United States – Measures Affecting Alcoholic and Malt Beverages, adopted June 19, 1992, BISD 39S/206; Panel Report on United States – Taxes on Automobiles, GATT Doc. DS31/R (October 11, 1994) (not adopted).

8. See, e.g., Panel Report on United States – Denial of Most-Favored-Nation Treatment as to Non-Rubber Footwear from Brazil, adopted June 19, 1992, BISD 39S/128.

9. Panel Report on EEC – Tariff Treatment of Citrus Products from Certain Mediterranean Countries, GATT Doc. L/5142 (June 17, 1981) (not adopted).

10. Panel Report on EEC – Member States' Import Regime for Bananas, GATT Doc. DS32/R (June 3, 1993) (not adopted); EEC – Import Regime for Bananas, GATT Doc. DS38/R (Jan. 18, 1994) (not adopted). See T. Christoforou, Multilateral Rules as a Constraint on Regional Rules: A Regional Perspective, in P. Demaret, J.-F. Bellis & G. Garcia Jimenez (eds.), *Regionalism and Multilateralism After the Uruguay Round: Convergence, Divergence and Interaction*, at 757, 766 (1997).

11. Panel Report on Republic of Korea – Restrictions on Imports of Beef – Complaint by the United States, adopted on November 7, 1989, BISD 36S/268.

12. This analysis of the *India QR* case is taken from a comment I presented to a conference in honor of Raymond Vernon, held at the Kennedy School in June 2000.

13. Understanding on Balance-of-Payments Provisions of GATT 1994, footnote 1; Understanding on the Interpretation of Article XXIV of GATT 1994, paragraph 12.

14. While it is true that a proposal to grant this authority in more explicit terms was not included in the understanding in the case of balance-of-payments measures, it is equally true that a proposal to limit this authority was not included in the case of Article XXIV. See

MTN.TNC/W/125 (Dec. 13, 1993), quoted in T. Christoforou, supra, at 764–65. However, given the clarity of the existing text, consideration of this ambiguous negotiating history is neither appropriate nor helpful under the standard rules for treaty interpretation.

15. Panel Report on Republic of Korea – Restrictions on Imports of Beef – Complaint by the United States, adopted on November 7, 1989, BISD 36/268, 304.

16. Id., at 302–03.

17. I would note, however, that the compliance Panel report in *Australia Leather* (not appealed because of prior agreement), which essentially concluded that implementation of the Panel report required the repayment of subsidies at issue, is an example of questionable intrusion by a Panel into governmental discretion, especially given the traditional practice in respect of remedies under GATT/WTO dispute settlement.

18. A failure to base a measure on a risk assessment has led Panels and the Appellate Body to conclude consequentially that the measure violates Article 2.2 (measure must be based on scientific evidence). In *Japan*, the Panel found that Japan had violated Article 2.2 without considering the risk assessment issue. The Panel in that case also found a violation of Article 7 (transparency) that was upheld by the Appellate Body. Violations of Article 5.6 (requirement to use less trade restrictive measures where feasible) were found by the Panels in *Salmon* and *Japan*, but were reversed on appeal.

19. This looser interpretation of Article 5.5 may be explained by its relationship to Article 2.3. If the third requirement of Article 5.5 means the same thing as Article 2.3, which provides that SPS measures shall not discriminate arbitrarily or unjustifiably between Members where similar conditions prevail and not be disguised restrictions on trade, then Article 5.5's requirement that Members "shall avoid arbitrary or unjustifiable distinctions" adds nothing to the SPS Agreement. A violation of Article 2.3 might be a violation of Article 5.5 (depending on whether there is an arbitrary or unjustifiable distinction between comparable situations), but a violation of Article 5.5 would always be a violation of Article 2.3. Thus, the added elements of Article 5.5 would have no real meaning. A looser interpretation of the third requirement can be viewed as giving Article 5.5 independent meaning. This explanation is contradicted, however, by the view of Panels and the Appellate Body that a violation of Article 5.5 is also a violation of Article 2.3.

20. Panel Report, *Salmon*, paras. 8.146-8.160.

21. Appellate Body Report, *Salmon*, paras. 159–78.

22. Compliance Panel Report, *Salmon*, paras. 7.86-7.108.

23. U.S. General Accounting Office, Textile Trade: Operations of the Committee for the Implementation of Textile Agreements, NSAID-96-186 (September 1996).

24. See Jeffrey L. Dunoff, The Death of the Trade Regime, *European Journal of International Law* 10 (1999), no. 4, at 733, 757–60.

25. Erwin Chermerinsky, *Federal Jurisdiction* (3rd ed. 1999), at 56.

26. Chermerinsky, at 59.

27. Chermerinsky, at 59–60.

28. Chermerinsky, at 57–59.

29. ICJ Reports 1970, p. 3.

30. ICJ Reports 1966, p. 6.

31. Appellate Body Report, *Bananas,* para. 136.

32. Id., at para. 138.

33. Of course, other values served by the standing requirement—avoiding controversial decisions, ensuring a full record for a decision and judicial economy—may apply, but they are discussed in more detail below under headings where they loom larger as justifications for issue-avoidance techniques. It is worth mentioning, however, that one fear expressed in respect of a lack of standing or legal interest requirement—a flood of cases or intermeddling—has not occurred in the WTO since the *Bananas* case.

34. Chermerinsky, at 126.

35. Chermerinsky, at 127–28.

36. Chermerinsky, at 132–40.

37. Questions of Interpretation and Application of the 1971 Montreal Convention arising from the Aerial Incident at Lockerbie (Libyan Arab Jamahiriya v. United States of America), Judgment, ICJ Reports 1998, p. 131, para. 45.

38. WTO Panels have also confronted the problem of replacement measures, where they have ruled on the replacement measure rather than the replaced measure. The issue in that situation, however, is more one of expansion of terms of reference than declining to rule on mootness grounds.

39. See reports cited in Panel Report, *Indonesia Autos,* para. 14.9, fn. 642.

40. Chermerinsky, at 114–17.

41. Chermerinsky, at 117.

42. Statute of the International Court of Justice, art. 38.

43. Border and Transborder Armed Actions, ICJ Reports 1988, p. 91 (para. 52).

44. ICJ Reports 1962, p. 15, 33–34.

45. Id., p. 98 (Judge Fitzmaurice).

46. See, e.g., Panel Report on United States – Measures Affecting the Importation, Internal Sale and Use of Tobacco, adopted October 4, 1994, BISD 41S/131, 174–75 at para. 118 (and cited cases).

47. *Malt Beverages,* op. cit.

48. Chermerinsky, at ch. 12 (abstention to avoid constitutional rulings or because of unclear state law); ch. 13 (abstention to avoid interference with state proceedings); ch. 14 (abstention to avoid duplicative litigation).

49. ELSI, ICJ Reports 1989, p. 15, 42–48; Interhandel, ICJ Reports 1959, p. 6, 26–29. This rule is of particular application when a nation is exercising its right of diplomatic protection of a national.

50. Panel Report on United States Imposition of Anti-Dumping Duties on Imports of Fresh and Chilled Atlantic Salmon from Norway, adopted April 27, 1994, BISD 41S/229.

51. 369 U.S. 186, 217 (1962).

52. Chermerinsky, at 146.

53. See generally Malcom N. Shaw, *International Law* (4th ed. 1997), at 753; Shabtai Rosenne, *The Law and Practice of the International Court, 1920–96* (3rd ed. 1997), sec. II.245.

54. Statute of the International Court of Justice, art. 38(1)(c).

55. Shaw, op. cit., at 78; see generally Legality of the Threat or Use of Nuclear Weapons (United Nations), ICJ Reports 1996 (e.g., discussion of various views on *non liquet* in Declaration of Judge Vereshchetin). There was a dispute between the judges in this case over whether the majority had in effect invoked *non liquet* in declining to answer if a state could use nuclear weapons in self defense if its survival were at stake.

56. See Pierre Pescatore, untitled article in Antonio Perez van Kappel & Wolfgang Heusel, Free World Trade and the European Union: The Reconciliation of Interests and the Review of the Understanding on Dispute Settlement in the Framework of the World Trade Organization 9, 21–22 (Academy of European Law, Trier).

57. These arguments should be distinguished from those concerned with the scope of the Panel's terms of reference, where Panels and the AB have insisted that the request for the Panel, which typically sets the Panel's terms of reference, must specify the measures at issue and the provisions of the WTO agreements that are alleged to have been violated. While Panels have allowed some leeway in respect of the measures specified, so as to include what might be called subsidiary or implementing measures, they have insisted that any such unspecified measure must be closely related to a specified measure, so as to give reasonable notice of the scope of the claim to the respondent and potential third parties. Similarly, Panels and the Appellate Body have not allowed complainants to invoke WTO provisions not specifically listed in the Panel request and have rejected those based on a general reference to an agreement or on a reference to other, unspecified provisions.

58. See, e.g., Panel Report, *Brazil Aircraft,* paras. 7.9-7.11

59. Appellate Body Report, *Brazil Aircraft,* para. 132.

60. Appellate Body Report, *Korea Dairy.*

61. Appellate Body Report, *Wool Shirts.*

62. Appellate Body Report, *Salmon,* paras. 223–24.

63. Appellate Body Compliance Report, *Brazil Aircraft,* para. 80.

CHAPTER 3

Limits of WTO Jurisprudence: Comments from an International Law and Human Rights Perspective

Ernst-Ulrich Petersmann

The two excellent reports by Prof. Howse (supra p. 11) and Prof. Davey (supra p. 43) both conclude that the WTO Appellate Body and WTO Panels have so far respected the customary rules of international treaty interpretation and can hardly be criticized for having exceeded their jurisdiction for the settlement of disputes among WTO Members and for the related clarification of WTO rules and protection of WTO rights.

1. Dynamic Treaty Evolution Based on Consensus

The Dispute Settlement Body (DSB) has so far never exercised its power *not* to adopt Panel and Appellate Body reports (cf. Articles 16:4 and 17:14 of the DSU), for instance, if the DSB should ever find that a Panel or the Appellate Body actually exceeded their limited jurisdiction. Dispute settlement rulings by the DSB are annually confirmed by the WTO General Council and by the bi-annual WTO Ministerial Conferences of all WTO Members. In view of this WTO treaty practice, one may doubt whether it is legally meaningful to claim an "excess of authority" by a Panel or by an Appellate Body report after their dispute settlement findings have been adopted by the DSB and endorsed by the WTO General Council and Ministerial Conferences. For it is recognized long since in international legal practice that international treaty law may evolve dynamically through subsequent treaty practice and may be modified through consensus-based practice even outside the formal treaty amendment procedures. While the power of WTO bodies remains legally limited, WTO member countries remain sovereign to confer additional powers on the WTO and to agree on new interpretations and modifications of WTO rules.

This chapter retains the form of the oral intervention at the conference without references to other relevant literature. The author is a former legal adviser in the WTO (1995-2000), GATT (1981-1995) and the German Ministry of Economic Affairs (1978-1981), and Chairman of the International Trade Law Committee of the International Law Association.

2. Human Rights and Other Constitutional Limits

Yet, other national and international tribunals (e.g., an ICSID or WIPO arbitral tribunal deciding on whether a WTO dispute settlement ruling or a national measure implementing WTO rules violated intellectual property rights) may find that a WTO dispute settlement ruling exceeded its authority by infringing national or international constitutional law (e.g., human rights to health and to food, human rights guarantees of "due process of law" and protection of property rights). There are currently several disputes among WTO Members about legal claims which have been submitted in part to WTO dispute settlement Panels[1] and in part to other international tribunals.[2] There have also been disputes where the WTO consistency of trade restrictions (e.g., EC restrictions on imports of bananas) was challenged simultaneously before national courts, the EC Court of Justice and in WTO dispute settlement bodies, resulting in mutually inconsistent judgments (e.g., EC Court of Justice decisions upholding the legality of EC import restrictions that had been previously declared illegal in WTO dispute settlement rulings binding on all EC institutions). Just as national constitutional courts in the EC have asserted the power to examine whether legal acts by the EC exceeded the limited EC competencies and may therefore produce no legal effects in the respective national legal system (e.g., in Germany), national courts and the EC Court may likewise examine whether WTO dispute settlement rulings, if they should exceed the limited WTO competencies, can validly interfere with rights protected by national or European constitutional law. In the absence of legal hierarchies between different international organizations and courts (such as the WTO Appellate Body, the ICJ, WIPO arbitration, and the World Bank's International Center for the Settlement of Investment Disputes), challenges of the limited WTO jurisdiction by other international organizations and tribunals cannot be excluded.

The customary rules of international treaty interpretation and Article 3:2 of the DSU require WTO dispute settlement bodies to construe WTO law with due regard to the context of WTO rules, including "any relevant rules of international law applicable in the relations between the parties" (cf. Article 31:3[c] of the Vienna Convention on the Law of Treaties). As virtually all WTO Members have recognized obligations under international treaty law as well as under international customary law to protect freedom, non-discrimination and other human rights in national and international relations, WTO dispute settlement bodies may find that human rights law and the customary rules of treaty interpretation require them to construe WTO rules (e.g., on intellectual property rights) in conformity with pertinent human rights obligations of the parties to the dispute (e.g., the 1966 UN Covenant on Economic, Social and Cultural Rights and its Article 15 on, *inter alia,* "protection of the moral and material interests resulting from any scientific, literary or artistic production of . . . the author"). In dispute settlement proceedings inside and outside the WTO, WTO Members may also claim that WTO legal guarantees of freedom, non-discrimination, rule of law and judicial protection reflect *human rights values* and an *opinio iuris* of WTO Members on how human rights and trade law should be mutually reconciled in transnational economic relations.

Even though *national law* cannot justify violations of WTO obligations, a domestic court or an international court may validly decide that human rights protected by international law must be given legal priority vis-à-vis WTO dispute settlement rulings limiting such human rights (e.g., a WTO arbitral ruling pursuant to Article 22:7 of the DSU authorizing "cross-retaliation" under the TRIPs Agreement in a manner resulting in a taking of private property rights without adequate compensation of the private right-holder). On the international level in WTO law, WTO Members have so far not been willing to recognize individuals as legal subjects entitled to invoke WTO rules in national and international courts. Yet, the universal recognition of "inalienable human rights" in national and international law limits the traditional freedom of governments to define or ignore individual rights by means of intergovernmental agreements. As in national and European constitutional law, an increasing number of human rights guarantees can be viewed today as constituting *erga omnes guarantees* and *general principles of law recognized by civilized nations* (in terms of Article 38:1[c] of the Statute of the International Court of Justice) which governments are no longer free to "withdraw" or disregard through intergovernmental agreements (including WTO rules and dispute settlement rulings). Since national and international human rights law recognizes human rights as "inalienable birthrights" preceding and limiting government powers and not conferred by governments, human rights can constitutionally limit national as well as international government powers.

3. WTO Judges and Judicial Deference

Which WTO rules justify claims that WTO dispute settlement findings should accord "deference" to policy decisions made by WTO Member governments? For instance, the general and security exceptions in WTO law (such as GATT Articles XX and XXI) reflect human rights values (such as the human right to protection of health underlying GATT Article XX[b]) which may justify WTO dispute settlement rulings according deference to national government discretion to balance different human rights values in the application of national safeguard measures. Yet, it should not be overlooked that the WTO guarantees of freedom of trade (e.g., in GATT Articles II, III and XI), non-discrimination and protection of property rights (e.g., in the GATS, TRIPs and TRIMs Agreements) may also be seen in a human rights perspective as protecting individual liberty rights, non-discrimination and property rights recognized in national and international law. Just as the European Court of Justice has accorded primacy to the protection of human rights over certain national restrictions of individual freedom and non-discrimination (e.g., in the field of Article 141 EC Treaty relating to sex equality and gender discrimination), WTO dispute settlement bodies may legitimately construe WTO guarantees of individual freedom and non-discrimination strictly so as to protect *individual freedom* and non-discrimination among producers, traders, and consumers *without* deference to discriminatory or unnecessary government restrictions.

The legitimacy of *judicial deference* may therefore depend on the relevant WTO rules and procedures concerned. The long tradition of protectionist, welfare-reducing abuses of trade policy powers for the benefit of rent-seeking pressure groups may be lawful under WTO law. From a human rights perspective, however, WTO rules promoting non-discriminatory freedom of mutually welfare-increasing trade transactions among citizens across frontiers appear more legitimate and more consistent with the human rights objectives of protecting freedom, non-discrimination and social welfare. The legal primacy of the WTO Agreement vis-à-vis "secondary WTO law" (including WTO "schedules of concessions") and the compulsory jurisdiction of the WTO dispute settlement system offer additional legal reasons why national policy discretion under GATT rules (e.g., for balance-of-payments measures pursuant to XVIII:B, free trade areas and customs unions pursuant to Article XXIV) has been rightly subjected to stricter judicial scrutiny in WTO jurisprudence than in the dispute settlement practice under the old GATT 1947 with its much less stringent separation between legislative, executive, and judicial powers. Also *domestic courts* may rightly conclude that the *due process* guarantees in WTO law (e.g., Articles 42 *et seq.* of the TRIPs Agreement) for national as well as international judicial review justify more effective judicial scrutiny of protectionist national trade restrictions than under the old GATT 1947.

The preceding comments illustrate that, for instance, due to the universal recognition of human rights and the stricter *separation of powers* and *rule of law* guarantees in WTO law (compared with the old GATT 1947), views about the appropriate "judicial policy" of WTO dispute settlement bodies may differ considerably. Trade diplomats interested in accommodating protectionist interest groups may claim that WTO Panels should grant as much deference to trade policy discretion of governments as it was usual in the "pragmatic" legal and dispute settlement practice under GATT 1947. WTO Panelists may argue, however, that the additional "checks and balances" of the WTO legal system (such as legal review of Panel reports by the Appellate Body, their political review by the DSB, possibility of authoritative interpretations by the General Council and WTO Ministerial

Conference) justify more "judicial activism" by WTO dispute settlement Panels. "Judicial economy" by Panels may make it impossible for the Appellate Body to decide on the legal claims within the very strict time-limits prescribed by the DSU if the Appellate Body wants to reverse Panel findings and to "complete its analysis" on the basis of the factual findings and legal claims recorded in the Panel report.

In contrast to WTO Panels, the Appellate Body may have good reasons for a higher degree of "judicial economy" (as it was practiced by most dispute settlement Panels under GATT 1947 where many Panels followed a policy of deciding "as little as necessary"). Many Appellate Body reports appear to limit their findings to those legal claims and legal interpretations whose clarification is indispensable for settling the dispute. Over time, just as constitutional courts in federal states (e.g., the U.S. Supreme Court) and the EC Court of Justice have progressively extended their judicial review of legislative and executive measures so as to protect human rights and other constitutional law principles more effectively, the WTO Appellate Body may also follow the example of the EC Court of Justice and rely more on *functional* and *systematic interpretations* of the law rather than on the so far characteristic focus of WTO jurisprudence on *literal interpretations* of the text of particular WTO provisions.

4. Arbitration within the WTO

There have been more than a dozen arbitral reports pursuant to Articles 21 and 22 of the DSU. However, the possibility of "expeditious arbitration within the WTO as an alternative means of dispute settlement" pursuant to Article 25 of the DSU has so far not been used in WTO practice. Article 25 seems to leave broad freedom to the WTO Members to agree on the subject-matter, procedures, and substantive law to be applied by the arbitral tribunal. In investment disputes under the GATS and intellectual property rights disputes under the TRIPs Agreement, for instance, mutually agreed arbitration under Article 25 of the DSU may offer an appropriate means of enabling arbitration awards that are consistent not only with WTO law but also with pertinent WIPO conventions, bilateral as well as multilateral investment agreements, and general international law rules (e.g., on state responsibility and reparation of injury). Mutually agreed arbitration under Article 25 of the DSU might be based on broad terms of reference justifying a broader conception of the judicial process than in the case of WTO Panel proceedings. "Judicial self-restraint" (e.g., *vis-à-vis* the judicial application of general international law rules on state responsibility in the WTO context) may no longer be seen as appropriate if the mutually agreed mandate requests arbitrators to decide disputes among WTO Members not only on the basis of WTO law but also with due regard to general international law (e.g., on reparation of injury caused by illegal "takings" of private property rights that may be protected not only by investment treaties and WIPO Agreements but also under GATS or the TRIPs Agreement).

5. Inherent Powers of Courts

One characteristic feature and necessary corollary of the quasi-judicial nature of dispute settlement in the WTO has been that both WTO Panels and the Appellate Body have recognized and accepted the legal need to fill gaps in the WTO dispute settlement procedures, for instance, as regards the power of WTO dispute settlement Panels to adopt *preliminary rulings,* accept *amicus curiae* briefs, clarify the "customary rules of interpretation of public international law" (Article 3:2 DSU), and decide on the legal relevance of general international law principles (e.g., on *prior exhaustion of local remedies*) for the interpretation of WTO rules. Arguably, the quasi-judicial nature and functions of WTO dispute settlement proceedings and the universal recognition of human rights in modern international law (including individual rights to effective legal and judicial remedies) confer additional authority and legitimacy on WTO dispute settlement bodies to secure *due process of law* and the effectiveness of WTO dispute settlement procedures. The adoption by the Appellate Body of "working procedures" pursuant to Article 17:9 of the DSU, and the adoption by the DSB of "Rules of conduct" for the settlement of disputes in December 1996, reflect the exercise of implied powers similar to those of other national and international judicial bodies. Whereas the interpretation and application of the old GATT 1947 was almost exclusively determined by *intergovernmental* decision-making processes, the dynamic evolution of WTO law is increasingly influenced also by *quasi-judicial* clarifications and progressive development of WTO rules through case-law.

The courageous admission in principle—yet very reluctant acceptance in practice—by the Appellate Body of *amicus curiae* briefs from non-governmental organizations (NGOs) illustrates beginnings of an indirect "dialogue" between the legislative and judicial branches of the WTO as well as with *civil society* representatives and NGOs. The future legitimacy of WTO law will not only depend on *intergovernmental rule-making* and *quasi-judicial dispute settlement procedures,* but also on increased *democratic participation* and on *deliberative democracy* in the WTO. Past experience with regional integration law (notably in the European Union) suggests that the needed democratic reforms of WTO law will hardly be politically possible unless individuals and economic operators, national judges and members of parliaments, as well as NGOs can more actively participate in WTO decision-making and dispute settlement processes and, thereby, can pressure governments to protect citizen interests and human rights more effectively across frontiers. Whereas trade diplomats like to perceive themselves as the "principals" who have to control the power delegated to the "judicial agents" of the WTO, citizens and national parliaments have good reasons to insist that, in democracies, the citizens and their parliamentary representatives are the true "principals" and sources of democratic legitimacy of national and international organizations. The democratic legitimacy of WTO rule-making and dispute settlement processes will increasingly depend on taking human rights and democracy more seriously by recognizing citizens and their *civil society* institutions as legal subjects and active participants of the WTO world trade, legal, and dispute settlement system.

NOTES

1. E.g., an EC complaint of November 2000 (see document WT/DS193/2) that Chile's exclusion of Spanish fishing vessels from Chilean ports violates GATT Article V; and a complaint by Honduras of June 2000 (WT/DS201/1) about an inconsistency with GATT Articles I and II and GATS Articles II and XVI of import restrictions imposed by Nicaragua in connection with a maritime border dispute.

2. Chile, for instance, requested a dispute settlement proceeding before the Law of the Sea Tribunal on the ground that Spain and the EC did not comply with their obligations under the Law of the Sea Convention to agree on rules for the protection of swordfish. Nicaragua submitted its maritime border dispute with Honduras and Colombia to the International Court of Justice.

Part II: Relevant Experience in the U.S. and the EC

CHAPTER 4

The Dormant Commerce Clause and the *Hormones* Problem

Donald H. Regan

It is obvious that no anti-discrimination regime can stop at forbidding explicit discrimination of the relevant sort. If only explicit discrimination is forbidden, lawmakers who want to discriminate can hide their discriminatory intentions behind facially neutral classifications that are nonetheless chosen because they differentially burden the protected class. So, we must be prepared to invalidate some facially neutral laws that have "discriminatory effect" or, as American lawyers often call it, "disparate impact." On the other hand, we cannot possibly invalidate all laws which have a disparate impact on a protected class; many perfectly reasonable laws adopted for completely innocent purposes will have such disparate impact. So, some laws with disparate impact must be upheld, and some must be invalidated. The question is how to draw the line. (I have intentionally not used the phrase "de facto discrimination." This common phrase could be used simply as a synonym for "disparate impact" and could be similarly neutral on the ultimate issue of illegality. But my impression is that for many trade lawyers, "de facto discrimination" tends to mean laws with disparate impact that are in fact illegal, for whatever further reason is determinative. In contrast, in American constitutional law "de facto discrimination" normally connotes the absence of illegality. So the phrase seems best avoided.)

As I say, the central question for this conference is how to decide which laws with disparate impact are illegal and which are not. But the first question that would occur to an American lawyer about the Arimani duck-meat law (see Appendix, p. 359) is a different one, namely, whether the law is preempted by federal statute or administrative regulation. I suspect a strong case could be made that it is so preempted, although I have not pursued the matter, because that is obviously not the issue primarily relevant to this comparative exercise. I shall discuss the status of the Arimani law under the dormant commerce clause, on the assumption that it is not preempted by statute or regulation. Still, the issue of statutory preemption is worth mentioning, since the possibilities for statutory preemption may affect our approach to issues about preemption by fundamental law. The United States has a central legislature with regulatory powers and a history of using them that go far beyond any analogue in the European Union or the WTO. It is possible that differences of this sort may either explain (empirically) or justify (normatively) different approaches to fundamental law preemption in the three systems.

In addition to the differences in institutional context, we cannot forget that the relevant legal texts in the three systems vary greatly in content and degree of specificity. The first duty of the judge is to apply the text that grounds her/his authority. The text the American judge is working with is so different from the texts that WTO tribunals are working with that there may not be much to be learned from American law about how disputes should be decided under, say, the SPS Agreement. (I would not say the same about the GATT itself.) If WTO tribunals were in the same situation as American judges—empowered by a text that is seen as giving them a mandate to create some trade-protective law but that offers no more specific direction—then I would recommend that WTO tribunals generally follow the American model (as I understand it) despite the differences in institutional context mentioned previously. As it is, I would merely urge, in the spirit of the American model and the text of the SPS Agreement itself, that the right of countries to choose their own level of SPS protection should not be reduced to an empty shell by excessively demanding standards for what constitutes a risk assessment, or scientific evidence, and so on. Given the text of the SPS Agreement, I find little to object to and much to praise in the Appellate Body's *EU – Hormones* decision,[1] but the result makes me uncomfortable.

So, I'm not sure whether comparison will prove useful. But my mandate is to discuss the American law, so on with it.

1. The Dormant Commerce Clause: Doctrine and Judicial Practice

Doctrine

The Commerce Clause of the United States Constitution gives Congress the power "to regulate commerce with foreign nations, and among the several states, and with the Indian tribes."[2] The states, unlike Congress, have whatever powers the Constitution does not forbid them. There is no provision of the Constitution that contains any explicit general limitation on the regulatory power of the states in favor of openness in trade; in that respect the Constitution differs fundamentally from the Treaty of Rome and the GATT (and later WTO agreements). It is well established, however, that the existence of the commerce power in Congress imposes some limits on state power even in the absence of any relevant legislation by Congress. The phrase "dormant commerce clause" (like the synonymous phrase "negative commerce clause") refers to the Commerce Clause as a source of such constitutional preemption. As far as I know, the origin of the phrase "dormant commerce clause" is Marshall's opinion in *Wilson v. Black Bird Creek Marsh*

Co., where he says the Delaware law is not "repugnant to the power to regulate commerce in its dormant state."[3]

I can simplify the necessary discussion of the dormant commerce clause by observing that the Arimani law forbidding the sale of hormone-fed duck meat (a) is not a tax (nor a law that might run afoul of even a generalized "multiple burdens" analysis), (b) is not a regulation of the interstate transportation/communication system itself (railroads, telephones, and so on), and (c) presents no issue of extraterritoriality.[4] Taxes, regulations of the transportation/communication system, and extraterritoriality all raise special issues which we would be required to attend to in a full discussion of dormant commerce clause doctrine. But in what follows I shall be discussing the dormant commerce clause as it applies to "core" cases that do not involve any such special considerations, like the Arimani duck case.[5]

The conventional wisdom takes as its scripture Justice Stewart's famous statement in *Pike v. Bruce Church, Inc.*: "Where the statute regulates evenhandedly to effectuate a legitimate local public interest, and its effects on interstate commerce are only incidental, it will be upheld unless the burden imposed on such commerce is clearly excessive in relation to the putative local benefits."[6] Or, as the conventional wisdom would be more likely to state matters: (1) if the state law discriminates against interstate commerce, it is invalid; (2) if the state law does not discriminate against interstate commerce but nonetheless burdens interstate commerce, then we must balance the local benefits of the law against the burden on commerce to see if the law is justified.[7]

There are many difficulties with Stewart's formulation, and with the conventional wisdom based on it. The most obvious difficulty is that they do not tell us what it is for a law to regulate "evenhandedly," or conversely, what it is for a law to "discriminate." Some things are clear. First, a law that is motivated by protectionist purpose is invalid. Second, a law that discriminates explicitly against foreign commerce is "virtually per se illegal,"[8] although the presumption of illegality may be overcome in the rare case where it can be argued that the explicit local/foreign discrimination is necessary to achieve a non-protectionist purpose.[9] But what about facially neutral state laws that have a discriminatory effect? We have already seen that we cannot invalidate all such laws. How then do we decide which such laws to uphold and which to invalidate? One obvious answer (the right answer, to my mind) is that we should invalidate the law if and only if it was motivated by a bad purpose. I shall say more about that later. But the standard suggestion at this point is that we should balance the local benefits of the law against the burden on commerce represented by the discriminatory effect.[10] Notice that this standard moves together the "discrimination" part of the conventional test and the "balancing" part. That is no great harm in itself, though it may lead us to wonder whether the view has been well thought through. It also brings forward another issue, whether balancing should be limited to those cases where there is discriminatory effect, or whether we should balance whenever there is a significant out-of-state cost from the statute, even if the statute is not discriminatory in any sense at all. (Here's an example: if Michigan, which has no tobacco-related industry of any sort, completely prohibited the sale of cigarettes, that would be a significant loss to tobacco farmers in Virginia and cigarette manufacturers in North Carolina; but there is no discriminatory effect.) The Pike test, as stated, clearly requires balancing even here, and so does the "virtual representation" argument for balancing favored by adherents of public choice theory (discussed in section 2). But there is not a shred of evidence that the Court has ever actually engaged in balancing in "core" cases where there is no discriminatory effect. (As I shall explain, I don't think the Court actually balances in any core case, but there is at least some evidence for their balancing in discriminatory effect cases.)

Judicial Practice

We have been discussing some of the difficulties in expounding the conventional wisdom, but in my view the conventional wisdom is wrong at a much more fundamental level. There is no place at all for balancing in dormant commerce clause analysis (in the core cases), and the fundamental notion of discrimination which is relevant is purposeful discrimination. In the core area of the dormant commerce clause, a law is unconstitutional if and only if it has a protectionist purpose. It's that simple. (As I shall explain below, this leaves room for, indeed accounts for, the "virtual per se rule" against explicit discrimination.) This is not just what I think the law should be. It is what I think the law is. This is the best summary of what the Court has actually been doing for at least the last sixty years, despite their claims to the contrary.

Of course, when I say "it's that simple," I mean the theory is simple.[11] I do not mean to suggest that it is always obvious whether there is protectionist purpose. No plausible theory can make every case an easy case. I shall say more in section 2 about how the purpose inquiry works, but one thing is worth saying immediately: outright assertions of protectionist purpose by legislators are neither necessary nor invariably sufficient for a finding of protectionist purpose. They are not necessary because the content and context of the law may make its bad purpose obvious even in the absence of any "smoking gun" in the legislative history. They are not invariably sufficient because a single statement by a single legislator, for example, may not reflect the thinking of her colleagues. Outright assertions of protectionist purpose are, of course, relevant, and they may in some cases be sufficient to show bad purpose. But in saying that the ultimate determinant of constitutional validity is purpose, I am not remotely saying that this sort of evidence is all that matters.

My claim that in the core cases a law violates the dormant commerce clause if and only if it has a protectionist purpose raises two obvious questions: (1) Given that the Court has explicitly announced a balancing test, what are my grounds for thinking they do not actually engage in balancing? (2) Could I possibly be right? Is it really plausible that the Court should so misdescribe its own behavior?

Let me take the second question first. There is a very natural way for the Court to misdescribe its own behavior: it states the relevant test at too high a level of generality.[12] There is a place for balancing in certain dormant commerce clause cases outside what I have called the "core," most particularly where the state law regulates the interstate transportation/communication system itself. In its statements of the dormant commerce clause test, the Court has generally not distinguished between such cases and my "core" cases, and a single test designed to cover both must necessarily mention balancing—but at the cost of misrepresenting the test the Court is actually applying to the larger part of the range of cases. Only recently has the Court noticed explicitly some of the distinctions among commerce clause cases that I suggest are crucial to understanding the Court's behavior; and in the process, the Court has intimated that balancing may indeed not be relevant in the core.[13]

We have seen how the Court might misdescribe its own behavior, but does it? What are my grounds for thinking the Court does not balance in core cases? After all, the famous Pike balancing test was announced in a core case (though the only significant precedents Stewart cites in support of the test are transportation cases). My grounds are a close reading of all the cases of the modern era (post-New Deal), not just looking for quotable quotes, but trying to see where and how in the opinions the cases are really being decided. I have developed my readings of all the major cases up to 1986 at length elsewhere,[14] and this is not the place for an extended recapitulation. But it may be useful to offer capsule discussions of some of the most famous cases, to give the flavor of my arguments.

The earliest core dormant commerce clause cases that are still regularly cited are *Baldwin v. G.A.F. Seelig, Inc.*[15] and *H. P. Hood & Sons v. Du Mond.*[16] In *Baldwin*, the Court struck down a New York statute which prohibited the sale in New York of out-of-state milk for which the producers had been paid less than New York's own domestic minimum price to producers. In *Hood*, the Court invalidated the New York Commissioner of Agriculture's refusal to allow a Massachusetts milk distributor that sold its milk in Boston to build a new milk receiving depot in New York; the Commissioner's nominal ground was that the new depot would cause "destructive competition." *Baldwin* and *Hood* are both regarded by most modern commentators as balancing cases, but in fact the Court does not even claim to balance in either case. The opinions are by Cardozo (*Baldwin*) and Jackson (*Hood*), two of the Court's greatest prose stylists, and they contain many purple passages about the importance of "economic union." But these oft-quoted passages are interlarded with references to tariffs, embargoes, customs duties, and the like (references that are often omitted when the passages are quoted). Those protectionist devices are the specific threats to "economic union" that both Cardozo and Jackson discuss. I think it is clear on an unprejudiced reading that in both cases what the Justices were concerned about, and what they thought they had identified, was thinly disguised protectionism.[17]

Consider next *Pike v. Bruce Church, Inc.* itself, where the Court famously does claim to balance. The facially neutral Arizona statute in the case required only that cantaloupes grown in the state be packed in approved containers. What Bruce Church, the cantaloupe grower, was actually challenging was an order under the statute by an Arizona official, requiring Bruce Church to pack their cantaloupes in Arizona instead of transporting them in bulk across the border to a packing shed in California. There was no claim that this order was necessary to ensure that the cantaloupes were packed in the proper sort of container; it was stipulated that California had an identical packing requirement. Rather, the Arizona official defended his order as necessary to ensure that the Arizona cantaloupes were labeled as grown in Arizona. This is an unusual set of facts, and Stewart's opinion meanders, despite its brevity. In the end, Stewart invalidates the order on the ground that it is an explicit local-processing requirement (as indeed it is), and that such local-processing requirements are "virtually per se illegal." This rationale is completely sound, but it is not a balancing rationale (not even if we have to decide at some point that there is no claim of local benefit adequate to override the presumption of illegality). The virtual *per se* rule which constitutes the case against the order is best understood as part of an anti-protectionism regime. The natural and best justification of the virtual *per se* rule is that explicit local-processing requirements, like other explicitly discriminatory commercial regulations, are virtually certain to be motivated by protectionist purpose. The reason is that non-protectionist purposes can normally be pursued without recourse to explicit discrimination. Pike announces a balancing test, but it is not a balancing case.[18]

Another famous "balancing" case, *Dean Milk Co. v. City of Madison*,[19] also involved an explicit local-processing requirement—in this case an ordinance of the city of Madison, Wisconsin, requiring that milk sold in the city as pasteurized to have been pasteurized and bottled within five miles of the city center. Again, Clark's opinion for the Court is a bit of a jumble, but in the end, it turns on the same sort of *per se* rule against explicit discrimination as Pike. Obviously, a full discussion would need to explain why explicit local geographical discrimination (as in Dean Milk) should be assimilated to explicit state-line discrimination (as in Pike); but equally obviously, the explanation would provide no support for a general balancing approach.[20]

Of the standard "balancing" precedents, the hardest to encapsulate briefly is *Hunt v. Washington State Apple Advertising Commission*,[21] in which the Court struck down a North Carolina statute that prohibited the use of any grades other than USDA (U.S. Department of Agriculture) grades on closed containers of apples sold in North Carolina. The effect of the statute was both to deprive Washington apple growers of the advantage of their specially prestigious state grading system (arguably preferred by buyers to the USDA system), and also to impose on Washington growers the extra cost of printing up boxes without Washington grades on them for sale in North Carolina—all to the advantage of North Carolina apple growers. The statute was facially neutral, and Chief Justice Burger, writing for the Court, explicitly said he did not need to find a protectionist purpose. Nonetheless, to my mind the opinion makes it clear both that there was a protectionist purpose and that Burger thought so. (He may have been unwilling to rely on protectionist purpose because of the absence of any finding in the district court's opinion.) In the present context it must suffice to mention two features of the opinion. First, Burger goes out of his way to quote a "glaring" statement by the North Carolina Agriculture Commissioner which suggests the Commissioner thought the purpose of the statute was protectionist;[22] this is the only instance in which he goes behind the district court's opinion to the record. Second, Burger's eventual argument that the statute achieves little or (probably) no local benefit is *a priori*. He argues that the statute could not possibly produce better informed purchasers (since it allows the sale of ungraded apples) and that it could not possibly achieve its putative goal of aiding consumers (since they never see the relevant containers). A case that is decidable by this sort of a priori argument is no precedent for judicial balancing in cases where there are genuinely contestable empirical issues about the law's effects. Also, what the Court can know *a priori*, the North Carolina legislature must have known, too. If the legislature knew they could not achieve their asserted objects, we can infer that they were attempting to disguise protectionism.[23]

Moving forward, *Edgar v. MITE Corp.*,[24] decided in 1982, was regarded by some as an important precedent for balancing. The Court invalidated an Illinois anti-takeover statute that was drafted in such a way that it could apply to transactions occurring entirely outside Illinois in the shares of a non-Illinois corporation with non-Illinois shareholders (if the corporation had its principal executive office in Illinois and at least ten percent of its stated capital and paid-in surplus were represented in Illinois). Justice White wrote a plurality opinion advancing three theories for invalidation: statutory preemption (by the federal Williams Act), extraterritoriality, and Pike balancing. Only one part of this opinion received five votes and became the official opinion of the Court, the part relying on Pike. Despite appearances, Edgar was not a significant precedent for Pike balancing. There would have been five votes for the result of invalidation even if only the preemption and extraterritoriality theories had been considered. The Justice whose vote made Pike the nominal theory of the Court (and the only Justice who relied solely on Pike) was Justice Powell, whose vote was not necessary to dispose of the case even though it was the crucial fifth vote for one particular theory. Powell actually thought the case was moot; furthermore, everything in his opinion suggests that he would have preferred to uphold the Illinois statute (!); and he says explicitly that his reason for voting for the Pike theory is that it is less restrictive of state power in this area than the other two theories in the running.[25] So, Edgar is not a genuine endorsement of Pike or of balancing.[26]

Further confirmation may be found in the next case involving a state anti-takeover statute, *CTS Corp. v. Dynamics Corp. of America*,[27] decided in 1987. The Indiana statute in *CTS Corp.* differed from the Illinois statute in *Edgar* in that it regulated voting rights acquired by transactions in the shares of Indiana corporations. This is an important difference, but neither this difference nor any other difference between the statutes suggested that they should fare differently on a balancing analysis. The Court in *CTS Corp.* upholds the Indiana statute, without any citation of *Pike* (except when summarizing the opinion below that they are reversing) and without any balancing (indeed, disclaiming any intention to second-guess the empirical judgments of the state legislature).[28] Powell writes for the Court, and in his opinion in *CTS Corp.* he never even acknowledges that there was an "opinion of the Court" in Edgar, although it was his vote that created it. He refers consistently to White's "plurality opinion." Perhaps even more remarkable, White, in his dissent in *CTS Corp.*, never mentions *Pike*, despite having written the Pike-based "opinion of the Court" in *Edgar* five years before. Both Powell and White focus in *CTS Corp.* on an issue of extraterritoriality—who is entitled to regulate the internal affairs of corporations? White also thinks the statute has a protectionist purpose. Balancing is nowhere in the picture.[29]

Since 1987, the Court has decided twenty-odd dormant commerce clause cases and invalidated eighteen statutes. In only one of those eighteen invalidations, *Bendix Autolite Corp. v. Midwesco Enterprises, Inc.*,[30] in 1988, does the Court even claim to balance; and it is doubtful whether there is really any balancing going on. The statute in issue tolls the statute of limitations for contract actions during any period when a defendant foreign corporation has not subjected itself to the general jurisdiction of the Ohio courts (even though the corporation may be amenable to suit during that period on all its Ohio-connected transactions under the Ohio long-arm statute). Kennedy, writing for the Court, says the Ohio law in question "might have been held to be a discrimination that invalidates without extended inquiry" (in effect, it might have been held to be patently unjustified facial discrimination, as Scalia says it is in his concurrence), but Kennedy says he "chooses" to go on and balance anyway, without explaining why. There is, in fact, reason to go on, though not in the balancing direction; the case is trickier than it seems, and the facial discrimination claim by itself does not get right to the heart of the matter. After all, if Midwesco (the foreign defendant) simply submitted to the general jurisdiction of the Ohio courts, it would get the full benefit of the statute of limitations, and it would be no worse off in respect of susceptibility to suit than any Ohio corporation or any corporation permanently present in Ohio. The problem is that it seems Midwesco, as a foreign corporation with no permanent presence, is entitled to be somewhat better off in respect of susceptibility to suit. But what is required to explain this entitlement, and with it the vice in the Ohio statute, is not balancing; it is arguments about due process and/or what we might call "multiple administrative burdens."[31] Kennedy's opinion does not make all of this clear; but his "balancing" discussion is as underdeveloped as Scalia claims in concurrence, and his opinion also clearly manifests the sort of "fairness" concerns I have indicated. I do not think it is balancing that really decides the case.

Those (except for *CTS Corp.*) are the standard precedents for balancing in "core" cases. All of them. I have necessarily given only capsule discussions of each case, but those are all the cases. There are many other cases in which the Court gives a general statement of dormant commerce clause doctrine that refers to balancing, but then invalidates the law under some other part of the test without claiming to balance. There are also a few cases in which the Court claims to balance but upholds the law under review. I do not count these as precedents for balancing. If the Court really engaged in balancing, these cases would obviously be important in helping us to see how balancing worked; but where the very existence of the balancing test is in controversy, a case does not help to establish the reality of the test unless balancing determines an invalidation. A test which never bites is no test at all. Aside from that, even in the cases that claim to balance and then uphold the law, there is no real balancing. The prime example is *Minnesota v. Clover Leaf Creamery Co.*,[32] in which the Court upheld a Minnesota statute which forbade the sale of milk in non-returnable plastic containers. Although the Court cites Pike and claims to balance, no "balancing" happens. Writing for the Court, Brennan notes that there is some discriminatory effect from the statute, which he says must be justified by some local benefit. But when it comes to the crucial issue of identifying the local benefits of the statute, Brennan refers back to his discussion of the benefits in the equal protection part of the opinion. However, in the latter, he said repeatedly that it was not for the Court to decide whether there really were any benefits, only whether the legislature might have thought so. (This is standard equal protection doctrine in the social/economic area.) In sum, Brennan never officially decides that there are any local benefits; nevertheless, he upholds the statute against dormant commerce clause challenge, and he upholds it in effect on the ground that the legislature thought there were benefits. That is not balancing; that is purpose analysis. The other cases that purport to apply *Pike* in the course of upholding a law do so even more cursorily.

One final observation. It is not always obvious in a particular case whether the Court is really applying a purpose test or balancing. This is not surprising, since all of the evidence that would be relevant to "discriminatory effect" balancing is relevant to a purpose inquiry as well. Evidence of discriminatory effect inevitably suggests discriminatory purpose; similarly, evidence that minimizes the claimed non-protectionist local benefit suggests that the real purpose was protectionism. If I conclude from the Court's somewhat equivocal record that they are looking at purpose and not balancing, one reason is that they often clearly don't balance and they never clearly do; another reason is that the purpose approach makes most sense, as I shall argue in the next section. I hope I have said enough about the cases to dispel the thought that I am merely imputing my own view to the Court in the face of the evidence. I have heard the suggestion that I am trying to read the Court's mind. In fact, I am reading their opinions—my radical idea is to pay attention to the whole opinion instead of just looking for the paragraph that is supposed to state "the test."

2. The Dormant Commerce Clause: Theory

I think the Court is right to eschew balancing and to rely entirely on an inquiry into legislative purpose in "core" dormant commerce clause cases. Since the most controversial part of my thesis is the rejection of balancing, it might seem natural to start with the case against balancing. But, in fact, there are surprising connections between the arguments for and against balancing and the arguments for and against purpose review—connections which go well beyond the crude point that if balancing and purpose review are alternatives, an argument against one is an argument for the other. In light of these connections, it makes best sense to start with the positive argument for purpose review.

Legislative Purpose, Efficiency, and the "Virtual Representation" Argument for Balancing

Why should we reject laws motivated by protectionist purpose? The central reason is that protectionism is inefficient. Protectionism can also embitter diplomatic relations and interfere with effective political integration, if that is a goal; but both in the contemporary United States, where political integration has progressed beyond the Framers' wildest imaginings, and in the WTO, where political integration is not a goal at all, the threat to efficiency is surely the front-line objection to protectionism. So we shall focus on that. It is presumably not necessary to explain here in detail why protectionism is inefficient, but I want to remind the reader of the central point so that she will have it before her/his mind as we proceed. If the only purpose of a law is to transfer market share from foreign producers to local producers (the commonest protectionist scenario), then the law will normally be transferring business from low-cost foreign producers to high-cost local producers. This results in a misallocation of productive resources. Local consumers will lose, and the loss to local consumers will exceed any benefit to local producers; the law is Kaldor-Hicks inefficient. To be sure, the law might still be justified from a local perspective if it is the only politically feasible way to achieve a desirable redistribution; but when we then consider that protectionism invites retaliation (which may be simply irrational, or may be for bargaining purposes), we see that the overall consequences of collective behavior if protectionism is allowed are likely to be bad everywhere.

It is crucial to see that the inefficiency of protectionism depends on the assumption that the purpose of the law in question is protectionist. Discriminatory effect flowing from a law which aims at and achieves some non-protectionist purpose does not suggest inefficiency in any way. For example, the law in *Minnesota v. Clover Leaf Creamery*, discussed above, was not inefficient, despite its discriminatory effect. The law transferred business from low-cost foreign producers (of non-returnable plastic packaging for milk) to high-cost local producers (of paper packaging).[33] But the low-cost foreign producers were actually higher-cost, and the high-cost local producers were lower-cost, once the external environmental costs of the two sorts of packaging, as evaluated by the Minnesota legislature, were taken into account. The point is quite general: if the law in question achieves some non-protectionist purpose of the legislature, then discriminatory effect which is unavoidably incidental to the achievement of that purpose raises no efficiency concern; it just reveals that foreign actors are greater contributors to the problem the law is aimed at.[34]

I have said that the law in *Clover Leaf* is efficient if we take into account the environmental costs of different kinds of milk packaging as evaluated by the Minnesota legislature. But why is the Minnesota legislature the appropriate body to evaluate those costs? The first answer, of course, is that one of the primary objects of a federal or quasi-federal system is to allow for a variety of evaluative judgments at the lower level of government. It is perfectly in order for Minnesota to attach a higher value to its environment than, say, Illinois attaches to its own. And it is perfectly in order if Minnesota therefore forbids non-returnable plastic milk containers in Minnesota while Illinois allows them in Illinois. But there is still a possible objection. It is often said that when the Minnesota legislature makes a decision that affects foreigners (out-of-staters), who are not represented in the Minnesota legislature, we need judicial oversight to take the interests of those foreigners into account. It is not enough, on this view, that Minnesota does not purposefully discriminate against foreigners; it is not enough that Minnesota acts on its own sincerely held non-protectionist values. If foreigners are made worse off by Minnesota's action, then even if that was no part of Minnesota's goal, courts must "balance" the foreign costs against the local benefits, to make sure the law is justified all things considered. We look to the court to give the affected foreigners "virtual representation" in the Minnesota legislative process.

This may seem like a strong argument, but in the present context, it is specious. To see why, forget about the dormant commerce clause for a moment, and consider a pair of simpler examples. Imagine Jones, who regularly buys his groceries at the Mom&Pop Grocery. If one day, while driving to the Grocery, Jones loses control of his car and drives through the front display window, we would regard it as appropriate for a court to intervene and to consider, perhaps by a sort of balancing of interests, whether Jones was negligent, and, if he was, to order compensation. Jones was not (or presumably not directly) taking Mom&Pop's interests into account in his decisions about how to drive, and in a sense the court forces the consideration of those interests. Here judicial "balancing" to protect interests other than the actor's makes sense. But consider now a different sort of interaction between Jones and the store. If Jones decides he wants a new breakfast cereal, which Mom&Pop don't carry, and if as a result he transfers his entire grocery shopping to the local Giant Supermarket, it would never occur to us to suggest judicial review of this decision, to see if the benefit to Jones really justifies the loss to Mom&Pop. We can stipulate that Jones neither consults Mom&Pop nor considers their interests when he transfers his custom to Giant, but even so we do not even consider intervening. Why not? One obvious reason is that the market context of the decision means that (unlike in the negligent driving case) an appropriate comparison of interests is actually being made, implicitly. By deciding what to stock and at what price to sell it, Mom&Pop effectively announce how much Jones's business is worth to them (even though they are not thinking of Jones in particular). By responding to Mom&Pop's price-and-availability announcement on the basis of his own interests, Jones makes the comparison between what it is worth to Mom&Pop to have him as a customer and what it is worth to him to shop elsewhere. The required "balancing" of interests is done by the parties' joint contributions, through the market mechanism, to the ultimate determination of where Jones will shop.

Now, Minnesota's decision not to buy non-returnable plastic milk containers is analogous, not to Jones's driving through Mom&Pop's window, but to Jones's taking his grocery business elsewhere. What would be analogous to the negligence case is, say, Minnesota's sending some noxious effluent into Wisconsin's aquifers; such a case wouldn't actually be treated under the dormant commerce clause, but it would definitely invite federal intervention to balance the states' interests. But just as judicial intervention is not needed when Jones abandons Mom&Pop for Giant, neither is it needed when Minnesota decides, on non-protectionist grounds, not to purchase plastic milk containers because they simply do not want them at the offered price (or, in this case, at any non-negative price). Minnesota's decision is a simple consumption decision, made by the state on behalf of all of its citizens, not to purchase particular goods; the market context allows us to infer that it is worth more to Minnesota to eschew the plastic containers than it is worth to the other states to sell them, just as the market context allowed us to infer that it was worth more to Jones to leave Mom&Pop than it was worth to them to keep him as a customer. The invisible hand of the market achieves its amazing welfare effects precisely because every market decision embodies this sort of local comparison of interests. (And as our parables remind us, decisions not to transact are as important for these purposes as decisions to transact.)[35]

It might be objected that I cannot properly rely on a market-based mechanism for comparison of the relevant interests when Minnesota is in fact interfering in the market. There may be individual Minnesota consumers who disagree with Minnesota's collective choice. That is true, but irrelevant. Minnesota is perfectly entitled to speak for all Minnesota consumers as a group; from the federal point of view, we presume that Minnesota efficiently promotes the various interests of its citizens. Minnesota is entitled to prevent some Minnesota citizens from inflicting externalities on other Minnesota citizens by buying the eco-noxious foreign containers—and in doing so it promotes efficiency even though it prevents some individual citizens from doing as they would like. Indeed, so far as the federal constitution is concerned, Minnesota is entitled to be paternalistic and to protect Minnesota citizens against themselves, if, for example, the buyers of the containers are the very people who will be hurt when the ecosystem is degraded—and in doing this also Minnesota is promoting efficiency, at least if the paternalistic intervention is well-judged. There are some limits, of course, on Minnesota's freedom to speak for its citizens. In the American system, there are constitutional limitations, though these are notoriously weak where economic regulation is involved. (In the international context there are basic human rights protections embodied in international agreements.) But in the present context the point is this: whatever Minnesota can impose on its citizens by way of a domestic economic restriction it can extend to interstate market transactions, provided the extension is not a disguise for protectionist motivation.[36] The undoubted fact that Minnesota can impose the restriction at home shows that it violates no basic constitutional right; and with that established, Minnesota is entitled to speak for its citizens as a group in the interstate economic arena. It can do this, as I say, to protect some citizens against others, or to protect citizens against themselves. And we properly regard Minnesota's collective choice as representing the relevant interests of its citizens.

I am not claiming that Minnesota invariably gets it right. But neither is Jones an infallible promoter of his own interests, nor Mom&Pop of theirs. Jones may be foolish to shop at Giant, or Mom&Pop may miscalculate. Still, no court is going to interfere. We sensibly presume Jones and Mom&Pop will do better at representing their own interests than a judge would. And we should presume the same of Minnesota. There may be failures in the political process, and, of course, such failures should be a matter of concern to Minnesotans. (Note, however, that we have set aside the sort of political failure which is most likely to affect interstate trade, by requiring that the law be motivated by something other than protectionism.) Even so, from the federal point of view we generally, and properly, presume that state political institutions do a better job of representing and reconciling in-state interests than federal institutions would. Absent some special reason for doubt (such as is reflected in various sorts of constitutional restriction), we should treat Minnesota governmental institutions as speaking authoritatively for Minnesota interests. And obviously, the mere fact that a state law has effects outside the state is not a reason to doubt that the law adequately represents the interests of citizens of the state. Of course, if the law has significant out-of-state effects, then pointing out that it authoritatively embodies in-state interests is not invariably a conclusive defense of the law. We would not allow Minnesota to dump untreated sewage into Lake Superior just because that is the best thing on balance for citizens of Minnesota. But now we are back to the main point of the last few paragraphs: when the out-of-state effects are mediated by a market context, as they are in the milk-packaging case, then it does suffice that the Minnesota law authoritatively embodies the interests of Minnesota citizens; the out-of-state interests are accounted for by the terms on which out-of-staters offer market transactions.

I think this is a powerful argument for why "virtual representation" by balancing is not required in "core" dormant commerce clause cases; powerful but simple in conception. Still, it took some years for it to filter gradually into my consciousness, and I can imagine that some readers may not be instantly persuaded. Let me therefore offer another argument, which is one of the intermediate forms in which this insight presented itself to me. If Minnesota dumps untreated sewage into Lake Superior, it is natural to say that it thereby harms or injures Wisconsin and Canada. In contrast, if Minnesota merely forbids the import of non-returnable plastic milk containers, it is not at all natural to say it harms or injures the manufacturers of such containers. To be sure, the manufacturers of such containers are worse off as a result of Minnesota's decision, but this worse-off-ness is not the result of a harming or injuring. Minnesota neither denies nor infringes any right of its would-be suppliers, no more than Jones denies a right of Mom&Pop when he turns to Giant. We might say the manufacturers are denied a benefit, and that would be nearer the truth than claiming they were harmed; but even that doesn't sound exactly right. The truth is just that they have lost a (collective) customer. It's the same with Jones. If he drives his car through Mom&Pop's window, he injures them; if he takes his custom elsewhere, he disappoints them, no more. Courts are in the business of preventing harms, not preventing disappointments—which is why they deal with Jones's negligent driving and Minnesota's sewage, but not with Jones's and Minnesota's decisions about what goods to purchase and from whom. (There is much more that might be said about the fairly deep relation between the "harm/disappointment" argument and the "market accounting of interests" argument, and about their overlapping ranges of application. But no more here.)

One last point about this "market accounting" argument. I have implicitly assumed that the argument applies to all "core" dormant commerce clause cases, and therefore explains why there is no need for balancing in any core case. I confess I have not thought all the way through to a demonstration of that assumption. What I can say is that the assumption is true for all the actual core cases that have produced Supreme Court decisions, and it seems intuitively right that it should be true for all core cases. But that is a loose end for the moment. Notice, on the other hand, that the assumption is not true of transportation/communication cases. Arizona's maximum train-length law, invalidated in *Southern Pacific Co. v. Arizona*,[37] may have reflected perfectly the interests of Arizona citizens, but there was no market context for Arizona's choice which gave the Court any reason to assume it reflected out-of-state interests as well.

The "Judicial Competence" Objection to Balancing, and Purpose Review as a Decision about Deference

Time to pause and take stock. We began with an argument in favor of purpose review, and that led us to a refutation of the standard argument for balancing. We saw that in core cases, balancing is unnecessary in principle; the protection it supposedly offers for out-of-state interests is not needed. At this point, the largely familiar judicial-competence argument against balancing may seem almost anti-climactic. But I want to rehearse it briefly, because it will lead us back to a richer understanding of purpose review.

In a nutshell, the Court should not balance because balancing requires judgments better left to the legislature. It is worth distinguishing two sorts of judgment. If we are going to balance the benefits and the costs of a law, we must first identify the actual consequences of the law; that is an empirical question. Then we must attach values to the various consequences and decide whether the overall consequences are good or bad on balance; that is a normative question. The commonest objection to balancing is that the courts are not competent to make the empirical judgments required; and that is often true. But another objection, and one which to my mind has even more force, is that the courts have no warrant to make the normative judgments required. In general, deciding what consequences are worth pursuing, and at what cost, is just what we have legislatures for.[38] And in a federal or quasi-federal system, the argument that courts should not make normative judgments in the standard run of cases is even stronger. As I have noted above, in such a system we have multiple legislatures at the lower level precisely so they can pursue different values. It would be inappropriate even for federal legislative institutions, if such exist, to impose a centralized value system without specific warrant. For courts to impose centralized values, without a clear necessity, is therefore doubly problematic.

Since I have particularly emphasized the case against judicial imposition of value choices by balancing, it is worth noting that there is one kind of case where the court might engage in a sort of degenerate "balancing" without being required to make any value judgment at all. That is the case where the court finds as an empirical matter that the law under review does not achieve any of the putative benefit. If there is really no benefit, then no normative judgment comparing values is required. Even here, however, we might think the court should not second-guess the legislature on the empirical judgment. The United States Supreme Court, for example, does not second-guess the legislature in applying the "rational basis/minimum scrutiny" test under the Equal Protection clause (applicable to social and economic legislation involving neither fundamental rights nor any suspect classification). As long as the Court does not believe the law was adopted for the bare purpose of discriminating against some unpopular group, then it suffices to uphold the law that "there is any reasonably conceivable state of facts that could provide a rational basis for the classification."[39] The Court does not decide for itself even the baseline empirical question of whether there is any actual benefit at all.

Perhaps this seems too draconian a self-limitation. Perhaps it seems there are some empirical judgments that the court can make as well as the legislature. Indeed, an example might be the question of whether, on the current scientific evidence, there is any danger at all to human health from eating hormone-added duck meat (or beef). I take it a central holding of the WTO Appellate Body's decision in *EU – Hormones* is that the SPS Agreement requires WTO tribunals to scrutinize legislative decisions on this sort of issue more closely than a United States court would do. Even so, the requirement on the legislature is primarily procedural. The Appellate Body does not say either that the tribunal may substitute its own judgment for the legislature's, or that the legislature must follow the dominant scientific view. Provided there is a risk assessment, a minority scientific view may suffice to support a restriction.[40] There is wisdom in the Appellate Body's restraint. To say the court can do as well as the legislature is not to say they can do better, and I see little reason to think they can. So, the case for judicial deference to the legislature may be at its weakest here, but it still seems preferable, other things being equal, that the decision be made by the more politically responsive body. This suggestion is strengthened when we remember that whatever danger the legislature is concerned with, it is unlikely that the tribunal can assert in good conscience that the probability associated with that danger is zero. Even the dominant scientific opinion of the moment may be wrong. As soon as there is a non-zero probability of harm, we have not just the empirical question of what the probability is, but also the normative question of how to respond to uncertainty. This seems to be a question the legislature should decide.

In sum, the argument against judicial balancing is an argument for deference to the legislature. We are now in a position to see that this deference argument against balancing and the efficiency argument for purpose review are like the negative and positive of a photograph. A finding of protectionist purpose on the part of the legislature does two things. It tells us that the law will result in inefficiency. It also undercuts the case for judicial deference: a legislative decision motivated by protectionism precisely fails to make empirical or normative judgments a court should respect. On the other hand, so long as the legislature's purpose is not protectionist, then their non-protectionist purpose, whatever it is, reflects their evaluation of the expected effects; their decision can be presumed efficient; and the court should defer. So, the inquiry into protectionist purpose determines at one and the same time whether there is an efficiency objection and whether deference is appropriate.

But can the courts identify protectionist purpose? In the American context, I unhesitatingly answer "yes".[41] As I have said before, the evidence the court may consider is not limited to outright expressions of protectionist purpose. The court can consider the structure of the law; the intuitive plausibility of the distinctions the law makes; the similarity to laws elsewhere; the zeal of the legislature for pursuing the asserted goal in other contexts; whatever is known about the support for the law and the political context outside and inside the legislature; the timing of the law; all in addition to legislative history to the extent it is available.[42] (It is also worth mentioning that legislators and other officials pursuing protectionism are often surprisingly candid about their motives—which becomes less surprising if we reflect that they want political credit.) It is irrelevant that the legislature, or even the particular legislative majority, is not all of one mind; the question is how to characterize the decision of the body as a whole. The connection that we have pointed out between the issue of protectionist purpose and the argument for deference may suggest a helpful formulation of the question: Did the legislature, within the usual limitations of legislative decision-making, make a decision on grounds that should be deferred to? If the law was supported by legislators with a variety of different purposes, then I suggest the question is roughly whether the contribution of protectionist purpose was a but-for cause of the adoption of the law. If it was, then the legislature as a body has not endorsed non-protectionist empirical and evaluative judgments that the court can defer to. (And if it was not, then they have.) What if it appears the legislature did not think at all, that they merely rubber-stamped the proposal of some lobbyist, or of some small set of members, or the views of their constituents? Then it is appropriate to take as the motivation of the legislature the motivation of that source. It is the legislature's prerogative not to think, but if they choose not to, they are responsible for the motivations of whomever they let do their thinking for them. Notice also that the question of the overall purpose of some law is quite different from the question of the legislature's "purpose" with regard to some very specific question like whether motorized roller-blades count as a "vehicle in the park." About a question like that, there may indeed be no actual legislative "purpose" in any sense; it is possible that nothing like that question occurred to anyone, and that the general principles that were agreed on do not settle it. But a law never lacks for overall motivation, either on the part of those who voted for it or on the part of those who secured the others' votes.

Nothing will make the decision what the legislature was really up to a mechanical one; but American judges are much better prepared for identifying legislative purpose than for making the decisions required under a balancing test. Aside from legal doctrine, the one thing American judges as a group can be presumed to be informed about and to have a feel for is politics. They have all been either elected themselves (in many state systems) or appointed by politicians. Despite their separation from day-to-day politics, American judges are definitely members of the political class. This argument has less force in the international context. Members of international tribunals are not likely to be political innocents, but neither can they have the insider's view of most of the systems whose laws they must review. On the other hand, the argument for deference may be correspondingly strengthened; in the abstract, international judges have even less warrant than domestic judges to second-guess the legislature's evaluations, if those evaluations are free of the taint of protectionism. So I am left thinking that, absent specific treaty provisions to the contrary, purpose review is to be preferred to anything like balancing even in the international context. (Are there further possibilities to consider, which are neither purpose review nor balancing? Obviously, there may be procedural requirements, such as the SPS Agreement imposes. Aside from that, I do not think there are other plausible substantive tests; but that is not a thesis I can argue here.)

3. The Dormant Commerce Clause and Dumb Duck Disease

Deciding the Arimani Duck Meat Case

So, after all that propaedeutic, is the Arimani law constitutional or not? Is it motivated by protectionist purpose? On this "record," it's hard to say (though I shall take a position presently). Some readers will take my hesitation as confirmation of the emptiness of the purpose test; but that would be a mistake. Aside from the fact that, as I said before, no plausible test can make every case an easy case, any judge faced with this case in the real world would know more about it than we are told. (I hope it is not necessary to say that while I express dissatisfaction as a "judge" with the "record" in the case, I am not in any way criticizing the authors of the hypothetical. Especially not, given how much I hate to write exams.)

For example, hormones are a real-world problem; there is no doubt that in some contexts the administration of hormones and hormone-like substances can cause or facilitate cancer and perhaps other morbid conditions. That means that, whether or not hormone residues in food pose a real danger, it is easy to imagine real-world anti-hormone laws like the EU's being adopted for non-protectionist reasons. But "dumb duck disease" is entirely hypothetical, which means it is impossible to have any feel at all for important aspects of the social and political context out of which this law is imagined to arise. It might be suggested that this lack of social and political context, even if it is far from the experience of the American judge, makes the hypothetical a good representation of the situation in which the international judge finds herself. That seems to me an exaggeration. International adjudicators are mostly citizens of the world. The basic sorts of danger that prompt countries to enact SPS measures are much the same around the world. Of course, there are local dangers, and local beliefs, and local politics—but I suspect that any record developed in an actual WTO proceeding would give the members of the tribunal more of a feel for the social and political background than can be gleaned from our hypothetical.

There is much else (aside from the general social/political context) that I would like to know about our case; but the one other thing I would most like to know about, and that I think I inevitably would know something more about in an actual case, is the nature of the Arimani "Institute for Public Health". Was their report produced by trained scientists attempting to do serious research (even if they may be self-selected for certain proclivities and also be under perfectly appropriate systemic pressures to be sensitive to risk—all of which I suspect describes the United States Environmental Protection Agency, for example), or was it produced by bureaucratic hacks merely parroting the government line? Perhaps I will be told that, in the international context, there is no way I would know which of these descriptions better fit the relevant Institute, but I find that hard to believe—and in any event this is something I need to know not just to apply the purpose test, but to decide whether there is "scientific evidence" under the SPS Agreement.

My decision, on the record as it stands? The Arimani law is upheld. State laws are entitled to a presumption of constitutionality; there is simply no evidence of protectionist purpose adequate to overcome that presumption. I assume that the Arimani Institute for Public Health does genuine science. It is hard to imagine why there is such a divergence of scientific opinion. If I were compelled to decide the scientific question on this very problematic record, I might say there is no danger from dumb duck disease. But happily that is not the question I must decide. The question is whether the Arimani law embodies a protectionist purpose. Possible dangers from hormone residues in food are not a comic-book fantasy, even if the best scientific evidence of the moment may suggest there is no danger. If either Arimani consumers or the Arimani legislature believe there is a danger from hormone-fed ducks, and if that, rather than protectionism, is the motivation for the law, the law must be upheld. There is, to be sure, discriminatory effect that benefits most Arimani duck producers (though the only political action by Arimani duck producers that we are informed of is a protest against the law by hormone-using producers). It is not surprising that there should be a correlation between consumer preferences or beliefs and the dominant practice in the local industry—there will be causal influences in both directions (as well as joint causes of both phenomena). Consumer distrust of hormones and industry avoidance of them are likely to be found together, even without assuming that the industry has stirred up the fears. It would be ironic if, in such a situation, the mere fact of discriminatory effect prevented the government from acting on consumers' concerns. It is not the function of the court either to educate the legislature in "good science" or to educate society to the merits of foreign products, provided those products are not excluded just because of their origin. The law is upheld.

Additional Questions

Let me now address the specific questions posed to Panelists. I shall take them in groups, with some rearrangement. Many of my answers are mere applications of what I have already said, but there is some new substance scattered through.

Questions 1, 3, 4
(About de facto *Discrimination)*
It absolutely matters that we are dealing with discriminatory effect (which I take to be what the question means by *de facto* discrimination) and not explicit discrimination. Explicit discrimination is virtually *per se* illegal. Discriminatory effect is relevant only as one sort of evidence of discriminatory purpose; in itself, it is not even a *prima facie* violation calling for justification. Discriminatory effect therefore does not trigger any requirement of "exoneration" (Question 4). On the other hand, weak causal linkages may tend to "exonerate" in the sense that when we are considering discriminatory effect as evidence of bad purpose, it seems likely that the more indirect the link between the putative innocent purpose and the discriminatory effect, the less persuasive is the discriminatory effect as evidence of bad purpose. Minnesota v. Clover Leaf Creamery may be an example, since the principal discriminatory effect of the Minnesota law was not in the market for milk packaging but in the market for inputs to milk packaging (plastic resins versus wood pulp).

Questions 2, 5, 6, 7 (in part), 10, 18, 21
(About the Relevance of Various Sorts of Evidence)
Since the ultimate question is whether the law was adopted with protectionist purpose, the relevance of evidence is tested by its relevance to that question. It is relevant whether there are other dangers from ducks (such as from feeding them in the park) that the legislature has not acted against; but it is a commonplace that the legislature may proceed "one step at a time" and that there may be many reasons for attacking one source of a danger but not another. If feeding in the park accounts for 2% of dumb duck disease, that will do little to show bad purpose. If feeding in the park accounts for 82%, I would certainly want some good explanation of why the legislature acted against the food-borne danger but not this one. The same general ideas apply to the failure to act against hormones in beef (although I take it hormones in beef do not cause "dumb duck disease"—it could be that hormones are a danger in duck meat but not in beef). Evidence from other countries is relevant precisely insofar as it may affect our view of the sincerity of the Arimani legislature. Similarly with the comparison to international or other widely adopted standards; here I think Arimania has more to gain from a showing that its concern is widespread than it has to lose from a showing that it is not. There is no question of Arimania being categorically required to justify its "deviation" from any other standards (except, of course, a controlling federal law, in which case the Arimani law is just preempted, no further questions asked).

Questions 7, 8, 15, 16, 17
(About How Judges Should Choose between "Efficiency" and "Democratic Legitimacy"—or How Much to "Defer" to Legislatures—in Domestic and International Contexts)

It is definitely not the role of the court to require in general that governments be efficient (though it is the court's role to suppress the specific inefficiency of protectionism). I would also emphasize that often where trade lawyers think there is a conflict between national autonomy and efficiency, there is actually no conflict. Conflicts between autonomy and trade-maximization are endemic, because nations have many reasons, including many non-protectionist ones, for restricting trade. But trade-maximization is not the same as efficiency, for reasons I sketched in section 2.[43] Efficiency normally requires that nations' non-protectionist choices be respected; in such cases, efficiency and autonomy point in the same direction, even if it is the direction of reduced trade.

As to the questions about the degree of deference, "deference" is a problematic concept; even what it might mean varies with different substantive views. In the purpose theory, for instance, "deference" is an all-or-nothing matter, and the crucial question about purpose is in effect a determination whether deference is appropriate or not. Pressed for an abstract answer to Questions 15 and 16 that might be relevant to other theories, I would be tempted to say there is no reason for international tribunals to be especially deferential, as long as they are exercising the powers delegated to them by treaty. (I admit to liking that deferential-seeming doctrine of treaty interpretation, *in dubio mitius*; but it seems to me there is a difference between, on the one hand, being restrained in the interpretation of the basic treaty obligation, as *in dubio mitius* recommends, but then enforcing the obligation straightforwardly, and, on the other hand, asserting a wide obligation but then being "deferential" case-by-case in enforcing it, which I find hard to justify. This distinction would obviously bear more discussion.) Tribunals should be careful not to overstep their authority; and they should be sensitive in applying the rules, whatever they are, to the variety of cultures. If the tribunals will do this, any remaining problems about the political acceptability of the world trading system must be dealt with by national governments: by improving the system, by educating people about its benefits, and by seeing that the benefits are in fact equitably distributed, both within and between nations.

Questions 9, 14
(The Seriousness of the Danger, the Precautionary Principle, and the Duty to Reexamine Legislation in Light of New Facts)

The seriousness of the danger matters precisely because it is relevant to the determination of purpose. Other things equal, the legislature is much more likely to have been genuinely motivated by what they perceived to be a serious danger than by a trivial one. The "precautionary principle" as such (that is, as an exception to some other duty) has no role in a purpose-based theory. But obviously a legislature may plausibly and innocently act against dangers for which the scientific evidence is slim (or in a narrow sense of "evidence," non-existent).

Since there is no "precautionary principle" in the purpose theory, there is no duty of reexamination associated with the precautionary principle. But the question about reexamination does raise an interesting problem for a purpose-based theory. Suppose a law was adopted with no bad purpose, but circumstances have changed enough since the law was adopted so that if it were readopted now, would we be strongly inclined to view it as motivated by protectionism? Obviously, non-repeal consciously motivated by protectionism is as inimical to the basic values of the system as a new protectionist law.[44] If the legislature is just unconscious, then we have in principle no ground of invalidity; but it is of course open to any injured party or nation to bring it to the legislature's attention that the law no longer serves any non-protectionist interest. At this point I think we might presume that non-repeal is motivated by protectionism and invalidate the law, unless the legislature acts in such a way as to persuade us that they genuinely believe in the continuing non-protectionist utility of the law. In this way, we can construct a limited "duty of reexamination" within the purpose theory.

Questions 11, 12, 13
(How to Decide Which Scientists to Believe)
The purpose-based theory does not require the judge to evaluate scientific reports in the sense of deciding who has the right answer. The only question is what the legislature might plausibly have relied on, a considerably easier question in most cases. Of course, considerations like the source and apparent persuasiveness of the report are relevant.

Questions 19, 20
("Less Restrictive Alternative" Analysis, and Labeling)
“Less restrictive alternative" analysis is relevant to both a purpose-based theory and a balancing theory, though it functions differently in the two contexts. It raises no new issue of principle in either. The existence of a less restrictive alternative is relevant in the purpose-based theory because the existence of an alternative which would achieve the full local benefit with less effect on trade suggests that the more trade-restrictive measure was chosen for its additional protectionist effect. But, of course, a crucial question is whether the legislature believed the alternative was fully adequate. Note that if they sincerely believed it was not, but the reviewing court is convinced that it is, then we have the same sort of situation as when the reviewing court

finds no benefit at all from a measure, contrary to the legislature's sincere belief. As I said before, judicial intervention is at its least objectionable here, since the result of invalidation can be reached by substituting the court's empirical judgment for the legislature's but without the need for an evaluative decision by the court. Even so, I would not intervene.

In the context of a balancing theory, where the court is already committed to making evaluative judgments, less restrictive alternative analysis has a wider scope, since the court can decide that even an alternative which does not achieve all the benefits of the local law should be preferred if the benefit that would be lost by moving to the alternative is less than the cost to trade that would be avoided. We might refer to this metaphorically as "balancing at the margin." This difference, between the way less restrictive alternative analysis fits into a balancing theory and the way it fits into the purpose theory, explains why less restrictive alternative analysis plays an independent role in, for example, American first amendment law (which involves balancing), but does not play an independent role, despite being regularly mentioned, in "core" dormant commerce clause cases.

Since Question 20 refers to labeling, let me close with a tendentious comment. Labeling is the all-purpose "less restrictive alternative" of the trade partisan. (Not specifically in this Question, where the point is implicitly made that the effects of labeling depend heavily on local conditions.) But it is a rare case in which labeling, even with a literate and consumer-conscious population, will fully achieve the goals of a broader prohibition. Labeling will do that only if (1) there are no concerns about external effects from the consumer's purchase or use of the product,[45] and (2) any harm to the consumer herself is one the legislature is willing to let her suffer if she chooses it voluntarily (the legislature is not required to be willing—international trade law contains no anti-paternalism principle). In sum, labeling is often less restrictive, but it is rarely a fully effective alternative.

NOTES

1. *EC Measures Concerning Meat and Meat Products (Hormones),* WT/DS26/AB/R and WT/DS48/AB/R (16 January 1998).

2. Art. I, §8, cl. 3.

3. 27 U.S. (2 Pet.) 245, 252 (1829).

4. As to extraterritoriality, the law does classify duck meat according to the production process, and it is sometimes suggested that "process-based" restrictions are extraterritorial. This is a mistake, in my view, but we need not discuss that here. See Robert Howse and Donald Regan, The Product/Process Distinction—An Illusory Basis for Disciplining "Unilateralism" in Trade Policy, *EJIL* 11 (2000), No. 2, 249–89. In this case, it is clear that the process of using growth hormones is forbidden because it is thought to affect the constitution of the meat itself at the

point of consumption. Such a prohibition is generally understood to be product-based in its essence.

5. Aside from taxation, transportation, and extraterritoriality, there is also no issue in the Arimani duck case about the "state as market participant" or Congressional authorization, doctrinal variations which are even further from our present concerns.

These categories (tax, transportation, extraterritoriality) are not arbitrary exclusions designed simply to create a residual class of cases about which I can claim that the Court does not balance. I have explained elsewhere why these categories are theoretically significant. See "The Supreme Court and State Protectionism: Making Sense of the Dormant Commerce Clause," *Michigan Law Review* 84 (1986), 1091–1287, at 1182–92 (transportation and taxation), and "Siamese Essays: (I) *CTS Corp. v. Dynamics Corp. of America* and Dormant Commerce Clause Doctrine; (II) Extraterritorial State Legislation," *Michigan Law Review* 85 (1987), 1865–1913, at 1873–84 (extraterritoriality). But even if the categories were not theoretically significant, they would be descriptively significant. The residual class that remains when these cases are excluded—what I now call the "core"—comprises most dormant commerce clause cases. If it is possible to identify by simple criteria a large class of cases in which the Court does not balance even though it says it does, that would be worth knowing even if the Court's behavior made no sense at all.

6. *Pike v. Bruce Church, Inc.*, 397 U.S. 137, 142 (1970).

7. Stewart talks about a test for "statutes"; I have formulated the conventional wisdom in terms of a test for any "law." Although Stewart may have allowed himself to be temporarily distracted in *Pike* by the fact that the challenge was not to the controlling statute but to an administrative order under that statute, it is clear that any authoritative norm is subject to the same basic dormant commerce clause test.

8. *City of Philadelphia v. New Jersey,* 437 U.S. 617 (1978).

9. *Maine v. Taylor,* 477 U.S. 131 (1986).

10. *Hunt v. Washington State Apple Advertising Commission,* 432 U.S. 333 (1977).

11. For two minor additions that do not change the fundamental principle, see the discussions in IV.B below of less restrictive alternative analysis (comments on Questions 19, 20) and the puzzle of significantly changed circumstances (comments on Questions 9, 14).

12. For other possible reasons, see Regan 1986, *supra* note 5, at 1284–87.

13. See the long footnote 12 in *General Motors Corp. v. Tracy,* 519 U.S. 278 (1997).

14. Regan 1986, *supra* note 5.

15. 294 U.S. 511 (1935).

16. 336 U.S. 525 (1949).

17. For fuller discussion, see Regan 1986, *supra* note 5, at 1245–52, 1262–68.

18. For fuller discussion, see Regan 1986, *supra* note 5, at 1209–20.

19. 340 U.S. 349 (1951).

20. For fuller discussion, see Regan 1986, *supra* note 5, at 1228–33.

21. 432 U.S. 333 (1977). For fuller discussion, see Regan 1986, *supra* note 5, at 1221–28.

22. 432 U.S. at 352.

23. And what if the legislature never thought at all, simply rubber-stamping a proposal from some lobbyist? The point is that whoever drafted the statute must have been motivated by protectionism, and the legislature either endorsed that motivation or made no substantive decision at all. In either case, a protectionist motive can be attributed to the legislature; there is no decision deserving of judicial deference. See section 2.

24. 457 U.S. 624 (1982).

25. 457 U.S. at 646 (Powell, J., concurring).

26. For fuller discussion, see Regan 1986, *supra* note 5, at 1278–83.

27. 481 U.S. 69 (1987).

28. 481 U.S. at 92.

29. For fuller discussion, see Regan 1987, *supra* note 5, at 1865–84.

30. 486 U.S. 888 (1988).

31. See, e.g., the discussion of *Allenberg Cotton Co. v. Pittman,* 419 U.S. 20 (1974), in Regan 1986, *supra* note 5, at 1188–89.

32. 449 U.S. 456 (1981).

33. I simplify slightly. The primary discriminatory effect was actually in the market for *inputs* to plastic and paper packaging, that is, plastic resins and wood pulp.

34. The phrase "unavoidably incidental to the achievement of that purpose" is included in the statement in the text to leave room for "less restrictive alternative analysis," of which more below (section 3, the discussion of Questions 19, 20). The statement in the text also assumes that the law *achieves* its non-protectionist purpose. If the law is so misguided as to achieve no benefit, then it is inefficient, though, of course, it may still be that the court should defer to the legislature's empirical determination that there is some benefit, as I shall argue below. Notice that a law which is inefficient because there is no benefit at all is inefficient whether or not it has an interstate discriminatory effect, so interstate discriminatory effect still is not the real ground of objection.

Incidentally, since I have argued that the inefficiency of protectionism is fundamentally tied up with purpose, I am moved to point out that even classic tariffs and import embargoes and the like are not inefficient if they are motivated by an intrinsic preference for autarky (which need not be based on crude xenophobia). In the real world, of course, protectionism is not normally the result of an intrinsic preference for autarky (which is why standard discussions never even mention this possibility); in the real world, protectionism is a collectively self-defeating attempt to secure local advantage at others' expense. Indeed, no state which joined the United States, and no country which has joined the EU or the WTO could possibly claim to have a significant intrinsic preference for autarky, so the point is of theoretical interest only. But it does remind us that, at bottom, efficiency is about satisfying preferences ("permissible" preferences, if you prefer, but there is no reason a non-xenophobic intrinsic preference for autarky should be impermissible).

35. Two further points: (1) Of course, the market mechanism will not work if there are significant third-party effects from Jones's decision to take his custom to Giant or from Minnesota's regulation of milk packaging (third-party effects which are not themselves mediated through further market relations). But there are not likely to be such effects in the Jones case, nor

in most cases like the Minnesota case. What the "virtual representation" theorist argues for in cases like this is virtual representation for the suppliers of plastic packaging to Minnesota, and *that* is just what we have shown is not necessary. - (2) Even if the market produces efficient results, we may, of course, disapprove of the distributive consequences. We might dislike the distributive consequences of Jones's taking his business to Giant, or of Minnesota's cutting off foreign plastics producers. But it would never occur to us to deal with the distributive consequences of Jones's decision either by saying he must continue to patronize Mom&Pop or by requiring him to compensate them for his defection. Nor should we deal with the distributive consequences of Minnesota's regulation by invalidating it (or requiring compensation).

36. Cf. the Note Ad Article III in the GATT.

37. 325 U.S. 761 (1945).

38. I speak of the general run of cases; there are cases, such as those involving basic rights or suspect classifications, where we precisely distrust the legislature to make acceptable normative judgments, and in such cases we turn to the courts as the only alternative.

39. *FCC v. Beach Communications, Inc.*, 508 U.S. 307, 313 (1993).

40. *Hormones, supra* note 1, at 194.

41. It is worth mentioning that, aside from the dormant commerce clause, purpose review is an established element of suspect classification equal protection law, establishment clause law, and free speech law.

42. For a similar list of considerations relevant to showing purpose, see *Village of Arlington Heights v. Metropolitan Housing Development Corp.*, 429 U.S. 252 (1977).

43. See also Howse/Regan, *supra* note 4, at 279–85.

44. For a rare real-world case where protectionist motivation for non-repeal may be identifiable, see *Kassel v. Consolidated Freightways Corp.*, 450 U.S. 662 (1981).

45. "Purchase" is relevant because the purchase itself will encourage future use of the process by which the product was produced, and that process may be the cause of a relevant externality. See Howse/Regan, *supra* note 4, at 262, 272–73.

CHAPTER 5

A U.S. Perspective on Ducks

Diane P. Wood

The Arimania case (see Appendix, p. 359) raises a number of interesting problems both for the initial tribunal that considers it and for an appellate court. Some of the more vexing issues that arise within the WTO system would be of little importance to a federal judge in the United States, while others are among the hottest questions under consideration in the courts today. Until very recently, almost all American observers would have said that the substantive issues presented would not pose serious issues, if we imagine that Arimania is one of the fifty constituent states of the United States. The Supreme Court's recent federalism revolution might be changing all that, although in an area as central to the federal government's power as interstate trade, it is equally possible that the revolution will not go that far. Procedurally, the questions for the U.S. judge are quite similar to the ones that the WTO Panels and Appellate Body have faced: who is entitled to participate in the proceeding; how liberally should the right to intervene be conferred; what is the role of *amicus curiae* and how many such parties should be permitted to express their views; how should complex scientific evidence be considered by judges who inevitably are not experts in the field; what interpretative principles are proper when considering the texts of statutes, regulations, and treaties; and finally, how much deference should be given to the original decision maker?

Because the substantive issues are relatively more straightforward, the paper considers them first, and then it turns to the procedural problems just identified. In spite of the many differences between the internal federal court system of the United States and the emerging judicial regime at the WTO, it appears that there are many areas in which useful comparisons are possible between the two, and that the appellate body in particular might be interested in the direction the U.S. courts are taking.

1. The Substantive Legality of Arimania's Law

There are two reasons why it is almost unthinkable that a state of the United States would try to pass legislation like the DDD Law in Arimania, or, if it were passed, that the law would survive for five minutes in a court challenge. The first is that both the area of food safety regulation and pharmaceutical regulation (even for animals) is pervasively occupied by the federal government. The Supremacy Clause of the U.S. Constitution would thus, in all likelihood, lead any federal or state court to find that the DDD Law was preempted by positive federal law and thus was unenforceable. In areas where federal law is said, in the phrase just used, to "occupy the field," the states are not permitted to regard federal standards as "floors" that they are entitled to exceed; instead, the courts will say that Congress deliberately chose both how much and how little it wanted in the way of regulation, and any state interference in any direction is preempted. Thus, during October Term 1999, the Supreme Court of the United States considered the question whether a railroad crossing that met the design specified under federal regulations might nonetheless be regarded as too unsafe under state law, and it answered with a resounding "no."[1] Another case considered the question whether cars that were not equipped with passive restraints (*i.e.,* airbags) at a time when federal regulations *permitted* but did not *require* passive restraints, might be held to be unsafe as a matter of state law.[2] Again, the Court said no: compliance with the federal regulation was enough. The Seventh Circuit Court of Appeals, on which I sit, recently followed these cases in a decision holding that compliance with design standards allowed by federal law for a bus was enough to protect the bus manufacturer from state tort liability.[3] Here, if duck growers in general were following relevant federal standards with respect to an authorized use of the growth hormone (which we assume had received the necessary regulatory approval at the federal level—otherwise it would violate federal law to use it at all), this line of cases indicates that the states could not impose additional requirements of their own.

The second reason why the DDD Law would be substantively doomed in the United States relates to the commerce clause issues discussed in more detail in Professor Regan's paper. A combination of the "dormant" commerce clause and the full faith and credit clause leads to a regime under which the states cannot impose this kind of barrier on interstate commerce. Indeed, the Supreme Court has gone so far as to say that one state cannot refuse to accept garbage generated in another state,[4] because there is actually interstate commerce in garbage. States cannot insist that milk be produced only within their borders on the basis of alleged concerns for milk purity and freshness.[5] Non-discriminatory rules, as long as they do not unduly burden interstate commerce, are permissible, but the bottom line is really that if the product is good enough to eat in Wisconsin, it's good enough to eat in Illinois.

The only caveat here relates to the Supreme Court's aggressive new line of cases resting on basic precepts of federalism. What is going on, in the view of many observers, is nothing less than a revolution. Ever since the New Deal, Congress has passed legislation that addresses national problems. Typically, it has relied on two sources of power: most frequently, it looks to the commerce clause, which is found in Article I of the Constitution;

occasionally, it relies on section 5 of the Fourteenth Amendment, which gives it the power to implement the guarantees of that amendment against state action that deprives persons of the equal protection of the law or violates due process principles. (The Fourteenth Amendment, as everyone will recall, is the middle of the three amendments to the U.S. Constitution passed in the wake of the American Civil War. Unlike most of the original Constitution and the amendments before the Thirteenth, it is specifically addressed to state action, it specifically gives federal protection to individuals whose rights are infringed by state actors, and it specifically confers on Congress the power to pass laws that restrict the states.) Until a few years ago, no one blinked an eye when Congress used its commerce clause powers in this way. But, starting with the *Seminole Tribe* decision in 1996,[6] the Supreme Court has been cutting back on federal commerce legislation in two ways: first, it has now definitively established the principle that Congress has no power to enact legislation that applies to the states using its Article I powers; second, it has now struck down in their entirety a number of laws passed under the commerce power on the theory that the link to interstate commerce is just too remote.

Why has the Court suddenly started taking such a restrictive view of Congress's Article I powers, and what does that mean for the WTO? The first question can be answered readily, though it is worth noting that this line of argument is quite controversial in the United States. Shortly after the country began operating under the Constitution of 1789, the Supreme Court decided a case in which federal jurisdiction was based on the language in Article III of the Constitution that permitted federal courts to hear disputes between an individual citizen of one state and another State *qua* State.[7] An uproar ensued that led to the enactment of the Eleventh Amendment to the Constitution.[8] Anyone who sat down and read the Eleventh Amendment would think that it simply repealed that controversial part of the Article III laundry list of jurisdictional grants, but she would be wrong. Instead, for many years the Supreme Court has seen in the Eleventh Amendment the embodiment of a kind of sovereign immunity principle for the states. Thus, for example, it has long been established that private individuals cannot sue a state in federal court for monetary relief. Recently, however, a razor-thin majority of the Court has taken the Eleventh Amendment much farther. In cases including *Florida Prepaid Postsecondary Educational Expense Board v. College Savings Bank,*[9] *College Savings Bank v. Florida Prepaid Postsecondary Educational Expense Board,*[10] *Alden v. Maine,*[11] and *Seminole Tribe of Florida v. State of Florida,*[12] it has transformed the Eleventh Amendment into a placeholder for a theory of absolute sovereign immunity for the states. (The scope of this immunity, incidentally, goes far beyond the sovereign immunity to which foreign nations are entitled under the Foreign Sovereign Immunities Act,[13] because their immunity is a restrictive one and, most significantly for present purposes, it does not extend to their commercial activities.) This means that private parties may no longer ensure that the states are living up to their obligations under federal law, if those obligations stem from one of the Article I powers: commerce, patents, copyright, post offices, bankruptcy, to name only a few. The federal government is still entitled to sue, because the Eleventh Amendment (for reasons the Court has not fully explained) did not diminish federal powers vis-à-vis the states. Still, the ability of injured parties in the United States as a whole to make sure that the states are not disrupting commercial obligations of the United States has been diminished.

Furthermore, as noted above, in several cases the Court has struck down federal legislation based on the commerce power, on the ground that it went too far. Three examples of this exist, and a fourth important environmental case was decided (though for the time being on non-constitutional grounds) in early 2001. The first was *United States v. Lopez,*[14] in which the Court decided that Congress had no power to pass a law criminalizing the possession of a gun within a certain distance of a public school. The second was *United States v. Morrison,*[15] in which the Court rejected extensive findings that Congress made when it passed the Violence Against Women Act and the many ways in which violence affected the interstate travel of women, including the use of weapons that had moved in interstate commerce and imposed demands on the national systems for health care, enforcement of court orders forbidding abusive spouses to harass women, and in other ways. Notwithstanding this record, the Court decided that the statute exceeded Congress's authority. The third case was *Jones v. United States,*[16] in which the question was whether a federal statute criminalizing arson when the property in question affected interstate commerce could be sustained. Once again, the Court said no. The 2001 case dealt with Congress's power to give authority to the federal environmental agencies (here, the Army Corps of Engineers) to regulate the use of lands that are used as habitat by migratory birds.[17] There, the Court decided that the Clean Water Act did not authorize the federal authorities to require the municipal Solid Waste Agency of Northern Cook County, Illinois, to obtain a permit to fill certain wetlands, because the statute itself did not reach beyond waters that were more literally "navigable." Because it rested the decision on a statutory theory, the Court did not reach the question whether Congress would have the power to impose federal regulation over such wetlands, and this therefore remains an open question. Many treaties exist that require the United States to do just that. Indeed, the site at issue in the Cook County case was home to more than 123 species of migratory birds, some of which are endangered, and so the question may yet arise in that very case.[18] Those who have an interest in the WTO and the United States's ability to implement its obligations under those treaties should watch the developments after the *Solid Waste Agency* case carefully.

Even given *SWANCC, Lopez, Morrison,* and *Jones,* it is hard to imagine that federal legislation in the area of food additives, agricultural use of hormones, or similar topics is at serious risk. The commerce clause was designed to create a single national market, and it has obviously succeeded beyond its drafters' wildest expectations. Thus, in the final analysis the substantive questions posed about the Arimani law would not be too difficult in the setting of the U.S. legal system. No greater deference attaches to *de facto* versus *de jure* discrimination (and no less). As a matter of proof, it might be easier to show that some kind of discrimination was occurring if DDD is also contracted by being close to ducks, but the absence of that fact would make very little difference.

2. Procedural Questions

Who Is Entitled to Participate in the Proceeding?

The decision about who is entitled to formal "party" status in a proceeding, no questions asked, can be a complex one. Professor Davey's paper offers a useful review of the rules of "standing to sue" in the United States, which govern the federal courts' treatment of this issue. But there is nothing obvious about those rules, and indeed many of the states follow different principles in their own courts, because they are not constrained by the formal "case or controversy" limitation on their power that Article III of the Constitution imposes on federal courts. The WTO is writing on a relatively clean slate here, and so it may be worth at least setting out the outer limits of the possible individuals, juridical entities, or political entities, that might have a clear right to participate.

At its narrowest (which is more or less where things seem to be right now), the only full parties are the complaining states or entities like the European Union. They are the contracting parties under the WTO agreements; they are the ones to whom other states made promises; and they are therefore the ones with the formal grievance. But if we allow the slightest degree of realism to intrude, it is plain that other actors are also deeply involved in the controversies. Indeed, they are visiting their national capitals, urging what is essentially the espousal of their private claims, and lobbying with respect to actions that should be taken.

So, expanding out from the strict right of states alone to participate, one could imagine a rule under which any party injured in fact from the challenged trade measure could participate. That in fact is the core, constitutional, dimension of standing recognized in the United States: injury in fact, caused by the action of the other party, and something that the judicial proceeding can redress.[19] The other dimensions of standing, such as the general rule prohibiting one party from asserting the rights of another, are known as "prudential" limitations and can be waived or overlooked in appropriate cases. (Thus, for example, doctors are sometimes allowed to assert the rights of their patients, as in the cases concerning access to reproductive technologies.[20] Or, in one of my favorite examples, bartenders were allowed to assert the right of eighteen-year-old boys who wanted to be permitted to purchase 3.2% beer just as their female counterparts could.[21])

How Liberally Should the Right to Intervene Be Conferred?

I distinguish rights of intervention from the right to be named as a party in the first instances, although the two ideas blend together at the margins. In the U.S. federal courts, the right to be a party is governed by Federal Rule of Civil Procedure 19 (in the sense of deciding who absolutely must be a part of the case, rather than who is permitted to be a party), and the right of intervention is governed by Federal Rule of Civil Procedure 24. Two kinds of intervention are recognized. The first is intervention of right, where the outcome of the proceeding will have such an important effect on the outsider's interests, and in some instances where a statute or rule acknowledges that interest, that the court must permit the outsider to join the litigation with full party rights. The other kind is permissive intervention, where the court may exercise its discretion in deciding whether or not to confer the functional equivalent of party status on the outsider. As things have stood since 1966, these inquiries have been pragmatic in nature, rather than focusing on formal legal categories.

What Is the Role of *Amicus Curiae*, and How Many of Them Should Be Permitted to Express Their Views?

This is a question that has been under active discussion in the Seventh Circuit. Two kinds of *amicus curiae* submissions arrive at the court: the first are briefs that all of the parties have agreed may be filed, and thus are submitted with consent; the second are briefs to which someone has objected. (It goes without saying that because judicial proceedings are public, the public in general knows that the litigation is under way, and a simple inquiry to the office of the clerk of the court will tell the prospective *amici* what the deadline is for the submission of the brief. A brief that supports the ultimate position of the appellant is due at the same time the party-appellant's brief must be filed; briefs supporting the appellee follow those timetables.[22])

The problems come with volume, repetition, and politicization of the judicial process. In high profile cases, the more *amicus curiae* briefs are filed, the more the judges must read. That may sound like an unimportant complaint, and perhaps it is for an appellate system with the caseload that the Appellate Body at the WTO now has, but in the federal appellate courts of the United States every little bit counts. At the Seventh Circuit, which covers only three states (Illinois, Indiana, and Wisconsin), annual filings are now running at about 3,400, for a court with 11 active judges, and the equivalent of 2.5 additional judges counting the assistance our senior judges generously give. Perhaps 1,800 of those 3,400 require serious disposition on the merits, after many are resolved on easy procedural points. We can all do the math, and if we must read more than the 200 pages or so each case requires, the burden can add up quickly.

The extra reading would be worth it if the *amicus* brief added a new perspective or revealed longer term implications of possible outcomes that the parties somehow did not bring to the court's attention. Indeed, such briefs are invaluable and we are delighted to receive them. But if the *amicus* brief simply rehashes the same points the party it is supporting has already made, it has very little value added for the case. I have seen instances in which the same lawyer more or less rewrote his brief for the *amicus.* The practice of the Seventh Circuit has had its critics, but we are likely to deny permission to file such a brief—even if it is proffered with the consent of all parties—because its costs outweigh its benefits.[23] The burden of reading is one problem, but a deeper and more serious one is the tone it gives to the proceeding. Judicial proceedings are not supposed to be like lobbying for legislation, where proponents of each side bring together as many different supporters as they can so that the legislature can see both how much people care and how many different groups support a point. Judicial proceedings are supposed to be decided on the law. It should not matter if fifteen groups support the appellant and no one has supported the appellee; if the law is on the appellee's side, the appellee should win; if it is not, that party should lose. Particularly when we are looking at a judicial manifestation of a hot-button political topic, such as abortion, affirmative action, or environmental clean-up, it is important not only to maintain impartiality, but also to maintain the appearance of impartiality. Paradoxically enough, *amicus curiae* briefs can damage the appearance of impartiality in those instances where they do not genuinely bring a different voice to the matter.

How Should Complex Scientific Evidence Be Considered by Judges Who Inevitably Are Not Experts in the Field?

The uses and misuses of scientific evidence have been the subject of books, treatises, and countless law review articles for a long time in the United States, and this is a topic that is of central importance to the review of Arimania's statute. The problem does not reveal any evidence on which Arimania relied before it enacted the DDD Law; to the contrary, it cites only "widespread fear that its citizens will be contaminated" if they consume the hormone-treated duck meat. After the law is passed, the opponents of the law "produce" (to whom?) the document attributed to Prof. Dr. Dr. h.c. Helmut von Entefleisch, in which he expresses the opinion that (1) the last known victim of DDD contracted the disease 98 years ago (September 2, 1902), and that (2) whatever risk there may be can be mitigated entirely by a diet rich in water and fruits. The problem also notes that no one would question Dr. von Entefleisch's "expertise." Last, *after* the legislation is passed and *after* Dr. von Entefleisch's opinion surfaces, the government goes out and obtains the reports from the governmental Institute for Public Health and the domestic group Industrywatch. On Karponia's side, the "Free Your Mind" report is prepared, from a purported neutral third party, or at least a third party physically located in a neutral third state, Neutronia.

The way this evidence would be received in a federal court of the United States is probably quite different from the way any WTO body would look at it. A word or two of background is necessary. First, we should distinguish between the way courts evaluate expert testimony in cases where the trial court (sometimes with, sometimes without a jury) is charged with the initial findings of fact, and the way courts look at expert testimony that an administrative agency has admitted in a proceeding before it. In the former case, the rules in federal court derive directly from the Federal Rules of Evidence, especially Rules 702 and 703, and the way the Supreme Court now construes those rules. This may be a district court, as it is in Social Security Disability appeals, or a court of appeals, as it is in appeals from decisions of the Federal Trade Commission or the Securities and Exchange Commission, for example. In the latter case, the reviewing court will almost always be guided by something like the "substantial evidence" standard found in the Administrative Procedure Act, under which the court must uphold the agency's determination if there is substantial evidence (*i.e.,* enough quantitatively to support a finding, and also qualitatively complete enough so as to leave no gaps in the reasoning process).[24] In deciding whether evidence was "substantial," a court will look back to the general rules for the admission of expert testimony, but it will give the agency the benefit of the doubt on questions like whether a finder of fact might have given too much weight to the expert's opinion. The assumption is that the agency knows what it is doing.

The general rules which are of direct importance in cases litigated in the courts and of indirect importance in our agency cases, used to ask only if the expert testimony was "generally accepted" in the relevant community of experts. While this had some benefits—*e.g.,* it had the effect of preventing juries or judges from hearing kooky theories that had never been substantiated—it also had the unfortunate effect of keeping away from the trier of fact the cutting edge theories by first-rate scientists that may not yet have achieved general acceptance. This was known as the *Frye* test, after the court of appeals opinion that first articulated it;[25] it is still the theory followed by many state court systems and is thus far from dead in the United States. But the *Frye* test was repudiated for the federal courts in an important 1993 decision of the Supreme Court, *Daubert v. Merrell Dow Pharmaceuticals, Inc.*[26] In *Daubert,* the Court replaced *Frye* with a test designed to ask more particular questions about the scientific validity of expert opinion. What methodologies did the scientist follow? Were they subject to any form of peer review? Are the tests pertinent to the problem at issue, in the sense that there is a good "fit" between the question the scientist is testing and the problem at hand? Has the expert done these kinds of things before outside the litigation context? While the problem of the "hired gun" may be less severe in Europe given the more inquisitorial nature of the judicial system, it is a serious one in the United States, and the problem implies that it could be a serious one for the WTO (at least in the facts we are given.)

At the very beginning (and even in the *Daubert* opinion itself), there were hints that *Daubert* may have established a more flexible test for the admission of expert testimony. Experience soon proved this wrong. Instead, as the Supreme Court roughly acknowledged in *Kumho Tire Co. v. Carmichael,*[27] the *Daubert* decision signaled the end of a permissive era in which practically any kind of "junk" science came in as "expert" testimony, and the start of an era in which trial judges took their role as gatekeepers far more seriously. Not only were the days of "hired guns" to be over, but the days of being swept away by someone's reputation when there was nothing of relevant substance being offered were also gone. The best example of that phenomenon that I know personally comes from an opinion of the Seventh Circuit written by my colleague Richard Posner, a person widely known for his extensive scholarship in law and economics, but whose scholarship and interests also run the gamut from the jurisprudence of Benjamin Cardozo, to Oliver Wendell Holmes, to an economic explanation of human sexual relations, to the complex relation between law and literature. The case was an antitrust case brought by small retail pharmacies against the large drug manufacturers and certain large wholesalers of drugs, in which the plaintiffs claimed that the large manufacturers had agreed among themselves to charge higher prices to the small stores and lower prices to the chains and to various hospital groups.[28] The plaintiffs wanted to use the expert testimony of Robert Lucas, a distinguished economist at the University of Chicago who had recently won the Nobel Prize for Economics. Judge Posner was unimpressed. Dr. Lucas, he held, was merely stating some truisms about the relation between market power and the ability of a firm to engage in the practice of economic price discrimination. As such, it contributed nothing to the case and was correctly rejected by the trial judge.[29]

Looking at the Arimania case, a federal court in the United States would find the initial law unsupported by anything but fear and superstition. But so what? Absent international obligations, democratically elected legislatures are entitled to pass whatever silly laws they wish. Here, of course, there is the SPS agreement, and so Arimania has, in fact, made a promise not to enact measures with a discriminatory effect that have no scientific basis. Is Dr. von Entefleisch's opinion something that tends to show there is *no* scientific basis? Not at all, as far as a U.S. court would see it. It is no better—indeed it is even less supported—than Dr. Lucas's opinion was in the *Brand Name Drugs* case. Dr. Lucas's only sin was in restating the obvious, whereas Dr. von Entefleisch has given no reason to believe that his methodologies were sound, that he monitored the tests, that additional information has not emerged to undermine his opinions, etc. Burdens of proof are certainly important here, too, but normally a complaining party has at least a burden of production to show that a measure does not comply with the WTO agreements. Dr. von Entefleisch's opinion neither adds nor subtracts from Karponia's position.

That leaves two reports on the table: the one from Free Your Mind, and the one from the government in Arimania. In principle, the source of a report should make no difference to the *Daubert* inquiry, as long as the science is sound. Governments regularly rely on reports from their expert scientific agencies, and there is nothing suspect in the process. Nor should it matter that Free Your Mind is located in a neutral "country" rather than in Karponia.

It is in this light that a U.S. court, whether reviewing the results of a trial or the conclusions of an administrative agency, would think about the minority support issue. A scientific position does not need to have attained general acceptance, but it must be soundly based. It must be the same kind and quality of research, as the Supreme Court put it in *Kumho Tire,* that the experts would have done in their ordinary work unrelated to litigation. Should it matter when the reports were generated? On the one hand, if they were not before the legislature when it acted, it is hard to say logically that this is why it passed the law as it did. On the other hand, suppose that the law was passed, and then before the case went to the WTO a Panel of the very best scientists in the world did a rigorously controlled study and found that DDD was invariably fatal to people, and that one portion of duck every two weeks was enough to increase 100-fold the risk of contracting it. Why should anyone care that the study was late, if it turns out that the law can meet the substantive standards imposed by the SPS agreement or other WTO instruments. Plainly, records must be closed at some time, but a reasonable case can be made for the proposition that it is time enough to close the record at the end of the challenge proceeding.

What Interpretative Principles Are Proper When Considering the Texts of Statutes, Regulations, and Treaties?

This, too, is a topic worth days, rather than minutes. Debate rages in the United States between those who insist that the plain meaning of the text should control in all instances, and who consider it virtually illegitimate to look beyond textual sources in construing written sources of law, and those who believe that context, the intent of the drafters, the kind of problem that was being targeted, and similar secondary sources matter. Naturally, for domestic interpretative questions, we do not have an authoritative document like the Vienna Convention on the Law of Treaties. The Vienna Convention does not answer all questions, but it does put an imprimatur on using the various sources it mentions. Those who argue against a more contextualist approach (including people like Justice Scalia on the Supreme Court and Judge Frank Easterbrook on the Seventh Circuit) point out that final legislative or treaty texts are usually the product of a complex series of compromises. Who can say what the ultimate "intent" of a multi-member body was, or what moved each individual voter in the majority finally to approve the language? Especially with an international treaty, they might add, it is important to stay very close to the text, lest one party impute a meaning to it that another would challenge.

How Much Deference Should Be Given to the Original Decision Maker?

I mean in this section to allude to the often-controversial *Chevron* doctrine in the United States.[30] Harking back to the last section, that doctrine provides that courts must construe legislation according to its plain meaning, even when they are reviewing actions of an administrative agency. But if there are genuine ambiguities, the court should defer to the interpretation given to the statute by those entrusted with its implementation—the expert administrative agency—rather than tackling it *de novo*. Interestingly for WTO purposes, the Court adopted this approach long after public choice doctrine had made perfectly clear the problem of regulatory capture that often afflicts agencies. Why defer to the National Labor Relations Board, for example, if it has been "captured" by organized labor? Why defer to the Commodities Futures Trading Commission, if the futures market advocates have taken it over? And yet both agencies (and many more) receive their *Chevron* deference. Pushing the analogy a bit, one could argue that the WTO Panels and Appellate Body should defer to the national agencies whose work they are reviewing, even though they know that national interest "capture" may have taken place there, too.

It is my impression that the Supreme Court is becoming somewhat more flexible in its application of *Chevron.* How else can one explain its decision in the 1999 Term to reject the Food and Drug Administration's expert determination that nicotine should be regulated as a drug, in favor of leaving the substance unregulated?[31] The Court reached this result by looking at the network of other laws Congress has passed over the years that pertain to tobacco and tobacco products. But the FDA was obviously aware of those other laws, too, and it is hard to say that one result or another was compelled. The Court may have simply softened the degree of deference it had previously said was called for under *Chevron.*

Another way in which *Chevron* deference was diluted has been in the Court's view of the kind of agency pronouncement that is entitled to deference. One might have thought that the Equal Employment Opportunity Commission is the expert agency in the field of employment discrimination and thus that its views on the proper implementation of statutes like the Americans with Disabilities Act and the Age Discrimination in Employment Act were clearly entitled to *Chevron* deference. But, in *Sutton v. United Airlines, Inc.,*[32] in which the Court found that the existence of disability [for purposes of the Americans with Disabilities Act] cannot be determined without taking into account any ameliorative measures the person uses, and in *Reeves v. Sanderson Plumbing Products, Inc.,*[33] in which the Court held that a plaintiff's case under the Age Discrimination in Employment Act had been dismissed too precipitously by the lower court, that is not what the Court did. To the contrary, in those cases, the Court implied that informal agency statements, while entitled to respect, do not trigger *Chevron* deference. If so, that means that *Chevron* itself does not require deference as often as many thought it did.

This more flexible version of *Chevron,* if carried out at the WTO level, might call for deference in those cases where the national authority has carried out its task in a procedurally appropriate way (the analog to the "notice and comment rulemaking" that the Court wanted to see in the domestic cases). And, as other papers offered here have suggested, such a rule would keep the WTO Panel and Appellate Body focused on manners inherently more susceptible to review than a reconsideration (even with lots of deference) to a highly complex factual record.

3. Conclusion

Some of these analogies to the practice of appellate courts in the United States may prove to be helpful for the work of the WTO and its nascent judicial bodies, and some may not. To the extent that the dispute resolution mechanism and the Appellate Body have already taken on the characteristics of courts, however, it is safe to say that the problems faced by other courts are well worth studying. The solutions to those problems will have to be compatible with the law governing the tribunals, in all instances, and so it will not be surprising to see the WTO tribunals chart a course that in some respects is unique to them. On the other hand, the WTO bodies will want to join their fellow courts in the important respects: impartiality, credibility, adherence to the rule of law, and respect for due process of law. Achieving this kind of reputation is the challenge the WTO tribunals face, as they are transformed from an essentially political dispute resolution system to a judicial one, and it is one that will be helped substantially through serious study and emulation of the best from the many different national court systems represented by the WTO members.

NOTES

1. Norfolk Southern Ry. v. Shanklin, 120 S.Ct. 1467 (2000).

2. Geier v. American Honda Motor Co., 120 S.Ct. 1913 (2000).

3. Hurley v. Motor Coach Industries, Inc., 222 F.3d 377 (7th Cir. 2000).

4. See City of Philadelphia v. State of New Jersey, 430 U.S. 141 (1977).

5. See, *e.g.*, West Lynn Creamery, Inc. v. Healy, 512 U.S. 186 (1994); Great Atlantic & Pac. Tea Co. v. Cottrell, 424 U.S. 366 (1976); Polar Ice Cream & Creamery Co. v. Andrews, 375 U.S. 361 (1964).

6. Seminole Tribe of Florida v. State of Florida, 517 U.S. 44 (1996).

7. See Chisholm v. Georgia, 2 Dall. 419 (1793).

8. The link between the *Chisholm* decision and the Eleventh Amendment was first noted in the Supreme Court's decision in Hans v. Louisiana, 134 U.S. 1 (1890).

9. 527 U.S. 627 (1999).

10. 527 U.S. 666 (1999).

11. 527 U.S. 706 (1999).

12. *Supra,* 517 U.S. 44.

13. See 28 U.S.C. §§ 1602–11.

14. 514 U.S. 549 (1995).

15. 529 U.S. 598 (2000).

16. 529 U.S. 848 (2000).

17. See Solid Waste Agency of Northern Cook County v. U.S. Army Corps of Engineers, 121 S.Ct. 675 (2001).

18. Full disclosure requires me to note that I watched this case with more than my usual interest, because I authored the court of appeals decision that was reversed. See 191 F.3d 845 (7th Cir. 1999).

19. See Friends of the Earth, Inc. v. Laidlaw Environmental Servs. (TOC), Inc., 528 U.S. 167 (2000); Lujan v. Defenders of Wildlife, 504 U.S. 555, 560 (1992).

20. See Planned Parenthood of Missouri v. Danforth, 428 U.S. 52, 62 (1976).

21. See Craig v. Boren, 429 U.S. 190, 193–97 (1976).

22. See Rules of the Supreme Court of the United States, Rule 37.

23. As former Chief Judge Richard Posner explained in NOW v. Scheidler, 223 F.3d 615 (7th Cir. 2000), "[t]he policy of this court is, therefore, not to grant rote permission to file an amicus curiae brief; never to grant permission to file an amicus curiae brief that essentially merely duplicates the brief of one of the parties . . . ; to grant permission to file an amicus curiae brief only when (1) a party is not adequately represented (usually, is not represented at all); or (2) when the would-be amicus has a direct interest in another case, and the case in which he seeks permission to file an amicus curiae brief may, by operation of stare decisis or res judicata, materially affect that interest; or (3) when the amicus has a unique perspective, or information, that can assist the court of appeals beyond what the parties are able to do." *Id.*, at 617.

24. Compare American Grain Trimmers, Inc. v. Office of Workers' Compensation Programs, 181 F.3d 810, 817–18 (7th Cir. 1999) (*en banc*).

25. See Frye v. United States, 54 App. D.C. 46, 293 F. 1013 (1923).

26. 509 U.S. 579 (1993).

27. 526 U.S. 137 (1999).

28. In re Brand Name Prescription Drugs Antitrust Litigation (II), 186 F.3d 781 (7th Cir. 1999).

29. *Id.*, at 786.

30. See Chevron USA Inc. v. Natural Resources Defense Council, Inc., 467 U.S. 837 (1984). One citation cannot do this doctrine justice, but this is not the place for exploring its full implications and limits.

31. See FDA v. Brown & Williamson Tobacco Corp., 120 S.Ct. 1291 (2000).

32. 527 U.S. 471 (1999).

33. 120 S.Ct. 2097 (2000).

CHAPTER 6

Deference—and Responsibility—by WTO "Judges"

Gary N. Horlick

The question of the degree of deference to be paid by WTO "judges" to national authorities seeking to protect the health of their residents is a central one, especially in the context of the failure of those same national authorities, acting in their capacity as WTO members, to provide a working legislative "process" to parallel—and overrule, where necessary—the dispute resolution process. But the importance of the question should not disguise its content—the question sounds quite differently when reworded as "how loosely should the WTO rules be applied to a Member taking protectionist action?" As with a number of legal questions, there is no *a priori* way to distinguish the two questions, which of course is why one has a dispute resolution mechanism.

As Rob Howse and Kalypso Nicolaidis have correctly pointed out, the question of the appropriate degree of deference has become intertwined with the legitimacy of the WTO itself. Whether this linkage is logically necessary (one can imagine an illegitimate organization with a properly deferential dispute settlement mechanism, and the reverse) may no longer be relevant.

Finally, one must take into account the likelihood that losing litigants and interest groups disappointed by decisions taken through a legitimate process will not forego complaining about the legitimacy of the process used.

A stylized version of the *Beef Hormone* case, similar although not identical to the Dumb Duck Disease hypothetically presented at the conference, reflects those phenomena. In some sense, the factual situation of the *Beef Hormone* was "too easy"—since there was no scientific evidence at all to support the challenged EU regulation, this permitted the Appellate Body to express great deference to national authorities (perhaps too much deference to national authorities relying on minority science—indeed, the *Beef Hormone* decision must be read in light of the subsequent Appellate Body decisions in *Australian Salmon* and *Japan Apples* which underline the requirement that the requisite assessment be done in a serious manner).

The comparative presentation was particularly interesting. As Judge Wood pointed out, the U.S. would never allow a state to do what Arimania does in the DDD hypothetical case (see Appendix, p. 359). The EU apparently spends considerable energy stopping member states from doing so (e.g., the current fuss with France over imports of British beef). Indeed, one

---

The views expressed here should be attributed solely to the author.

of the reasons why there is a WTO (and why one would have to be invented if it did not exist) is to prevent countries from segmenting world markets—and to provide governments with a reason for telling domestic constituencies why they cannot do so. Put another way, the fact that the EU, for whatever non-science-based reasons, refuses to comply with the *Beef Hormone* decision is not a reason to water down the SPS rules. It may well be a reason to rethink what is, in effect, a focus on trade barriers as the nearly exclusive remedy for non-compliance in the current WTO system. A more logical system would isolate those cases where compliance is truly impossible politically, and then find ways to compensate the injured party for the harm done by the WTO-inconsistent practice.

Finally, both scholars as well as politicians have an obligation to listen to not only the loud voices of different interest groups, but also to the interests of those who have benefited, or will benefit in the future, from the astonishing success that the global trading system—an ideologically impure mix of profit seekers, governments, and non-profit private sectors organizations—has had in terms of meeting the basic human needs of better nutrition and health for hundreds of millions of people. Since 1947, life expectancy around the world has increased more than 50 percent—one of the best crude indicators of human health and nutrition. The world's population has doubled and we are now capable of feeding it better than ever in history. Science has eliminated former plagues, such as smallpox, and parents in much of the world no longer watch childhood colds kill their young children. Science has provided the means to increase food production far faster than Dr. Malthus ever suspected, and has provided medical remedies and procedures which would have been considered miracles 50 years ago. Trade spread these benefits around the world, whether by movement of goods, movement of ideas, or movement of people. Scientifically engineered rice varieties from a lab in the Philippines have eliminated the scourge of famine from Asia, not just the Philippines.

The furor over GMO foods (to be more precise, genetically engineered food—genetic modification of foods is approximately as old as agriculture itself) is a worrisome foretaste of future fights: The voices of well-fed opponents—and proponents too, for that matter—resounded through decision-making and scholarly circles earlier and more loudly than those of the hundreds of millions of inhabitants of the planet who might well benefit from greater crop yields, less food lost to pests, and so on.

CHAPTER 7

The Agency Model of Judging in Economic Integration: Balancing Responsibilities

Joel P. Trachtman

1. The Problem of Judicial Decision in "Vertical Federalism" Cases

Every society has "judges" who are called upon to decide cases. These roles may be informal, but in modern industrial society, there are many varieties of formal judging roles. Formal judging roles place individuals in an agency relationship with the rest of society: they receive delegated social authority to decide cases.

The vocation of judging has many facets; the essence of judging is to exercise delegated social authority. Where society's mandate is very specific, judges have the luxury of simply determining the facts and applying specific laws to the facts they have found. Where society's mandate is more general, judges have a more creative, more discretionary role. However, it is important to recognize that even where the mandate is general, judges still act as society's agent. The descriptive and normative question left concerns the breadth of discretion-accorded judges.

The scope for this discretion, and the way that it is constrained, are social choices. They are choices that are made explicitly when a legislator determines the specificity of a statute or the scope of judicial review. However, it is unrealistic to assume that society does not also make these choices implicitly, and *sub rosa.*[1] In many cases, we can give specific instructions to judges. However, in other circumstances, generality may be efficient, or transfer of "hard" choices to the judicial branch, perhaps with its air of false inevitability, may be efficient.[2]

I thank Bob Hudec for helpful conversations in connection with the ideas expressed herein, but he shares no responsibility for my views. I also thank other participants in the World Trade Forum 2000 at which these issues were thoughtfully discussed. joel.trachtman@tufts.edu

Defining the Judicial Mandate

Where the role of the judge is not precisely defined, what should we tell him or her about how to behave? A purported strict constructionist would argue that the judge should apply only the law as specifically written. This position is often associated with positivism, but is not quite positivism: positivism requires a judge to follow his or her mandate from society—it is possible the mandate could extend beyond what is specifically written. This is contrasted with natural law theory, in which the judge is expected to perceive and translate the emanations of natural law into positive law. For the enlightened positivist, authority comes from society mediated by governmental processes, but courts are part of the process, and legislatures use courts as their agents and may give them more or less discipline, supervision, or precision of instructions, depending on the circumstances.

Even where legislatures purport to be very specific, or to make their commands "formally realizable," in von Ihering's words,[3] there is always room for interpretation, for splitting hairs. This is a natural social process. Thus, even a seemingly simple norm such as Article III of GATT requires judgment. This can be seen in connection with the definition of "like products," as discussed more fully below. Why is this important? It shows that judgment, and yes, balancing, broadly speaking, are always with us. This was pointed out by the Appellate Body in the *Shrimp/Turtle* case when it referred to its search for a "line of equilibrium." Other examples from the U.S. domestic system are the law of tort, where judges decide on responsibility as between individuals, as in the law of nuisance, or the U.S. approach to choice of law, and prescriptive jurisdiction, which call for judicial balancing of multiple factors.

Trade-off Devices

Elsewhere, I have developed a taxonomy of "trade-off devices": mandates to central judges to invalidate local laws under specific circumstances.[4] In each of the U.S., the EU and the WTO, these trade-off devices appear in combination, rather than alone, and each category of trade-off device conceals considerable latitude for heterogeneity. Thus, despite the list of only six categories, far more combinations and variations are possible.

1. *National treatment rules.* A national treatment rule is a type of anti-discrimination rule that examines whether different legal standards are applied to comparable cases, as between the domestic and the foreign. National treatment rules entail surprising complexity. In order to deal with more difficult cases, they sometimes incorporate some of the tests set forth below in this list.

2. *Simple means-ends rationality tests.* These tests consider whether the means chosen is indeed a rational means to a purported end. Simple means-ends rationality testing is often combined with limitations on ends. Analytically, simple means-ends rationality testing is included in all of the tests described below in this list, and is sometimes used as a proxy to detect discrimination.
3. *Necessity or least trade-restrictive alternative tests.* This type of test goes a significant step beyond simple means-ends rationality testing. It inquires whether there is a less trade-restrictive means to accomplish the same end. The definition of the end is often outcome-determinative. In some cases, necessity testing is qualified by requiring that the means be the least trade restrictive alternative that is *reasonably available.* In addition, necessity testing is sometimes combined with limitations on the categories of ends permitted.
4. *Proportionality.* Proportionality *stricto sensu*[5] inquires whether the means are "proportionate" to the ends: whether the costs are excessive in relation to the benefits. It might be viewed as cost-benefit analysis with a margin of appreciation, as it does not require that the costs be less than the benefits. Proportionality may be either static or comparative, in the same way as cost-benefit analysis. A comparative approach to proportionality testing would include in its calculus the costs and benefits of alternative rules.
5. *Balancing tests.* Balancing tests purport to decide whether a measure that impedes trade is acceptable, balancing factors that may be delimited by practice or legislation, or that may be unlimited. When it is unlimited, balancing may be viewed as a kind of amorphous or imprecise cost-benefit analysis.[6] More charitably, and perhaps more correctly, it may be viewed as a kind of cost-benefit analysis that recognizes the difficulty of formalizing the analysis, and seeks to achieve similar results informally.[7] It should be noted that the term "balancing test" is sometimes used broadly to include least trade-restrictive alternative analysis, proportionality, or cost-benefit analysis.
6. *Cost-benefit analysis.*[8] Static cost-benefit analysis in the context at hand[9] juxtaposes the regulatory benefits of regulation with the trade costs of regulation, as well as other costs of regulation, and would strike down regulation where the costs exceed the benefits. Cost-benefit analysis in this context may be viewed as stricter scrutiny than the domestic cost-benefit analysis that has recently become popular in the U.S., as it adds a cost dimension not normally included: detriments to trade. Adding trade detriments to the calculation would presumably have the marginal effect of causing some regulation to fail a cost-benefit analysis test. It is worth comparing static cost-benefit analysis, simply juxtaposing the costs and benefits of a single rule, with a more dynamic comparative cost-benefit

analysis, comparing the net benefits of multiple rules, and recommending the rule with the greatest net benefits.

Blurred Distinctions between Anti-Discrimination and Other Tests
In order to make a case of discrimination, in U.S. law, EU law or WTO law, or any law, it is necessary to claim that like things are treated differently (or that different things are, inappropriately, treated the same). It has become clear in both WTO law and U.S. law that the determination of the "likeness" of products, producers or services involves discretion. At least one GATT Panel, the Wine and Beer Panel, has recognized the potentially extensive effects of the like products issue.

The Panel recognized that the treatment of imported and domestic products as like products under Article III may have significant implications for the scope of obligations under the General Agreement and for the regulatory autonomy of contracting parties with respect to their internal tax laws and regulations: once products are designated as like products, a regulatory product differentiation, e.g., for standardization or environmental purposes, becomes inconsistent with Article III even if the regulation is not "applied . . . so as to afford protection to domestic production."[10]

An important recent example is the Panel decision in the *Asbestos* case,[11] in which the Panel, surprisingly, found that powerful carcinogenicity does not suffice to render asbestos "unlike" other types of insulation. This approach, if extended, would find virtually all regulation to violate the national treatment provisions of article III.

In *General Motors v. Tracy*,[12] the Supreme Court recognized this problem, in connection with its attempt to determine whether two kinds of producers were "like" enough to invoke the anti-discrimination norm of the dormant commerce clause. The inquiry was extraordinarily substantive, and involved the exercise of substantial judgment. This case illustrates that a balancing inquiry not terribly different in scope from that which would be involved in an undue burdens inquiry may be necessary in connection with a discrimination inquiry.[13] This fact alone raises substantial questions about the argument against balancing based on judicial limitations.

Exceeding the Mandate

In particular contexts, we might find that a judge exceeded his or her mandate. This analysis is a narrow legal one: what, descriptively, is the scope of the mandate, and by comparison, what has the judge done? When they level this type of critique, scholars play a role in assisting legislatures in monitoring and disciplining courts to inhibit *ultra vires* action. In other contexts, we might find that the mandate assigned to the judge is too broad– not that the judge has erred, but that society has erred in assigning him or her too much discretion. This is a different question, and it is a normative institutional critique: the judge *should* not be assigned this type of discretion. In order to successfully make this latter critique, it is necessary to engage in comparative institutional analysis: which institutional alternative would be better?

In a context where judges have exercised a certain discretion for a substantial period of time, where the legislature has had occasion to curtail the scope of judicial discretion, it may be appropriate to assume that the legislature has, implicitly, approved the judicial activity.

In the context of the interpretation of the U.S. commerce clause, and specifically its application to state laws that have the effect of restricting trade with persons in other states, we have a hybrid circumstance. It is unrealistic to think in terms of amending the commerce clause, and the U.S. Supreme Court is in charge of interpreting the commerce clause, with no direct legislative oversight. However, the U.S. Congress has the authority to authorize a state to engage in activity that otherwise would violate the commerce clause.[14] Thus, in particular circumstances, Congress wields a legislative veto on negative Supreme Court action under the commerce clause. Congress also wields a limited legislative veto on positive Supreme Court action under the commerce clause (upholding a state or local law). Assuming the state or local activity sufficiently affects interstate commerce, Congress may legislate a direct or indirect prohibition of the state or local activity. This federal legislation will be supreme over state or local legislation. So, importantly, the question before us in the U.S. context, as contrasted with the WTO context,[15] is largely one of bureaucratic burden of action: should Congress be required to act to invalidate state action, or can the courts take an initial action? When viewed this way, this argument is not about the absolute power of the court versus the legislature. Rather, it is an interstitial argument about bureaucratic dynamics, susceptible to analysis by a social choice methodology.

Thus, in the U.S. context, there is little ground to argue that our Supreme Court has usurped a clear constitutional or legislative mandate. However, some argue that there is no mandate for the dormant commerce clause at all.[16] The majority of the Supreme Court believes that the U.S. Constitution is plastic enough to accommodate judicial balancing under the commerce clause. There are no serious proposals to amend the Constitution to restrain this judicial balancing.

2. Legitimacy and Beyond: Rules, Standards and Customization of Outcomes

There are initially two main ways of considering the choice between decision-making in legislatures and in courts: through the rhetoric of legitimacy, and through a comparison of more specific rules and less specific standards.

I believe, instrumentally speaking, that legitimacy refers to two characteristics: (i) the effectiveness of the relevant institution in aggregating and transmitting individual preferences, and (ii) the perception of constituents of such effectiveness, based on such factors as the transparency and procedural regularity thereof, as well as less substantive public relations considerations. While legislatures are viewed as the fount of legitimacy *par excellence,* other institutions may have intrinsic legitimacy, or may be "delegated" legitimacy from the legislature. Courts often have a combination of intrinsic and delegated legitimacy. Furthermore, as we consider effectiveness in transmission of preferences, we must consider cost-effectiveness. Here, the second way of considering the choice between decision-making in legislatures and in courts enters the equation. This is the parameter of rules versus standards.

In any legal system, legislators must choose between rules and standards.[17] While courts can make rules and legislators can follow standards, the more typical vocation of courts is to apply rules, which are more specific *ex ante,* or to apply standards, which are less specific, and thus provide greater *ex post* discretion. So, we can think of more specific rules as denying discretion to courts, and more general standards as granting discretion to courts. But the literature regarding rules and standards considers parameters beyond legitimacy.

Rules and Standards

In the rules versus standards literature, a law is a rule to the extent that it is specified in advance of the conduct to which it is applied. Thus, a law against littering is a rule to the extent that "littering" is well-defined. Must there be an intent not to pick up the discarded item? Are organic or readily bio-degradable substances covered? Is littering on private property covered? Is the distribution of leaflets by air covered? Any lawyer knows that there are always questions to ask, so that every law is incompletely specified in advance, and therefore incompletely a rule.

A standard, on the other hand, is a law that is farther toward the other end of the spectrum, in relative terms. It establishes general guidance to both the person governed and the person charged with applying the law, but does not specify in detail in advance the conduct required or proscribed. The relativity of these definitions is critical. It is more apparently and intentionally incompletely specified in advance. Familiar constitutional standards in the U.S. legal system include requirements like "due process," prohibitions on uncompensated "takings," or prohibitions on barriers to interstate commerce. A well-known statutory standard is "restraint of trade" under the U.S. Sherman Act. It is worth noting that the distinction between a rule and a standard is not necessarily grammatical or determined by the number of words used to express the norm; rather, the distinction relates to how much work remains to be done to determine the applicability of the norm to a particular circumstance. Furthermore, this distinction assumes, with H. L. A. Hart, and contrary to certain tenets of critical legal theory, that language may be formulated to have core meanings, penumbral influence and limits of application.[18] If all language were equally indeterminate, there would be no distinction between a rule and a standard.

Incompleteness of specification may not simply be a result of conservation of resources. It may be a more explicitly political decision to either agree to disagree for the moment, to avoid the political price that may arise from immediate hard decisions, or to cloak the hard decisions in the false inevitability of judicial interpretation. It is important also to recognize that the incompleteness of specification may represent a failure to decide how the policy expressed relates to other policies. This is critical in the trade area, where often the incompleteness of a trade rule relates to its failure to address, or incorporate, non-trade policies.

Obviously, each law is comprised of a combination of rules and standards. However, it will be useful to speak here generally of rules as separate from standards.

The Costs and Benefits of Rules and Standards

Rules are more expensive to develop than standards, *ex ante,* because rules entail specification costs, including drafting costs and negotiation costs, as well as the strategic costs involved in *ex ante* specification. In order to reach agreement on specification—in order to legislate specifically—there may be greater costs in public choice terms.[19] This is particularly interesting in the trade context, where treaty-making would be subjected to intense domestic scrutiny, while application of a standard by a dispute resolution process would be subjected to reduced scrutiny. On the other hand, NGOs have sought in this connection to enhance transparency in dispute resolution. Finally, rules require clear decision; standards may serve as an agreement to disagree, or may help to mask or mystify a decision made.[20] Under standards, both sides in the legislative process may claim victory, at least initially.

Rules are generally thought to provide greater predictability. There are two moments at which to consider predictability. The first is the ability of persons subject to the law to be able to plan and conform their conduct *ex ante,* sometimes known as "primary predictability."[21] The second moment in which predictability is important is *ex post,* after the relevant conduct has taken place. Where the parties can predict the outcome of dispute resolution—where they can predict the tribunal's determination of their respective rights and duties—they will spend less money on litigation. This type of predictability is "secondary predictability." Both types of predictability can reduce costs. While rules appear to provide primary and secondary predictability, tribunals may construct exceptions in order to do what is, by their lights, substantial justice, and thereby reduce predictability. It may be difficult to constrain the ability of tribunals to do this. Furthermore, as noted below, game theory predicts that some degree of uncertainty—of unpredictability—may enhance the ability of the parties to bargain to a lower cost solution. Thus, simple predictability is not the only measure of a legal norm; rather, we must also be concerned with the ability of the legal norm to provide satisfactory outcomes. In economic terms, we must be concerned with the allocative efficiency of the outcome. We consider allocative efficiency below as we consider the institutional dimension of rules and standards.

As we consider the relative allocative efficiency of potential outcomes, we must recognize that there is a temporal distinction between rules and standards. Standards may be used earlier in the development of a field of law, before sufficient experience to form a basis for more complete specification is acquired. In many areas of law, courts develop a jurisprudence that forms the basis for codification—or even rejection—by legislatures. With this in mind, legislatures (or adjudicators) may set standards at an early point in time, and determine to establish rules at a later point in time.[22] It is clear that a rule of *stare decisis* is not necessary to the development of a body of jurisprudence by a court or dispute resolution tribunal.[23] It is also worth noting that in a common law setting, or any setting where tribunals refer to precedents, the tribunal may announce a standard in a particular case, and then elaborate that standard in subsequent cases until it has built a rule for its own application.

Kaplow points out that where instances of the relevant behavior are more frequent, economies of scale will indicate that rules become relatively more efficient. For circumstances that arise only infrequently, it is more difficult to justify promulgation of specific rules. In addition, rules provide compliance benefits: they are cheaper to obey, because the cost of determining the required behavior is lower. Rules are also cheaper to apply by a court: the court must only determine the facts and compare them to the rule.

The Institutional Dimension of Rules and Standards

Another distinction between rules and standards, often de-emphasized in this literature, is the institutional distinction: with rules, the legislature often "makes" the decision, while with standards, the adjudicator determines the application of the standard, thereby "making" the decision. Again, it is obvious that these terms are used in a relative sense (this caveat will not be repeated). Economists and even lawyer-economists seem to assume that the tribunal simply "finds" the law, and does not make it. Of course, courts can make rules pursuant to statutory or constitutional authority: the hallmark of a rule is that it is specified *ex ante,* not that it is specified by a legislature. However, at least in the international trade system, rules are largely made by treaty, and standards are largely applied by tribunals. On the other hand, Prof. Regan's work shows that the U.S. Supreme Court has made some distinctions in the way that it balances, and the extent to which it balances, that may have precedential value and may move the jurisprudence toward the "rule" end of the spectrum.

Of course, the difference between legislators and courts is an important one, and may affect the outcome.[24] The choice of legislators or courts to make particular decisions should be made using cost-benefit analysis. Such a cost-benefit analysis would include, as a critical factor, the degree of representativeness of constituents: which institution will most accurately reflect citizens' desires? There are good reasons why such cost-benefit analysis does not always select legislatures. First, there is a public choice critique of legislatures. Second, even under a public interest analysis, legislatures may not be efficient at specifying *ex ante* all of the details of treatment of particular cases. Third, the rate of change of circumstances over time may favor the ability of courts to adjust. Finally, we must analyze the strategic relationship between legislators and courts. Thus, in order fully to understand the relationship between rules and standards, the tools of public choice or positive political theory[25] should be brought to bear to analyze the relationship between legislative and judicial decision-making.[26]

The Strategic Dimension of Rules and Standards

It is not possible to consider the costs and benefits of rules and standards separately from the strategic considerations that would cause states to select a rule as opposed to a standard. Johnston analyzes rules and standards from a strategic perspective, finding that, under a standard, bargaining may yield immediate efficient agreement, whereas under a rule, this condition may not obtain.[27] Johnston considers a rule a "definite, ex ante entitlement" and a standard a "contingent, ex post entitlement." Like Kaplow, he does not here consider the source of the rule, whether legislature or tribunal.

Johnston notes the "standard supposition in the law and economics literature . . . that private bargaining between [two parties] over the allocation of [a] legal entitlement is most likely to be efficient if the entitlement is clearly defined and assigned ex ante according to a rule, rather than made contingent upon a judge's ex post balancing of relative value and harm."[28] Johnston suggests this supposition may be incorrect:[29] "[W]hen the parties bargain over the entitlement when there is private information about value and harm, bargaining may be more efficient under a blurry balancing test than under a certain rule."[30] This is because under a certain rule, the holder of the entitlement will have incentives to "hold out" and decline to provide information about the value to him of the entitlement. Under a standard, where presumably it cannot be known with certainty *ex ante* who owns the entitlement, the person not possessing the entitlement may credibly threaten to take it, providing incentives for the other person to bargain. Johnston points out that this result obtains only when the *ex post* balancing test is imperfect, because if the balancing were perfect, the threat would not be credible. This provides a counter-intuitive argument for inaccuracy of application of standards.[31] Interestingly, further research as to the magnitude of strategic costs under rules and under standards might suggest that over time, rules provide some of the strategic benefits of standards. This might be so if tribunals develop exceptions to rules in a way that introduces uncertainty to their application. This increased benefit would of course be countervailed to some extent by the reduction of predictability that the development of exceptions would entail.

3. Balancing by Judges

As Regan discusses (*supra*, p. 91), judges engaged in balancing have both empirical tasks and normative tasks. The empirical tasks involve identifying the factors required to be balanced and assessing them. Thus, in the case of a *Pike* balancing test, local benefit and external cost must be identified and assessed. I say "assessed," rather than "measured," because these categories are not readily capable of commensuration, and also are subject to the impossibility of interpersonal (or interstate) comparison of utility. However, the point here is that we often use government, and courts as part of government, to engage in these activities. We appoint them to do so as preference revelation devices. Regan makes two kinds of arguments: descriptive and normative.

Descriptive Arguments

The first argument has two parts: (i) the Supreme Court is gradually shrinking from balancing, and (ii) the Supreme Court, while talking the talk of balancing, has generally not walked the walk of balancing. Prof. Regan has considered these cases with a nuanced understanding. However, in order to support his thesis, he has found it necessary to emphasize some aspects of cases, and de-emphasize others, and he has constructed some heroic distinctions in order to establish a category of so-called "core" cases in which, he argues, balancing does not occur. Moreover, even accepting Regan's characterization of the cases, and further accepting that "discriminatory intent" is the sole target of dormant Commerce Clause analysis, it is not clear that the Court's approach should change. Regan charges that the Court uses the rhetoric of balancing as a "mask" for its identification of discriminatory intent, where the Court cannot actually articulate the discriminatory intent, or only suspects the discriminatory intent. If discriminatory intent and failure of the *Pike* balancing test indeed coincide, then it is not necessarily appropriate to abandon the *Pike* balancing test. Rather, the *Pike* balancing test may be the judicial mechanism that allows Regan's main prescription—to attack discriminatory intent—to be effected.

One inconsistency in Regan's descriptive argument is that he excludes certain types of dormant Commerce Clause cases, suggesting that the fact that balancing occurs in transportation and taxation cases, as opposed to movement of goods cases, should not be taken as evidence that balancing is used generally. This distinction seems problematic. First, there is little substantive basis for treating transportation services differently from trade in goods or other services: one might posit circumstances in which energy-based goods, or financial services, would be more important to the national common market than transportation services.[32]

Second is the fact that the Commerce Clause contains no basis for this distinction. It is difficult to make the argument for judicial passivity in connection with Commerce Clause balancing, while suggesting that courts be active enough to craft, with no support within the text of the Commerce Clause, a special category of commerce subject to balancing. However, those of us who are normatively open to a more active role for the judge may welcome the ability of judges to craft specific tests for particular types of circumstances. I will suggest below that this is natural in the evolution of law: we begin with a more general standard and, as we gain experience, we may engage in greater specification. While the tax and transportation cases are still characterized by standards, as opposed to rules, they are characterized by specialized standards that appear to fit those circumstances. However, this judicial activity does not necessarily argue, and does not seem to argue, for the abandonment of standards in other areas.

Normative Arguments

Regan's second argument is a normative one: that courts are simply unsuited for balancing. Here, while I am not prepared to advance an affirmative argument that courts *are* suited for balancing in this particular context, I find Regan's argument against balancing unconvincing. This type of normative argument should be based on positive evidence of the effects of the institution being criticized and the institution being proposed as a substitute. Regan argues that legislatures should do all the balancing. As this is not the way society has arranged itself—courts often balance[33]—the principle of conservatism would suggest that the burden of scholarly proof be placed on the proponent of change.

There is the possibility of strong and highly inefficient externalization without discrimination.[34] It is safe to assume that cases will exist where local legislators will not take full account of the concerns of outsiders. It is obvious that there will be circumstances in which it will make sense for states, collectively, to establish institutions that will require local legislators to take some account of the concerns of outsiders. This is the reason for a federation. Regan seems to accept that the federal government in the U.S. would want to restrain states under some circumstances, but he cannot believe that we would allocate relatively broad discretion to courts to determine the circumstances.

Prof. Regan argues that inefficiency of protectionism depends on protectionist purpose. This is simply wrong (unless it is tautological by virtue of a purposive definition of protectionism). He suggests that *Clover Leaf Creamery* illustrates this proposition, but it only does if one assumes that the Minnesota legislature's rule itself was efficient. If instead, the Minnesota law imposed costs on foreign producers in excess of the benefits to Minnesota, it would, by definition, be inefficient. Prof. Regan seems to attempt to support his assumption by asserting, without support, that Minnesota "is entitled to act on its own evaluations of consequences." However, this simply begs the question of whether Minnesota has this unrestricted entitlement under the U.S. Constitution. If we interpret the dormant Commerce Clause as including an "undue burdens" test, Minnesota does not have this entitlement. Importantly, Regan seems to accept intrusions on this type of entitlement in transport and tax cases.

In the end, we might presume that all trade inhibiting effect that is not justified under a balancing test must be based on protectionist motivation. It is in this sense that Regan's descriptive analysis of U.S. Commerce Clause jurisprudence rings true. But this is not an argument for abandoning balancing in favor of a more limited scrutiny.

4. Conclusion

Of course, as we consider an agency model of judging, we must recall that when we ask the question "what do judges maximize," the answer, as given by Richard Posner, is "the same thing everybody else does in their position."[35] Despite this, society uses judges to engage in all sorts of balancing. I have tried to show in this paper that judicial balancing is not necessarily bad, and that it could, under certain circumstances, be efficient in the U.S. federal, European Union, or WTO contexts. More subtle theoretical analysis, and extensive empiricism, would be necessary to support a decision.

NOTES

1. *See* Richard B. Collins, *Economic Union as a Constitutional Value,* 63 N.Y.U.L. Rev. 43 (1988). *See also* Camps Newfound Owatonna Inc. v. Town of Harrison, 520 U.S. 564, 595 (1997) (Scalia, J. dissenting, *citing* H. P. Hood & Sons, Inc. v. Du Mond, 336 U.S. 525, 539 (1949)): "We have often said that the purpose of our negative-commerce-clause jurisprudence is to create a national market. As Justice Jackson once observed, the 'vision of the Founders' was "that every farmer and every craftsman shall be encouraged to produce by the certainty that he will have free access to every market in the Nation, that no home embargoes will withhold his exports, and no foreign state will by customs duties or regulations exclude them.'"

2. It is important to specify what I mean by "efficient." I use a standard neo-classical approach, but this approach is not limited to narrow wealth maximization. Thus, we look at the maximization of the full range of individual preferences in context. Transfer of hard choices to the judicial branch may be efficient from a public choice standpoint, under circumstances of other constraints in the quality of decision-making. For a discussion of the problem of international regulatory protectionism from a public choice standpoint, *see* Alan O. Sykes, Regulatory Protectionism and the Law of International Trade, 66 *U. Chi. L. Rev.* 1 (1999).

3. For the use of this term in English, *see* Duncan Kennedy, Form and Substance in Private Law Adjudication, 89 *Harv. L. Rev.* 1685, 1687–89 (1976), *citing* R. von Ihering, Der Geist des Romischen Rechts, 50–55, 84 (1883).

4. Joel P. Trachtman, Trade and . . . Problems, Cost-Benefit Analysis and Subsidiarity, 9 *Eur. J. Int'l L.* 32 (1998).

5. Nicholas Emiliou, The Principle of Proportionality in European Law: A Comparative Study 6 (1996). A wider definition of proportionality developed in the EU context includes three tests: (i) proportionality *stricto sensu,* (ii) a least trade-restrictive alternative test, and (iii) a simple means-ends rationality test. This article will consider only the narrower type of proportionality.

6. *See* Michael E. Smith, State Discriminations Against Interstate Commerce, 74 *Cal. L. Rev.* 1203, 1205 (1979) ("The Justices take all relevant circumstances into account and render judgment according to their overall sense of the advantages and disadvantages of upholding the regulation."). At their most precise, balancing tests are the same as cost-benefit analysis. *See* Earl M. Maltz, How Much Regulation is Too Much—An Examination of Commerce Clause Jurisprudence, 50 *Geo. Wash. L. Rev.* 47, 59–60 (1981).

7. "If we had a way of quantifying all the appropriate inputs, and a way of comparing them, and a theory that told us how to do so, we would not call it balancing. Rather, it would be called something like 'deriving the most cost-effective solution,' or just 'solving the problem.' " Stephen E. Gottlieb, The Paradox of Balancing Significant Interests, 45 *Hastings L.J.* 825, 839 (1994). *See also* T. Alexander Aleinikoff, Constitutional Law in the Age of Balancing, 96 *Yale L.J.* 943, 1002–1004 (1987).

8. There is an important distinction between judicial balancing and cost-benefit analysis. Cost-benefit analysis has two forms. The first form simply examines the costs and benefits of a particular policy, to determine whether the latter exceed the former. The second, which is equivalent to potential Pareto efficiency analysis (also known as Kaldor-Hicks efficiency analysis), seeks to determine whether there is an alternative policy which has greater net benefits (or lesser net costs). U.S. courts do not purport to engage in either of these analyses. Rather, under *Pike v. Bruce Church,* they seek to determine whether the putative local benefit is greater than the external cost. This is an incomplete test from an economic standpoint. There may be local costs, or external benefits, that would be taken into account under an economic analysis.

Other parameters may be considered, such as whether there is a less trade-restrictive alternative; that is, whether it is possible to reduce external costs without diminishing local benefits. As I have analyzed these distinctions at great length elsewhere, I will not review them here.

9. For more general and technical treatment of cost-benefit analysis, *see, e.g.*, Peter S. Menell & Richard B. Stewart, Environmental Law and Policy 81–160 (1994); D. Pearce & C. Nash, The Social Appraisal of Projects: A Text in Cost-Benefit Analysis (1981); R. Tresch, Public Finance: A Normative Theory (1981); Edith Stokey & Richard Zeckhauser, A Primer for Policy Analysis (1978); E.J. Mishan, Cost-Benefit Analysis (1976); H. Raiffa, Decision Analysis (1968). *See also* the recent special issue of *The Journal of Legal Studies* devoted to cost-benefit analysis, beginning at 29 *J. Leg. Studs.* 837 (2000) (including papers by W. Kip Viscusi, Amartya Sen, Martha Nussbaum, Richard Posner and Gary Becker).

10. United States Measures Affecting Alcoholic and Malt Beverages, 39 B.I.S.D. 279, at 294, para. 5.72 (1992). *See* Gerald C. Berg, An Economic Interpretation of "Like-Product", 30 *J. World Trade* 195 (1996).

11. Report of the Panel, European Communities–Measures Affecting Asbestos and Asbestos-Containing Products, WT/DS135/R, 18 September 2000, paras. 8.130-8.132 (holding that risk to health is not a factor in determining "likeness" under art. III of GATT).

12. 519 U.S. 278 (1997).

13. *See* Trachtman, *supra* note 6.

14. Wardair Canada, Inc. v. Florida Dep't of Revenue, 477 U.S. 1, 12–13 (1986); Northeast Bancorp., Inc. v. Board of Governors, 472 U.S. 159, 174–75 (1985); Western & Southern Life Ins. Co. v. State Bd. of Equalization, 451 U.S. 648, 652–53 (1981); Prudential Ins. Co. v. Benjamin, 328 U.S. 408, 421–27 (1946).

15. The WTO has legislative capacity, by virtue of its ability to make decisions, amend treaties and establish new treaties, but this legislative capacity is quite different in effectiveness from U.S. federal legislative capacity, or even EU legislative capacity.

16. For this argument, *see* General Motors Corp. v. Tracy, 519 U.S. 278, 312 (1997) (Scalia, J., concurring). *See also* Martin H. Redish & Shane V. Nugent, The Dormant Commerce Clause and the Constitutional Balance of Federalism, 1987 *Duke L.J.* 56.

17. For an introduction to the rules versus standards discussion in law and economics, *see* Louis Kaplow, General Characteristics of Rules, in Encyclopedia of Law and Economics (B. Bouckaert & G. De Geest, eds. 1998); Louis Kaplow, Rules Versus Standards: An Economic Analysis, 42 *Duke L.J.* 557 (1992). *See also,* Cass R. Sunstein, Problems with Rules, 83 *Cal. L. Rev.* 955 (1995). In international trade law, "standards" has a specific meaning, referring to product standards. This meaning is separate from the sense in which "standards" is used here.

18. H. L. A. Hart, The Concept of Law, chap. VII (2d ed. 1994). *See also* Frederick Schauer, Playing by the Rules (1991).

19. See Gillian K. Hadfield, Weighing the Value of Vagueness: An Economic Perspective on Precision in the Law, 82 *Cal. L. Rev.* 541, 550 (1994), citing Linda R. Cohen & Roger G. Noll, How to Vote, Whether to Vote: Strategies for Voting and Abstaining on Congressional Role Calls, 13 *Pol. Behav.* 97 (1991).

20. Kenneth W. Abbott & Duncan Snidal, Why States Act Through Formal International Organizations, 42 *J. Conflict Resol.* 3 (1998).

21. For this use of the terms "primary predictability" and "secondary predictability", *see* William F. Baxter, Choice of Law and the Federal System, 16 *Stan. L. Rev.* 1, 3 (1963).

22. See Kaplow, The General Characteristics of Rules, supra note 17, at 10.

23. David Palmeter & Petros C. Mavroidis, The WTO Legal System: Sources of Law, 92 *Am. J. Int'l L.* 398 (1998).

24. *See* Neil Komesar, Imperfect Alternatives (1994).

25. *See, e.g.*, John Ferejohn & Barry Weingast, A Positive Theory of Statutory Interpretation, 12 *Int'l Rev. L. & Econ.* 263 (1992). *See also* Sunstein, supra note 17, at 973.

26. Robert Cooter & Josef Drexl, The Logic of Power in the Emerging European Constitution: Game Theory and the Division of Powers, 14 *Int'l Rev. L. & Econ.* 307 (1994)

27. Jason Scott Johnston, Bargaining under Rules versus Standards, 11 *J. L. Econ. & Org.* 256 (1995).

28. *Id.* (citations omitted).

29. *See also* Carol Rose, Crystals and Mud in Property Law, 40 *Stan. L. Rev.* 577 (1988); Joel P. Trachtman, Externalities and Extraterritoriality, in Jagdeep Bhandari & Alan O. Sykes, Economic Dimensions in International Law (1997).

30. Johnston, supra note 27, at 257.

31. *Id.* at 272.

32. Regan argues that these are distinct because there is a national interest beyond avoiding state protectionism in connection with transportation cases, but not in connection with movement of goods cases. However, the national benefits of a common market in goods are surely as important as an unimpeded national transportation system. *See, e.g.*, Collins, supra note 4.

33. An important example, from a U.S. domestic perspective, is choice of law, where the modern approach entails quite a bit of interest analysis, or balancing. On a horizontal level, choice of law is quite similar to the vertical question at issue here: which government should be empowered, and which should not. Tort law, both in the U.S. and abroad, is similar. Tort allocates responsibility between individuals: it determines when the vertically next level–the state–will intervene to restrain or require compensation. On this basis, it is analogous to the question of whether the central government will intervene to restrain. As the seminal U.S. torts scholar, Prosser, stated: "In tort law the responsibility for answering the unanswered questions falls to the courts." P. Keeton, D. Dobbs, R. Keeton & D. Owen, Prosser and Keeton on the law of torts 19 (5th ed. 1984 & Supp. 1988). Under a rules and standards analysis, all decisions are hybrids. Judges operate in a mixed environment where some of their decisions are dictated by rules, and some of their decisions involve greater discretion pursuant to standards.

34. *See, e.g.*, Sykes, supra note 5, at 30:

> [R]egulatory protectionism need not be deliberate. Regulators may act often with limited information, or without meaningful input from those affected by their decisions. This problem is likely to be particularly acute when those disadvantaged by regulation are foreign firms. International legal agreements that prohibit regulatory protectionism, such as the TBT and SPM Agreements of the WTO, require central governments to pay much greater heed to the implications of their regulations for trade. In significant part, these agreements may be aimed not just at deliberate cheating but also at the costs of inattention and inadvertence in a

diffuse bureaucracy. Otherwise, the unwitting destruction of joint surplus through regulations that unnecessarily burden foreign suppliers may become a serious problem. Efforts to avoid such problems by international agreement ensure that protection is afforded only where it is, on balance, politically valuable, and only in a manner that destroys as little surplus for well-organized interest groups as possible.

35. Richard A. Posner, What Do Judges Maximize? (The Same Thing Everybody Else Does), 3 *S. Ct. Econ. Rev.* 2 (1993).

CHAPTER 8

The EC Response

Piet Eeckhout

1. Procedural Issues (or Courts and Legislatures)

In an EC context, the case as presented concerns trade between Member States, and legislation of a Member State which affects the free movement of goods. Most of the following analysis will therefore concentrate on the application of Articles 28 and 30 EC to facts such as those concerning the rearing of ducks in Arimania. However, it must be emphasized from the outset that this is not the only type of situation in which the European Court of Justice (hereafter the Court) may be asked to review legislation which lays down requirements to be met by products for the purpose of protecting public health: the Court has also reviewed legislation adopted by the EC itself, such as the EC directive banning the use of hormones in the production of beef.[1] But there are significant differences between these two types of review, of national and of Community legislation. Before embarking upon the analysis of the actual case in a context of intra-Community movement of goods, it is therefore appropriate to touch upon those differences, which are important for appreciating and assessing the kind of review which the Court exercises.

First some points of procedure. In those cases where the Court is asked to review national legislation, it, as a matter of fact, has no jurisdiction formally to strike down such legislation. The Court of Justice has no formal jurisdiction over legislation of a Member State. In substance, nonetheless, the Court does exercise review, in two types of action.

The first is where the European Commission brings an infringement action against a Member State under Article 226 EC, for failure to implement certain Treaty obligations. In such cases, the Court may examine national legislation, so as to check its conformity with rules of EC law. Here, the Court treats such legislation almost as a factual matter; what it is concerned with is establishing an infringement of EC law, and it does not matter whether such an infringement results from legislation or other types of official action. Also, the Court cannot actually invalidate national legislation which is not in conformity with EC law. It is up to the Member State concerned to draw the necessary conclusions from the Court's judgment, which may encompass amendment or repeal of incompatible legislation. The judgment may also be relied upon by individuals invoking the direct effect and supremacy of EC law so as not to have the incompatible legislation applied. A national court may give effect to such a claim, but again that does not mean that the incompatible legislation is formally struck down. EC law principles merely require that incompatible national legislation is disapplied, so as to give full effect to the EC law rules in issue.[2] It may be noted that the infringement action under Article 226 EC comes close to WTO dispute settlement.[3]

The second type of action is where the Court delivers a preliminary ruling on a question of interpretation of EC law (Article 234 EC). Very often such a question is in substance a question on the compatibility of national legislation with a provision of the EC Treaty or of EC legislation. The typical case is that where, before a court of a Member State, an individual argues that national legislation is incompatible with EC law and relies on the direct effect of European law. The national court may then refer a question of interpretation of the relevant EC law provision to the Court, but very often it is, in substance, asking the Court to rule on the compatibility issue itself. Formally, the Court has no jurisdiction to establish such an incompatibility, but, again in substance, the Court's ruling is often a ruling on incompatibility. There are nonetheless limits to the review of national legislation which the Court exercises in such preliminary rulings cases. Among those limits is the circumstance that it is for the referring court to establish the facts and to describe the national legislation in issue. Even though the Court is not strictly bound by the reference, it is the case that the Court has no autonomous fact-finding competence in the framework of the preliminary rulings procedure. Also, it is for the referring court to apply the ruling delivered by the Court of Justice. It is therefore for the referring court actually to establish the incompatibility, and to disapply the incompatible national legislation (see above). This also means that the Court may leave some of the review work to the national court. Here the Court's practice varies. Some preliminary rulings are so detailed and precise as to leave no room for maneuver by the referring court, which merely applies the Court's judgment. Other rulings, however, are more open-ended; they may, for example, formulate the principles which the national court needs to apply, but leave the application of those principles to the facts of the case to that court. This may mean that the Court of Justice does not establish (in)compatibility, and that one is obliged to look for the final judgment of the court which has made the reference to find out whether the national legislation in issue was considered to be compatible with EC law or not.[4]

Those are the two types of action in which the Court reviews national legislation, and most of the judgments which are referred to in the following analysis of the Arimania case were delivered in an action of either type. I will not systematically refer to the differences between the two types of action, but the reader should be aware of those differences, particularly as regards factual review, which is much more limited under the preliminary rulings procedure than it is in an infringement action.

The Court also reviews Community legislation. Such legislation may have a content similar to the legislation of a Member State. To take the facts of the Arimania case, Arimania may either be an EC Member State, or it may be the EC itself; the legislation banning the use of hormones may be national legislation or EC legislation. It would, however, be erroneous to think that the review exercised by the European Court of Justice is necessarily similar. On the contrary, the parameters of the judicial review of Community legislation are rather different from those of the Court's review of national legislation.[5]

First, in contrast with its lack of jurisdiction over national legislation, the Court does have the authority formally to strike down Community legislation. It may do so in an action for annulment under Article 230 EC, which, in the case of general normative action, cannot be brought by an individual but only by another Member State or one of the Community institutions;[6] or it may do so in a preliminary ruling on a question of validity of a piece of Community legislation, which is the individual's route towards judicial review of Community legislation. The effect of annulment and invalidity rulings is identical.

Secondly, the substantive parameters of review of Community legislation are also rather different from those of review of national legislation, in particular in the context of a case such as the Arimania legislation, which concerns trade issues. If the Court were confronted with such a case, and Arimania was an EU Member State, then the Court would obviously review the legislation on the basis of Articles 28 and 30 EC, concerning the free movement of goods between Member States. If, on the other hand, Arimania was the EC itself, then the legislation would not *prima facie* interfere with the free movement of goods in the internal market; by laying down common rules on the rearing of ducks it would actually remove obstacles to trade and create a level playing-field. Therefore, the EC Treaty provisions on the free movement of goods would not seem to be in issue. Judicial review of such EC legislation is more likely to be centered on either issues of competence and subsidiarity, or issues of fundamental rights and proportionality.[7] It is easy to see that this is an entirely different context. Given that achieving a single market and upholding the primacy and uniformity of EC law remain two of the most important functions of the EU, it is not surprising that the Court of Justice generally exercises more stringent review of national legislation interfering with free movement between Member States than of Community harmonizing legislation which has the effect of replacing divergent national legislation with common rules.

Thirdly, but no doubt related to the previous point, the Court has adopted a deferential standard of review of EC legislation where issues of competence, fundamental rights, and particularly proportionality are involved. The Court emphasizes the margin of political discretion for the EC legislature, and exercises limited judicial review. An example is the *Working Time Directive* case, a challenge by the United Kingdom against a social policy directive, where the Court held:[8]

> As to judicial review [of the conditions imposed by the principle of proportionality], however, the Council must be allowed a wide discretion in an area which, as here, involves the legislature in making social policy choices and requires it to carry out complex assessments. Judicial review of the exercise of that discretion must therefore be limited to examining whether it has been vitiated by manifest error or misuse of powers, or whether the institution concerned has manifestly exceeded the limits of its discretion.

Such dicta are also found in cases involving a challenge to EC legislation in the sanitary and phytosanitary field, such as the *BSE* case.[9]

Most of the following analysis of the Arimania case refers to case law concerning Member State legislation and the free movement of goods. Where, on occasion, reference is made to judgments involving judicial review of EC legislation, the reader should bear in mind the different parameters of such review.[10]

2. Indistinctly Applicable Measures

The Arimania legislation is clearly caught by Article 28 EC. It is a classic measure having equivalent effect to a quantitative restriction on imports. The leading case for such measures is the well-known *Cassis de Dijon* case,[11] where the Court extended the scope of Article 28 to so-called indistinctly applicable measures which hinder the free movement of goods. An indistinctly applicable measure is a measure which applies without distinction to domestic and imported goods. Since *Cassis de Dijon* there have been a lot of cases involving national measures which impose requirements to be met by products, of the kind of the Arimania legislation, and the Court consistently considers such measures to be caught by Article 28 EC. There is, thus, no doubt whatsoever that the Court would rule to the same effect if the Arimania legislation were to come before it. The *Keck and Mithouard* judgment, which is regarded by many to limit the scope of Article 28, clearly left the *Cassis de Dijon* approach intact. The Court stated in *Keck:*[12]

> It is established by the case law beginning with "Cassis de Dijon" . . . that, in the absence of harmonization of legislation, obstacles to free movement of goods which are the consequence of applying, to

> goods coming from other Member States where they are lawfully manufactured and marketed, rules that lay down requirements to be met by such goods (such as those relating to designation, form, size, weight, composition, presentation, labeling, packaging) constitute measures of equivalent effect prohibited by Article [28]. This is so even if those rules apply without distinction to all products unless their application can be justified by a public-interest objective taking precedence over the free movement of goods.

The Arimania case contains some questions concerning the distinction between *de iure* and *de facto* discrimination. In EC law on the free movement of goods, those concepts are no longer in use. There has been a time when the Court often referred to material or covert discrimination ("discrimination matérielle"), but since *Cassis de Dijon* the emphasis is really on the question whether a national measure operates as a restriction to intra-Community trade or not. As *Cassis de Dijon* established that indistinctly applicable measures may also be caught by Article 28, the Court is no longer looking for a form of discrimination as a precondition for finding a trade restriction. However, the answer as to what constitutes a restriction is obviously very difficult. It transcends the free movement of goods, as the other basic internal market freedoms (of persons, services, and capital) have also been interpreted as going beyond a mere prohibition of discrimination. It is not a question which could be fully answered here. By way of comment, nonetheless, I would say that the most difficult dimension of the question is determining the boundaries of the restriction concept. There is a question in the Arimania case asking whether all cases of *de facto* discrimination (even remotely so) should be punishable. It would seem obvious, for various reasons, that there must be boundaries, even in the EC with its far-advanced idea of an internal market. But where exactly those boundaries are located has not been determined yet, and the Court of Justice continues to struggle with borderline cases, both in the field of free movement of goods,[13] and in other areas of free movement.[14]

The Arimania case also raises the question whether the fact that we deal here with a *de facto* and not *de iure* discrimination already makes us adopt a more pro-deference stance. In EC law on the free movement of goods, the (similar) question whether a national measure is indistinctly applicable or not is indeed of considerable importance for the analysis of that measure's compatibility with the free movement of goods. In *Cassis de Dijon*, the Court extended the scope of Article 28 EC to indistinctly applicable measures, but balanced that extension by introducing the concept of "mandatory requirements," a notion referring to public-interest objectives taking precedence over the free movement of goods. In effect, those mandatory requirements are an extension of the express exceptions to the free movement of goods provided for in Article 30 EC. In contrast with Article 30, however, the list of mandatory requirements is completely open-ended, as any non-economic public-interest objective may trump the free movement principle, provided the restriction is proportionate to the objective pursued. But mandatory requirements can only be relied upon in case of an indistinctly applicable measure, not where imports are treated differently from domestic products. The Court continues to uphold that approach, despite invitations to drop the distinction between indistinctly and distinctly applicable measures, and to apply the mandatory requirements also to the latter.[15]

3. Justification

As explained above, there is no doubt that the Court of Justice would hold that the Arimania legislation is caught by Article 28 EC. The difficult question, under EC law, is whether the legislation is justified on grounds of public health.[16] This section has two subsections, one on the public health justification as such, and one on the principle of proportionality, which is of paramount importance for the actual application of the public health justification (or any other justification, for that matter). It is nonetheless obvious that in practice the types of justification and proportionality are closely intertwined. Inevitably, therefore, there will be mutual overlap between the subsections.

Approach to Public Health Issues

Article 30 EC permits prohibitions or restrictions on imports justified on grounds of the protection of health and life of humans. The EC Treaty thus expressly provides for the public health exception. In addition, the Court has mentioned public health as one of the mandatory requirements capable of justifying indistinctly applicable measures in the *Cassis de Dijon* case.[17] This is potentially confusing, but the *Cassis de Dijon* reference would now appear to be an isolated instance. Where public health issues are at stake the Court consistently refers to Article 30 EC, and in *Aragonesa* the Court stated that, as the express exceptions in Article 30 have broader scope than the mandatory requirements, it is not necessary to consider whether public health protection is also in the nature of an imperative requirement.[18]

De Peijper was the first meaningful case in which the Court addressed the public health exception. It held that health and the life of humans rank first among the property or interests protected by Article 36 (now Article 30) and that it is for the Member States, within the limits imposed by the Treaty, to decide what degree of protection they intend to assure.[19] That set the tone for further case law, in which the Court consistently takes as a starting-point a measure of deference to the discretion of Member States. As we will see, however, that deferential approach is generally counter-balanced by a fairly strict proportionality test.

In the Court's case law on the free movement of goods, there are no cases which are very similar to the Arimania case. What comes closest is the strand of cases on the use of additives in foodstuffs. Most of those stem from the 1980s, culminating in the *German Beer* case,[20] where the Court brought the various principles of its previous rulings together. There are only a few judgments posterior to *German Beer,* and the reasons therefore may be that (a) the Court's case law had sufficiently clarified the law, and (b) most national legislation on foodstuffs had gradually come to be replaced by EC legislation.

The *German Beer* case partly concerned an absolute ban on the marketing of beers containing additives. The German government argued that such a ban was justified on public-health grounds. It considered that in view of the dangers resulting from the utilization of additives whose long-term effects were not yet known and in particular of the risks resulting from the accumulation of additives in the organism and their interaction with other substances, such as alcohol, it was necessary to minimize the quantity of additives ingested. Since beer is a foodstuff of which large quantities are consumed in Germany, the government considered that it was particularly desirable to prohibit the use of any additive in its manufacture, especially in so far as the additive was not technologically necessary and could be avoided if only the ingredients laid down in the German legislation were used.[21]

The Court, after having established that the prohibition was an obvious barrier to importation, examined whether it was justified under Article 36 (now Article 30). It referred to its earlier *Sandoz* judgment, where it was held that "[i]n so far as there are uncertainties at the present state of scientific research it is for the Member States, in the absence of harmonization, to decide what degree of protection of the health and life of humans they intend to assure, having regard however to the requirements of the free movement of goods within the Community."[22] The Court added that Community law does not preclude the adoption by the Member States of legislation whereby the use of additives is subjected to prior authorization. Such legislation meets a genuine need of health policy, namely that of restricting the uncontrolled consumption of food additives. However, the Court continued, the application to imported products of prohibitions on marketing products containing additives which are authorized in the Member State of production but prohibited in the Member State of importation is permissible only in so far as it complies with the requirements of Article 36 EC (now Article 30). The Court then referred to the principle of proportionality which underlies the last sentence of Article 36 (now Article 30), whose effect is that prohibitions on the marketing of products containing additives authorized in the Member State of production but prohibited in the Member State of importation must be restricted to what is actually necessary to secure the protection of public health. And, in line with previous case law, the Court held that the use of a specific additive which is authorized in another Member State must be authorized in the case of a product imported from that Member State where—in view, on the one hand, of the findings of international scientific research, and in particular of the work of the Community's Scientific Committee for Food, the Codex Alimentarius Committee of the FAO and the WHO, and, on the other hand, of the eating habits prevailing in the importing Member State—the additive in question does not present a risk to public health and meets a real need, especially a technical one.[23]

There are a number of important elements in this analysis. The first is the deference in principle to the level of protection which a Member State chooses to set, particularly in case of uncertainties in the present state of scientific research. Secondly, the deference appears to be qualified by the principle of mutual recognition—or perhaps one should speak of the presumption of mutual recognition. The Court refers to the limits imposed by Article 36 (now Article 30) in the case of imported products lawfully manufactured in another Member State, where the use of the relevant additives is authorized. Such products do not have to be admitted solely on the basis that they are lawful in the Member State of exportation, but the fact that they *are* lawful in that State clearly leads to closer scrutiny of the reasons for not tolerating them on the market of the Member State of importation. Thirdly, such closer scrutiny needs to take place on the basis of (a) findings of international scientific research, both at EC and international level, and (b) the eating habits prevailing in the importing Member State. Finally and crucially, the overall test is whether, in the light of the above, the additive in question presents a risk to public health and meets a real need, especially a technical one. Some of those ingredients of the Court's analysis call for some further comments.

The concept of risk lies at the basis of allowing Member States to adopt measures which operate as a trade restriction. However, the Court has made no real attempt at defining the type of risk required, and has dealt with the question on a case-by-case basis. In *German Beer*, Advocate General Slynn argued that in its previous case law the Court had developed a notion of "serious risk" or "real danger" to public health.[24] The concept of "serious risk" was indeed mentioned in cases such as *Van Bennekom* and *Kaasfabriek Eyssen;*[25] and in *Melkunie* and *Heijn*, the Court referred to "real danger" and "major risk" respectively.[26] However, it is not altogether clear that by using those notions the Court actually required a serious risk as the cornerstone for the public health exception in Article 30. There is no particular emphasis on serious risk, and there are other cases which point in the opposite direction. In *Sandoz,* for example, a case concerning the use of vitamins in foodstuffs, the Court spoke of a risk that could not be excluded and approvingly referred to EC legislation which testified "to great prudence regarding the potential harmfulness of additives, the extent of which is still uncertain in respect of each of the various substances, and leave a wide discretion to the Member States."[27] In *Muller*, the Court referred to the EC directives on food additives, which it described as showing great prudence in regard to the potential harmfulness of such substances, the underlying principle being that the uncontrolled consumption of additives with food should be restricted as far as possible; and the Court approvingly characterized this as "a legitimate aim of health policy."[28] Such language does not emphasize a concept of serious risk, but suggests elements of the so-called precautionary principle. The Court adopted a similar approach in the much more recent *BSE* case, in which the United Kingdom challenged a Commission decision banning all exports of beef subsequent to scientific reports which could not exclude a link between the mad cow disease and the human Creutzfeldt-Jakob disease. The Court emphasized that there was great uncertainty as to the risks, and stated that "where there is uncertainty as to the existence or extent of risks to human health, the [EC] institutions may take protective measures without having to wait until the reality and seriousness of those risks become fully apparent." In support of that position, the Court referred to Article 130r EC (now Article 174), paragraphs 1 and 2, on the aims of EC environmental policy, where there is emphasis on a high level of protection, also as regards public health, and on taking preventive action.[29] The Court did not, however, expressly refer to the precautionary principle, which is also mentioned in Article 174(2), nor did it refer to what is now Article 152, on public health, which mentions the prevention of human illness and diseases. Thus, the precautionary principle is not defined by the Court.

Veiled reference to the precautionary principle can also be found in the recent *Kemikalieinspektionen* case, concerning a Swedish prohibition, subject to individual exemptions, of all use of a chemical substance, trichloroethylene, in industrial processes. The Court referred to evidence of carcinogenic effects produced by the International Cancer Research Agency, set up by the WHO, as well as to recent German and American studies. In the light of this evidence, which boiled down to "suspicions that trichloroethylene can cause cancer in humans," the Court was satisfied that there was a sufficiently serious health risk.[30]

To link this to some of the questions in the Arimania case, the Court's occasional reference to serious risk does suggest that the seriousness of the externality is to some extent an issue, and that the Court would be inclined to adopt a different attitude if DDD is deadly or simply causing slight fever. As to the precautionary principle, the Court may be hesitant to give it more weight than it has done so far, in view of its continuing concern to ensure that there is a well-operating internal market. The Court has also touched upon the question whether, once the precautionary principle has been invoked, there should be an obligation to re-examine periodically the issue. In *BSE*, the Court approvingly referred to the preamble of the Commission's decision, where it was stated that the export ban was temporary and an emergency measure, and that there was a need for the significance of the new information and the measures to be taken to be subjected to detailed scientific study and, consequently, a need to review the contested decision following an overall examination of the situation.[31]

The Court holds that risk assessment must be based on (international) scientific research and on the eating habits in the Member State of importation. The latter is fairly obvious, but the Court will rather strictly review, under the heading of proportionality, defenses based on differences in eating habits.[32] As to scientific research, the Court would not generally engage in a deep discussion of the findings of such research. That may partly be due to the fact that there seem to have been very few cases where there were clearly conflicting views in scientific research. It may, however, also be due to the fact that the Court does not see it as its task strictly to review such findings. When reading the relevant case law, one is under the impression that, in case of inconclusive scientific research, the Court would err on the safe side, and would acknowledge that there are uncertainties justifying protective action by a Member State. The clearest statements were made in *Motte,* again a case on additives. There the Court repeated that Member States must take into account the results of international scientific research and, in particular, the work of the EC's Scientific Committee for Food. Nevertheless, the Court said, it must be emphasized that the opinions of the Committee do not have binding force. In addition, the fact that a figure for the acceptable daily intake of an additive was indicated showed that the use of that substance was liable to create a risk beyond a certain threshold and failed to remove uncertainties arising from the differences between the eating habits in the different Member States. The opinions of the Committee could not therefore abrogate the responsibility of national authorities for the protection of health in the absence of binding rules and effective supervisory measures at the EC level.[33] It would thus seem that the Court does consider that it may be wiser to adopt a pro-deference stance in cases of scientific disagreement. Scientific analysis is, in any event, something which does not lend itself easily to judicial review, much like certain other factors of policy-making, such as foreign and security policy, where the Court has also adopted a pro-deference stance.[34]

That does not, however, mean that mere allegation by a Member State is sufficient. In *Commission v. Italy,* on inspections on imports of fish, the Court held that the Italian government had failed to establish that the consumption of fish containing nematode larvae that are dead or devitalized as a result of appropriate treatment is dangerous to human health. In particular, the Italian government had not adduced any actual evidence to refute the Commission's argument that the findings of international scientific research confirm that the ingestion of dead or devitalized nematode larvae constitutes no risk to health.[35] The case of *Van der Veldt,* concerning imports of bread in Belgium from the Netherlands, is similar. The Dutch bread contained slightly more salt than the maximum provided for under Belgian legislation, and the Belgian authorities argued that this might lead to excessive consumption of salt. The Court replied that this was general conjecture which did not prove that increasing salt intake by a small amount poses a risk for public health. The risk must be measured, the Court said, not according to the yardstick of general conjecture, but on the basis of relevant scientific research.[36]

As regards the use of additives in foodstuffs, however, the Court does not only refer to scientifically assessed risk, but acknowledges that in case of uncertainty additives can be banned if they do not meet "a real need, especially a technical one." That is an interesting notion which appears to be rather particular to the Court's case law. It was first mentioned in *Sandoz,* on the use of vitamins, where it seemed to come out of the blue.[37] The Court discussed the "need" requirement more fully in *Motte,* where it referred to its origin, namely a 1980 report of the EC's Scientific Committee for Food. In that report, the Committee stated that for an additive to be authorized it must be established that the use for which it is intended corresponds to a need which may be technological or economic or again, as far as flavoring and coloring matters are concerned, organoleptic or psychological; and the Court integrated that policy guideline in its general test for review of Member States' policies on the authorization of additives.[38] As can be seen from the above description, the need requirement is interpreted rather liberally, which is confirmed by the *German Beer* case, where Advocate General Slynn was satisfied that preservatives could be "needed" to prolong the shelf-life of beers, or that additives could be needed in the light of consumers' preferences as regards color, flavor or amount of foam, even though it was uncontested that at least certain types of beer could perfectly be produced without additives.[39]

4. Proportionality, Due Process, and Legitimacy

As was mentioned, the starting-point in the Court's case law is invariably the recognition of a measure of discretion for Member States to take action aimed at protecting public health. However, that discretion is counter-balanced by the application of the principle of proportionality which, in this field, much as in other fields, appears to be the Court's tool for exercising significant review of measures interfering with the free movement of goods. The principle of proportionality is of course well known, even if it cannot be defined with great precision.[40] But it is generally accepted that the following elements form part of the proportionality test as operated by the Court in a context of exceptions to free movement. The measure under review must be appropriate for achieving a valid regulatory purpose; it must also be necessary for achieving that purpose; and among possible alternatives the least restrictive measure must be chosen. In the context of public health protection, the Court would subsume those elements under the final phrase of Article 30 EC, prohibiting arbitrary discrimination or a disguised restriction on trade, but there is no particular emphasis on the wording of that phrase.

The care taken by the Court to review measures on the basis of proportionality is complemented by insistence on what may be termed due process requirements. Member States must not only adopt the least restrictive measure, but they must also ensure that traders are able, for example, to request authorization of a particular additive and to pursue their claim by administrative and judicial process.

It is difficult to categorize those parts of the case law which turn on proportionality and due process, as those elements are quite fact- and case-specific. It may therefore be best to provide a fairly descriptive overview which does no more than to illustrate the Court's approach.

The Court emphasized proportionality and due process in *Sandoz,* on vitamins. That judgment is particularly instructive as regards the requirements which may and may not be imposed on the importer of the product. The Court did not accept that the authorization to market the foodstuffs in question was subject to proof by the importer that the product is not harmful to health. Since Article 36 (now Article 30) is an exception, to be strictly interpreted, it is for the national authorities to check in each instance that the measure contemplated satisfies the criteria of Article 36. Accordingly, although the national authorities may ask the importer to produce information in his possession, they must themselves assess whether authorization must be granted. Also, authorization to market cannot be made subject to proof by the importer that the marketing of the product in question meets a market demand, because the whole purpose of the free movement of goods is to ensure for products from the various Member States access to markets on which they were not previously represented.[41]

The *German Beer* case very much turned on proportionality.[42] There was no dispute that the German authorities could in principle ban certain additives, but the general prohibition on the use of any additives was clearly disproportionate. After having set out the general test for the approval of additives (see above), the Court recalled that, by virtue of the principle of proportionality, traders must be able to apply, under a procedure which is easily accessible to them and can be concluded within a reasonable time, for the use of certain additives to be authorized by a measure of general application. Furthermore, it must be open to traders to challenge before the courts an unjustified failure to grant authorization. The Court also repeated that, without prejudice to the right of the competent national authorities of the importing Member State to ask traders to produce the information in their possession which may be useful for the purpose of assessing the facts, it is for those authorities to demonstrate that the prohibition is justified on grounds relating to the protection of the health of its population.

The Court then addressed proportionality proper. It pointed out that the German rules on additives applicable to beer result in the exclusion of all the additives authorized in the other Member States and not the exclusion of just some of them for which there is concrete justification by reason of the risks which they involve in view of the eating habits of the German population. The Court then described the German government's defense. As regards the harmfulness of additives, the German government, citing experts' reports, had referred to the risks inherent in the ingestion of additives in general. It maintained that it was important, for reasons of general preventive health protection, to minimize the quantity of additives ingested, and that it was particularly advisable to prohibit altogether their use in the manufacture of beer, a foodstuff consumed in considerable quantities by the German population. However, the Court replied, it appeared from the table of additives authorized for use in the various foodstuffs submitted by the German government itself that some of the additives authorized in other Member States for use in the manufacture of beer were also authorized under the relevant German rules, for use in the manufacture of all, or virtually all, beverages. Mere reference to the potential risks of the ingestion of additives in general and to the fact that beer is a foodstuff consumed in large quantities, the Court held, does not suffice to justify the imposition of stricter rules in the case of beer. Advocate General Slynn also made some interesting statements in that regard; for example, it seemed to him disproportionate to seek to justify rules which exclude the whole of society from beer other than nationally produced beer because some additives may constitute a risk for a person who drinks in excess of 1,000 liters of beer a year or for an alcoholic already suffering from cirrhosis of the liver. Accepting that such persons may need protection there were other ways of achieving it, medical advice as to quantum and self-restraint to name only two.[43]

This can be linked to some of the questions in the Arimania case. For the Court, it would be relevant under proportionality that DDD is also contracted by feeding ducks and that Arimania would not be taking action against it. As to the question whether it is the role of the judge to impose an obligation on governments to be efficient, the EC law principle of proportionality clearly does require some measure of efficiency, and it is the courts' role to review on the basis of proportionality. Such review is not based on the letter of the existing legal texts—proportionality as a general principle of EC law being the creature of the Court of Justice—even though in the context of free movement of goods and the protection of public health the prohibition of arbitrary discrimination and disguised restrictions on trade in Article 30 EC may be construed as suggesting elements of proportionality.

The Court's reference in *German Beer* to the fact that some of the prohibited additives are accepted for all other beverages would suggest that, in the Arimania case, the fact that growth hormones are also used in beef and that no action is taken against such practices would matter, depending, of course, on the degree of similarity of the public health risk.

The Court also discussed proportionality in *Commission v. Italy,* as regards health inspections on imports of fish, rejecting here some of the Commission's claims. It was not disputed that the consumption of fish infested with larvae that have not been devitalized entails dangers to public health. The Court agreed with the Italian government that the measures less restrictive of trade suggested by the Commission were not capable of guaranteeing effective protection of public health. Labeling intended to inform consumers of the presence of live nematodes in fish was not a satisfactory solution where, as in this case, a product was involved which constituted a risk factor for human health. No more was a prohibition on consuming raw fish an effective measure for protecting public health, as it would have been impossible to ensure that it was complied with in practice. This was also true of a requirement imposed on consignees of the products in question that fish infested with nematodes had to be subjected to appropriate treatment to ensure that the larvae were devitalized.[44]

One can see here that the Court does engage in examining what is the least restrictive alternative (see the Arimania question), and that it does construct the counterfactual, or at least rejects the counterfactual suggestions by the Commission.

5. Concluding Comments

By way of conclusion, some thoughts about the issues of democratic legitimacy and political acceptability to which the Arimania case refers. In an EC context, the Court of Justice does show sensitivity towards policy decisions at national level which result from democratic processes. At the same time, the Court considers it to be its function to ensure that the internal market really works and the free movement of goods is generally guaranteed. The Court is very much aided in the difficult task of striking a balance by the fact that the EC itself may and does develop policy and adopt legislation. The case law on additives, it seems to me, is fed by an underlying dialogue between scientific research, in particular at EC level, EC legislation incorporating principles and rules based on such research, and research and decision-making at national level. The Court particularly interacts with the EC legislature which, through the adoption of harmonization directives, develops law on issues of public health protection, risk, scientific evidence, and regulatory intervention. Here the difference with the WTO context is striking. At WTO level, there is no general legislature. The WTO dispute settlement organs cannot interact with the WTO legislature. They are constrained to referring to other forms of international "legislation," developed for example in the FAO or in the WHO, which have the disadvantages of not being integrated with the WTO's work, of not always being coherent in the absence of an overarching structure and setting, and of themselves raising legitimacy issues.

It is submitted that the EU has reached an appropriately balanced system in this respect. The European Court of Justice does exercise significant judicial review, particularly where it applies the proportionality principle. The legitimacy of doing so, however, results from the Court's interference being embedded in a political and legal system where there is mutual respect, and checks and balances, between national legislatures and executives, the EC legislature and executives, national courts, and the EC courts. A system, also, where there are basic constitutional principles on free trade and its limits, *as well as* detailed legislation where appropriate. The lesson for the WTO would appear to be that, rather than focusing on the role of the dispute settlement organs, more attention should be paid to the legislative gap. There is nothing wrong with a judiciary exercising significant review—in fact it is rather meaningless to have a judiciary which would be unable to do so—provided there is a political counterpart. How to construct a WTO legislature is a subject for another day.

NOTES

1. Case C-331/88 *Fedesa and Others* [1990] ECR I-4023.

2. See Joined Cases 314 to 316/81 and 83/82 *Procureur de la République v. Waterkeyn* [1982] ECR 4337.

3. What comes even closer is the action between Member States under Article 227 EC, but very few cases are brought under this procedure.

4. See, e.g., Case C-368/95 *Familiapress v. Bauer Verlag* [1997] ECR I-3689.

5. See also J. Scott, "On Kith and Kine (and Crustaceans): Trade and Environment in the EU and WTO," Harvard Jean Monnet Working Paper, pp. 29–30, and N. McNelis in this volume, p. 225.

6. Due to the restrictions on standing in Article 230, paragraph 4.

7. See, e.g., *Fedesa,* cited in note 1, and Case C-180/96 *UK v. Council* [1998] ECR I-2265 (the *BSE* case).

8. Case C-84/94 *UK v. Council* [1996] ECR I-5755, para. 58.

9. *BSE,* cited in note 7, paras. 60 and 96–97.

10. For further analysis of some of the differences see P. Eeckhout, "The European Court of Justice and the Legislature," 18 *Yearbook of European Law* (1998), pp. 1–28.

11. Case 120/78 *Rewe v. Bundesmonopolverwaltung für Branntwein (Cassis de Dijon)* [1979] ECR 649.

12. Joined Cases C-267/91 and C-268/91 [1993] ECR I-6097, para. 15.

13. In my view, the *Keck and Mithouard* saga itself constitutes such struggling.

14. See, with respect to free movement of workers, Case C-190/98 *Graf v. Filzmoser Maschinenbau,* judgment of 27 January 2000; see in particular the Opinion of Advocate General Fennelly of 16 September 1999, which provides an excellent analysis of the case law.

15. See in particular the Opinion of Advocate General Jacobs of 26 October 2000 in Case C-379/98 *PreussenElektra AG v. Schleswag AG,* where, in view of the fundamental importance for the analysis of Article 28 EC of the question whether directly discriminatory measures can be justified by imperative requirements, the Advocate General urges the Court clarify its position. He then concentrates on the imperative requirement of environmental protection, where he sees specific reasons in favor of a more flexible approach (see paras. 229–33 of the Opinion).

16. For an overview, see P. Oliver, *Free Movement of Goods in the EC* (Sweet and Maxwell 1996), at pp. 203–17, and S. Pardo Quintillán, "Free Trade, Public Health Protection and Consumer Information in the European and WTO Context," 33 *JWT* (1999), pp. 149–53.

17. Cited in note 11.

18. Joined Cases C-1/90 and C-176/90 *Aragonesa de Publicidad Exterior and Publivía* [1991] ECR I-4151, para. 13.

19. Case 104/74 [1976] ECR 613, para 15. In the recent *Kemikalieinspektionen* judgment the Court recalled that "the health and life of humans rank foremost among the property or interests protected by Article 36 [now 30] of the Treaty;" see Case C-473/98 *Kemikalieinspektionen* v *Toolex Alpha,* judgment of 11 July 2000, para. 38.

20. Case 178/84 *Commission* v *Germany* [1987] ECR 1227. See also Joined Cases C-13/91 and C-113/91 *Debus* [1992] ECR I-3617.

21. See para. 39.

22. Case 174/82 *Sandoz BV* [1983] ECR 2445.

23. *German Beer,* cited in note 20, paras. 40–46.

24. At 1256.

25. Case 227/82 *Van Bennekom* [1983] ECR 3883, para. 40, and Case 53/80 *Officier van Justitie v. Kaasfabriek Eyssen* [1981] ECR 409, para. 13.

26. Case 97/83 *Melkunie* [1984] ECR 2367, para. 18, and Case 94/83 *Heijn* [1984] ECR 3263, para. 13.

27. Cited in note 22, paras. 12 and 15.

28. Case 304/84 *Ministère public v. Muller* [1986] ECR 1511, para. 22.

29. *BSE,* cited in note 7, paras. 99–100. See also Case T-199/96 *Bergaderm and Goupil v. Commission* [1998] ECR II-2805, para. 66.

30. Cited in note 19, paras. 41–45.

31. Para. 101.

32. Again *German Beer* (cited in note 20) is an example, see paras. 48–49.

33. Case 247/84 *Motte* [1985] ECR 3887, para. 20. See also *Melkunie,* cited in note 26, para. 18.

34. See, e.g., Case C-70/94 *Werner v. Germany* [1995] ECR I-3189, in particular Opinion of Advocate General Jacobs, paras. 42–43; Case C-120/94 *Commission v. Greece* [1996] ECR I-1513, again Opinion of Advocate General Jacobs; Case C-273/97 *Sirdar v. The Army Board, Secretary of State for Defense,* judgment of 26 October 1999.

35. Case C-228/91 *Commission v. Italy* [1993] ECR I-2701, para. 28.

36. Case C-17/93 *Van der Veldt* [1994] ECR I-3537, paras. 16–17.

37. Cited in note 22.

38. Cited in note 33, para. 21.

39. Cited in note 20, at 1254.

40. See generally T. Tridimas, *The General Principles of EC Law* (OUP 1999), chapters 3 and 4; various contributions in E. Ellis (ed.), *The Principle of Proportionality in the Laws of Europe* (Hart Publishing 1999).

41. Cited in note 22, paras. 21–27.

42. Cited in note 20, paras. 45–49.

43. Cited in note 20, at 1257.

44. Cited in note 35, para. 36.

CHAPTER 9

To What Extent Is the Description of the U.S. Law Made by Professor D. H. Regan Applicable in the EC Context?

Michel Waelbroeck

Professor Regan (p. 91) has given us an analysis of the U.S. law on restrictions to interstate commerce that rests essentially on two propositions.

The first proposition is that a state measure that produces a restrictive effect without being facially discriminatory—what we Europeans would call an "indistinctly applicable measure"—must be presumed to be legal unless it can be shown that it was "motivated by a bad purpose," in other words, that the real objective pursued by the legislator was protectionist.

The second proposition is that, whatever the courts may have said they were doing, in reality they do not apply a balancing test when deciding on the lawfulness of a state measure having a restrictive effect.

I intend to examine whether these two propositions reflect the attitude adopted by the European Court of Justice when deciding on the compatibility with the EC Treaty of restrictive measures adopted by Member States. I shall show that this is not so. At the same time, I shall discuss whether the Court should adopt the "Regan propositions" in its future case law. Let me say at once that my answer will be negative.

1. The "Protectionist Purpose" Test

It is clear that the Court does not base its examination of restrictive State measures exclusively on an examination of their purpose. In my opinion, the Court is correct in doing so.

First, as has already been stressed by several participants today, it is not always easy to detect the "real" purpose for which a measure was adopted. Even admitting, as Professor Regan does, that "purpose" is not limited to "subjective intent" but can be gathered from circumstantial evidence such as the structure of the law, the plausibility of the distinctions it draws, the legislator's zeal in pursuing the asserted goal in other contexts, the political context, the timing of the law, etc., the fact is that, in many instances, it is difficult for the Court to come across sufficient hard evidence to be able to come to the conclusion that the "real" motive pursued by the legislator, whatever it may officially say, is to discriminate against foreign products or producers. In addition, such a finding may be politically sensitive, taking into account national susceptibilities, which are still strong in the EC context.

Second, the historic dimension must not be lost sight of. It sometimes happens—as in the case of the Belgian legislation concerning the shape of margarine packages or the German law concerning the ingredients from which beer can be produced—that a measure is adopted for a genuinely lawful motive, such as the protection of consumers, but that this motive loses its importance over time as circumstances change. Can it be said that the measure, although unchanged in the statute book, has become protectionist at a certain point in time? If so, when?

Third, and more importantly, measures with no identifiable protectionist purpose have been struck down by the European Court when they brought about an unjustifiable restriction of trade and could not be justified by overriding considerations of general interest (so-called "mandatory requirements"). This happened, for instance, to the French law prohibiting the import and sale of substitute milk powder,[1] even though it did not have any protectionist intent or effect. (Indeed, substitute milk powder can be manufactured just as easily in France as in other Community countries, and milk is the object of overproduction throughout the Community and not only in France.)

Fourth—and this will bring me to my next point, i.e., the appropriateness of the balancing test—there can be a concurrence of motivations behind a single measure, some of which may be legitimate, while others may have a protectionist character. Without some balancing act, it is impossible to decide such cases.

2. The Suitability of Balancing by Courts

In innumerable cases, the European Court has applied the "proportionality" test, which is indisputably a balancing act. Indeed, according to this test, the Court checks whether a restrictive State measure is appropriate to reach a certain public interest objective, whether it does not impose a greater burden than necessary to achieve that objective, and whether there does not exist a less restrictive alternative to achieve the objective.

In many of these cases, the Court's decision has come out against the compatibility of the State measure with the Treaty. The Court did not feel inhibited by an asserted lack of competence to make the empirical judgments required—and indeed I do not see any reason why the Court should have felt so inhibited. I shall give a few examples.

Duplication of Controls

In a steady line of cases since the *Biologische Produkten* case,[2] the Court has held that although Member States are allowed under the Treaty to require that the sale of certain potentially harmful products such as pesticides, be subject to prior approval, Member States are obliged to take due account of the results of tests carried out in other Member States with a view to obtaining approval there. Indeed, requiring the duplication of tests already conducted in another Member State imposes a disproportionate burden on trade between Member States.

Existence of Less Restrictive Alternative

Often the Court will say that a State measure reserving a sales designation to products produced according to certain norms (allegedly to prevent deception of consumers) is "disproportionate" where the same result—e.g., information of consumers concerning ingredients, quality, production methods etc.—can be achieved by a simple label. This was already the reasoning in the notorious *Cassis de Dijon* case.[3] It has been repeated in a long line of cases since then, including recently the French *Foie Gras* case.[4]

Internal Inconsistency

When the legislator prohibits—allegedly for a reason of general interest such as the protection of public health—the use or sale of a given substance in certain circumstances but not in others where the presence of the substance would be potentially equally damaging, the Court has been quick to denounce the internal inconsistency in the legislator's approach and to consider the ban as disproportionate. Indeed, in such cases, the ban is not appropriate to reach the public interest objective sought since the very existence of situations where it is not imposed belies the need to impose it in others. A famous example of this type of reasoning is provided by the *German Beer* case.[5]

Restrictive Effect Disproportionate by Comparison with Protected Objective

Where the State measure, although pursuing a legitimate objective such as the protection of the environment, imposes a burden on imported products that is disproportionate with regard to the objective it seeks to attain, the Court does not hesitate to strike it down, as it did in the *Danish Bottles* case.[6] In that case, the Court upheld on environmental grounds a Danish law requiring beer and soft drinks to be sold in reusable containers and made subject to a deposit, although this law made it more costly for foreign products to be marketed in Denmark because of the need to set up a recycling system involving the transportation of empty containers over larger distances than when a Danish producer was involved. Nevertheless, the Court considered as disproportionate the requirement that the containers conform to types approved by the Danish authorities. The Court stressed the expense which this measure imposed on foreign producers, since it obliged them to use special containers for their sales to Denmark.

3. Conclusion

To conclude it appears that the European Court of Justice does not require proof that a national measure was motivated by a protectionist purpose but applies the following three-pronged test:

1. is the measure apt to impose a burden on imports that is greater than any burden it may impose on domestic products?[7]
2. can the measure be justified by overriding considerations of public interest?
3. is the measure proportionate to the public interest objective it purports to achieve?

Only if the latter two questions draw an affirmative answer will the measure pass muster under the Court's case law. In my submission, this case law gives appropriate deference to the Member States' legitimate objectives, whilst allowing the Community to continue to develop successfully.

NOTES

1. Commission v. France, case 216/84, [1988] ECR 793.
2. Frans-Nederlandse Maatschappij voor Biologische Produkten, case 272/80, [1981] ECR 3277.
3. REWE-Zentral v. Bundesmonopolverwaltung für Branntwein, case 120/78, [1979] ECR 649.
4. Commission v. France, case C-184/96, [1998] ECR I-6197.
5. Commission v. Germany, case 178/84, [1987] ECR 1227.
6. Commission v. Denmark, case 302/86, [1988] ECR 4607.
7. Keck and Mithouard, cases C-267 and 268/91, [1993] ECR I-6097.

Part III: The Review of Health Standards in the WTO

CHAPTER 10

Does the WTO Stand for "Deference to" or "Interference with" National Health Authorities When Applying the Agreement on Sanitary and Phytosanitary Measures (SPS Agreement)?

Joost Pauwelyn

The record of WTO dispute adjudicators in respect of "deference to" *versus* "interference with"[1] decisions by national authorities in the field of health protection under the Agreement on the Application of Sanitary and Phytosanitary Measures (SPS Agreement) is mixed.[2] This paper offers some arguments in support of either side in the deference *versus* interference debate.

1. Deference to National Health Authorities

Several elements could support a statement that the SPS Agreement *does* give considerable leeway to Members maintaining measures allegedly justified on health grounds.

No Minimum Level of Risk Required

The SPS Agreement gives complete pre-eminence to health over trade. As soon as *some* health risk exists, a measure addressing this risk can, in principle, be taken. Each Member has, indeed, complete freedom to decide on the *level of risk* it can accept.[3] In theory, even a zero risk level could be justifiable.[4]

A WTO Panel *cannot,* therefore, strike down a measure simply because it considers the risk involved to be "minimal." Nor can a Panel strike down a measure following a cost-benefit analysis showing, for example, that the "trade or other welfare costs" linked to the measure manifestly outweigh its proven "health benefits." No matter how high the costs resulting from the restriction (in terms of, for example, higher consumer prices), as long as the restriction mitigates a health risk it can, in principle, be maintained. Under no circumstance can a reduction in the level of health protection be imposed.[5] A

The views set out in this paper are strictly personal. Thanks to Gabrielle Marceau and Erik Wijkstrom for very useful comments. joost.pauwelyn@wto.org

measure can only be found to be "too restrictive to trade" when there is an alternative measure that is not only *less trade restrictive* but also achieves the *same level of health protection* as that achieved by the measure in place.[6] However, as long as the alternative does not meet that level, a Panel cannot find a violation in this respect.

In other words, it would seem impossible for the WTO to state, in the moot case (see Appendix, p. 359), that even though there is a risk of "duck fever," since the risk is so small or since "duck fever" is such a minor disease, Arimania's health measure is inconsistent with the SPS Agreement (see Question 9).

This approach may be quite novel in the WTO legal system. When it comes to protective measures under GATT Article XX, for example, the stated "not more trade-restrictive than necessary test" may arguably imply some form of balancing act between, on the one hand, for example, "environmental benefits" and, on the other, "trade costs"; a balancing act that could allow a Panel to question the level of environmental protection sought by the Member concerned.[7] Under the SPS Agreement, however, this possibility is explicitly ruled out.[8]

Case law will determine whether the same route will, nevertheless, be taken under GATT Article XX. Especially when it comes to the protection of health or the environment, it would seem difficult, in policy terms at least, to take a different route, i.e., for Panels to openly scrutinize the *level* of health or environmental protection sought under GATT Article XX. A different route may be taken, however, under other paragraphs of Article XX, for example, Article XX(d).[9]

As a matter for future changes to the SPS Agreement, a distinction between different types of health concerns could, however, be considered. When it comes to protecting *human* health, it may be justified that *any* health risk, however small, trumps trade benefits. When a politician explains to an audience that there is only one cancer risk in a million, the reply shouted from the audience "I hope *you* are the one," explains all. However, at least when addressing the health or life of *animals* or *plants,* one could perhaps reconsider the current "guillotine approach" (of "risk established, measure justified") and move towards a more economic analysis for the imposition of SPS measures. Should there, indeed, not be circumstances where an import ban cannot be maintained because the *actual* welfare costs linked to *having* the ban manifestly outweigh the *potential* costs of *not having* the ban, i.e., the risk of a relatively harmless animal or plant disease entering the country? Or should Members, in these circumstances, be allowed to maintain a "zero risk" level even if it implies a huge economic welfare loss affecting, among other things, the jobs and livelihoods of many people? In the legal system of the European Communities, this issue is referred to as the criterion of "proportionality."

It is interesting to note that the SPS Agreement already makes a distinction between human health, on the one hand, and animal and plant health, on the other. Only in respect of animal and plant health, not human health, need certain economic factors be considered in the risk assessment that is required in support of a measure (SPS Article 5.3). However, the economic factors referred to in Article 5.3 (e.g., loss of production in case of disease entry) are all factors that may *support* the introduction of a trade restriction, i.e., factors on the "benefits-side" of the health measure. What is argued here is that Members—and arguably also Panels—should perhaps be *under an obligation* to take account also of economic factors on the "costs-side" of the health measure, i.e., the social welfare that is foregone because of the banning of a certain product.[10] This would occur, not in the risk assessment phase (a more or less scientific exercise where, for example, it would be found that two in one million casualties would occur if the product were allowed for import), but in the so-called risk management phase (where, for example, the cost of the two casualties is compared to the costs of keeping the product out; and where it may be required that if the cost of keeping the ban in place manifestly outweighs that of the two casualties, the ban cannot be maintained).

An obligation along these lines would, indeed, put some form of "efficiency" requirement on governments considering the imposition of health measures, as referred to in Question 7.

The Member *Challenging* the Health Measure Bears the Burden of Convincing the Panel of the Validity of Its Claims

Introducing health measures is explicitly recognized as a WTO Member's *right*. It is no longer framed in terms of an *exception* to free trade principles. As a result, it is for the Member *challenging* a health measure to prove that the measure is *inconsistent* with the SPS Agreement.[11] In other words, it is for the complainant to prove that the measure is maintained *without* sufficient scientific evidence, is *not* based on a risk assessment or *is* more trade-restrictive than required to achieve its acceptable level of protection. Even if the defendant maintains a measure that *deviates* from an internationally accepted standard, it remains with the complainant to prove that there is *no* scientific justification for the measure (see Question 21).[12]

All of this clearly works in favor of the Member imposing the health measure. These are elements in support of "deference to" national health authorities.

Since the burden of proof rests on the complainant, in case the scientific evidence before a WTO Panel is in *equipoise,* i.e., if the evidence in support and against the health measure is, according to the Panel, equally strong, the health measure will stand.

This approach is a clear departure from GATT Article XX. Once the complainant has established a violation of, say, GATT Article XI (prohibiting quantitative restrictions), it is *for the defendant* to invoke the GATT Article XX defense of, say, health protection or the conservation of exhaustible natural resources. As a result, it is also *for the defendant* to prove that the conditions required under GATT Article XX are met, i.e., to prove that the measure is "necessary" to protect health, or "relates to" the conservation of exhaustible natural resources.

It should be noted, however, that the application of the burden of proof concept in SPS cases, rather than ensuring deference to national health authorities, may actually work *against* the Member imposing the health measure. It is, indeed, sufficient for the complainant to raise a *prima facie* case or presumption that, say, the measure is *not* based on a risk assessment. "When that *prima facie* case is made, the burden of proof moves to the defending party, which must in turn counter or refute the claimed inconsistency."[13] In practical terms—depending, of course, on what one requires for a *prima facie* case to be raised—this may well mean that the heaviest burden will rest on the Member that introduced the health measure (i.e., the burden to rebut an arguably easily established presumption of inconsistency with the SPS Agreement).

Two points could be noted in this respect.[14] First, the actual burden of proof (in the sense of the burden of finally convincing the Panel; not the burden to submit evidence to the Panel) should never shift and always rest on the complainant: it is for the complainant (not the defendant) to convince the Panel; in case of doubt, the health measure should stand.

Second, the burden to simply produce evidence in support of one's claims and arguments (as opposed to the actual burden of proof) may shift from one party to the other and back (in particular, with the use of presumptions).

However, since a mere presumption raised by the complainant that has not been rebutted by the defendant would, under current case law, effectively lead to the invalidation of the health measure, the "standard," "level" or "quantum" of proof required for such presumption to be created should be *high* (in SPS cases perhaps higher than under other WTO agreements). This would mean, for example, that when a Member claims that a measure is *not* maintained with sufficient scientific evidence (SPS Article 2.2), it does not suffice that this Member simply points at the measure and the SPS provision concerned for the *prima facie* case to be established and the burden to shift to the defendant. To give some meaning to the fact that the actual burden of proof rests on the complainant, the Member challenging the measure should, in addition, be required to submit itself some scientific evidence showing that the measure is *not* founded in science.

If no further clarification is made on this issue by Panels or the Appellate Body, this open question of "what is required for a presumption to be raised" could well be abused by Panels or the Appellate Body alike to justify a predetermined outcome. To that extent, one could question the usefulness of the presumption technique altogether in that it raises more questions than it solves.

A more practicable alternative could be for a Panel to simply ask itself: "Has the complainant convinced us of the existence of the fact or the validity of its claim?" If not, the health measure should stand. The focus could then directly be on "what do we require to be convinced," i.e., the "standard" or "level" of proof (e.g., preponderance of evidence, beyond reasonable doubt, etc.), not the altogether different notion of burden of proof.

Minority Scientific Opinions May Be Sufficient

The obligation under the SPS Agreement to only maintain health measures with "sufficient scientific evidence" (Article 2.2) that are "based on" a risk assessment (Article 5.1), has been interpreted in case law as a requirement for a "rational or objective relationship" between the health measure, on the one hand, and the scientific evidence and risk assessment put forward by the Member enacting the measure, on the other.[15]

In respect of the requirement that health measures be "based on" a risk assessment (Article 5.1), the Appellate Body in *EC – Hormones* added the following:

> We do *not* believe that a risk assessment has to come to a *monolithic conclusion* that coincides with the scientific conclusion or view implicit in the SPS measure. The risk assessment could set out both the prevailing view representing the "mainstream" of scientific opinion, as well as the opinions of scientists taking a divergent view . . . In most cases, responsible and representative governments tend to base their legislative and administrative measures on "mainstream" scientific opinion. In other cases, equally responsible and representative governments may act in good faith on the basis of what, at a given time, *may be a divergent opinion coming from qualified and respected sources*. By itself, this does not necessarily signal the absence of a reasonable relationship between the SPS measure and the risk assessment, *especially where the risk involved is life-threatening in character and is perceived to constitute a clear and imminent threat to public health and safety*.[16]

In respect of the requirement that health measures not be "maintained without sufficient scientific evidence" (Article 2.2) the Appellate Body in *Japan – Varietals* added what follows:

> Whether there is a rational relationship between an SPS measure and the scientific evidence *is to be determined on a case-by-case basis and will depend upon the particular circumstances of the case, including the characteristics of the measure at issue and the quality and quantity of the scientific evidence.*[17]

Of course, the crucial message in these findings is that, in principle, even a minority scientific opinion, such as the one by Dr. von Entefleisch in the moot case, could, in principle, satisfy the quantum of scientific evidence required under the SPS Agreement. In other words, there is no need to find, for example, that at least a majority of the scientific community is in favor of a proposed health measure. *A fortiori,* the fact that there are dissenting scientific opinions does not prevent a Member from imposing the measure. This is the reason why the above quotes are placed here in support of a statement that considerable "deference" is given under the SPS Agreement.

Once this crucial statement is absorbed, however, it becomes apparent that certain conditions may be linked to upholding a health measure supported only by minority opinions. As noted in the above-quoted passage from *Japan – Varietals,* this will depend on a case-by-case examination (see Question 12).

First, reference is made to the "characteristics of the measure." In *EC – Hormones,* for example, it was stated that minority opinions may well be sufficient "where the risk involved is life-threatening in character and is perceived to constitute a clear and imminent threat to public health and safety." Could this mean that in case of an alleged or perceived "lower risk," either in terms of quantity or quality or both, the required quantum of scientific evidence increases (see Question 9)? In other words, will a "lower risk" (in the moot case, duck fever as opposed to DDD; or, more generally, animal or plant health as opposed to human health) require more scientific evidence? For example, what if the risk is the same, in terms of quantity, for a certain event occurring to humans (one in every one million die), animals (one in every one million die) and plants (one in every one million die), would the same amount and quality of scientific evidence be required for a ban to be consistent with the SPS Agreement? Or would a distinction be made based on the *quality* of the risk involved, i.e., human health as opposed to animal or plant health?

Second, reference is made to the "quality" of the scientific evidence. In *EC – Hormones,* there is mention of "qualified and respected sources." Does this mean that if the minority evidence does not come from a reputable or independent source—say, a retired scientist who could well have been paid to come to certain conclusions, or evidence backed up only by scientists employed by the government imposing the measure—the measure cannot pass the test under the SPS Agreement? On the basis of what criteria should Panels decide that one source is "better" than the other? The evidence provided by Dr. von Entefleisch in the moot case would, for example, not seem to meet the required standard, but who is the Panel, composed almost exclusively of lawyers and economists, to say that Dr. von Entefleisch is not a "qualified and respected source"?

Third, reference is made to the "quantity" of the scientific evidence. Obviously, minority opinions may vary in quantity, ranging from anything between 49% of the scientific community to close to 0%. The bigger the minority, the more likely that it is found to be sufficient.

How these three conditions will interact may provide another interesting development. Would it, for example, be enough if, say, 30 % of the scientific community supports the measure, but this 30 % seems to be the less reputable or less credible part of the community and the risk at stake is "only" a minor disease?

In any event, it could be submitted that an examination of these three conditions may well require a degree of "interference with" national regulatory regimes that was not expected when enunciating the position that minority opinions can validate a health measure under the SPS Agreement.

It should also be recalled that evidence in support of a measure has to be specific enough, i.e., it has to address the particular kind of risk at stake (e.g., in terms of specific substance, residue levels, etc.). For example, in *EC – Hormones* the evidence required had to address the carcinogenic or genotoxic potential of hormone residues in meat derived from cattle to which hormones had been administered for growth promotion purposes; studies showing the existence of a general risk of cancer related to hormones generally (not at the low residue levels reached in case of beef production) were not enough.[18] In this sense, in the moot case, the study made by Arimania's Public Health Institute explaining in general terms why DDD can be dangerous and even deadly may not be relevant or specific enough in support of the more specific situation of banning growth hormones in duck production.

Finally, it should be noted that—notwithstanding Articles 2.2 and 5.1 set out above—Members can impose provisional health measures on the basis of a precautionary approach, if such measure is:

(1) imposed in respect of a situation where "relevant scientific information is insufficient" and
(2) adopted "on the basis of available pertinent information."[19]

However, such a provisional measure may not be maintained unless the Member which adopted it:

(1) "seek[s] to obtain the additional information necessary for a more objective assessment of risk," and
(2) "review[s] the . . . measure accordingly within a reasonable period of time."[20]

Since Article 5.7 has been characterized as a "qualified exemption"[21] it would seem that the Member imposing the provisional measure has the burden of proving that the four elements above are met.

Deference in the Interpretation of Legal Obligations under the SPS Agreement

When it comes to interpreting a Member's obligations under the SPS Agreement, the Appellate Body in *EC – Hormones* has referred to the principle of *in dubio mitius* as a supplementary means of interpretation *in deference to* the Member whose SPS obligations are being examined.[22] According to this principle, if the meaning of a term is ambiguous, the meaning which is less onerous to the party assuming an obligation is to be preferred.

It is interesting to note that neither the Appellate Body, nor any Panel, has subsequently referred to this principle even in cases where the ordinary meaning of a treaty term was unclear. Indeed, the rules enunciated in Articles 31 and 32 of the Vienna Convention on the Law of Treaties (provisions that do not mention the *in dubio mitius* principle) have always been referred to. It is unclear whether this principle will play a role in future case law.

2. Interference with National Health Authorities

In contrast to the four sections of the previous chapter, several points can be raised in support of a thesis that the SPS Agreement, as it has been applied in case law, requires a great deal of "interference with" national regulatory authorities. Some of these points have already been hinted at in the previous chapter. Three more points are addressed below.

No Requirement of Discrimination

The SPS Agreement was found to apply to all SPS measures affecting international trade and this *independently from the GATT.*[23] Before the entry into force of the SPS Agreement, health regulations only had to be justified once a prior violation of one of the GATT principles had been found.[24]

Article XX(b) of GATT (allowing for measures "necessary to protect human, animal or plant life or health") is, indeed, only activated once a violation of, say, the non-discrimination provisions (in Articles I or III of GATT) has been established. Such violation of Article III, for example, requires a finding that, first (to take the example of *EC – Hormones*), imported hormone treated beef is "like" domestic non-hormone treated beef and, second, imported hormone treated beef is treated "less favorably." It is only if these two findings can be made that Article III is violated and Article XX comes into play.[25]

Under the SPS Agreement, in contrast, all disciplines apply even if *no* prior discrimination has been found. This means that a health measure can be inconsistent with the SPS Agreement even if it does not discriminate, either *de jure* or *de facto,* between imports and domestic production or between imports from different origins (see Questions 1 and 3). The mere fact that the health measure is *not based on science* is, in principle, sufficient for it to be invalidated under the SPS Agreement.

At this juncture, the question could be asked, however, whether "economic efficiency" in and of itself (apart from science) should at some point be considered enough to justify an SPS measure (although under the current SPS agreement this would not seem to be the case). The science-based requirement in the SPS Agreement seems to assume that if a measure is not based on science, it is, by default, disguised protectionism. But could there not be measures that are *not* based on science, *or* protectionist (if one believes the Appellate Body that is what the EC hormone ban is,[26] though to many, it looks like a bad example)? In other words, if a trade restrictive measure is proven to be *not* protectionist, but based on other "externalities" such as, to take one example, genuine consumer preferences (not government imposed ones), could one not say that it should be allowed? It could be argued, indeed, that such type of measure will, for the country in question, be the most "efficient" one in economic terms, that is when taking into account all externalities including consumer preferences (costs related to allowing imports *against* such preferences may outweigh the economic benefits of allowing imports, benefits that may not actually exist since consumers do not want the product).[27]

Economists may not agree with this (why not let consumers decide for themselves?). For, in essence, it is a political argument: if a population genuinely does not want a certain product *and* requests its government to do something about this, and this urge is not the result of trade protectionism, should a democratic (national as well as international) system not allow a ban (or other restriction) on such products? It would seem so, unless, of course, one sees "free trade" as some basic constitutional right, such as human rights, that should trump democracy. But this seems difficult to support: it is for free traders, not constitutional judges, to convince the public of the advantages of free trade. The problem is then to define the "genuineness" of a population's concerns or risk perceptions. The procedural risk assessment obligations referred to below—with due importance being given to risk communication—may serve this objective quite well (and actually be equipped better in this respect than the substantive science-based requirements now highlighted in SPS case law).

In addition, it should be recalled that the SPS Agreement does repeat the traditional MFN and national treatment obligations in its Article 2.3. However, even if a health measure has a disproportional effect on imports, as long as it is justified in science, this discriminatory impact should not, in itself, invalidate the health measure. Indeed, the discrimination would then, following the terms of Article 2.3, not be "arbitrary or unjustifiable." In this sense, science trumps the non-discrimination provisions.

Standard of Review by Panels: "Objective Assessment of the Facts"

Panels have to make an "objective assessment of the facts" (DSU Article 11). They cannot conduct a *de novo* review (for example, they cannot conduct their own risk assessment and on that basis tell the defendant what measure she should have taken). On the other hand, they cannot either give total deference to the findings of national authorities.[28] The Appellate Body found that this standard of "objective assessment" is only breached in the event a Panel, in the assessment of factual evidence, was to make an "egregious error that calls into question the good faith of the Panel."[29]

To make an "objective assessment" by Panels possible, all three SPS Panels have sought the advice of scientific and technical experts.[30] These experts did not act as a tribunal within a tribunal, required to come forward with a consensus view, but were appointed in their individual capacity. The opinions of the experts do not bind the Panel. In *Japan – Varietals,* the Appellate Body noted that the "comprehensive nature" of a Panel's authority to seek information from external sources suggests that Panels have a "significant investigative authority."[31]

However, the Appellate Body also found that scientific evidence submitted by experts appointed by the Panel cannot be used by the Panel as the basis for a finding of an inconsistency with the SPS Agreement in the event the complaining party itself had not first established a *prima facie* case of inconsistency based on specific legal claims asserted by it.[32] It is, in other words, not for the Panel or the experts to make the case of the complainant. This is where the Panel's inquisitorial functions end and the adversarial role of WTO dispute settlement prevails. In some cases, however, it may be questionable whether "what the parties argued" should prevail over the "obvious truth on the matter." Should Panels always disregard obvious solutions or alternatives (even those falling within the ambit of a claim raised by the complainant itself) simply because they have not been specifically put forward by the parties?

The above suggests that Panels, though not conducting a *de novo* review, have considerable authority in reviewing national regulatory processes. One author pointed out that in anti-dumping matters the WTO explicitly requires Panels to give deference to such processes (pursuant to Article 17.6 (i) of the Anti-Dumping Agreement), whereas in SPS matters no such deference is called for.[33]

In the area of dumping, however, many of the WTO obligations are of a procedural nature and an anti-dumping measure can only be imposed following several steps in a procedure strictly defined in the Anti-Dumping Agreement. But it is true that also for the substantive decisions, say, on whether there is dumping or injury, any "unbiased and objective" evaluation of the facts made by the national authority when it introduced the measure, needs to be accepted by the Panel (even if the Panel might have reached a different conclusion). In the area of dumping, the Panel is, indeed, restricting itself to checking, with quite a degree of deference, what the national authorities did *prior to* or *at the time of* the imposition of the measure. It is inconceivable for a dumping Panel to gather itself evidence on, for example, the existence of dumping or the likelihood of injury; all it can do is go through the evidence used by the national authority itself.

In the SPS area, in contrast, one often sees that Members first enact health measures and then, *ex post facto,* attempt to justify them. In two of the three SPS cases so far (*EC – Hormones* and *Japan – Varietals*), most of the evidence examined by the Panel was, indeed, not the evidence that the EC or Japan had before them when enacting the health measure but rather the evidence that they had gathered *ex post facto* or even only for the purpose of the Panel proceedings.[34] Combine this with a Panel's "significant investigative authority" through gathering advice from its *own* scientific experts, and it becomes apparent that often Panels may indeed be called upon to somehow conduct their own assessment of whether *at the time of the Panel's decision,* say, hormones in beef production are safe. This exercise is, indeed, far more intrusive than simply examining what a Member has done when it enacted the measure and asking the question of whether, at that time, the Member made an "unbiased and objective" evaluation of the facts.[35]

In case this rather extensive authority of Panels were to upset Members, an alternative may be to re-focus the SPS Agreement the way the Anti-Dumping Agreement is written, i.e., to set out internationally the different steps national health authorities have to follow when they want to enact health measures, what factors they have to look at, what evidence and from whom they have to gather, etc. Once such procedures are imposed internationally, the standard of review in respect of health measures could then be lowered to checking whether a Member has followed, as under the

Anti-Dumping Agreement, the different procedural steps and made an "unbiased and objective" evaluation of the facts in respect of the substantive decisions required.

One way of "filtering" protectionist concerns from genuine health or other concerns—the problem referred to earlier—may well be to put such strict obligation on WTO members to go through detailed procedures, mainly risk analysis procedures, step by step, including detailed risk communication. If all sections of the population are involved in such analysis (domestic producers as well as importers and consumers), then one would expect such exercise to lead to a fair and democratic result. This is perhaps where the WTO could and should stop: to only impose procedural risk analysis obligations (in the hope and assumption that they will lead to democratic, non-protectionist measures, especially if combined with SPS Articles 5.5 and 5.6 type of obligations), not a substantive obligation to base SPS measures on science.[36]

Consistency in Levels of Acceptable Risk

It is often difficult to establish whether a health measure is, as alleged by the Member imposing it, genuinely introduced to counter a health risk or simply a disguised restriction on trade. One way out may be to make a comparison between different situations that raise similar risks. To find out then, for example, whether in the moot case Arimania is really banning *growth hormones in ducks* for health purposes or simply doing so to protect its own duck producers (less than 20% of whom were previously using such hormones), one may well examine whether Arimania is as much concerned for its consumers' health when it comes to growth hormones in *beef* production (Question 10) or to *feeding ducks* in the national park (Question 5). If these two other situations raise similar risks, but Arimania does nothing in respect of these situations, one could, indeed, start to doubt whether Arimania's health concerns in respect of hormones in duck production are genuine.

This technique of comparison—although it raises the difficult question of whether situations pose similar risks—would, indeed, seem to be the most objective way of getting at the genuine intent behind measures allegedly taken for health purposes. It requires, however, close scrutiny of national regulatory processes and in-depth "interference" by adjudicators.

The technique has, nevertheless, been incorporated in Article 5.5 of the SPS Agreement. It is, in effect, the bite of the SPS Agreement. The obligation, contained in Article 5.5, is the following:

> [E]ach Member shall avoid arbitrary or unjustifiable distinctions in the levels it considers to be appropriate in different situations, if such

distinctions result in discrimination or a disguised restriction on international trade.

Article 5.5 aims, indeed, at avoiding situations where a Member—without making explicit origin-based distinctions—imposes a very high level of protection for one situation while at the same time it is very lenient in respect of another and this even though both are equally "dangerous" (or the former is even more dangerous than the latter). Even if, in such circumstances, the selected SPS measures equally apply to imports *and* domestic production they will, nevertheless, be inconsistent with the SPS Agreement in the event the distinction made is

1. between (at least) equally "dangerous" situations;
2. "arbitrary or unjustifiable"; *and*
3. results in "discrimination or a disguised restriction on international trade."

On the second element of Article 5.5, clearly, in the event one situation poses *higher* risks than the other, any distinction in treatment that is proportional to the difference in risk would seem "justifiable."

Moreover, coming back to the economic analysis suggested above, it may be feasible that a Panel accept as a justification for distinguishing between different situations that pose the *same or very similar* risks, the argument that in one situation the *costs of imposing a ban* (e.g., higher consumer prices) are much higher than in the other; and, as a result, only in the latter situation the ban was imposed, not the former.

This seems to be what the Appellate Body had in mind when saying that the EC could not possibly ban natural hormones in things like broccoli, so that the distinction made between these hormones and growth promotion hormones in beef was found to be "justifiable" under Article 5.5. The economic cost of banning natural hormones or enforcing a maximum residue level for natural hormones would simply be too high (contrary to banning growth promotion hormones in beef). Here the "economic cost or risk" somehow outweighs the "scientific risk" (resulting in one product being allowed for import, not the other).

The same could happen in case banning a given product, because of risk *X*, would cause so much economic harm that it is not "worth" banning the product for the risk involved (say, banning the product would simply mean that consumers cannot buy it, since it is not domestically produced, or would, more generally, dramatically raise consumer prices). At the same time, another product may represent the same risk *X*, but there the economic cost of banning it may not be so high (since, for example, the product is "not essential" or can be substituted). Could this distinction in treatment (ban – no ban, for the same risk) be justified under Article 5.5 on economic cost grounds? It would seem plausible, as long as the economic justification for the distinction is not related to trade protectionism.[37]

The third element under Article 5.5 (the distinction results in "discrimination or a disguised restriction on international trade") is crucial and subject to much debate. The Appellate Body in *EC – Hormones* stressed that it is *not* enough for this element to be met that there is an arbitrary or unjustifiable discrimination *between situations* which results in a trade restriction, even if such product discrimination is manifest.[38] In addition, elements of discrimination *between WTO Members* or protectionism of domestic production need to be proven (referred to as "warning signals" and "additional factors"). On that ground, the Appellate Body—after having found an "arbitrary or unjustifiable" distinction in the way the EC deals with hormones in cattle and antimicrobials in swine—concluded that the third element was *not* met and thus no violation of Article 5.5 could be found:

> We are unable to share the inference that the Panel apparently draws that the import ban on treated meat and the Community-wide prohibition of the use of the hormones here in dispute for growth promotion purposes in the beef sector were not really designed to protect its population from the risk of cancer, but rather to keep out U.S. and Canadian hormone-treated beef and thereby to protect the domestic beef producers in the European Communities.[39]

In *Australia – Salmon,* on the other hand, the Appellate Body confirmed the Panel's finding of a violation of Article 5.5. The Appellate Body concluded that Australia, by banning imports of salmon products but allowing imports of herring used as bait and live ornamental finfish—which represent similar, if not higher, risks of disease introduction—acted inconsistently with Article 5.5.[40] In so doing, it made the following instructive statement:

> [A] finding that an SPS measure is not based on an assessment of the risks to human, animal or plant life or health—either because there was no risk assessment at all or because there is an insufficient risk assessment—is a strong indication that this measure is not really concerned with the protection of human, animal or plant life or health but is instead a trade-restrictive measure taken in the guise of an SPS measure, i.e., a "disguised restriction on international trade."[41]

Should this be read as a departure from the Appellate Body findings in *EC – Hormones?*

Additional factual elements may need to be referred to for the establishment of an Article 5.5 violation, in particular when it comes to proving that the distinction (which was found to be "unjustifiable" under the second element, say, on scientific risk-related grounds) results in "discrimination or a disguised restriction on international trade," under the third element. One such factual element may be that, in the moot case, *prior* to the imposition of the ban domestic duck production with growth hormones amounted to less than 20 %, whereas foreign duck production with growth hormones amounted to much more (in particular in Karponia where it represents more than 98 %). In other words, the *effect* of the ban was much harsher on imports than on domestic producers. This *de facto* discrimination may be an important element under Article 5.5 (assuming, of course, that the distinction made by Arimania between hormones in duck—a ban—and hormones in beef—no limitations—was first found to be "unjustifiable" under the first element).

The objective of consistency in respect of a Member's "acceptable level of risk" may, however, be very difficult to achieve given current practice. The idea implicit in Article 5.5 seems to be that a Member first fixes the level of health risk it is willing to accept in a given field, say, one casualty in a million when it comes to cancer risk. Subsequently, when a new and different situation arises where a cancer risk is alleged, the Member concerned is supposed to examine the new situation, evaluate the risk it involves, say, 0.01 or five casualties in a million and decide, respectively, to allow the use of the substance or ban it. In practice, however, it seems that very few countries have defined the level of health risk they can accept in any detail. What mostly seems to happen is that regulators decide cases on an *ad hoc* basis, depending on both scientific evidence and all types of consumer and producer pressures without, however, any built-in requirement of consistency.

It seems, therefore, that one major challenge will be to conduct a wide debate within each Member as to what types and level of risk should be acceptable. There is, indeed, a need for consumers to realize that "zero risk" does not exist and that scientists will never be able to exclude the presence of risk (they can only find that given a number of trials there is *X* risk or that in that number of trials the adverse affects did not occur; they cannot exclude, however, that in future or other trials the risk event may still occur). Once such acceptable level of risk is set and defined in sufficient detail, it will become easier for policy-makers to take decisions, using the level as benchmark instead of being under political pressure to ban everything unless a finding of no risk is made (see the recent UK-France beef war within the EU).

Such approach would focus a lot on consumer information and risk communication. Much depends, however, on what role the government should play in the area of health protection: should it ban all risky products (assuming the consumer cannot decide for her-/himself) or should it inform the consumer about risk so that she can make her/his own informed decision?

Especially in the event case law or the SPS agreement itself would move away from the "science based" requirement, as suggested above (procedural "risk assessment" obligation rather than substantive "science-based" one), Article 5.5 is where one's focus should be. Even if SPS were left unchanged, case law shows us that people, especially economists, need to think urgently about how to fill in the details of Article 5.5. The "warning signals" and "additional factors" currently used in case law to find "discrimination" under the third element of Article 5.5 are neither convincing nor predictable criteria.

NOTES

1. The word "deference" is used here in its more general sense of giving national authorities more possibilities for imposing certain measures; not in its stricter sense related to the notion of "standard of review."

2. See my contribution on The WTO Agreement on Sanitary and Phytosanitary (SPS) Measures as Applied in the First Three SPS Disputes, *JIEL* (1999), 641–64.

3. "The determination of the appropriate level of protection . . . is a *prerogative* of the Member concerned and not of a Panel or of the Appellate Body" (*Australia – Salmon,* Appellate Body Report, adopted on 6 November 1998, WT/DS18/AB/R, para. 199).

4. "[T]he 'risk' evaluated in a risk assessment must be an ascertainable risk . . . This does not mean, however, that a Member cannot determine its own appropriate level of protection to be 'zero risk.'", ibid., para. 125.

5. All of this is subject, of course, to the elements of "interference" discussed below, in particular the SPS obligation related to "consistency in levels of health protection" and the SPS obligation to ensure that the measure is not "more trade-restrictive than required" to achieve the chosen level of health protection. However, subject to somehow being consistent in the level of health protection chosen for different situations and to selecting a measure that is not more trade-restrictive than necessary to achieve this level, the selection of the level in and of itself *cannot* be challenged under WTO rules.

6. SPS Article 5.6.

7. See Trachtman, Joel, Trade and . . . Problems, Cost-Benefit Analysis and Subsidiarity, *EJIL* 9 (1998), 32–85, at 71.

8. The TBT Agreement is not as explicit as the SPS Agreement when it comes to making the determination of the "level of protection" a prerogative of Members but comes close to it by referring to this prerogative in its preambular paragraph 6.

9. In this respect, it is interesting to note that in the Panel report on *Korea – Beef* (WT/DS169/R), Korea failed to successfully invoke Article XX(d) because it was unable to convince the Panel that there were no alternatives to a dual retail system for domestic and imported meat that would prevent deceptive practices in the beef retail market. In so finding, it would seem that the Panel somewhat lowered the degree of protection against deceptive practices sought by Korea. Indeed,

to resort to labeling, record-keeping, prosecution, and fines may go some way to avoiding retailers to misrepresent imported beef as domestic beef. Nevertheless, the same level of protection would not seem to be met as that achieved by bluntly requiring the different types of meat to be sold in separate shops. Much is a consequence also of the difference in burden of proof under Article XX as opposed to that under the SPS and TBT Agreements, discussed below.

10. Clearly, under the SPS Agreement it is perfectly *lawful* for Members to make such cost-benefit analysis, i.e., to say that no trade restriction will be imposed because of its related costs (as long as the Member is consistent in this approach, see below). Indeed, only in the event trade restrictions *are* imposed does it become feasible that a complaint be brought under the SPS Agreement. What is suggested here is that there should perhaps be an *obligation* on Members to take account of economic costs related to a health measure, allowing Panels to strike down a measure in case this obligation has not been fulfilled.

11. Appellate Body report on *EC – Hormones,* adopted on 13 February 1998, WT/DS26/AB/R, para. 98.

12. Ibid., para. 104.

13. *EC – Hormones,* Appellate Body report, op. cit., para. 98.

14. See my contribution on Evidence, Proof and Persuasion in WTO Dispute Settlement – Who Bears the Burden? *JIEL* 1 (1998), 227–58.

15. In respect of Article 2.2, Appellate Body report on *Japan – Varietals,* adopted on 19 March 1999, WT/DS76/AB/R, para. 21. In respect of Article 5.1, Appellate Body report on *EC – Hormones,* para. 193.

16. Para. 194 (underlining added). The Appellate Body reiterated this view in respect of the "rational or objective relationship" in Article 2.2 in *Japan – Varietals,* para. 77.

17. *Japan – Varietals,* Appellate Body report, paras. 73 and 84 (italics by the author, footnote omitted).

18. *EC – Hormones,* Appellate Body report, para. 200.

19. *Japan – Varietals,* Appellate Body report, para. 89.

20. Ibid.

21. *Japan – Varietals,* Appellate Body report, para. 80.

22. *EC - Hormones,* Appellate Body report, footnote 154.

23. *EC – Hormones,* Panel reports, para. 8.36 (U.S. Panel) and para. 8.39 (Canada Panel)

24. For example, Report of the Panel on *Thailand - Restrictions on Importation of and Internal Taxes on Cigarettes,* adopted on 7 November 1990 (DS10/R), 37S/200.

25. A prior violation of GATT Article XI (prohibition on quantitative restrictions), without there being discrimination, would also suffice for Article XX to be activated. However, at least in the field of food safety, SPS measures are most likely to be applied equally to both domestic and imported products (as the measure in *EC – Hormones*). As a result, the Ad Note to GATT Article III makes Article III and not Article XI applicable to such SPS measures.

26. Op. cit., para. 245.

27. One could argue then that the measure is no longer a true SPS measure since it is not there to protect against "health risks." But that, of course, is the major issue: are "health risks" to be limited to "scientific risks," or should they include also other, non-scientific perceptions of "risk" such as social or cultural ones?

28. *EC – Hormones,* Appellate Body report, para. 117.

29. *EC – Hormones,* para. 133.

30. On the basis of Article 13 of the DSU and Article 11.2 of the SPS Agreement.

31. *Japan - Varietals,* Appellate Body, paras. 127–29.

32. Ibid., para. 129.

33. Charnovitz, Steve, Environment and Health Under WTO Dispute Settlement, 14 *International Trade Reporter* (1997), p. 913: "The WTO is in the odd position of deferring to national judgments of economic interest, but not to national judgments of health interest."

34. It is true that when these measures were first enacted, the SPS Agreement did not yet exist and thus neither the EC nor Japan had any obligations under it. Even though with the entry into force of the SPS Agreement, one could expect that new SPS measures are taken only *subsequent to* a scientific evaluation, many so-called health measures continue to be taken without much of a prior risk assessment. It is, however, very doubtful that a Panel would strike down such SPS measures in case there is evidence in their support *at the time of the Panel's decision* on the simple ground that *at the time of their introduction* there was no such evidence.

35. This difference between SPS and dumping examinations by Panels is also to a great extent due to the substance being examined: in SPS, science, an evolving, dynamic substance; in dumping, economic data related, mostly, to the past; a substance that, by definition, is static.

36. Panels, for one thing, would feel much more at ease when checking on "procedures" than they now do when checking on "science." After all, very few *national* legal systems impose an explicit, court-enforced, obligation on governments to base SPS measures on science. This should not mean, of course, that science has no role to play in SPS issues; it clearly has and should for regulators, but perhaps not so much before a court. The science-based requirement also lacks the comparative aspect found under the Article 5.5 consistency requirement. It basically asks trade lawyers/diplomats to make a scientific judgment where scientists themselves cannot reach one.

37. Such cost-benefit analysis should not allow, for example, for domestic protectionism in the sense of "[T]he hormone risk for beef and pork is the same but since I have domestic beef producers but no domestic pork producers, I only ban beef imports, not pork imports."

38. Appellate Body, para. 240, reversing the Panel report, paras. 8.203, 8.216 and 8.241 (U.S. Panel), and paras. 8.206, 8.219, and 8.244 (Canada Panel).

39. Op. cit., para. 245. One author derived from this that "the EC's good intentions save its measures from an Article 5.5 violation" (Hurst, David, Hormones: European Communities – Measures Affecting Meat and Meat Products, 9 *EJIL* (1998), p. 182) and is of the view that the Appellate Body transformed the analysis under SPS Article 5.5 "into an unprincipled inquiry into the intent of the Member imposing a measure."

40. Op. cit., paras. 178 and 240.

41. Op. cit., para. 166.

CHAPTER 11

Some Issues of the SPS Agreement

Mitsuo Matsushita

1. Applicable GATT/WTO Provisions in Cases Dealing with Food Safety Issues

In the GATT/WTO framework, the following are the main provisions of major agreements which may be applied to situations in which a national regulation for food safety is at issue. First, provisions of the SPS Agreement (Agreement on the Application of Sanitary and Phytosanitary Measures) are applicable. These are specifically designed to control sanitary and phytosanitary measures (SPS measures) enforced by Members. Secondly, Articles I, III and XX (b) of the GATT are applicable. Article I provides for the most-favored nation treatment (the MFN principle) and Article III provides for the national treatment. Article XX (b) provides for an exception to the prohibition of restrictions if a restriction in question is based on the protection of life and health of human beings, animals, and plants. Besides the above, Article XI, which prohibits quantitative restrictions of import and export trade exercised by Members, may apply if a measure in question restricts imports of foods, animals, and plants.

Among the above, however, provisions of the SPS Agreement seem to be the most relevant since the SPS Agreement is specifically designed to deal with issues of food safety and import. If there is a conflict between a provision of the GATT and a provision of the SPS Agreement, the latter prevails. If there is no conflict and both provisions overlap, presumably both apply. If there is no conflict and the coverage of both is different, both apply. However, provisions in the GATT as above mentioned are general in nature and provisions in the SPS Agreement are specific and much more detailed as regards food safety and import matter.

2. Provisions of the SPS Agreement

As stated in the Preamble of the SPS Agreement, provisions of this Agreement are an elaboration of Article XX (b) of the GATT 1994.

Coverage of the SPS Agreement

Article 1 states that this Agreement applies to all SPS measures which may, directly or indirectly, affect international trade. SPS measures to which the Agreement applies are, according to Annex A of the Agreement, measures (a) to protect human or animal life from risks arising from additives, contaminants, toxins or disease-causing organisms in their foods; (b) to protect human life from animal-carried diseases; (c) to protect animal or plant life from pests, diseases, or disease-causing organisms; (d) to prevent or limit other damage to a country from the entry, establishment or spread of pests.

Basic Rights and Obligations

Article 2 is entitled as "Basic Rights and Obligations" and contains the general principles of the Agreement. Article 2.1 provides that Members are entitled to take SPS measures necessary for the protection of human, animal or plant life or health provided that such measures are not inconsistent with the provisions of this Agreement. Article 2.2 states that any SPS measure shall be applied only to the extent necessary to protect human, animal or plant life or health, is based on scientific principles and is not maintained without sufficient scientific evidence. Article 2.3 provides that SPS measures shall not arbitrarily or unjustifiably discriminate between Members where identical or similar conditions prevail, including between their own territory and that of other Members. It also provides that such measures shall not be applied in a manner which would constitute a disguised restriction on international trade. Article 2.4 states that SPS measures which conform to provisions of the Agreement are presumed to be in accordance with provisions of the GATT 1994.

Provisions in Article 2 establish the general principles underlying the whole structure of this Agreement according to which provisions—especially those in Article 5 (referred to later)—of the Agreement should be interpreted.

Harmonization

Article 3 is concerned with harmonization of SPS measures among Members. For this purpose, this Article establishes three requirements.

Article 3.1 requires that Members shall base their SPS measures on international standards, guidelines, or recommendations if they exist except as otherwise provided for in Article 3.3 (referred to later). Article 3.2 provides that SPS measures which conform to international standards, guidelines or recommendations be presumed to be consistent with provisions of this Agreement and of the GATT 1994. In spite of Articles 3.1 and 3.2, however, Article 3.3 stipulates that Members may introduce and maintain

SPS measures which result in a higher level of sanitary or phytosanitary protection than measures based on the relevant international standards, guidelines or recommendation, if there is a scientific justification, or as a consequence of the level of sanitary or phytosanitary protection a member determines to be appropriate in accordance with the relevant provisions of paras. 1–8 of Article 5.

Assessment of Risk and Determination of the Appropriate Level of Sanitary or Phytosanitary Protection

Article 5 is the core provision in the SPS Agreement. It provides that a country which enforces a higher SPS standard than international standards must perform risk assessment to justify the higher SPS standard.

Article 5.1 states that SPS measures that Members enforce shall be based on an assessment of the risks to human, animal, or plant life or health. Article 5.2 stipulates that, in the assessment of risks, Members shall take into account available scientific evidence; relevant processes, and production methods; relevant inspection, sampling, and testing methods; prevalence of specific diseases or pests; existence of pest- or disease-free areas; relevant ecological and environmental conditions; and quarantine or other treatment.

Article 5.3 states that, in the risk assessment, a country shall take into account as relevant economic factors such as the potential damage in terms of loss of production or sales in the event of entry or spread of a pest or disease and the costs of control or eradication in the territory of the importing country.

Article 5.3 requires that, in risk assessment, each Member shall avoid arbitrary or unjustifiable distinctions in the levels it considers to be appropriate in different situations, if such distinctions result in discrimination or a disguised restriction on international trade.

Furthermore, Article 5.6 provides that Members shall ensure that SPS measures are not more trade-restrictive than required to achieve their appropriate level of sanitary or phytosanitary protection, taking into account technical and economic feasibility.

Lastly, Article 5.7 allows Members to take a precautionary measure. It states that, where relevant scientific evidence is insufficient, a Member may provisionally adopt SPS measures on the basis of available pertinent information, including that from the relevant international organizations as well as from SPS measures applied by other Members. However, it requires that, in such cases, Members shall seek to obtain the additional information necessary for a more objective assessment of risk and review the SPS measure accordingly within a reasonable period of time.

Relationship between the Provisions of the Agreement

A fundamental feature of the SPS Agreement is a compromise between the two propositions, i.e., the right of each Member to take its own SPS measures it sees appropriate and the requirement that Members conform to international SPS standards. If a measure conforms to the SPS Agreement, it is presumed to be consistent with the GATT 1994. If a measure conforms to international SPS standards, it is presumed to be consistent with the SPS Agreement and the GATT 1994.

What is the relationship between Article 2 and Article 5? As explained earlier, Article 2 provides for the general principles in respect of the enforcement of SPS measures by Members and Article 5 lays down specific requirements of risk assessments with regard to SPS measures. It seems that Article 2 is a larger circle and Article 5 is a smaller and concentric circle within that larger circle. Therefore, Article 5 is a subset of Article 2. In this sense, a measure which infringes Article 5 seems to infringe Article 2 as a matter of logical necessity.

Article 5.1 which provides that an SPS measure be based on a risk assessment corresponds to Article 2.2 which provides that an SPS measure be based on scientific principles and is not maintained without sufficient scientific evidence and for a part of it.

Article 5.2 provides that Members, in taking SPS measures, shall make sure that they take into account available scientific evidence and this seems to correspond to Article 2.2. This raises the question of whether or not "available scientific evidence" as provided in Article 5.2. is the same as "sufficient scientific evidence" as provided for in Article 2.2. It may be that "available" signifies merely a possibility of making use of a piece of evidence while "sufficient" means "enough" or "full." In this interpretation, even if a piece of evidence satisfies the requirement of Article 5.1, this may not satisfy that of Article 2.2.

Article 5.5 obligates Members to avoid arbitrary or unjustifiable distinction in the level it considers to be appropriate in different situations, if such distinctions result in discrimination or a disguised restriction on international trade. This seems to correspond to Article 2.3 which states that SPS measures be not discriminatory and arbitrary. In this regard, there may be a similar issue of whether the scope of Article 2.3 is wider than that of Article 5.5.

Article 5.6 requires that SPS measures be no more restrictive than necessary. This corresponds to Article 2.3. Here again, there may be a similar problem of whether or not the scope of Article 2.3 is wider than that of Article 5.6.

Considering that Article 2 provides the general principles whereas Article 5 stipulates specific application of the requirements of Article 2, there are items covered by Article 2 but not by Article 5. Therefore, it may be that Article 2 can provide an independent cause of action.

Lastly a question is whether or not a violation of Article 5.5 is independent from a violation of Article 5.6. Since Article 5.5 deals with "discrimination" contained in a measure whereas Article 5.6 is concerned with "excessiveness" of a measure, they deal with different subject matters and a violation of one does not necessarily establish a violation of the other.

3. Steps of Analysis in SPS Cases

The above description of the relevant provisions of the SPS Agreement suggests that the following steps be taken in analyzing the factors involved in the case.

The first step is to inquire whether the measure in question (the measure) is based on international standards (Articles 3.1 and 3.2). If the measure is based on international standards, the compatibility of the measure with the GATT 1994 and the SPS Agreement is presumed. The party challenging the measure must bear the burden of proving that the presumption is overturned.

Secondly, if the measure is not based on international standards, the question is whether it can be scientifically justified (Articles 3.3 and 5.1-5.8). In connection with this, it should be examined whether a risk assessment was performed in respect of the measure (Articles 5.1., para. 4 of Annex A).

Thirdly, if a proper risk assessment is performed and the measure is justified, it should be examined whether the measure amounts to arbitrary or unjustifiable distinctions relating to the level of protection (Art. 2.3 and 5.5).

Lastly, if the above requirements are satisfied, we need to examine whether the measure is excessive or not.

Only once all of the above requirements are satisfied, the measure is justified under the SPS Agreement.

There have been three decisions of the DSB regarding issues of SPS measures. These are the *EC Hormones* case,[1] the *Australian Salmon* case,[2] and the *Japan Varietals* case (the *Apples* case).[3] In the following pages, an analysis will be made from the standpoint of how, under the current interpretations and precedents, a Panel and the Appellate Body "will" decide the case as opposed to how they "should" decide it, i.e., our inquiry is to determine "what is law" rather than "what ought to be law." Although an academic or a lawyer can construct his/her interpretation of a provision of a WTO agreement different from that made by Panels and the Appellate Body and claim that this is the right interpretation, it is Panels and the Appellate Body which are empowered to rule on a case. Although the WTO Ministering Conference and the General Council are authorized to adopt an official interpretation of a provision of a WTO agreement,[4] this seldom happens. We can, therefore, safely say that precedents established by Panels and the Appellate Body provide legal certainty and predictability.

Although past rulings of Panels and the Appellate Body are not binding on subsequent Panels and the Appellate Body in disposing of cases, they serve as valuable guidance for them and, in fact, Panels and the Appellate Body make every efforts to follow the precedents when disposing of a case.

4. A Hypothetical SPS Case

Arimania's Measure

Let us take up a hypo and see how provisions of the SPS Agreement are applied to SPS cases. The essential facts of our hypo are as follows (see Appendix).

(a) Article 1 of the legislation in Arimania, an imaginary Member of WTO, prohibits all sales of food consumption of ducks and duck meat products treated with growth hormones in the territory of Arimania. (b) Article 2 states that the sales ban is not discriminatory. (c) An unofficial document is presented which is signed by an authority on DDD (Prof. Dr. Dr. h.c. Helmut von Entefleisch) according to whom DDD is a mere fiction. (d) A report of the government Institute for Public Health in Arimania explains in a very systematic manner why DDD can be dangerous and even deadly if certain conditions are met and the fact that the domestic Industry Watch points out that only 88.12% of the domestic production is hormone-free. (e) The report of "Free your mind," a neutral institution, requested by the government of Karponia to examine the issue states that there is no danger at all from eating hormone-treated duck meat, DDD belongs to the past and a person consuming at least 3 kilograms of duck meat daily for an uninterrupted five years has a less than 2 % chance to incur fever for a week.

Thus Karponia challenges the measure of the government of Arimania and a petition is filed with the Dispute Settlement Body of the WTO. The DSB established a Panel which made its findings and an appeal was taken to the Appellate Body.

Analysis of the Case

De Facto *Discrimination and* De Jure *Discrimination*

Under the SPS Agreement, an SPS measure is judged according to whether it complies with the requirements of the Agreement as above described. Generally, a measure is judged according to whether: (a) it is based on international standards, (b) if not, it is based on a proper risk assessment, (c) if yes, it is not discriminatory or arbitrary nor constitutes a disguised restriction of trade, and (d) it is not excessive.

Such an examination is made according to Article 2.3 and Article 5.5 of the SPS Agreement. Article 2.3 requires that Members ensure that their SPS measures do not arbitrarily or unjustifiably discriminate between Members where identical or similar conditions prevail. Article 5.5 requires that each Member shall avoid arbitrary or unjustifiable distinctions in the levels it considers to be appropriate in different situations, if such distinctions result in discrimination or a disguised restriction on international trade. The role of a Panel and the Appellate Body in interpreting Articles 2.3 and 5.5 of the SPS Agreement is not to take a pro-deference or anti-deference attitude but to make an objective assessment of facts and to seek to find the correct interpretation of the provisions.

Are All Cases of De Facto *Discrimination Punishable?*

To determine that an SPS measure constitutes a *de facto* discrimination, Article 5.5 of the SPS Agreement indicates that three constituent elements be established, i.e., (a) the Member imposing the measure in question has adopted its own appropriate levels of sanitary protection against risks to human life or health in several different situations, (b) those levels of protection are arbitrary or unjustifiable in their treatment of different situations, and (c) the arbitrary or unjustifiable differences result in discrimination or a disguised restriction of international trade.

When a Panel assesses facts involved to determine whether the SPS measure in question is arbitrary or unjustifiable and results in discrimination or a disguised restriction of international trade, an analysis of quantitative as well as qualitative factors is necessary to make a proper comparison between the difference levels of protection. A *de minimus* difference in treatment, for example, may not constitute a violation of Article 5.5.

In the *Hormones* case, the Appellate Body stated that the fact that the European Communities banned the use of hormones in raising cattle for the production of meat while it did not take any measure regarding endogenous hormones in some foods such as eggs, meat, and broccoli did not amount to an unjustifiable discrimination. It decided, however, that the fact that it banned the use of hormones in raising cattle for meat while allowing calbadox (a chemical substance used to raise swine which is carcinogenic) to be used in the swine industry constituted an unjustifiable discrimination. Involved in this case was a total ban applied to hormone-treated beef as opposed to an unlimited allowance given to pork meat in which calbadox is used. This seems to suggest that, if the difference in those two situations is not as extreme as it is in this case, there may have been a room for a different conclusion.

In the *Hormones* case, one of the issues was whether the European Communities was in violation of Article 5.5 of the SPS Agreement by banning the use of hormones in raising cattle and the import of hormone-treated meat (absolute prohibition) while taking no measure with respect to calbadox used to raise swine (unlimited allowance) although both substances were regarded as carcinogenic. The Appellate Body stated in its report that this difference in the level of protection with regard to hormones was unjustifiable. In reaching this conclusion, the Appellate Body weighed qualitative and quantitative factors surrounding this case.

As shown by the Panel and the Appellate Body in the *Hormones* case, a determination of whether an SPS measure amounts to a violation of Article 5.5 requires a close examination of the facts in each case on a case-by-case basis. It is clear that such a determination of whether an SPS measure is in conformity with Article 5.5 is made not in abstract but in the context of particular factual situations of each case.

The assumption in our hypo is that the use of hormones is prohibited in Arimania to combat DDD and an import is also banned. Superficially, there is no discrimination with regard to the domestic use of hormones and the prohibition of import of meat treated with hormones. In both situations, the prohibition applies. The fact that DDD is contracted by being close to ducks and Arimania takes no action against this possibility does not seem to be an unjustifiable discrimination. It is true that Arimania establishes different levels of protection in two similar situations, i.e., the total ban in hormone-treated duck meat and the unlimited permission of being close to ducks. However, there is no reason to assume, without more evidence, that this distinction between one level of protection and the other level of protection has the effect of discriminating between different situations. The Appellate Body finding in this regard is relevant.

In the *Hormones* case, the Panel found that the European Communities violated Article 5.5 of the SPS Agreement by banning the use of hormones in raising cattle while taking no measure in respect to endogenous hormones in foods such as eggs and broccoli and thereby establishing an unjustifiable difference in the level of protection. The Appellate Body reversed this finding by stating that there was a fundamental distinction between added hormones and naturally occurring hormones and the prohibition of naturally occurring hormones would amount to an excessive intervention into the process of nature and ordinary course of human life. This situation involved in our hypo is somewhat akin to, although not exactly the same as, the situation involving the distinction between added hormones and naturally occurring hormones. To require the population of Arimania by law to stay away from ducks altogether seems to be too much of an interventionist approach and amounts to absurdity. Even if feeding ducks is responsible for 82% of all DDD casualties, a legal requirement of not feeding ducks is extra-ordinary. In this type of situation, perhaps warnings issued by the government are more appropriate.

Seriousness of Externality

When a Member of the WTO imposes an SPS measure of which the standard is higher than those established in international standards, the Member must conduct a risk assessment to determine whether that measure can be justified on the basis of scientific evidence. Generally, a risk assessment is a matter of science, i.e., a scientific determination of whether, for example, a substance causes hazard to life and health of humans, animals or plants.

However, often scientists and medical doctors differ from each other as to the question of whether or not a certain kind of substance is risky or safe when used in foods. There may be conflicting pieces of scientific evidence regarding the question of whether the substance causes risk to life or health and, when it causes risk to life or health, to what extent. When faced with conflicting pieces of evidence as regards risk involved in the consumption of a certain kind of food, the government of a Member must choose the majority, the minority or, under some circumstances, just one scientific opinion in adopting an SPS measure. If a dispute arises under the SPS Agreement with regard to this measure, a Panel and the Appellate Body must decide whether the measure is based on a proper risk assessment.

There is a distinction between issues of protecting the life and health of humans and those of animals and plants. Article 5.3 of the SPS Agreement states that, in assessing the risk to animal or plant life or health and determining the measure to be applied for achieving the appropriate level of sanitary or phytosanitary protection from such risk, Members shall take into consideration economic factors such as, for example, the costs of control or eradication and the relative cost-effectiveness of alternative approaches to limiting risks.

As shown in the above provision, economic and cost factors are relevant in risk assessment when it comes to the protection of life and health of animals and plants. There is no similar provision regarding the life and health of humans. It seems to follow from this that, when it comes to the matter of human life and health, Members need not take into account cost-efficiency factors of the protective measures. Members can enforce an SPS measure as long as it is scientifically justified.

In the *Hormones* case, the Appellate Body stated that, although in most cases governments tend to base their legislative and administrative measures on mainstream scientific opinion, a divergent opinion can be relied on as a basis of risk assessment. The Appellate Body states that a divergent and minority opinion can be relied on "especially where the risk involved is life-threatening in character and is perceived to constitute a clear and imminent threat to public health and safety."

The above statement seems to suggest that, in evaluating risk assessment conducted by the government of a Member, a minority view or even the view of one scientist among many can play an important role when the subject matter being examined relates to "life-threatening" situations. This would mean that the seriousness of externality surrounding the case at hand affects a determination of whether a risk assessment is appropriate.

In our situation, the question of whether DDD is deadly or simply causing slight fever should affect the decision of a Panel and the Appellate Body when reviewing the appropriateness of risk assessment. If DDD is deadly, even a minority view or a single view regarding the dangerousness may play a decisive role in upholding the SPS measure in question.

However, if a substance is deadly, there should be consistency in prohibiting the use of it. For example, if the government of a Member entirely prohibits the use of a substance which is determined to be risky when it is used in one type of food, it should prohibit the use of it in all other types of food. Therefore, if the government of a Member prohibits the use of hormones in ducks while taking no measure against the use of it in beef, this constitutes an infringement of Article 5.5 of the SPS Agreement as discussed already.

Risk Assessment

Article 5.3 of the SPS Agreement requires that a Member conduct a risk assessment to support an SPS measure it takes when that measure establishes a higher standard of protection. When a Panel examines whether a SPS measure of a Member is based on a proper risk assessment, it often faces the situation in which pieces of scientific evidence in regard to the risk in question is indecisive. There may be majority and minority views on the subject matter and, in some cases, views may be equally divided.

Article 13 of the Dispute Settlement Understanding confers a wide range of power to Panels in deciding which evidence to accept and base its decision on. In case of conflict of views regarding the appropriateness of an SPS measure, it is the power of a Panel to choose among conflicting pieces of evidence and decide the case as long as it stays in the scope of objective assessment of facts as provided for in Article 11 of the DSU. Panels have to decide the case on a case-by-case basis and there is no abstract rule to decide whether a majority or minority view should be accepted. Factors such as the craftsmanship of the report and the reputation of the research institute have to be taken into account and be weighed together. There is no pre-judged criterion to determine what factors should be relied upon when considering which scientific view should prevail.

The nationality of a research institute is not necessarily a reason for accepting or rejecting the report. Even a report published by a scientific institute of the Member of which an SPS measure is being challenged or of the Member which challenges the SPS measure may provide a basis for Panels' judgment as long as that institute's neutrality is established.

Precautionary Principle

Article 5.7 of the SPS Agreement recognizes the precautionary principle according to which Members may provisionally adopt SPS measures in cases where relevant scientific evidence is insufficient. Therefore, Members can rely on this provision and impose an SPS measure even in the absence of sufficient scientific evidence. However, Article 5.7 suggests that a precautionary measure can be applied only on the basis of this provision and it should meet the requirements of this provision.

The second sentence of Article 5.7 states that Members shall seek to obtain the additional information necessary for more objective assessment of risk and review the SPS measure accordingly within a reasonable period of time.

When the result of risk assessment conducted by a Member shows that there is a sharp division of views regarding the risk involved in the use of a substance, that Member can rely on Article 5.7 and apply an SPS measure provisionally even if the scientific evidence available is insufficient. It is, of course, incumbent upon that Member to seek to obtain the additional information and review the measure within a reasonable period of time.

Democratic Legitimacy and Political Acceptability

Although it is true that WTO bodies are not based on representation of national constituencies, the Ministerial Conference and the Council of the WTO are represented by the governments of all Members and decisions are made by consensus. Therefore, voices of Members are deemed to be reflected in decisions of WTO bodies including the Dispute Settlement Body. As far as SPS measures are concerned, it is the SPS Agreement which reflects the wills and intentions of the Members of the WTO. Panels and the Appellate Body operate on the basis of the confidence bestowed on them by Members to implement this Agreement. It is, therefore, the duty of Panels and of the Appellate Body to interpret provisions of the SPS Agreement as they are written and put them into effect.[5]

In light of the above principle, Panels and the Appellate Body should not make their findings on the "political" basis of whether it is a political view of a national constituency or an international community. They owe their allegiance only to WTO agreements which they are charged to interpret and apply.

Evidence from Other Constituency

Article 5.1 of the SPS Agreement requires that an SPS measure of a Member be based on risk assessment when it establishes a higher standard of protection than those established in international standards. The question here is the meaning of "based on." In the *Hormones* case, the Panel held that the meaning of "based on" is the same as "conform to" and a Member enforcing an SPS measure should conduct its own risk assessment and should come up with sufficient scientific evidence to support the proposition that the measure in question conforms to the result of risk assessment.

The Appellate Body reversed this finding and held that risk assessment can be interpreted more broadly. The meaning of "based on" can be a situation where the measure in question is wholly or partly backed up by risk assessment and the risk assessment does not necessarily have to be the result of scientific research of that Member. If, for example, an SPS measure imposed by a Member can be backed up by scientific evidence established by an institute in another country, it should be sufficient as long as this evidence is good enough to support the measure in question.

It seems to be reasonable to argue that an SPS measure enforced by a Member needs only to be supported by sufficient scientific evidence which exists somewhere. Risk assessment does not necessarily have to be conducted by the Member enforcing the measure. All that is required is that the measure has sufficient scientific basis. However, it may be true that a substance used in foodstuff which causes hazard to life and health of humans in one state may not cause the same hazard in another state or, even if it causes a similar hazard, the degree of seriousness is much smaller. This may be because of the difference in dietary habits and climatic conditions. Therefore, the fact that there is evidence of hazard to human life or health caused by a substance in one state cannot automatically be transplanted to another state in order to support the proposition that the same hazard exists there, too. Conversely, the fact that there is no hazard caused by a substance when used in foodstuff in one state does not automatically guarantee that there is no risk of that substance in another state.

5. A Note on Article XX (b) of GATT 1994—The *Asbestos* Case

Article XX (b) of GATT 1994 provides for an exception to prohibitions of GATT 1994 if a measure under challenge is necessary to protect human life and health. In the recent *Asbestos* case,[6] the issue was whether this exception applied to a French measure prohibiting the sale and import of asbestos for the reason of protecting human life and health. The Panel which dealt with this issue made a ruling which granted an exception to this French measure under Article XX (b). An appeal was taken to the Appellate Body by the appellant, Canada. At the time of writing this paper, the Appellate ruling has not come yet. Although involved in this case was the issue of product safety rather than food safety, the ruling of the Panel has some implications for food safety issues. Therefore, a brief analysis of this case is made below.

An Outline of the Case

The issues involved in this case are whether a French measure prohibiting the sale and import of asbestos: (a) amounts to a measure which is covered by the Agreement on Technical Barriers to Trade (TBT Agreement), (b) falls under Article III: 4 of GATT 1994, and (c) constitutes a nullification and impairment of the benefit of tariff concessions under GATT. The Panel ruled that the French measure: (a) did not amount to a measure under the TBT Agreement except for some situations provided for in the Decree in which limited uses of asbestos were permitted, (b) fell under the prohibition of Article III: 4 of the GATT 1994, (c) fell under the exception as provided for in Article XX (b) of GATT 1994, and (d) did not amount to a nullification and impairment under Article XXIII (b) of GATT 1994. Although every issue is an important one, only the item (c) is examined below.

The French Measure in Question and the Panel's Findings

Involved in this case was a French decree which prohibited the sale and importation of asbestos. This was Decree No. 96-1133 of 24 December 1996, issued by the Prime Minister of the Government of the French Republic, which banned asbestos, implemented pursuant to the Labor Code and the Consumer Code (hereafter it is referred to as "Decree"). Article 1 of the Decree prohibited, among others, the manufacture, processing, sale, and import of all varieties of asbestos fibers regardless of whether these substances have been incorporated into materials, products or devices and any product containing asbestos fibers. Article 2 provided for an exception, under strictly confined circumstances, to certain existing materials containing chrysotile fiber when no substitute for that fiber is available.

Canada brought a petition to the Dispute Settlement Body of WTO alleging that the Decree was in violation of Article 2 of the TBT Agreement and Articles XI and III:4 of GATT 1994. It further alleged that, if the Decree was not in violation of the above articles, still Article XXIII:1 (b) of GATT 1994 (non-violation claim) applied.

The Panel found that the Decree was not covered by the TBT Agreement, except for the aspect of it which dealt with exceptions, for the reason that the Decree prohibited asbestos fibers at all stages and did not specify the characteristics, the processes of production methods for asbestos fibers and asbestos-containing products in accordance with Annex 1 Article 1 of the TBT Agreement. Canada did not bring a claim regarding the aspect of the Decree which related to the exceptions. The Panel found that asbestos and products containing asbestos on the one hand and their substitutes on the other were like products and the Decree did not accord treatment to asbestos and products containing it no less favorable than the treatment accorded to substitutes and, therefore, constituted a violation of Article III of GATT 1994 which provides for the national treatment for like products in respect of laws, regulations, and other measures.

EC, the respondent, invoked Article XX (b) and claimed that the Decree fell under the exception provided for in that article.

General Principles of Article XX (b) of GATT 1994

The Panel notes that, considering the ruling of the Appellate Body regarding the burden of proof on exceptions in Article XX of GATT 1994 in *United States-Reformulated Gasoline,*[7] EC, which invokes, bears the burden of proving that: (a) the policy in respect of the measures for which Article XX is invoked falls within the range of policies designed to protect human life or health and (b) the inconsistent measures for which the exception is invoked are necessary to fulfill the policy objective.

With respect to (a) above, the Panel states that the words "policies designed to protect human life or health" imply the existence of a health risk and the question is whether chrysotile asbestos poses a risk to human life or health. On (b) above, the Panel notes that the assessment as to whether the measure in question is necessary should be based on whether there is any other measure consistent with provisions of GATT 1994 or less inconsistent with them.

Application of Article XX (b) of GATT 1994 to the Decree

EC argued that, in prohibiting the placing on the market and use of asbestos and products containing it, the Decree seeks to stop the spread of the risks to human life and health due to asbestos and thereby reduce the number of deaths due to exposure to asbestos fibers among the French population. The Panel notes that the carcinogenicity of chrysotile fibers has been acknowledged for some time by international bodies, carcinogenicity was confirmed by exports consulted by the Panel and that there is sufficient scientific evidence to show that there is a serious carcinogenic risk associated with the inhalation of chrysotile fibers.

For the above reasons, the Panel concluded that EC has made a *prima facie* case for the existence of a health risk in connection with the use of chrysotile asbestos and this *prima facie* case has not been rebutted by Canada. Therefore, according to the Panel, EC has shown that the policy of prohibiting chrysotile asbestos implemented by the Decree falls within the range of policies designed to protect human life or health and satisfies one of the requirements for the exception under Article XX (b) of GATT 1994.

Necessary

The Panel cites the Panel Report in *Thailand-Tobacco*[8] which defined the test of necessity under Article XX (b) as a situation in which there is no alternative measure consistent with GATT or less inconsistent with it to employ to achieve its health policy objectives. In the context of the case before the Panel, the question is whether controlled use of the products in question is sufficiently effective in the light of France's health policy objectives and whether it constitutes a reasonably available measure. Canada argued that, if asbestos are used in controlled circumstances, i.e., for example, in the form of encapsulation in cement products etc., its hazard can be effectively controlled and this constitutes an alternative which is consistent with provisions of GATT or less inconsistent with it. On this issue, the Panel, after taking into consideration pieces of evidence produced to the Panel, states that, in view of the difficulties of application of controlled use, an official in charge of public health policy might reasonably consider that controlled use did not provide protection that was adequate in relation to the policy objective and that controlled use based on international standards would not seem to make it possible to achieve the level of protection sought by France.

The Panel concludes that, in the light of France's public health objectives as presented by EC, the latter has made a *prima facie* case for the non-existence of a reasonably available alternative to the banning of chrysotile and chrysotile cement products and recourse to substitute products, that Canada has not rebutted the presumption established by EC and that the decree satisfies the conditions of Article XX (b) of GATT 1994.

Introductory Clause (Chapeau) of Article XX of GATT 1994

Chapeau of Article XX of GATT requires that, even if a measure satisfies the requirement for exception under (b), it does not amount to (i) means of arbitrary or unjustifiable discrimination between countries where the same conditions prevail or (ii) disguised restriction on international trade.

Regarding the question of whether the Decree is a means of arbitrary or unjustifiable discrimination between countries where the same conditions prevail, the Panel points out that the word "discrimination" in the chapeau covers both discrimination between products coming from different supplier countries and discrimination between domestic and imported products. It also points out that the word “discrimination” in the chapeau cannot logically refer to discrimination as envisaged in Article III by which a violation of a substantive rule can be demonstrated since, if otherwise, the exception in Article XX (b) would be rendered meaningless. Therefore, the less favorable treatment of asbestos as compared with substitute fibers identified by Canada is not relevant for establishing the existence of discrimination under Article XX. Therefore, the question is limited to discrimination between suppliers of asbestos, between domestic and foreign countries or between a foreign country and other foreign countries.

The Panel says that, as argued by EC, the Decree covers products originating in any country, including France, where the same conditions prevail and the text of the Decree confirms this. In the Decree, only the product in question is mentioned, without any reference to its origin. The Panel concludes that EC has made a *prima facie* case for its argument that the Decree does not constitute, in its application, arbitrary or unjustifiable discrimination and that Canada has not rebutted the presumption established by the *prima facie* case made by EC, according to which the Decree does not introduce discrimination.

The final question of the chapeau is whether the Decree is a disguised restriction on international trade. On this, the Panel cites a few words from *United States –Reformulated Gasoline* ("that concealed or unannounced restriction . . . in international trade does not exhaust the meaning of 'disguised restriction' ") and states that a measure which is unpublished does not satisfy this second requirement of the chapeau. The Panel further notes that the Decree was published in the Official Journal of the French Republic on 26 December 1996 entering into force on 1 January 1997 and that the Decree applies unequivocally to international trade, since as far as asbestos is concerned both importation and exportation are prohibited.

The Panel also states that the core of the concept of "disguised restriction" is "disguised" rather than "restriction" and that, in deciding whether a measure amounts to a disguised restriction, the kinds of considerations pertinent in deciding whether the application of a particular measure amounts to "arbitrary or unjustifiable" may also be taken into account. Since the Panel has not found any discrimination, it considers that it is unnecessary to determine whether there is a discrimination that amounts to a disguised restriction on international trade.

The Panel notes that there is always the possibility that measures such as those contained in the Decree might have the effect of favoring the domestic substitute product manufacturers and that this is a natural consequence of prohibiting a given product and in itself cannot justify the conclusion that the measure has a protectionist aim, as long as it remains within certain limits. It mentions that the information made available to it does not suggest that the import ban has benefited the French substitute fiber industry to the detriment of third country producers, to such an extent as to lead to the conclusion that the Decree has been so applied as to constitute a disguised restriction on international trade.

Comments on the Asbestos Case

As mentioned earlier, the Preamble of the SPS Agreement declares that Members desire "to elaborate rules for the application of the provisions of GATT 1994 which relate to the use of sanitary or phytosanitary measures, in particular the provisions of Article XX (b) . . ." From this, it follows that the SPS Agreement is an implementation of Article XX (b). There is a sharp contrast between this and the TBT Agreement in which there is no similar provision. Therefore, Article XX (b) and the SPS Agreement should be regarded as constituting one package of rules and be read together.[9] In fact, provisions of the SPS Agreement should be regarded as part of Article XX (b). In the *Asbestos* case, the Panel rejected the claim of Canada that provisions of the TBT Agreement should apply and instead applied Article XX (b) of GATT 1994. If a claim for application of the SPS Agreement is raised together with Article XX (b), a similar rejection of a Panel to apply the SPS Agreement is problematic.

Article XX (b) has been invoked several times but, in the past, Panels denied the granting of exception due to the fact that the measure in question either did not fall within one of the categories for exception or did not satisfy the requirements of the chapeau. The *Asbestos* case is the first one in which the Panel granted exception from the prohibition of Article III of GATT 1994 on account of Article XX (b).

The Necessity Test

In *Thailand-Tobacco,*[10] Thailand argued that the ban imposed on U.S.-made tobacco due to the fact that some hazardous additives were incorporated in it fell under Article XX (b) of GATT 1994. The Panel recognized that smoking caused risk to human health and efforts to reduce smoking fell under Article XX (b). The Panel stated that Article XX (b) recognized that the importance of protecting human health outweighed the benefit of free trade. However, the Panel did not grant exception because, in its judgment, the ban did not satisfy the requirement of necessity. Likewise, in *United States-Tuna/Dolphin,*[11] the Panel ruled that the U.S. measure to protect dolphins fell under Article XX (b) but did not satisfy the requirement of necessity. In *United States-Reformulated Gasoline*, the U.S. government argued that the measure to control the quality of gasoline which was designed to control air pollution by harmful emission from automobiles amounted to Article XX (b). The Panel stated that this measure fell under Article XX (b) but did not satisfy the requirement of necessity. In contrast, the Appellate Body in this case held that the U.S. measure fell under Article XX (g) but did not satisfy the requirements of the chapeau.

As seen above, the previous Panels which dealt with the question of applicability of Article XX (b) held that, although the measures in question would be given exception under (b), the total exception from the prohibition of GATT 1994 was denied due to the fact that Panels ruled that the measures in question did not satisfy the requirement of necessity.[12]

In the *Asbestos* case, the Panel ruled that the French measure mustered the test of necessity. Does this Panel modify the necessity test that was enunciated by the previous Panel? It seems that there is difference between the factual situation surrounding this case and those specific to the previous cases. In the previous cases, the measure in question could have been replaced by a less restrictive measure. For example, in *Thailand-Tobacco*, the import ban could have been replaced by requiring certain kinds of labeling or representation of product contents. In *Tuna-Dolphin*, the United States government could have negotiated with other governments so that those governments could take a measure similar to that of the United States to protect dolphins and accomplished the object of the measure without any unilateral imposition of import ban.

Compared with the previous cases, the *Asbestos* case seems to represent the situation in which the only alternative method of protecting human health from the hazard of asbestos was a controlled use of it. However, there was sufficient scientific evidence that the controlled use of asbestos did not accomplish the objective of totally protecting human health from harms of asbestos. It seems, therefore, the distinction between the ruling of the Panel in the *Asbestos* case and the rulings of Panels in other cases come from differences of factual conditions. There seems to be no fundamental change in the interpretation of the necessity test.

Arbitrary or Unjustifiable Discrimination and Disguised Restriction

Chapeau of Article XX requires that a measure which falls under one of the categories for exception be not (a) arbitrary or unjustifiable or (b) disguised restriction of trade. The relationship between (a) and (b) remains unclear. In *United States-Reformulated Gasoline*, the Appellate Body stated that (a) and (b) impart meanings to each other. It seems that the areas of coverage of those two do not entirely overlap but these two are closely related to each other. In fact, often disguised restrictions involve some forms of discrimination.

In *United States-Imports of Tuna*,[13] the issue was an import restriction imposed by the United States on tuna and tuna products. The Panel stated that the U.S. measure fell under Article XX (d) of GATT 1947 and that, since this measure was applied to products not only from Canada but also from Costa Rica, Ecuador, Mexico and Peru, it was not arbitrary or unjustifiable discrimination. Similarly in *United States-Auto Springs*,[14] the Panel held that the United States measure was not discriminatory since it applied to all import of the product in question. In the *Asbestos* case, the Panel disposed of the issue of whether the French Decree was arbitrary or unjustifiable or disguised restriction of trade simply by stating that the Decree was not discriminatory and there was no counter-proof to this.

With regard to disguised restriction of trade, the Panel in the *Asbestos* case ruled that the French Decree did not amount to that for the reason that it was published in the form of a decree. In making this ruling, the Panel followed the precedent in *United States-Tuna/Dolphin*[15] in which a similar ruling was handed down. However, it may be too simplistic to state that the disclosure and publication of a decree automatically qualifies it to be not a disguised restriction of trade. There may be a situation in which a published decree operates as a hidden restriction of trade. For example, a published law or regulation of a state may require that a product contain certain substances in order for this product to be given a permission for industrial uses. But the industry in that state may have an overwhelming competitiveness in this product compared with substitutes in which industries in other states enjoy a higher level of competitiveness. This kind of published regulation may have a hidden effect and/or purpose of restricting trade and thereby excluding substitutes from the domestic market in order to protect a domestic industry. Therefore, a functional approach in which Panels examine actual functions of products to each conclusion seems to be more reasonable.

NOTES

1. EC-Measures Concerning Meat and Meat Products (Hormones), Report of the Panel, WT/DS26/R/U.S.A, 18 August 1997; Report of the Appellate Body, AB-1997-4, WT/DS26/AB/R, WT/DS48/AB/R, 16 January 1998.

2. Australia-Measures Affecting Importation of Salmons, Report of the Panel, WT/DS18/R, 12 June 1998; Report of the Appellate Body, AB-1998-5, WT/DS18/AB/R, 20 October 1998.

3. Japan-Measures Affecting Agricultural Product, Report of the Panel, WT/DS76/R, 27 October 1998; Report of the Appellate Body, AB-1998-8, WT/DSD76/AB/R, 22 February 1999.

4. Article IX:2 of the Marrakesh Agreement Establishing the World Trade Organization states: "The Ministerial Conference and the General Council shall have the exclusive authority to adopt interpretations of this Agreement and of the Multilateral Trade Agreements."

5. Article 31 of the Vienna Convention states that a treaty interpreter shall interpret a provision of a treaty in accordance with the ordinary meaning of the word of the treaty, its context, and its objective.

6. European Communities-Measures Affecting Asbestos and Asbestos-Containing Products, WT/DS/35/R, 18 September 2000.

7. United States-Standards for Reformulated and Conventional Gasoline, Appellate Body and Panel Report, adopted on 20 May 1996, WT/DSD2/9.

8. Thailand-Restrictions on Importation of and Internal Taxes on Cigarettes, adopted on 7 November 1990, BISD 37S/200.

9. See Brazil-Measure Affecting Desiccated Coconut, Report of the Panel, WT/DS22/R, 17 October 1996; Report of the Appellate Body, AB-1996-4, WT/DS22/AB/R, 21 February 1997. In this case, the Appellate Body stated that Article VI of GATT 1994 (on subsidies and countervailing duties) and the SCM Agreement (The Agreement on Subsidies and Countervailing Measures) are inseparable and constitute one package of rules.

10. See note 8, supra.

11. United States-Restrictions on Import of Tuna, circulated on 3 September 1991, not adopted, BISD 359/155; United States-Restrictions on Imports of Tuna, circulated on 15 June, not adopted, DS29/R.

12. On the necessity test in regard of Article XX (d), see United States-Section 337 of the Tariff Act of 1930, adopted on 7 November 1989, BISD 36S/345.

13. United States-Prohibition of Imports of Tuna and Tuna Products from Canada, adopted on 22 February 1982, BISD 29S/108.

14. United States-Imports of Certain Automotive Spring Assembles, adopted on 26 May 1983, BISD 30S/107.

15. See note 11, supra.

CHAPTER 12

Comment on the "WTO Response"

Steve Charnovitz

Thank you for the opportunity to comment on the excellent papers by Joost Pauwelyn and Mitsuo Matsushita. This is my first opportunity to meet Mr. Pauwelyn whom I have considered (based on his significant scholarship) to be among the most thoughtful of the new generation of WTO law analysts. I want to highlight some areas of agreement and disagreement between the two papers, and offer a few comments of my own.

1. GATT vs. SPS

Professor Matsushita characterizes the SPS provisions as more specific and detailed than those of the GATT, and suggests that it should be sufficient to examine the hypothetical under SPS rules. Mr. Pauwelyn contends that the SPS Agreement "gives complete pre-eminence to health over trade," and that this SPS approach may be quite novel in the WTO legal system. He contrasts SPS with GATT Article XX which he says states a "not more trade-restrictive than necessary test" that could lead a Panel to balance trade versus health under GATT (but not under SPS).

Neither author evaluates the hypothetical under GATT rules, so let me try to do so. A ban on the *sale* of ducks treated with growth hormones ought not to be a violation of GATT Article III:2, and hence should be GATT-consistent. Nevertheless, one can imagine a Panel finding a national treatment violation on the grounds that all ducks are "like" products regardless of their health effects on consumers. Were that to happen, then the defendant country should be able to justify the measure as necessary to protect human health under Article XX(b). In considering Article XX(b), I assume that the Panel would apply a least-GATT-inconsistent test and not a least-trade-restrictive test. Although these tests are commonly confused, they are not synonymous and can lead to different results. The idea of a least trade-restrictive test goes back at least as early as the Abolition Convention of 1927. But despite its influence in the case law of the European Community, this test has never been adopted and applied by a GATT or WTO Panel as of the end of 2000. So I do not necessarily agree with Joost Pauwelyn that the GATT presupposes more balancing between health and commerce than does SPS.

Even if the measure passes GATT review, it could be challenged under SPS, as both authors note. This procedural posture suggests that it would be adequate to analyze a disputed health measure under SPS, while omitting a similar review under the GATT. Unless there is an international standard involved, it is hard to conceive of a situation where a measure would be consistent with SPS but inconsistent with the GATT.

Let me also note that I am not in complete agreement with Joost Pauwelyn's interesting observation that the SPS Agreement "gives complete pre-eminence to health over trade." For unlike the GATT, the SPS Agreement does have a least-trade-restrictive principle in SPS Article 5.6. Of course, the text of this provision appears to be deferential to the choices of a government on its "level of sanitary or phytosanitary protection." How that provision will be applied in tough cases remains to be seen. In my view, the implementation of SPS Article 5.5 by WTO Panels (particularly Salmon) has not accorded complete pre-eminence to health over trade.[1] Rather, it has favored commerce and some notional idea of policy consistency over health concerns. (See further discussion below.)

Finally, in Professor Matsushita's paper, he says that as stated in the Preamble of the SPS Agreement, the SPS provisions are an elaboration of Article XX(b) of GATT. It is true that the SPS Preamble says this. Nevertheless, in my view, giving any effect to these inartfully written words by WTO Panels will simply lead to mischief. For example, these words might be read as narrowing the scope of Article XX(b).

2. Adequacy of Risk Assessment

Professor Matsushita seems to accept the risk assessment as sufficient, but Mr. Pauwelyn expresses the concern that the assessment may not be specific enough to the situation of growth hormones in ducks. We probably don't have enough information to know for sure.

3. SPS Science Requirement

On the moot case (see Appendix), Mr. Pauwelyn suggests that even a minority scientific opinion, such as the one by Dr. von Entefleisch, could satisfy the quantum of evidence required. But he also notes that this determination depends on a case-by-case examination. Professor Matsushita takes greater note of the distinction between the SPS requirements in Articles 2.2 and 5.1, and points out that science evidence may be sufficient for Article 5.1 but not for Article 2.2. He also makes the important observation that Article 2 can provide an independent cause of action. Furthermore, he underlines that "[i]t is the power of a Panel to choose among conflicting pieces of evidence and decide the case as long as it stays in the scope of objective assessment."[2]

I do not doubt that Panels will do this type of choosing (if they haven't already), and the Appellate Body may have done so in the *Hormones* case in rejecting Dr. Lucier's concerns about the one-in-a-million risk for women of getting breast cancer. The SPS Agreement seems to suggest such a vetting process in the requirement of "adequate" scientific evidence (Article 2.2) and in making available scientific expertise to the Panel (Article 11.2). This dimension of the gatekeeper role of the WTO Panelists will be explored further in future cases.

It is hard to view the WTO or SPS as being a promoter of public health and safety. Thus, I believe that it is deceptive for the WTO to claim on its web page that "safety concerns are built into the WTO agreements" and that the purpose of WTO provisions on product standards "is to defend governments' rights to ensure the safety of their citizens."[3] Defend from whom? The WTO?

I am also troubled by Professor Matsushita's suggestion that a Panel should consider factors such as the "reputation of the research institute" and whether the institute is "closely affiliated" with the government imposing the SPS measure. I see no reason to impugn a food safety institute that is part of a government.

4. Regulatory Consistency

Mr. Pauwelyn notes, I believe correctly, that the SPS requirement for regulatory consistency (Article 5.5) requires "in depth interference" and is the provision with the "real bite" in the SPS Agreement. He and Professor Matsushita reach the same conclusion on Question 10 that a ban on duck meat but not beef could violate SPS.

I would guess that they are right about how a Panel would rule. And that's probably the way the Panel ought to rule given the text of Article 5.5. But I doubt that WTO rules should have been written with such a sharp bite directed at health-related laws.

It is true that Article 5.5 does not outlaw policy inconsistency alone. For a measure to violate Article 5.5, it must not only seek arbitrary or unjustifiable differences in levels of risk avoidance, but it must also be discriminatory or a disguised restriction on international trade. This sounds like a stringent test, but in practice Panels have found it easy to detect what they perceive to be discriminatory behavior.

The logic behind Article 5.5 is that because policy inconsistency is irrational, one can infer from it that governments are motivated by protectionism. The problem with this approach is that irrational government action is too common to serve as a reliable indicator of protectionism. In pointing this out, I surely don't mean to defend irrational public policy. But before the WTO attacks disguised health policies, it should do more to eliminate undisguised protectionist trade policies such as tariffs and quotas. Furthermore, many national protectionist policies (such as antidumping) are internally inconsistent and lack any scientific basis, yet they are still permitted by the WTO.

5. Sovereignty and Deference

A few of the posed questions use the term "deference" (Questions 1, 13, 15, 16); one of the questions uses the term "sovereignty" (Question 8). These questions can be asked regarding the role of the judge. They can also be asked regarding the nature of the international commitment.

What is the role of the WTO judge? I don't think she ought to resist encroaching sovereignty. The governments have decided in writing the treaty to dilute their sovereignty to some extent. Similarly, because the WTO is a set of disciplines on governments, the judge should not defer to a defendant government as to whether the defendant has violated these disciplines. If there is space for deference in the judge's role, it would only be in delineating facts. What is the standard of review on the facts? The Appellate Body says it is "objective assessment of the facts." This seems to imply very little (if any) deference to an administrative determination by the defendant government on facts. (But the Antidumping Agreement, Article 17.6 does have an exception to this.)

Similarly, I would not favor the judge being deferential to a government's view of the nature of its obligation within the WTO treaty. That's one reason why the statement in the DSU (Article 3:2) that WTO recommendations and rulings "cannot add to or diminish the rights and obligations provided in the covered agreements" cannot be taken seriously. In every WTO case I've seen, the government litigants come in with very different views as to their respective "rights and obligations." And they can't both be right. So in many disputes, one government's *ex ante* expectations on its "obligations" are being changed, and new obligations are being added by WTO dispute settlement.

Of all the administrative determinations supervised by the SPS agreement, the ones relating to Equivalence may be the most deserving of deference. SPS Article 4.1 states that importing countries shall accept SPS measures of an exporting country's government if that government "objectively demonstrates" to the importing country's government that its measures achieve the importing State's chosen level of SPS protection. While the use of the term "objectively" suggests less than complete deference, a Panel ought to accord considerable deference to a regulatory agency's review of foreign regulatory practices.

NOTES

1. Steve Charnovitz, The Supervision of Health and Biosafety Regulation by World Trade Rules, *Tulane Environmental Law Journal* 13 (2000), 271, 283–85, 291.

2. See Matsushita in this volume, p. 202.

3. World Trade Organization, "10 Common Misunderstandings about the WTO".

CHAPTER 13

Comment on Facial Non-Discrimination in the WTO

David Palmeter

In its 1851 decision in *Cooley v. Board of Wardens,* the Supreme Court held that the United States Constitution precludes individual states from enacting laws on commercial subjects that are "in their nature national, or admit only one uniform system, or plan of regulation."[1] That was the start of what is known as "dormant commerce clause" jurisprudence in the United States, a jurisprudence that has led Prof. David P. Currie to observe, "the confused body of decisions handed down in this field . . . suggests the depth of the can of worms that *Cooley* . . . opened up and that we have never since succeeded in closing."[2] The WTO is unlikely to escape opening a comparable "can of worms." Indeed, it probably already has done so.

In the United States, the Constitution gives Congress the authority to regulate commerce, both with foreign nations and among the states.[3] This power is viewed as a peremptory power, one that allows Congress to override any contrary state law. Enactment of legislation is an active or "non-dormant" exercise of the commerce power. But even in the absence of congressional legislation, *Cooley* held that States may not take action that would unduly interfere with foreign or interstate commerce. This is what is referred to as the "dormant" commerce clause. It is a prohibition on certain State action even in the absence of congressional action.

If the statement of the nature of the dormant commerce clause is simple, its application has proven to be anything but that. The first glimpse of the can of worms was foreshadowed less than 20 years after *Cooley* was decided. *Woodruff v. Parham* upheld a state law because, "[t]here is no attempt to discriminate injuriously against the products of other states."[4] This rationale of non-discrimination provoked a dissent from Justice Samuel Nelson, who observed that a tax by a Northern state on "all sales of cotton, tobacco, or rice . . . would be a tax without any discrimination; and yet it would be in fact, in its operation and effect, exclusively upon these Southern products."[5] Nelson's example, by the way, did not betray a Southern concern. He was a Northerner, from Cooperstown, New York.

Justice Nelson posed a problem that has existed in dormant commerce clause jurisprudence since the 1860s—the problem of facially neutral measures that are discriminatory in effect. The case law developed in response to the issues that have arisen in the near century and a half since then is the can of worms noted by Prof. Currie. It has provided material with which generations of constitutional law professors have been able to torment hapless students, challenging them to make some kind of sense of the mish-mash of decisions that has emerged.

The problem is that in any federal system, or in any system resembling a federal system, there are two or more law-enacting bodies. In the United States, the two are the Federal Government and the State governments. The federal system in the United States, as the commerce clause attests, is intended to provide for an internal common market, for internal free trade. But conflicts often arise between the goals of free trade and State autonomy when states attempt to regulate economic activity within their territory.

The problem is not confined to the United States. It is present as well in the European Communities—as exemplified in the *Cassis de Dijon* case[6] and in questions of subsidiarity. And it is present and growing in the World Trade Organization—the *Beef Hormones* and *Alcoholic Beverages* cases being prime examples.[7] The legal structures in the U.S., the EC, and the WTO are different; the legal texts also are different; but the problems are often the same. In the United States, the question posed is whether a State measure is an unconstitutional interference with interstate commerce, or a valid exercise of the State's police power. In the WTO, there are more questions because there is more relevant text. Generally, however, the questions are (1) whether a measure is inconsistent with the national treatment requirements of Article III and, if so, whether it nonetheless is permitted under Article XX; and (2) whether a measure embodies an "arbitrary or unjustifiable" distinction that results in "discrimination or a disguised restriction on international trade" under Article 5.5 of the SPS Agreement.

The can of worms appears because tribunals—courts in the United States, Panels, and the Appellate Body in the WTO—are not always candid as to the bases of their decisions. This lack of candor, understandable on the part of a tribunal that does not want to cast aspersions on the motives of lawmakers, can lead to apparent inconsistencies that, when enough accumulate, can accurately be called a can of worms.

In his discussion of the question whether consistency is required to justify a measure, Joost Pauwelyn quotes two examples from Appellate Body reports. In *Hormones*, the Panel had concluded that the EC's ban on hormones constituted a disguised restriction on international trade. The Appellate Body disagreed:

> We are unable to share the inference that the Panel apparently draws that the import ban on treated meat and the Community-wide prohibition of the use of the hormones here in dispute for growth promotion purposes in the beef sector were not really designed to protect its population from the risk of cancer, but rather to keep out U.S. and Canadian hormone-

treated beef and thereby to protect the domestic beef producers in the European Communities.[8]

In *Australia – Salmon,* however, the Appellate Body concluded that Australia's ban on imports of salmon, while allowing imports of other species that represented similar, if not higher, risks, was a disguised restriction:

> [A] finding that an SPS measure is not based on an assessment of the risks to human, animal or plant life or health—either because there was no risk assessment at all or because there is an insufficient risk assessment—is a strong indication that this measure is not really concerned with the protection of human, animal or plant life or health but is instead a trade-restrictive measure taken in the guise of an SPS measure, i.e., a "disguised restriction on international trade."[9]

Mr. Pauwelyn suggests that these statements might be inconsistent. Perhaps, but not necessarily. The Appellate Body has said that "the goal set is not absolute or perfect consistency, since governments establish their appropriate levels of protection frequently on an *ad hoc* basis and over time, as different risks present themselves at different times. It is only arbitrary or unjustifiable inconsistencies that are to be avoided."[10] What seems clear from these statements is that, in both instances, the Appellate Body was looking at the motivation of the authorities in enacting the measure. Indeed, in deciding whether a measure is or is not a "disguised restriction," some look at motive or purpose seems inevitable. This, however, simply seems to push the question further back, but does not eliminate it: how is it decided that a particular inconsistency is or is not "arbitrary or unjustifiable"?

The Appellate Body, like the Supreme Court, understandably seems reluctant simply to say that, in the one instance they believed the explanation of the defending party that its purpose was not protectionist, and in the other they did not. One technique for avoiding this explanation is to frame the issue in different terms, as the Appellate Body did in *Hormones:* "The implementing measure must be shown to be *applied in such a manner* as to result in discrimination or a disguised restriction on international trade."[11] The phrase "applied in such a manner" avoids the need to cast aspersions on anyone's motives or purpose. After all, the effect of the application could be entirely inadvertent.

As Donald Regan points out, however, while the Supreme Court gives many explanations, a detailed examination of the cases reveals that, "[i]n the core area of the dormant commerce clause, *a law is unconstitutional if and only if it has a protectionist purpose.* It's that simple."[12] This view is consistent with the view of Daniel Farber and Robert Hudec, who note that "common sense tells us that most tribunals are likely to be strongly affected by their perceptions about the motive of the government that enacted the measure."[13]

Mitsuo Matsushita's analysis, while not addressing the protectionist purpose issue directly, is consistent with that of Prof. Regan, Prof. Farber, and Prof. Hudec. He notes that the role of Panels and the Appellate Body is "to make an objective assessment of the facts and to seek and to find the correct interpretation of the provisions."[14] He goes on to observe that, "[a] *de minimus* difference in treatment . . . may not constitute a violation. . . "[15] One reason for this might be that a *de minimus* difference in treatment is not likely the result of a protectionist purpose.

In *Hormones,* however, the difference was more than *de minimus,* and was found to be—in the terminology of the SPS Agreement, "unjustifiable." In particular, Prof. Matsushita notes, the fact that the European Communities banned the use of a hormone in raising cattle but permitted its use in raising swine, was unjustifiable. "In reaching this conclusion," he writes, "the Appellate Body weighed qualitative and quantitative factors surrounding this case."[16]

Prof. Matsushita's point is particularly interesting in light of the portion of the *Hormones* determination quoted by Mr. Pauwelyn.[17] When the issue was simply whether the facially neutral ban on hormones in beef was really designed to keep out imported beef, the Appellate Body was remarkably sympathetic to the EC. It referred to "the depth and extent of the anxieties experienced within the European Communities" about the issue, and the "dangers of abuse" of added hormones.[18] It considered the internal political, legal, and administrative problems of the EC:

> A major problem addressed in the legislative process of the European Communities related to the differences in the internal regulations of various Member States of the European Union (four or five of which permitted, while the rest prohibited, the use for growth promotion of certain hormones), the resulting distortions in competitive conditions in and the existence of barriers to intra-community trade. The necessity for harmonizing the internal regulations of its Member States was a consequence of the European Communities' mandate to establish a common (internal) market for beef.[19]

This sympathy did not extend, however, as Prof. Matsushita notes, to a situation in which the EC permits a hormone to be given to swine but prohibits its use in beef.

Prof. Matsushita, of course, was a Member of the Division of the Appellate Body that decided *Hormones,* so his comments are understandably and quite properly reserved, and tied very much to the language of the SPS Agreement. Still, if the Appellate Body noted that a hormone was banned in cattle but not in swine, and if it weighed the qualitative and quantitative factors surrounding the case, is it not fair to say that it looked into what was "really going on," and detected a protectionist purpose?

The intuitive appeal of a search for protectionist purpose can be seen from looking at the question from an advocate's point of view. What lawyer, presenting a case involving an allegation of *de facto* discrimination from a facially neutral measure, would not welcome evidence of a protectionist intent? What lawyer, defending such a case, would welcome such evidence? Advocates are likely to agree with Prof. Hudec:

> The normal response of most tribunals . . . is to decide the case as best they can by making a seat-of-the-pants judgment about whether the defendant government is behaving correctly or incorrectly—a process of judgment known in some circles as the "smell test." Once the tribunal comes to a conclusion about who should win, it fashions an analysis, in terms of the meaningless criteria it has been asked to apply, that makes the case come out that way.[20]

Nevertheless, tribunals often are reluctant to question the motives of legislatures. This sensitivity might be heightened in the case of international tribunals who are asked by complainants to find, in effect, that the intentions of a government were not necessarily what that government said they were. Euphemisms will be sought. Actions—how is a measure "applied"?—will be examined. "Aims" and "purposes" will be minimized, if not avoided, wherever possible. But, in the words of Prof. Hudec, "[t]his does not mean . . . that the 'aims and effects' approach has been exterminated. It simply means that it will remain underground."[21]

NOTES

1. 53 U.S. (12 How.) 298, 319.

2. David P. Currie, The Constitution in the Supreme Court: The First Hundred Years, 1789 to 1888, (Chicago 1985), p. 331.

3. Art. I § 8.

4. 75 U.S. (8 Wall.) 123, 140 (1869).

5. Id., at 145.

6. Case 120/78 [1979] ECR 649, [1979] 3 CMLR 494. See generally, Todd J. Friedbacher, "Motive Unmasked: The European Court of Justice, the Free Movement of Goods, and the Search for Legitimacy," 2 *European Law Journal* 226 (Nov. 1996).

7. *EC-Measures Concerning Meat and Meat Products (Hormones), Complaint by the United States,* WT/DS26/R/USA (18 August 1997), *Complaint by Canada,* WT/DS48/R/Can (18

August 1997), *EC Measures Concerning Meat and Meat Products (Hormones),* AB-1997-4, WT/DS26/AB/R, WT/DS48/AB/R (16 January 1998) (adopted 13 February 1998); *Japan-Taxes on Alcoholic Beverages,* WT/DS8/R, WT/DS10/R, WT/DS11/R (11 July 1996); *Japan-Taxes on Alcoholic Beverages,* AB-1996-2, WT/DS8/AB/R, WT/DS10/AB/R,WT/DS11/AB/R (4 October 1996 (adopted 1 November 1996).

8. *EC-Measures Concerning Meat and Meat Products (Hormones),* AB-1997, note 7 supra, para. 2.45.

9. *Australia-Measures Affecting Importation of Salmon,* AB-1998-5, WT/DS18/AB/R (20 October 1998) (adopted 6 November 1998), para. 166.

10. *Hormones,* para. 213.

11. Id., para. 215.

12. See Regan in this volume, p. 94.

13. Daniel A. Farber and Robert E. Hudec, Free Trade and the Regulatory State: A GATT's Eye View of the Dormant Commerce Clause, 47 *Vanderbilt Law Review* (Oct. 1994),1401, 1439.

14. See Matsushita in this volume, p. 199.

15. See Matsushita in this volume, p. 199.

16. Id.

17. See footnote 8, supra.

18. *EC-Measures Concerning Meat and Meat Products (Hormones),* AB-1997, note 7 supra, para. 2.45.

19. Id., citing Article 7a of the Treaty Establishing the European Community.

20. Robert E. Hudec, Requiem for an "Aims and Effects" Test, 32 *International Lawyer* 619 (1998), reprinted in Robert E. Hudec, *Essays on the Nature of International Trade Law* 359, 376 (London, 1999).

21. Id., 377.

CHAPTER 14

The Role of the Judge in the EU and WTO: Lessons from the *BSE* and *Hormones* Cases

Natalie McNelis

What follows is a tale of two cases, both involving trade in beef, both involving allegations that the beef in question was not fit for human consumption. In both cases, the European Union (EU) institutions imposed a total ban on trade in the products concerned, and both cases gave rise to litigation, one before the European Court of Justice (ECJ), and the other before the World Trade Organization (WTO) Appellate Body.[1] And here is where the paths of these two cases diverge—the ECJ upheld the first ban; the WTO Appellate Body struck the second one down. Key to these outcomes were the different standards of judicial review that were applied in the two cases. While these different standards of review are already indicated in the terms in which they are described—"manifest error" for one case, "objective assessment" for the other—those terms do not fully encapsulate the standard of review. Rather, the standard of review is to be found in the relationship of the "judge" to the "judged." This paper will explore the reasons why these two cases came to dissimilar ends, and what can be learned from them about the role of the judge in the EU and WTO.

1. Mad Cows and Englishmen

The unfortunate beast at the center of the first of our two tales is a cow struck down with a disease that was once particularly prevalent among cows in the United Kingdom—bovine spongiform encephalopathy (BSE), also known as "mad cow disease." Back in 1996, there was a discovery that there was a potential risk that BSE could jump the species barrier and cause a similar

---

Correspondence address: Wilmer, Cutler & Pickering, Rue de la Loi 15 Wetstraat, B-1040 Bruxelles; Email: natalie.mcnelis@wilmer.com. This paper is a further development of an idea contained in my part of a longer piece on the precautionary principle, written with my colleague Axel Desmedt. I would like to thank him for his invaluable contribution in the formation of many of the ideas further developed herein. I am also grateful to him and Frédéric Louis for taking the time to read and provide insightful comments on a draft of this paper. Finally, thanks go to Bradley Williams for his helpful research assistance. Errors and omissions are entirely the responsibility of the author.

disease (Creutzfeld Jakob Disease, or CJD) in human beings that consumed affected beef.[2] CJD is a degenerative brain disease which is fatal, and for which there is no known cure.

In light of this discovery, the European Commission adopted a decision establishing emergency measures to protect against BSE/CJD by imposing, on a temporary basis, a total ban on exports of bovine animals, bovine meat and derived products from the United Kingdom to the other Member States of the EU and to third countries.[3] In its decision, the Commission said that, although it could not yet take a definitive position with regard to the danger of BSE to human and animal health, it also could not exclude the possibility of those dangers. Therefore, under the circumstances and as an emergency measure, it found a temporary ban necessary. The Commission explicitly called for further detailed scientific studies, and noted that the decision would be reviewed once all the relevant elements were examined.

This ban was challenged in the Community courts in two cases[4] on the basis of a laundry list of grounds, some of which were: that the Commission had failed to observe the limits placed on its powers by the directives at issue,[5] disregarded the principle of the free movement of goods, misused its powers, breached the principle of proportionality, infringed the Common Agricultural Policy and relied on an inappropriate legal basis for its actions.

In two judgments handed down on the same day, the ECJ upheld the Commission's decision to impose the ban. The Court said that such a decision fell within the Commission's considerable discretion to take measures within the ambit of the Common Agricultural Policy.[6] Although it acknowledged that such measures do impinge on the free movement of goods, the Court said that they are not necessarily contrary to Community law, considering that they are based on directives the very aim of which is to ensure the free movement of agricultural products.[7] As to the allegation that the Commission breached the principle of proportionality, the Court first reviewed the elements of that principle (measures adopted by Community institutions must not exceed the limits of what is appropriate and necessary in order to attain the objectives legitimately pursued by the legislation in question, when there is a choice between several appropriate measures recourse must be had to the least onerous, and the disadvantage caused must not be disproportionate to the aims pursued).[8] It then produced language that the EU has since lauded as an endorsement of the precautionary principle:

> Where there is uncertainty as to the existence or extent of risks to human health, the institutions may take protective measures without having to wait until the reality and seriousness of those risks become fully apparent.[9]

The Court went on to hold that in view of the seriousness of the risk and the urgency of the situation, the Commission did not react in a manifestly inappropriate manner by imposing the general ban, and consequently did not breach the principle of proportionality.[10]

Having similarly dismissed all of the other grounds of challenge of the Commission's decision, the Court upheld its validity. The ban was temporarily imposed, and indeed the EU has now lifted it[11]—an outcome the implications of which will be further discussed at the end of this article.

2. The Fatted Calf

A cow, too, stands at the center of our next tale—this one, presumably, mentally sound but physically perhaps a bit outsized. The cow here has been treated with growth hormones, a process prevalent in the U.S. and Canadian beef industries.

In the 80s, the EU outlawed administering hormones to cattle for growth promotion purposes, and prohibited import of "hormone beef" from third countries.[12] This was at least ostensibly due to health concerns, although there were allegations that the restrictions were rather intended to protect the EU beef industry—both from foreign competition and from a possible fall in demand due to consumer concerns, whether or not they were well-founded.[13]

The U.S. and Canada subsequently challenged this import ban at the WTO, claiming in particular that it was in violation of the WTO Agreement on the Application of Sanitary and Phytosanitary Measures (the SPS Agreement).[14]

Two Panels and the Appellate Body agreed that the EU ban was a violation of the SPS Agreement.[15] In particular, the Appellate Body said that although WTO Members are free to determine what level of sanitary protection they wish to maintain ("The right of a Member to determine its own appropriate level of sanitary protection is an important right. . . ."),[16] that right is not "absolute or unqualified."[17] According to the Appellate Body, compliance with Article 5.1 SPS, which requires that Members "ensure that their sanitary or p' ytosanitary measures are based on assessment, as appropriate to the circumstances, of the risks to human, animal or plant life or health," is a counterbalance to the right to choose a level of protection. In that regard, the Appellate Body said:

> Article 5.1 . . . requires that the results of the risk assessment must sufficiently warrant—that is to say, reasonably support—the SPS measures at stake. The requirement that an SPS measure be "based on" a risk assessment is a substantive requirement that there be a rational relationship between the measure and the risk assessment.[18]

Although the Appellate Body granted that governments do not necessarily have to follow "mainstream" scientific opinion, in its examination of the evidence brought to bear, it did not believe that any risk assessment that "reasonably supports or warrants" the measures was furnished to the Panel.[19] In that regard, the Appellate Body, like the Panels, did not find general studies submitted by the EU convincing:

> The 1987 IARC [International Agency for Research on Cancer] Monographs and the articles and opinions of individual scientists submitted by the European Communities constitute general studies which do indeed show the existence of a general risk of cancer; but they do not focus on and do not address the particular kind of risk here at stake—the carcinogenic or genotoxic potential of the residues of those hormones found in meat derived from cattle to which the hormones had been administered for growth promotion purposes—as is required by paragraph 4 of Annex A of the SPS Agreement. Those general studies are in other words relevant but do not appear to be sufficiently specific to the case at hand.[20]

Thus, the Appellate Body went on to uphold the Panels' conclusion that the EU's hormone ban was in violation of its obligations under the SPS Agreement. It recommended that the Dispute Settlement Body request the EU[21] to bring its measures into conformity with its WTO obligations.

3. Why Such Different Outcomes?

There are undeniable similarities between these two cases: we have the same actor (the EU institutions), the same product (beef), the same type of measure (a total ban) and the same type of justification for the measure (serious concerns about public health)—and yet, the cases come to opposite conclusions.

There are important differences in the facts of these cases and in the applicable legal provisions, and these elements partly explain this parting of the ways. However, it is submitted that there is another compelling cause of this disparity that merits examination. It lies in the standard of review that the adjudicators applied in the two cases, and more specifically, in the different relationship of the judge to the "judged" in the EU and WTO.

Different Risks

First, one way to reconcile *BSE* and *Hormones* could be that there was simply more to the *BSE* case than the *Hormones* case, and that is why the ECJ upheld the BSE ban while the WTO struck the hormone ban down. After all, scientists declared that there was a probable link between consumption of BSE beef and CJD, and CJD is a horrific, fatal disease. Meanwhile, proof of the dangers of hormones was threadier, and even if there were a danger, the consequences were somehow less alarming—it seems that every day, we learn that one or another substance is possibly carcinogenic, especially if consumed in large quantities. Perhaps if the WTO had treated the *BSE* case, it also would have upheld the ban; perhaps if the ECJ had been the judge of the *Hormones* case rather than the WTO Appellate Body it, too, would have struck down the EU institution's actions.

One cannot be so sure of such hypotheses, especially as far as *Hormones* is concerned. The ECJ actually treated the hormones case itself back in the 80s, in the *Fedesa* case,[22] and unlike the WTO Appellate Body, the ECJ backed the Council up in its ban of hormone beef. (Granted, the ECJ did judge this case ten years earlier than the WTO Appellate Body. The fact that even ten years later the EU still could not come up with convincing proof might very well have led the ECJ to a different conclusion if it decided the case today.) In *Fedesa,* in a preliminary ruling from a UK court that arose in the context of a case brought by the Fédération Européenne de la Santé Animale[23] (Fedesa), the ECJ examined the legality of one of the very directives that was at issue in the WTO case, Directive 88/146, which prohibited the use of certain hormones. The Court affirmed the legality of this directive, dismissing arguments that it infringed the principle of legal certainty in view of the lack of scientific evidence demonstrating the danger to human health of using the hormones in question, and it dismissed arguments based on proportionality. Rather, the Court held that the Council was within the limits of its discretion to adopt this ban, and even went so far as to say that this was so even if the action was in response not to threats to health, but to concerns expressed by the European Parliament and several consumer organizations that such threats could exist.

Temporary Measures

A second potential explanation of the difference in outcome between the *BSE* and the *Hormones* case is that the BSE ban was explicitly a temporary, emergency measure while the *Hormones* ban was not. In imposing the export ban in the *BSE* case, the European Commission said that it could not take a definitive position with regard to the danger of eating BSE-tainted beef, but it also could not exclude that danger. Therefore, as a precaution, the EU imposed a ban, but explicitly called for further scientific studies and indicated that its measures would be adapted if those studies showed adaptations were merited. (Indeed, as will be discussed below, the EU has since seen fit to lift the ban—not because studies showed that the BSE threat was unreal, but rather because the Commission was convinced that precautions taken by the

UK are sufficient to protect against that threat.) The ECJ upheld this "precautionary" approach.

Again, one could argue that, had the *BSE* case come to the WTO, the WTO Appellate Body would have judged like the ECJ and upheld the measure. Indeed, the BSE ban might very well have passed muster under Article 5.7 SPS, which permits Members to take provisional measures where relevant scientific evidence is insufficient, as long as they seek additional information so that they can make a more objective assessment of risk and review the measure within a reasonable period of time. Thus, perhaps the BSE ban, explicitly provisional, would have been judged the same in the two fora. Incidentally, the EU's hormones ban, in place since the 80s, was long-term and not of a temporary nature, and the EU did not attempt to argue that its measures were provisional within the meaning of Article 5.7 SPS.

4. The Standard of Review and the Relationship between the Judge and the "Judged"

It is submitted, however, that the reason why the *BSE* and the *Hormones* cases came out differently is more profound than that; it lies rather in the different standards of review applicable to each case. Indeed, an indication of the different standards of review is already seen in the expressed standards of review: in the *BSE* case, the bar for the judge to overturn the authority's measure was set very high, "manifest error." Meanwhile in the WTO *Hormones* case, the "objective assessment" standard of review (although not adequately defined)[24] in any event granted the EU less discretion. However, the standard of review is not fully encompassed in the terms that are used to describe it. More importantly, the standard of review is an outgrowth of the relationship between the judge and the actor being judged.

Standard of Review in the *BSE* Case—"Manifest Error"

In the *BSE* case, the measures at issue were based on rules that were rooted in the Common Agricultural Policy, an area where the Commission has broad discretion. Indeed, in coming to its decision the Court said:

> [S]ince the Commission enjoys a wide measure of discretion, particularly as to the nature and extent of the measures which it adopts, the Community judicature must, when reviewing such measures, restrict itself to examining whether the exercise of such discretion is vitiated by a manifest error or a misuse of powers or whether the Commission did not clearly exceed the bounds of its discretion.[25]

Similarly, when the Court turned to consider the plea based on breach of the general principle of proportionality, the Court held that in its judicial review of compliance with the principle of proportionality in this case, it had to take account of the fact that the Community legislature has a discretionary power which corresponds to its political responsibilities under the Common Agricultural Policy. As a consequence, the Court said that the legality of a measure adopted in that sphere can be affected only if the measure is manifestly inappropriate to the objective sought.[26] The Court concluded:

> [I]n view of the seriousness of the risk and the urgency of the situation, the Commission did not react in a manifestly inappropriate manner by imposing, on a temporary basis and pending the production of more detailed scientific information, a general ban on exports of bovine animals, bovine meat and derived products. Consequently, the Commission has not breached the principle of proportionality.[27]

Thus the standard of review in the *BSE* case was very deferential to the European Commission—"manifest error," "manifestly inappropriate." (Incidentally, this was also the Court's standard of review in its hormones case, *Fedesa,* mentioned above.) In that light, it is not surprising that the ECJ upheld the Commission's actions, as the standard of review was nearing total deference. Granted, the ECJ's job was eased by the fact that the grounds for the ban in the *BSE* case did seem to be founded; there was evidence that a potential risk existed, and the consequences if that risk were real were very serious indeed.

Standard of Review in the WTO *Hormones* Case—"Objective Assessment"

In the WTO *Hormones* case, the EU argued that the Panels had employed the wrong standard of review in considering the case. For the EU, the two alternative goalposts are "*de novo* review" versus "deference." *De novo* review allows a Panel complete freedom to come to a different view from that of the competent authority of the Member whose act is being reviewed. Under a "deference" standard, the Panel should not redo the investigation, but rather should examine whether the procedure required by the relevant WTO rules had been followed.[28]

The EU argued that the Panel should adopt a "deferential 'reasonableness' standard" when reviewing a Member's determination that a particular inference from the available data is scientifically plausible.[29] It considered that this standard is applicable in all "highly complex factual situations."[30] It was the EU's conviction that the Panel had instead substituted its judgment for that of the EU. The EU went further to say that the Panel's conclusions were so wrongful that they did not constitute an "objective assessment of the facts."[31]

The WTO Appellate Body pointed out that the SPS Agreement is silent as to the appropriate standard of review, and said that where a standard of review is specifically assigned—in the Anti-dumping Agreement—it is specific to that agreement and does not apply to the SPS Agreement. The Appellate Body said that the standard of review applicable to the SPS Agreement "must reflect the balance established in that Agreement between the jurisdictional competences conceded by the Members to the WTO and the jurisdictional competences retained by the Members for themselves."[32]

The Appellate Body said that the standard of review applicable to the SPS Agreement is "articulat[ed] with great succinctness but with sufficient clarity" in Article 11:

> [A] Panel should make an objective assessment of the matter before it, including an objective assessment of the facts of the case and the applicability of and conformity with the relevant covered agreements . . . [33]

The only other guidance given by the Appellate Body in this regard is to say that "the applicable standard is neither de novo review as such, nor 'total deference'."[34] Therefore, the most we can say is that the standard of review is somewhere in-between.

Looking at the facts of the *Hormones* case, one could say that the standard of review employed by the Appellate Body in fact came pretty close to the "reasonableness" standard the EU asked for. In fact, the Appellate Body even uses the word "reasonably" in its holding:

> [T]he results of the risk assessment must sufficiently warrant—that is to say, reasonably support—the SPS measure at stake. The requirement that an SPS measure be "based on" a risk assessment is a substantive requirement that there be a rational relationship between the measure and the risk assessment.[35]

However, the requirement that the evidence "sufficiently warrant" the measures and that there be a "rational relationship between the measure and the risk assessment" is not exactly the kind of deference the EU was looking for. And indeed, the EU ended up losing the case. The Appellate Body looked into the evidence, and contrary to the EU Council, it found that it did not reasonably support the total ban that the EU imposed.

The Standard of Review Is Not Encapsulated in the Terminology

In explaining the different outcomes of our two cases, then, one could point to the fact that the standard of review in the *BSE* case was on its face more deferential ('manifest error') than in the *Hormones* case ('objective assessment'). However, it is submitted that the difference in the expressed standard of review does not tell the whole story. The *BSE* case and WTO *Hormones* case probably did come to different ends in part because of the different standards of judicial review to which they were subject. However, the standard of review is not embodied merely in the terms that are used to describe it. In particular, the words that the Appellate Body used in *Hormones* give us little guidance as to the standard of review it deemed appropriate in that case.

Semantics aside, the real standard of review is a function of the relationship of the judge and the "judged." To explain, the ECJ did not uphold the EU's ban in the *BSE* case simply because its hands were tied by the "manifest error" standard of review. In fact, it is submitted that the ECJ would have upheld the BSE ban regardless of whether the standard of review was stringent or lax.

Similarly, it is put forward, the WTO Appellate Body would have struck down the EU's ban in the *Hormones* case whether the standard of review was described as "objective assessment" or "manifest error." After all, in the WTO *Hormones* case, several studies had been submitted which specifically looked at the issue of the risk of eating beef that came from cattle to which growth hormones had been administered. All of those studies concluded that, as long as good veterinary practice was observed, eating such beef was safe. As mentioned above, the evidence that the EU said cast doubt on this conclusion came from general opinions and articles that, unlike the aforementioned studies, did not look at the particular issue of whether eating food containing residues of hormones could pose a health risk.[36] Therefore, even if the standard had been a "manifest error," the WTO Appellate Body probably could have found it—it would have said that since there was *no* evidence in favor of the ban, imposing it rose to the level of a "manifest error."

By the same token, if the WTO Appellate Body had wanted to uphold the EU ban, it also could have done so—it could have given more credence to those general studies, which it admitted "indeed show the existence of a general risk of cancer";[37] it could have emphasized the Members' right to choose whatever level of protection they see fit; it could have explicitly endorsed the precautionary principle, even outside of Article 5.7. In fact, the standard of review was actually expressed in the terms that the EU wanted, a kind of administrative law "reasonableness" standard, but the EU still lost the case.

The Standard of Review Lies Rather in the Role of the Judge and His Relationship to the "Judged"

Regardless of the expressed terminology, the real standard of review lies in the relationship between the judging entity and the actor "judged." In the one case, we have the ECJ judging an act of one of its sister institutions—the *BSE* case. In the other case, we have the WTO Appellate Body judging the act of a fraction[38] of its 130-odd Members—the *Hormones* case. Here lies the root of the two disparate outcomes.

BSE—the "Insider" Looking "In"

First, in the *BSE* case, we have an "insider" looking "in": the ECJ was in the position of judging an act of a member of its own "family," the European Commission. There were many reasons for the Court to give the Commission the benefit of the doubt. Both institutions are on the same team, and they have been playing together for a long time. This is not to say that the Court would hesitate to overrule an act of the Commission; it does so all the time.[39] However, to some extent the Court knows and "trusts" the Commission, especially in this kind of circumstance. After all, the Commission is a special institution—it is traditionally the guardian of the EC Treaty and the Common Market. It has in the past tirelessly attacked restrictions to free movement in the EU.[40] Therefore, there is a presumption that if the Commission imposes a rule that impinges on the free movement of goods within the EU, it probably has a pretty good reason for doing so.[41]

Furthermore, in the *BSE* case, the measure in question also hit home. The Commission imposed a ban on exports of products from one of its own Member States, the United Kingdom. The suspicion that there was a protectionist purpose behind the measures is undercut when the measure is imposed by the Commission and not another Member State.[42] Skepticism aside, the Commission acts not for the interest of one Member State, but for the interest of the EU as a whole. In such a context, and in view of the persuasive facts of the *BSE* case, it is not surprising that the ECJ upheld the BSE ban.

Hormones—the "Outsider" Looking "In"

Meanwhile, the WTO *Hormones* case was rather an instance of an "outsider" looking "in"—the WTO Appellate Body judging an act of an EU institution.

First of all, there is no particularly special relationship between the WTO Appellate Body and the EU institutions. Rather, the EU is simply one group out of the WTO's more than 130 (sometimes unruly) Members. In fact, within that group, the EU's reputation, especially after the *Bananas* case, is blemished.[43]

Therefore, when looking at the acts of the EU institutions, the WTO Appellate Body does not start from the assumption that a ban imposed by such an institution is rational and does not have a protectionist purpose. In fact, even though the hormone ban also affected the European industry, there was quite some suspicion in the *Hormones* case that the EU's rules were, at least in part, motivated by a desire to protect the European beef industry at the expense of Canadian and American competitors. Protectionism, and suspicion of protectionism, go a long way toward making the difference.[44]

With such factors in mind, it is not surprising that in the *Hormones* case, the WTO Appellate Body was less deferential with regard to the EU Council than the ECJ was with regard to the EC Commission in the *BSE* case. To use an analogy, to some extent, when the ECJ looks at the Commission, it is like the principal judging a fellow teacher. When the WTO Appellate Body looks at the EU, it is rather like the principal disciplining a student.

5. Sovereignty and Other Sacred Cows

Having laid out the contention that there are different standards of review at work here, and that those different standards are a function of the relationship between the judge and the judged, the question then arises: in light of the EU example, is the standard that the WTO Appellate Body applied in the *Hormones* case appropriate? If not, what would be the appropriate standard of review for such a case?

The "BSE Standard" Is Too Deferential for the WTO

If one tries to draw a parallel in the relationships between the judge and the "judged" in the EU versus the WTO, the standard we saw in the *BSE* case (and in the EU's own hormones case, *Fedesa*) is probably too deferential for the WTO. In the *BSE* case, the relationship between the ECJ and the Commission was marked by a number of factors that made its lenient standard of review appropriate—in particular, both institutions are on the same "side" and the Commission is a special institution that traditionally guards the Common Market. These elements are not a feature of the relationship between the WTO Appellate Body and the EU.[45]

A Better Parallel Is the ECJ Judging EU Member States, the WTO Judging Its Members

In that light, perhaps a closer parallel[46] to the WTO judging the EU is not the standard of review that the ECJ applies when it judges the EU institutions, but rather the standard the ECJ applies when it judges one of its own Member States under the rules on the free movement of goods.[47] Like WTO Members, the EU Member States are sovereign States.[48] They represent their national interest first, and they are not above the occasional instance of protectionism.

Where the ECJ has judged Member State restrictions to the free movement of goods in the EU premised on protection of the public health, it has acknowledged that:

> [T]he health and life of humans rank first among the property or interests protected by Article 36[49] and it is for the Member States, within the limits imposed by the Treaty, to decide what degree of protection they intend to assure . . . [50]

The ECJ has also said:

> [I]n so far as there are uncertainties in the present state of scientific research with regard to the harmfulness of a certain substance, it is for the Member States, in the absence of full harmonization to decide what degree of protection of the health and life of humans they intend to assure, in the light of specific eating habits of their own population, having regard for the requirements of the free movement of goods within the Community.[51]

That has not stopped the ECJ from being extremely critical where Member States base restrictions on the need to protect human health. For example, in the *German Beer* case,[52] Germany had *inter alia* imposed a total ban on the use of additives in beer. Germany argued that the restriction was necessary to protect the health of its citizens, given in particular its population's proclivity to beer. Germany argued that:

> [I]n view of the dangers resulting from the utilization of additives whose long-term effects are not yet known and in particular of the risks resulting from the accumulation of additives in the organism and their interaction with other substances, such as alcohol, it is necessary to minimize the quantity of additives ingested.[53]

To support that point, the German government cited experts' reports that spoke to the risks inherent in the ingestion of additives in general.[54] Yet the Court was not convinced. The Court referred to the findings of international scientific research,[55] in particular the work of the Community's Scientific Committee for Food, the Codex Alimentarius Committee of the UN Food and Agriculture Organization and the World Health Organization, which indicated that the additives did not present a particular risk.[56] The Court indicated that, to prove the existence of a genuine risk, Germany would have had to submit specific studies to that effect, as "[m]ere reference to the potential risks of the ingestion of additives in general and to the fact that beer is a foodstuff consumed in large quantities does not suffice . . . "[57]

The Court ultimately overturned the German ban, calling it disproportionate to its aims. In so doing, the Court noted that use of the additives was permitted in other Member States and, damningly, was allowed by Germany itself in beverages other than beer.[58] Furthermore, the Court found Germany's exclusion of all the additives in question, rather than a few of them for which there might be concrete justification for such exclusion in light of the eating habits of the German population, highlighted the ban's disproportionate nature. Finally, to the Court, the lack of proportionality was also shown by the fact that the challenged rules did not lay down a specific procedure whereby traders could obtain authorization to use certain additives.

Already, one can point to similarities in the ECJ judging EU Member States and the WTO judging its Members; we can hear echoes of the *German Beer* case in *Hormones.* Both cases involved a total ban of a foodstuff due to health concerns, and in both cases the country concerned cited scientific uncertainty about the long-term effects of consuming the product as a justification for drastic measures. Evidence contained in general studies was in both cases pitted against contrary evidence from more specific studies. Finally, while in both cases the judges recognized the primacy of public health interests and acknowledged that it is for the State to determine its own appropriate level of protection, they still overruled the respective State measures.

A Caveat: The WTO Is Not the EU

While, as stated above, the WTO should probably not be as deferential as the ECJ sometimes is when judging its institutions, it is submitted that the WTO should neither be as demanding of its Members as the ECJ is of its Member States. This parallel between the ECJ judging the EU Member States and the WTO judging its Members should not be taken too far—the WTO is not the EU.

It was mentioned above that both the EU Member States and the WTO Members are sovereign States. However, EU law has direct effect, and the Member States of the EU have ceded some of their sovereignty to the EU. As the ECJ put it in the 1964 case *Costa v. ENEL:*

> By contrast with ordinary international treaties, the EEC Treaty has created its own legal system which, on the entry into force of the Treaty, became an integral part of the legal systems of the Member States and which their courts are bound to apply.

> By creating a Community of unlimited duration, having its own institutions, its own personality, its own legal capacity and capacity of representation on the international plane and, more particularly, real powers stemming from a limitation of sovereignty or a transfer of powers from the states to the Community, the Member States have limited their sovereign rights and have thus created a body of law which binds both their nationals and themselves.[59]

Direct effect and a limitation of sovereignty are decidedly *not* a feature of the WTO, where direct effect has steadfastly been refused (in particular by the U.S. and EU) and where sovereignty is sacrosanct.

Further, the goals of the EU reach much further than those of the WTO. The EU strives for a more and more far-reaching union, and this also permits its Court to be more exigent. The EU Member States have committed themselves to that goal, and in that regard they are required to accord some trust to the rules and procedures of their EU partners.[60] Moreover, while admittedly the EU Member States may be primarily driven by national interest, they also understand their interest in the success of the whole. The existence of such an interest in the WTO is more diffuse and harder to quantify—and it is not widely known or understood, especially by individual citizens. Moreover, the WTO Members are not necessarily inclined to defer to the rules of other WTO Members. And, unlike the EU, the WTO does not have such an overarching goal of an ever-closer union. The WTO is, at its basis, simply a market-liberalizing arrangement, and its adjudicators are limited by that scope.

Undoubtedly, it is also easier for the EU Member States to grant credence to the rules of their neighbors. When one compares the membership of the EU to the WTO, one sees that the EU has fifteen Member States that are in fact rather homogeneous: they are all European, all Western, all developed. Moreover, the ECJ judges, coming from that same background, are also perhaps more competent to evaluate arguments about, for example, the habits of the German population. The WTO, on the other hand, has more than 130 Members. Its Members span the globe, and many have little more in common than the fact that they all belong to the WTO. Thus the WTO judges are also to a certain extent constrained by the diversity of the WTO Membership in a way that the ECJ is not.

Furthermore, the WTO Appellate Body does not have the legitimacy with regard to its Members that the ECJ has with regard to the EU Member States. The ECJ is better placed to evaluate the consequences of its judgments, and its judgments are more likely to be accepted by a Community closely linked to it (geographically, politically, ideologically) than are similar judgments of the WTO. The ECJ is firmly established as the highest court of the EU, and talk of disrespect of an ECJ judgment is very rare indeed.

Meanwhile, the vitriolic reactions of many citizens to the WTO in general indicates that the dictates of its Panels and Appellate Body, especially when they could impact the health of individuals, are likely to continue to meet with strident opposition. Perhaps the WTO will in time reach a level of legitimacy comparable to the ECJ—but it is simply not there yet.

6. Conclusion

To sum up, we have explored the relationship between two cases, which despite their similarities, came to opposite conclusions. The explanation for these results is partly due to the different facts of the cases, particularly because the risk of BSE was more compelling, and the proof more weighty, than in *Hormones.* If we look beyond the facts of the cases, however, we see that more determinant of the outcomes were the different standards of review that were applied in these two cases. While one can point to the terms in which those standards were described—"manifest error" for *BSE,* "objective assessment" in *Hormones*—those terms do not encapsulate the standard of review. Rather, the standard of review is a function of the relationship of the "judge" to the "judged". If that is true, then perhaps the relationship of the ECJ to one of its institutions, which we explored in the *BSE* case, is not the proper parallel to the WTO vis-à-vis one of its Members. Perhaps then the proper parallel is rather to the ECJ judging one of the EU Member States. Indeed, one can already see a certain similarity in cases of the ECJ judging a Member State, as in the *German Beer* case, and the WTO judging a Member, as in *Hormones.*

However, while this does seem to be a more appropriate parallel to draw, it is submitted that the WTO must be less interventionist in judging its Members than the ECJ is when judging its Member States. The EU's goals are far loftier than those of the WTO, and in the EU, Member States have explicitly accepted some limitation of their sovereignty so that such goals may be achieved. Meanwhile, the WTO's goals are humbler, and WTO Members have steadfastly refused any encroachment on their sovereignty. Finally, the WTO does not—yet—have the legitimacy of the EU and its institutions. For those reasons, it is submitted that for the WTO Appellate Body to be as intrusive as the ECJ is in judging its Member States would be a bridge too far.[61]

7. A Final Reflection: Subsequent Sanity Where Mad Cows Roam?

In July 1999, satisfied that measures and safeguards were sufficient to guarantee the safety of British beef, the European Commission decided to lift the ban on exports of beef and beef products from the United Kingdom.[62]

Meanwhile, the *Hormones* controversy rages on. Despite the WTO Appellate Body ruling declaring its measures unlawful, the EU is unyielding in its refusal to admit hormone beef to the EU market. The U.S. is retaliating against the EU. This dichotomy raises the question: why was it possible for the EU to reach some resolution of the *BSE* case, while the *Hormones* case remains intractable?

One cause, it seems fair to say, was that in the *BSE* case the political pressure on the EU to reassess its precautionary trade restrictions was more sustained than in the *Hormones* case. Furthermore, the *BSE* case faced the EU squarely with two competing interests about both of which it was sincerely concerned, the health of its own people on the one hand, and on the other hand, the trading interests of one of its own members. In such a situation, the EU was forced to balance these interests continuously and eventually modify trade-restrictive measures.

In the *Hormones* case, while the international community and the WTO might be pressuring the EU to change its stance, internal pressures are heavily weighted to the other extreme—EU consumers do not want hormone-beef—and the EU has stood by them. Continuing to draw a parallel between WTO Members and EU Member States, even though the Commission has seen fit to lift the BSE ban, there is still resistance at EU Member State level. Like the EU with respect to *Hormones,* France has refused to comply with the Commission's order to end the BSE embargo.[63]

It is submitted that where the burden of a risk (however minimal) is internal, and the benefit of lifting a ban is largely external, it will always be difficult for an authority to justify to its population taking a less trade-restrictive stance. Perhaps for cases like *Hormones* to ever come to a BSE-like resolution, the internal benefit of the less trade-restrictive measures must be more readily apparent to the citizen.

NOTES

1. The hormone ban also gave rise to litigation in the ECJ, see discussion of the *Fedesa* case below.

2. In March 1996, the Spongiform Encephalopathy Advisory Committee stated that eating beef from cattle that had BSE was the most likely cause of certain cases of CJD in humans, see ECJ, Case C-180/96 *UK v. Commission* [1998] ECR 2265, para. 9.

3. Commission Decision 96/239, OJ 1996 L 78/47. The ban also extended to exports of beef and related products from the UK to third countries. That the ban also covered third countries was an element that was vehemently challenged before the ECJ, on the grounds that the Commission did not have the power to enact such a far-reaching measure (see in particular ECJ, Case C-180/96 *UK v. Commission* [1998] ECR 2265, para. 16 ff). The Council defended the worldwide nature of the Commission's ban by saying that it made deflections of trade (such that exported beef could find its way back to the EU) impossible, and it added that "it would have been indefensible to apply dual standards, depending on whether the products were destined for the Community or

for third countries." (ibid., at para. 22). The Court upheld the worldwide nature of the ban, but supported its decision on the danger of possible re-importation to the EU if the ban were not worldwide.

4. ECJ, Case C-180/96 *UK v. Commission* [1998] ECR 2265 and reference for a preliminary ruling in ECJ, Case C-157/96 *The Queen v. Ministry of Agriculture, Fisheries and Food* [1998] ECR I-2211. The first was a direct action for annulment of the EU ban, brought by the UK against the Commission, and the second was a preliminary ruling pursuant to a question about the validity of the EU measures from the UK High Court, in a case in which farmers had sued the UK Ministry of Agriculture for acts based on the EU ban.

5. In particular, Council Directive 90/425/EEC of 26 June 1990 concerning veterinary and zoological checks applicable in intra-Community trade in certain live animals and products with a view to the completion of the internal market (OJ 1990 L 224/29) and Council Directive 89/662/EEC of 11 December 1989 concerning veterinary checks in intra-Community trade with a view to the completion of the internal market (OJ 1989 L 395/13), as amended.

6. Title II of the EC Treaty, Articles 32 to 38 (ex Articles 39 to 43 and 46). For the convenience of the reader, the following excerpts from those provisions are provided:

According to Article 32, "The common market shall extend to agriculture and trade in agricultural products. . . . The operation and development of the common market for agricultural products must be accompanied by the establishment of a common agricultural policy."

Article 33 goes on to say that "the objectives of the common agricultural policy shall be: . . . to increase agricultural productivity . . . to ensure a fair standard of living for the agricultural community . . . to stabilize markets . . ."

Next, Article 34 provides: "In order to attain the objectives set out in Article 33, a common organization of agricultural markets shall be established. This organization shall take one of the following forms, depending on the product concerned: (a) common rules on competition; (b) compulsory coordination of the various national market organizations; (c) a European market organization. . . . The common organization established in accordance with paragraph 1 may include all measures required to attain the objectives set out in Article 33. . . .The common organization shall be limited to pursuit of the objectives set out in Article 33 and shall exclude any discrimination between producers or consumers within the Community."

Then, Article 35: "To enable the objectives set out in Article 33 to be attained, provision may be made within the framework of the common agricultural policy for measures such as: . . . joint measures to promote consumption of certain products."

Finally, Article 37 provides that "In order to evolve the broad lines of a common agricultural policy, the Commission shall . . . convene a conference of the Member States with a view to making a comparison of their agricultural policies . . . Having taken [that] into account . . . the Commission shall submit proposals for working out and implementing the common agricultural policy . . . The Council shall, on a proposal from the Commission and after consulting the European Parliament, acting by a qualified majority . . . replace the national market organizations by the common organization," provided that the "common organization offers Member States which are opposed to this measure and which have an organization of their own for the production in question equivalent standards . . . such an organization ensures conditions for trade within the Community similar to those existing in a national market . . ."

7. ECJ, Case C-180/96 *UK v. Commission* [1998] ECR 2265, at para. 63.

8. Ibid., at para. 96. See also ECJ, Case C-331/88 *Fedesa and Others* [1990] ECR I-4023, para. 13, and Joined Cases C-133/93, C-300/93 and C-362/93 *Cripoltoni* [1994] ECR I-4863, para. 41.

9. Ibid., *UK v. Commission,* at paras. 99 and 63 respectively.

10. Ibid., at paras. 110 and 111.

11. Commission Decision 1999/514, OJ 1999 L 195/42.

12. Council Directive 81/602/EEC of 31 July 1981 (OJEC 1981 L 222/32); Council Directive 88/146/EEC of 7 March 1988 (OJEC 1988 L 70/16); Council Directive 88/299/EEC of 17 May 1988 (OJEC 1988 L 128/36). These directives were later repealed and replaced by Council Directive 96/22/EC of 29 April 1996 (OJEC 1996 L 125/3).

13. WTO Panel Report, *EC – Measures Concerning Meat and Meat Products (Hormones), Complaint by the United States,* WT/DS26/R/USA, adopted 13 February 1998, paras. 26 and 31. This is not to question the sincerity or the seriousness of those concerns. In fact, in the early 90s, a Belgian veterinarian was murdered by assassins linked to what is known in Belgium as the "hormone mafia," because of his role in enforcing the ban on the use of growth hormones by cattle breeders in the EU.

14. Ibid. and WTO Panel Report, *EC – Measures Concerning Meat and Meat Products (Hormones), Complaint by Canada,* WT/DS48/R/CAN, adopted 13 February 1998. In particular, they argued that these measures:

- directly and indirectly affected international trade;
- were not based on an assessment of risk and were consequently inconsistent with Article 5.1 SPS;
- were maintained without sufficient scientific evidence in contravention of Article 2.2 SPS;
- were not justified as a "provisional" measure under Article 5.7 SPS;
- breached Articles 2.2 and 5.6 SPS in that they were not based on scientific principles;
- were not applied only to the extent necessary to protect human life or health and were more trade-restrictive than required to achieve the appropriate level of sanitary protection;
- arbitrarily or unjustifiably discriminated between Members where identical or similar conditions prevailed, in contravention of Article 2.3 SPS;
- constituted a disguised restriction on international trade, in breach of Article 2.3 SPS;
- contravened Article 3.1 SPS because they were not based on the relevant international standards, guidelines or recommendations and that this departure from international standards was not justified by Article 3.3 SPS;
- were based on arbitrary or unjustifiable distinctions in the levels of protection in different situations, resulting in discrimination or a disguised restriction on international trade in contravention of Article 5, para. III (2).

15. Ibid. and Appellate Body Report, *European Communities – Measures Affecting Meat and Meat Products (Hormones),* WT/DS26/AB/R, adopted 13 February 1998.

16. Appellate Body report, at para. 172.

17. Ibid., para. 173.

18. Ibid., para. 193.

19. Ibid., para. 208.

20. Ibid., para. 200.

21. The Appellate Body, of course, refers to the "European Communities", but for consistency the abbreviation EU will be used throughout this paper.

22. ECJ, Case 331/88, *The Queen v. Minister of Agriculture, Fisheries and Food and Secretary of State for Health, ex parte: Fedesa and others ('Fedesa')*, [1990] ECR I-4023. The EU's hormones regime was also the subject of a number of other cases before the ECJ, brought by companies, the UK government and non-governmental organizations (see ECJ, Case 160/88, *Fedesa v. Council*, [1988] ECR 6399; ECJ, Case 160/88R, *Fedesa v. Council*, [1988] ECR 4121; ECJ, Case 34/88, *Cooperative agricole de l'Anjou et du Poitou and others v. Council*, [1988] ECR 6265; ECJ, Case 376/87, *Distrivet SA v. Council*, [1988] ECR 209; ECJ, Case 68/86, *UK v. Council*, [1988] ECR 855).

23. Which translates to the European Federation of Animal Health.

24. See Axel Desmedt, Hormones: "Objective Assessment" and (or as) Standard of Review, 1 *Journal of International Economic Law* 695 (1998).

25. ECJ, Case C-180/96 *UK v. Commission* [1998] ECR 2265, para. 39.

26. Ibid., para. 61.

27. Ibid., para. 75.

28. Appellate Body report in *Hormones*, para. 111.

29. Ibid., para. 14.

30. Ibid., para. 15.

31. Ibid., para. 17.

32. Ibid., para. 115.

33. Ibid., para. 116.

34. Ibid., para. 117.

35. Ibid., para. 193.

36. Ibid., para. 198, 199.

37. Ibid., para. 200.

38. The fifteen Member States of the EU are WTO Members, as is the EU (the European Communities) itself.

39. See for example, ECJ, Joined cases C-289/96, C-293/96 and C-299/96 *Kingdom of Denmark, Federal Republic of Germany and French Republic v. Commission of the European Communities* [1999] ECR I-1541 (where the ECJ annulled a Commission regulation registering "feta" as a protected geographical indication and designation of origin); ECJ, Joined cases C-68/94 and C-30/95 *French Republic and Société commerciale des potasses et de l'azote (SCPA) and Entreprise minière et chimique (EMC) v. Commission of the European Communities* [1998] ECR I-1375 (the *Kali und Salz* case, where the Court overruled a Commission decision in the context of merger control); and CFI (European Court of First Instance), Cases T-30, 36 and 37/91 *Solvay and ICI v. Commission of the European Communities* [1995] ECR II-1775 (the *Soda Ash* cases, where the Court reversed the Commission on rights of the defense and access to the file).

40. Some examples of other cases in which the Court has found a restriction to the free movement of goods in the EU not to be justified on public health grounds are in the *Cassis de Dijon* case, cited below (minimum alcohol content), *Commission v. Germany*, Case 153/78

[1979] ECR 2555 (a prohibition on importing meat products manufactured in one Member State from animals slaughtered in another Member State), *Gilli and Andres,* Case 788/79 [1980] ECR 2071 (prohibition on the importation and sale of vinegar other than wine vinegar) and *Kelderman,* Case 130/80 [1981] ECR 527 (prohibition on the sale of bread containing more than a certain amount of dry matter).

41. In fact, the measures the Community institutions took over hormones could be seen as ensuring free movement in the Community, see Joanne Scott, On Kith and Kine (and Crustaceans): Trade and Environment in the EU and WTO, in Joseph Weiler, *The EU, the WTO, and the NAFTA, Towards a Common Law of International Trade?* (Oxford, England: Oxford University Press 2000) 125, at 160:

> [T]he European Court exhibited greater deference than the WTO dispute settlement organs in reviewing the scientific basis of Council acts prohibiting hormones in beef. [footnote omitted] It should, however, be stressed that the reluctance of the Court to second-guess legislative policy choices occurred in the context of an act conceived as facilitating rather than impeding market integration. Indeed, had the measures not been enacted, the different approaches adopted by the Member States to the administration of hormones in farming might have resulted in market fragmentation as a result of Member State recourse to Article 30 EC Treaty exception (formerly Article 36).

42. But, one might say, the hormone ban also affected European producers. However, use of hormones in the European beef industry was never as prevalent as in the U.S. and Canadian industries. Unlike the measures taken in the *BSE* case, which made all exports from one Member State impossible, the hormone ban only required some European producers to change their policies.

43. *European Communities - Regime for the Importation, Sale and Distribution of Bananas* ('*Bananas*'), complaints by Ecuador, Guatemala, Honduras, Mexico and the United States (WT/DS27, Appellate Body report and Panel report, as modified by the Appellate Body, adopted on 25 September 1997). In *Bananas,* in spite of the fact that both a Panel and the Appellate Body found that the EU's banana regime was not WTO-consistent, the EU has so far failed to bring its regime into conformity, leading to WTO-authorized retaliation by the United States and Ecuador against the EU, to the tune of US$191.4 million and US$201.6 million respectively.

44. Incidentally, Professor Donald Regan argues that this is also true in the United States, where what counts for the U.S. Supreme Court in considering a State restriction on the free movement of goods is whether the rule in question has a protectionist purpose, see Donald Regan, The Supreme Court and State Protectionism: Making Sense of the Dormant Commerce Clause, 84 *Michigan Law Review* 1091 (1986), a point of view that he maintains today, following his presentation at this World Trade Forum conference.

45. In fact, the EU did not go so far as to ask for a "manifest error" standard of review in *Hormones*, but it did seek a "reasonableness" standard. That language sounds like a U.S. administrative law standard of review—but the EU before the WTO is not in the position of an administrative agency.

46. I am indebted here to the thinking of Marco Slotboom on this issue, in his article, The *Hormones* case: an Increased Risk of Illegality of Sanitary and Phytosanitary Measures, 36 Common Market Law Review 471 (1999), at 486–91.

47. The EU free movement of goods, which is directly based on the GATT rules, springs from Article 28 EC Treaty, which says: "Quantitative restrictions on imports and all measures having equivalent effect shall be prohibited between Member States."

Article 29 provides the same rule for exports. Derogations from these rules are possible, in particular on the basis of Article 30 EC Treaty:

> The provisions of Articles 28 and 29 shall not preclude prohibitions or restrictions on imports, exports or goods in transit justified on the grounds of public morality, public policy or public security; the protection of health and life of humans, animals or plants; the protection of national treasures possessing artistic, historic or archeological value; or the protection of industrial and commercial property. Such prohibitions or restrictions shall not, however constitute a means of arbitrary discrimination or a disguised restriction on trade between Member States.

The Court has also recognized in its *Cassis de Dijon* line of cases a series of "mandatory requirements" in addition to the grounds of justification expressly set out in Article 30, such as consumer protection, the prevention of unfair competition and the protection of the environment. (ECJ, Case 120/78 *Rewe-Zentral v. Bundesmonopolverwaltung für Branntwein ('Cassis de Dijon')* [1979] ECR 649).

48. However, as will be discussed below, when one speaks of sovereignty it must be kept in mind that the EU Member States have accepted much more far-reaching encroachments on their sovereignty than the WTO Members have.

49. EC Treaty, now Article 30.

50. ECJ, Case 104/75 *De Peijper* [1976] ECR 613, para. 15.

51. See for example ECJ, Case C-174/82 *Sandoz BV* [1983] ECR 2445, para. 16, ECJ, Case C.272/80, *Frans-Nederlandse Maatschappij voor Biologische Producten* [1981] ECR 327, para. 12, ECJ, Case C-227/82 *van Bennekom* [1983] ECR 3883, para. 38 and ECJ, Case C-178/84, *Commission v. Germany* [1987] ECR 1227, para. 41.

52. ECJ, Case C-178/84, *Commission v. Germany* [1987] ECR 1227.

53. Ibid., para. 39.

54. Ibid., para. 48.

55. In so doing, the Court confirmed earlier decisions in which it emphasized that the proportionality test obliges a Member State to take into account the results of international scientific research. See ECJ, Case 247/84 *Motte* [1985] ECR 3887, para. 24.

56. Ibid., para. 44.

57. Ibid., para. 49. This requirement of specific studies was confirmed in a subsequent judgment, ECJ, C-17/93, *Van der Veldt,* [1994] ECR 3537, para. 17, where the Court struck down a Belgian food safety norm whereby bread could not contain more than 2% salt, thus prohibiting imported bread containing 2.11 to 2.17% salt.

58. But see ECJ, Case 247/84 *Motte* [1985] ECR 3887 (where the ECJ upheld a Belgian rule prohibiting the use of colorants for use in lumpfish roe, although those colorants were authorized in Belgium for use in other foodstuffs).

With regard to the issue of consistency, after five years of deliberation, the WTO SPS Committee recently completed draft guidelines on risk "consistency", guidelines on which there was "fairly general agreement". The aim of this text is to give national authorities WTO guidelines to help them to treat risk consistently in their food safety, animal and human health measures, as is required by Article 5.5 SPS (as reported in the WTO's *Focus* Newsletter of March/April 2000).

59. ECJ, Case 6/64 *Costa v. ENEL* [1964] ECR 1141.

60. See for example ECJ, Case C-5/94 *The Queen and Ministry of Agriculture, Fisheries and Food, ex parte Hedley Lomas* [1994] ECR I-2553.

61. On 25 July 2000, a Panel upheld a French ban on white asbestos from Canada. While the Panel found that the ban was a violation of Article III:4 GATT, it found it justified under the public health exception of Article XX(b) GATT. This was the first time that the WTO has endorsed a trade ban on the basis of health concerns (WTO Panel Report, *European Communities – Measures Affecting Asbestos and Asbestos-Containing Products,* WT/DS135/R, report made public 18 September 2000, not yet adopted). On 23 October 2000, Canada notified the Dispute Settlement Body of its decision to appeal the case, and the appeal is currently pending.

62. Commission Decision of 23 July 1999, OJ L 195/42.

63. Indeed, on 4 January 2000, the Commission filed suit against France for its failure to lift the ban. It threatened to do the same against Germany, but Germany finally complied with the EU rule. France, for its part, brought an action against the Commission in December 1999 claiming that the Commission failed to observe the precautionary principle in removing the ban. Both cases are pending before the ECJ (Action brought on 29 December 1999 by the French Republic against the Commission of the European Communities, ECJ, Case C-514/99 OJ 2000 C 63/18 and Action brought on 4 January 2000 by the Commission of the European Communities against the French Republic, ECJ, Case C-1/00 OJ 2000 C 63/19).

CHAPTER 15

Commentary on Natalie McNelis' Paper

Merit Janow

Ms. McNelis has produced a very interesting article, obliging us to think structurally and institutionally about the relationship between the judge and the judged. This is an important perspective and illuminating when considering issues as politically sensitive as health- and safety-related matters and indeed the degree of deference to be accorded to national measures by various bodies, including the WTO. In a period of time when the WTO's DSB is still establishing its legitimacy (and track record on covered matters), the questions of standard of review and deference go to the central question of the allocation of power between national governments and international organizations. Here, let me briefly offer a comment on two dimensions of the paper: first, an area where I might differ slightly in emphasis from the author and then, several general observations about the SPS and WTO law itself.

On the first dimension, there was one legal difference in the two cases that I thought was likely to be more critical to explaining differences in outcomes than appeared to be the author's own assessment. Namely, whether the differences in outcome by the ECJ versus the WTO could be explained by the applicable legal standards of review that were contained in each of the agreements. McNelis makes a very interesting argument as to why the expressed standard of review does not explain the different outcomes. One wonders if this might be better illustrated in the context of other cases than the one before us—*BSE* and *Hormones*. Here, and particularly informed by the facts of the two cases, the difference in legal standard of review seems to go quite far in explaining differences in outcome. Specifically, the concept of "manifest error" which is contained in the Common Agricultural Policy (CAP) does indeed appear to give a high degree of deference to the EC's own determination. This is in contrast to the expectation of an "objective assessment" contained in Article 11 of the SPS. The author notes that the guidance by the Appellate Body as of that time on the meaning of "objective assessment" was slim, meaning that this was neither *de novo* review nor total deference, which is accurate. And, one's understanding of the different outcomes is enhanced by the added institutional perspectives of the role of the EC v. ECJ in contrast to WTO. Nevertheless, when coupled with applicable facts of each case, this difference in legal standard appears significant.

Second, with respect to WTO law, let us recall that the very purpose of the SPS Agreement was a negotiated outcome to ensure that there is some scientific basis for the introduction of trade restrictions at the national level. EC restrictions on U.S. hormone-treated beef have been a point of U.S.-EU trade tension for many years—indeed predating the conclusion of the SPS Agreement. Presumably the EU knew (or might have expected) that the SPS Agreement would be used for challenging those EU practices. Of course, nations can introduce health measures with limited scientific evidence by invoking the precautionary principle, under article 5.7 of the SPS Agreement, which the EU did not. But, on matters before the WTO under the terms of the SPS, a WTO Panel must defer so long as the importing member determinations are based on scientifically plausible accounts of cause and effect. To decide *among* scientifically plausible alternatives might, on the other hand, be second-guessing matters of science policy beyond the intended reach of the agreement. Put differently, it seems fully consistent with the WTO's legitimate goal to foster transparency, in this case of fact-finding, to require full disclosure when sanitary measures that restrict flows of trade are introduced. Parties should be stating the reasons and the basis for restrictions.

McNelis also makes some important observations about differences between the ECJ and the WTO with respect to the direct effect of covered agreements. She argues that the WTO must be less interventionist than the ECJ given the mandate of each institution. Indeed, the purposes of WTO rules are not squarely to oblige market integration, but rather to reduce government interventions of a trade-distorting nature. Hence, the WTO for the most part only pulls in the direction of integration and harmonization. One such example arises in the SPS which seems to require that members base their sanitary or phytosanitary measures on international comparisons, where they exist (see Article 3 of SPS.) This can be seen on the one hand as a safe harbor provision, but it might also be seen as a provision to encourage a degree of soft harmonization of systems. In the SPS context, that agreement identifies the CODEX as a reference for food safety, while recognizing that nations may chose to conform to that standard or pursue higher or different standards as well.

A further contribution of this paper is that the very subject matter considered (beef hormones/BSE) obliges us to ask anew: are there matters that are outside of the WTO or should be? What types of matters, if any, should be framed in terms of a political question? To a degree, this question has already been asked and answered satisfactorily in two ways: first, WTO members themselves can identify the applicable international restrictions. For example, members can reserve the right to determine matters deemed to be non-justiciable and outside of the competence of the WTO. This is already possible in the context of GATT Article 21, national security exception. This is perhaps the closest analogue to what is called political question doctrine in the United States, although that stems from a separation of powers doctrine. Further, in matters of interpreting judicial hierarchy, WTO members can choose to invoke the precautionary principle. However, once a WTO member elects not to invoke that principle, it hardly seems sensible to exclude matters *ex ante* in dispute settlement because they are sensitive. That being said, there is still room for improvement in all stages of WTO dispute settlement, including the first, where improved consultation mechanisms, perhaps through expanded mediation and other methods, might prove useful.

CHAPTER 16

Commentary on Natalie McNelis' Paper

George A. Bermann

Natalie McNelis' "tale of two cases"—essentially a comparison between the European Court of Justice's treatment of the European Commission's ban on beef exports from the UK with the WTO's treatment of the Community's own ban on the import of hormone-treated beef—is both instructive and provocative. We observe the Court of Justice sustaining the export ban on UK beef as consonant with the principle of free movement of goods and the principle of proportionality, and as a justifiable exercise of the precautionary principle. By contrast, the Community's ban on the import of hormone-treated beef was found by both the WTO Panel and Appellate Body to run afoul of the SPS Agreement, and in particular its requirement that covered measures be objectively based on a scientific risk assessment reasonably justifying those measures.

Although the cases display numerous differences (different facts, different legal measures, different legal texts, different justification standards), on the basis of which their outcomes might be reconciled, McNelis urges us to dig deeper for a truer explanation. She finds the doctrinal difference in justification standards particularly misleading. True, the Court of Justice appears to have required only that the challenged measure not be "manifestly inappropriate" for achievement of the end in view, while the WTO positively demanded that the challenged measure be objectively justified. But McNelis doubts the outcome would have been any different even if the two adjudicatory institutions had employed identically worded judicial review formulas. What matters more, in McNelis' view, is that the Community court was judging a measure of a Community institution (hence acting as "insider"), while the WTO adjudicators were judging a measure of a participating State (hence acting as "outsider").

The "insider/outsider" thesis is an important and original one. Fortunately it can be further tested by comparing the Court of Justice as "insider" and "outsider" judge: insider when assessing the legality of the export ban on British beef, outsider when assessing the legality of a comparable Member State measure. Suppose, in the face of the "mad cow disease" outbreak, the Community had not acted promptly, but a Member State (say, France), acting unilaterally, had barred imports of British beef. If that measure were challenged in the Court of Justice, would the Court have applied stricter scrutiny to the French measure than it applied in fact to the

Community measure? Would it have taken a dimmer view of the French measure than it took of the Community measure? Since, in my view, the answer to both questions is yes, the "insider/outsider" thesis appears to be supported.

The thesis is also supported in American law. The federal courts are decidedly more tolerant of restrictions on interstate commerce when they are imposed by Congress or other federal authorities than when they are imposed by individual states. Notions of separation of powers allow market-partitioning measures by Congress to pass constitutional muster when comparable measures by the states would run afoul of the supremacy or, more likely, the dormant commerce clause. By the same token, were the Appellate Body ever called upon to adjudicate the legality of GATT rules as such, it would likely be more lenient than it has shown itself to be in adjudicating the legality of member state rules.

Let us remember, however, that while it impeded the flow of a particular good between Member States, the Community's import ban on British beef was nevertheless, like so many Community measures, still a harmonization measure, in the sense that it purported to harmonize Member State market regulation. To that extent, the ban promoted the free movement of goods and, thereby, market integration. Is it fair to compare the WTO's judgment of a measure (the European ban on hormone-treated beef) that neither was nor even purported to be a harmonization or other market integration measure with the Court of Justice's judgment about a measure of that sort? We had better, perhaps, compare the WTO outcome with a Court of Justice case in which the Community measure in question was not, and did not purport to be, of a market integration character. Think, for example, of those cases in which a Commission regulation authorizes the imposition by one Member State of emergency duties on imports from another Member State. The fact is that the Court has not shown itself particularly indulgent toward Community measures of that stripe.

We also need to recognize that the "insider/outsider" distinction does not operate identically in all contexts. McNelis acknowledges as much ("the WTO simply is not the EU"), though in doing so she may be laying undue emphasis on institutional considerations and insufficient emphasis on political ones. McNelis thus cites both the direct effectiveness of EU law and the Member States' transfer of legislative sovereignty to the Community—features absent in the WTO legal system. But is the fact that EU law is capable of having direct effect a good reason to render judicial review of Member State legislation in the Court of Justice *more* stringent? Arguably, that fact suggests that the Court's review should be *less* stringent. As for the Member States' ceding of legislative sovereignty to the EU, I would have thought that, too, a good reason for the Court to make its review of Member State legislation less exacting. After all, the very transfer of legislative authority to the Community renders the Community capable of enacting harmonization measures whose effect is presumably to foster market integration. A polity that enjoys legislative prerogatives of this character has correspondingly less need to give direct effect to the basic treaty provisions, and certainly less need to give them highly rigorous direct effect.

I would invoke different features of the Community law system in explaining why the "insider/outsider" distinction works differently in the EU and in the WTO contexts. There is, first, the undeniable heterogeneity issue. The European Court of Justice works within a grouping of States that are incomparably less diverse, economically and otherwise, than the States that constitute the WTO system. I would suggest that stringent judicial policing of Member State rules that restrict market access becomes more difficult to maintain the more widely the States that comprise the grouping diverge from one another in relevant respects.

More generally, the EU, its ups-and-downs notwithstanding, has an integrative Community-building ethos. (The force of this ethos is something that may have been sacrificed in the terminological shift from European "Community" to European "Union.") The more integrative the *telos* within the grouping, the more likely it is that the adjudicatory bodies of the grouping will participate in that *telos,* and adjust their scrutiny of component State measures accordingly.

While I agree that, all circumstances considered, we can expect the review of Member State trade restrictions by the European Court of Justice to be less deferential than review of national restrictions by the WTO, I also think we need to recognize the existence of factors that potentially point in the opposite direction. Consider the fact that EU law renders offending Member State laws, for all practical purposes, unenforceable, while WTO law, even while condemning them, essentially renders them only potentially more costly to the enacting State. Arguably, where Member State laws, once condemned, will be virtually unenforceable, the court may be lead to read more gently in its assessments.

The United States is once again an instructive example. Curiously, the U.S. exhibits not only the two institutional features that McNelis emphasizes (viz. direct effect of federal law and the transfer by the States of legislative competences to the federal government), but also the two more political features that I have emphasized (viz. an integrative "nation-building" ethos and a relative homogeneity). The U.S. therefore has all the characteristics we have associated with forceful judicial policing of the internal market. Yet, under virtually any account of U.S. Supreme Court dormant commerce clause jurisprudence, the federal courts tend to show greater tolerance of potentially restrictive state measures than the European Court of Justice shows toward comparable Member State restrictions. The U.S. example suggests that the "insider/outsider" distinction does not tell us the whole story, so far as the stringency of judicial review of trade-impeding state measures are concerned.

The U.S. example may also serve to remind us that text (or lack thereof) does, after all, matter. The U.S. Constitution simply does not contain a rigorous textual prohibition on State measures that potentially inhibit interstate commerce. The WTO Agreement contains something more, and the European Community Treaty, of course, considerably more again. Should the presence or absence of text affect the stringency of judicial review of trade-impeding State measures? Democratic legitimacy reasoning suggests that it should.

We can conclude, I think, that McNelis is entirely right in suggesting that spatial relations (as in "insider/outsider") do matter when it comes to judicial scrutiny of trade-impeding measures, but that other factors matter as well—however difficult it may be to reach agreement in identifying the factors that matter and determining how much they do. I would be highly reluctant, both for descriptive and normative reasons, to omit text from among those factors.

CHAPTER 17

National Health Regulations and the SPS Agreement: The WTO Case Law of the Early Years

Henrik Horn and Petros C. Mavroidis

1. Introduction

Much of the policy debate about the WTO has centered on the conflict, real or alleged, between domestic health regulations and the agreements in the WTO. Several high profile disputes have rather recently dealt with such issues, such as the *European Communities - Measures Affecting the Importation of Hormone-Treated Beef* dispute, the *Australia - Measures Affecting Importation of Salmon* dispute, and the *Japan - Measures Affecting Agricultural Products* disputes. The purpose of this paper is to distil the more important aspects of the legal text and the ensuing case law, and to very briefly discuss the problems confronting the adjudicating bodies of the WTO in the health context.

In terms of the number and the importance of disputes, the most important agreement for the trade and health link is the Agreement on Sanitary and Phytosanitary Measures (SPS), even though both the Agreement on Technical Barriers to Trade (TBT) and Art. XX GATT (and XIV GATS) are relevant, as witnessed by the *Asbestos* dispute between France and Canada.

Under the SPS Agreement, it is clear that health measures that affect trade are usually adopted on "scientific evidence". They can also be adopted without scientific evidence, by invoking the "precautionary" principle. If adopted on scientific evidence and subsequently contested by affected WTO Members, the role of the judge will be to review the quality of the scientific evidence. As has been shown amply in, e.g., the *Hormones* dispute, this is not a simple exercise. The SPS Agreement advances a model to deal with this issue; it is, however, drafted in such a general language that it all becomes a matter for interpretation. With respect to the use of the "precautionary"

We would like to thank Richard Baldwin, Eyal Benvenisti, Claus-Dieter Ehlermann, Lorenzo Sigismondi, Joost Pauwelyn, Bill Sage, Alex Stein, and participants in the Fourth World Trade Forum Conference held in Bern on August 21 and 22, 2000, for very useful discussions.

principle, the SPS Agreement is quite laconic. Hence, once again interpretation is sought. The WTO adjudicating bodies have recently been quite active in this respect, as will be discussed below.

With respect to treatment of health-related obstacles to trade under the SPS Agreement, the thesis advanced in this paper can be captured in two observations:

1. The current SPS Agreement-test asks up-front the question: "Is a trade-obstructing legislation health-based, in the sense of does it help to promote a health-related objective?"
2. By adopting trade-obstructing, even though health-based, legislation, WTO Members might be aiming at more than one bird with one stone. Through a consistency-requirement, the SPS Agreement distinguishes between consistent and inconsistent trade-obstructing health-based policies, that is, in a sense it distinguishes between genuine and not genuine health concerns.

The heart of the paper is a presentation and a subsequent critical evaluation of this second part. For consistency between different measures can only be appreciated once comparability between these has been established, and, as this paper aims to demonstrate, some of the elements necessary to establish comparability according to the SPS Agreement are very hard to evaluate.

It should be emphasized that health-based obstacles to trade liberalization can be also addressed by invoking other WTO Agreements, especially the GATT and the Technical Barriers to Trade (TBT) Agreement. The relationship between the three agreements has not been clarified in WTO jurisprudence so far, however. It is clear from its text that the SPS Agreement is *lex specialis* to the TBT Agreement and must take precedence over it. The relationship, on the other hand, between the GATT and the TBT Agreement and the GATT and the SPS Agreement has not been so far clarified in WTO practice.[1] Moreover, the fact that the SPS Agreement takes precedence over the TBT Agreement does not mean that the latter is irrelevant as far as health-related disputes are concerned: the SPS Agreement deals with sanitary and phytosanitary measures only, and these form a sub-set of measures with potential health impact that can potentially be part of a "technical regulation" or a "standard," that is, the ambit of the TBT Agreement. But while WTO case law with respect to health-related issues now exists in both the GATT and the SPS Agreement, WTO adjudicating bodies have shown a certain reticence to interpret the TBT Agreement.

The next section provides a positive account of the most important provisions of the SPS Agreement paying particular attention to those already interpreted by the WTO adjudicating bodies. It also discusses the emerging case law from a more principled level, pointing to some inherent problems facing international trade regulations in the context of health. The SPS Agreement has so far proved to be the most frequently used *forum* to address health-based trade disputes. The *Asbestos* case is evidence that even in the GATT an SPS-inspired standard is slowly evolving. Section III discusses the case law presented in Section II and concludes that for good reasons (uncertainty, asymmetry of information, increased agency costs) a deferential standard of review is most appropriate when the international judge is dealing with health-related issues.

2. SPS and Its Interpretation in Case Law[2]

Art. 3.2 SPS makes it clear that if a health measure is based on an *international standard,* there is a presumption that the measure at hand is compatible with the WTO.[3] But the article does not oblige countries to follow these standards: indeed, Art. 3.3 SPS allows countries to adopt their own standards. In such circumstances, however, they cannot benefit from the presumption under Art. 3.2 SPS and will have to, if challenged, absolve the burden of proof to demonstrate that their measures are WTO-compatible. The rest of the paper deals with the case where a WTO Member has decided not to follow an international standard.

Generally speaking, a Member can, according to Art. 3.3, enact a national regulation that is more restrictive than the international standard provided there is *"scientific justification"*, or provided it is consistent with the procedural requirements laid out in Art. 3.5. Some of the key issues (risk, risk assessment, scientific evidence, non-discrimination, coherence) have been already interpreted in the WTO case law. We will below discuss these issues in turn.

"Risks . . ." (Art. 5.1 SPS)

In order to interpret the notion of risk assessment, one must first have a clear idea about the meaning of "risk". The notion of "risky" as opposed to "risk-free" is, in a sense, not very interesting in the SPS context: it is almost impossible to rule out the possibility that a certain product might cause a certain harm. It might seem a ludicrous idea to anyone that such a connection might exist, one might lack any theory or empirical evidence that would suggest such causality, but it might still exist. This might seem a sophist type of argument, but is actually of much more relevance, as will be seen. When evaluating "riskiness", the problem of the adjudicating bodies thus becomes one of distinguishing levels of risk that are positive, but still not enough to justify a certain measure, from levels that are sufficiently high. Their task is thus not to judge whether products are risk-free or not.

The *Hormones* Appellate Body report[4] acknowledges this point (upholding a previous finding by a Panel) when it states that:

> [T]he Panel opposes a requirement of an "identifiable risk" to the uncertainty that theoretically always remains since science can *never* provide *absolute* certainty that a given substance will not *ever* have adverse health effects. We agree with the Panel that this theoretical uncertainty is not the kind of risk which, under Article 5.1, is to be assessed. (§186, emphasis in the original)

The *Hormones* Appellate Body report also notes that:

> The ordinary meaning of "potential" relates to "possibility" and is different from the ordinary meaning of "probability". "Probability" implies a higher degree or a threshold of potentiality or possibility. (§184 op. cit.).

This point was confirmed by the Appellate Body in the *Salmon* dispute:

> As stated in our Report in European Communities – Hormones, the risk evaluated in a risk assessment must be an ascertainable risk; theoretical uncertainty is "not the kind of risk which, under Article 5.1, is to be assessed."[5]

And:

> [I]t is not sufficient that a risk assessment conclude that there is a *possibility* of entry, establishment or spread of diseases and associated biological and economic consequences. (§123 op. cit.)

Hence, a risk in the context of Art 5.1 is more than a mere possibility. This does not mean, however, that the Appellate Body believed that there should be a minimum level of risk involved in order for a permanent measure to possibly be lawful (on this issue, see also *infra* at 1.3.5):

> To the extent that the Panel purported to require a risk assessment to establish a minimum magnitude of risk, we must note that imposition of such quantitative requirement finds no basis in the SPS Agreement.

"Measures Are Based on . . . an Assessment . . . of the Risks . . ." (Art. 5.1 SPS)

Now turn to the notion of risk assessment. The *Hormones* Panel report[6] made a distinction between risk assessment and risk management. We should note first that the term "risk assessment" is already defined in Annex A of the SPS Agreement:

> The evaluation of the likelihood of entry, establishment or spread of a pest or disease within the territory of an importing Member according to the sanitary or phytosanitary measures which might be applied, and of the associated potential biological and economic consequences; or the evaluation of the potential for adverse effects on human or animal health arising from the presence of additives, contaminants, toxins or disease-causing organisms in food, beverages or foodstuffs.

The *Hormones* Panel report understood this term as follows: "An assessment of risk is, at least for risks to human life or health, a *scientific* examination of data and factual studies; it is not a policy exercise involving social value judgments made by political bodies" (§8.94 op. cit., emphasis in the original).

The Panel distinguishes from "risk assessment", as defined above, "risk management" which is the second step in a decision by a WTO Member to enact an SPS measure. That is, after a risk assessment has been carried through and provided that a Member face an ascertainable risk as defined above, the Member can choose its appropriate level of sanitary or phytosanitary protection.[7] As the Panel implies, WTO Members, provided that they respect the disciplines laid out in Art. 5.4–5.6 SPS, are free to choose the level of protection that seems appropriate to them. This finding is in line with the finding of the Appellate Body that WTO members can legitimately pursue a zero-risk policy.

The Appellate Body did not accept this reasoning, however. §181 of the cited report states:

> We must stress in this connection that Article 5 and Annex A of the SPS Agreement speak of "risk assessment" only and that the term "risk management" is not to be found either in Article 5 or in any other provision of the SPS Agreement.

We should note, however, that this finding by the Appellate Body can only have formal and not substantial consequences: as we understand it, the notion of appropriate risk management must be understood as equivalent to the notion of maintaining the appropriate level of sanitary or phytosanitary protection. The operative consequence of such discretion is that, if a proper risk assessment has been made, WTO Members are free to choose their optimal level of protection (for instance, Members might have different attitudes toward, or economic possibilities of, risk reduction). Through the use of the term "risk management", the Panel report reflects precisely that regulatory diversity is consistent with the SPS Agreement, and while the Appellate Body report refutes the use of the term "risk management", it does not cast any doubt on the proposition as such.[8]

The notion of risk assessment was further clarified in the *Salmon* Appellate Body report. There, in a passage often quoted in subsequent case law, the Appellate Body states:

> [W]e consider that . . . a risk assessment within the meaning of Article 5.1 must:
>
> 1. *identify* the diseases whose entry, establishment or spread a Member wants to prevent within its territory, as well as the potential biological and economic consequences associated with the entry, establishment or spread of these diseases;
>
> 2. *evaluate the likelihood of entry,* establishment or spread of these diseases, as well as the associated potential biological and economic consequences; and
>
> 3. evaluate the likelihood of entry, establishment or spread of these diseases *according to the SPS measures which might be applied.* (§121 op. cit.)

So, according to this definition, a risk assessment involves the establishment of a likelihood of entry of an identified disease, and of a causal relationship between the SPS measure at stake and the occurrence of the disease, in the sense that its measure will mitigate the identified risks.

Now, for a permanent SPS measure to be WTO-compatible it must be *based on* a risk assessment. The exact meaning of the words "based on" is discussed in the *Hormones* litigation. Two aspects of the term have been interpreted: the time dimension and the extent of the overlap between the SPS measure enacted and the risk assessment. With regard to the time dimension, the Panel report in the *Hormones* litigation holds for the proposition that[9]

> [T]he Member imposing a sanitary measure needs to submit evidence that at least it actually *took into account* a risk assessment when it

enacted or maintained its sanitary measure in order for that measure to be considered as *based on* a risk assessment.[10]

Hence, according to this view, the lawfulness of a measure depends on the *decision process* leading to the measure: scientific evidence not used in the decision process is irrelevant even if it would as such support the measure (§8.115 of the report). The Appellate Body reversed the Panel's findings in this respect and ruled that a WTO Member can lawfully enact a measure even when it cannot offer a basis of risk assessment at the moment of enactment of such measure, provided that a basis can be offered if and when the measure is challenged before a WTO adjudicating body.

The *Hormones* Appellate Body report, again reversing the Panel report, made it clear that "based on" should not be understood to mean that the SPS measure must be absolutely conform to the risk assessment. A certain margin of discretion in favor of the WTO Member enacting legislation must be acknowledged. The relevant passage reads:

> We are unable to accept this interpretation of the Panel. In the first place, the ordinary meaning of "based on" is quite different from the plain or natural import of "conform to." A thing is commonly said to be "based on" another thing when the former "stands" or is "founded" or "built" upon or "is supported by" the latter.[11] In contrast, much more is required before one thing may be regarded as "conform[ing] to" another: the former must "comply with," "yield or show compliance" with the latter. The reference of "conform to" is to "correspondence in form or manner," to "compliance with" or "acquiescence," to "follow[ing] in form or nature."[12] A measure that "conforms to" and incorporates a Codex standard is, of course, "based on" that standard. A measure, however, based on the same standard might not conform to that standard, as where only some, not all, of the elements of the standard are incorporated into the measure. (§163 op. cit.)

Both the Panel and the Appellate Body report referred to the use of international standards. Hence, it is clear that national SPS measures based on international standards can pass the test of WTO legality even if they reflect only elements of an international standard.

"Shall Take into Account Scientific Evidence . . ." (Art. 5.2 SPS)

The SPS Agreement[13] imposes on all WTO Members concerned an obligation to base their measures on scientific evidence. Art. 2.2 SPS reads:

> Members shall ensure that any sanitary or phytosanitary measure is applied only to the extent necessary to protect human, animal or plant life or health, is based on scientific principles and is not maintained without scientific evidence, except as provided for in paragraph 7 of Article 5.

The term "scientific evidence" is not *a priori* clear. Indeed, what exactly is scientific evidence? The *Hormones* Panel report did not discuss the issue in great detail. In §8.130 of the report, though, we note that general information not relating specifically to the subject matter under discussion might be disregarded as impertinent. Hence, the report advances a *specificity* criterion in judging whether advanced arguments are to be regarded as scientific evidence, but without explaining exactly which level of specificity is necessary for an opinion to qualify as such evidence.

The Appellate Body *Hormones* report gave a general definition of scientific evidence:

> [A] process characterized by systematic, disciplined, and objective enquiry and analysis, that is, a mode of studying and sorting out facts and opinions. (§187 op. cit.)

While this, for many situations, is a too general definition to be operational, the report importantly stated that *minority scientific opinions* may suffice for a WTO Member to have absolved its burden under the SPS:

> Article 5.1 does not require that the risk assessment must necessarily embody only the view of a majority of the relevant scientific community. In some cases, the very existence of divergent views presented by qualified scientists who have investigated the particular issue at hand may indicate a state of scientific uncertainty. Sometimes a divergence may indicate a roughly equal balance of scientific opinion, which may itself be a form of scientific uncertainty. In most cases, responsible and representative governments tend to base their legislative and administrative measures on "mainstream" scientific opinion. In other cases, equally responsible and representative governments may act in good faith on the basis of what, at a given time, may be a divergent opinion coming from qualified and respected sources. (§194)

But while a minority opinion may suffice, it must fulfill a form of *"sufficient degree of insight"* criterion. When examining an oral statement by an expert (Dr. Lucier) invited to testify before it in the same dispute, the Appellate Body notes that:

> [T]his opinion by Dr. Lucier does not purport to be the result of scientific studies carried out by him or under his supervision focusing specifically on residues of hormones in meat from cattle fattened with such hormones. Accordingly, it appears that the single divergent opinion expressed by Dr. Lucier is not reasonably sufficient to overturn the contrary conclusions reached in the scientific studies referred to by the European Communities that relate specifically to residues of the hormones in meat from cattle to which hormones had been administered for growth promotion. (§198)

While it is somewhat unclear why the Appellate Body dismissed the opinion of the expert, the term "accordingly" used by the Appellate Body seems to suggest that the reason was the fact that Dr. Lucier had not previously conducted research on the issue, and could therefore not be trusted to be sufficiently well informed about the issue.

The Appellate Body report on *Hormones* thus provides certain guidance concerning the definition of "scientific evidence," but an operational definition for WTO disputes still remains to be provided.

Factors Other Than Scientific Evidence That Can/Should Be Taken into Account According to Art. 5.2 SPS

Art. 5.2 SPS lists the factors to be taken into account when assessing risk. It mentions: available scientific evidence; relevant processes and production methods; relevant inspection, sampling, and testing methods; prevalence of specific diseases and pests; existence of pest- or disease-free areas; relevant ecological and environmental conditions; and quarantine or other treatment.

In a notorious passage in its *Hormones* report, the Appellate Body interpreted the objective function of the list:

> [T]o the extent that the Panel purports to exclude from the scope of a risk assessment in the sense of Article 5.1, all matters not susceptible of quantitative analysis by the empirical or experimental laboratory methods commonly associated with the physical sciences, we believe that the Panel is in error. Some of the kinds of factors listed in Article 5.2 such as "relevant processes and production methods" and "relevant inspection, sampling, and testing methods" are not necessarily or wholly susceptible of investigation according to laboratory methods of, for example, biochemistry or pharmacology. Furthermore, there is nothing to indicate that the listing of factors that may be taken into account in a risk assessment of Article 5.2 was intended to be a closed list. It is essential to bear in mind that the risk that is to be evaluated in a risk assessment under Article 5.1 is not only risk-ascertainable in a science

> laboratory operating under strictly controlled conditions, but also risk in human societies as they actually exist, in other words, the actual potential for adverse effects on human health in the real world where people live and work and die. (§187 op. cit.)

Hence, it seems that the Appellate Body in this passage, on the one hand, opts for a hands-free attitude vis-à-vis national SPS measures (by allowing WTO Members to view the factors mentioned in the list not necessarily from a strict scientific angle); on the other, it also adopts the position that the list of Art. 5.2 SPS is not exhaustive, and that factors that are not mentioned in the list can be taken into account when a WTO Member assesses a risk.

At this stage, we are in the dark as to *which* other factors can be taken into account (beyond those mentioned in Art. 5.2 SPS) or as to *how* the factors mentioned can in practice be evaluated from a non- (or less) scientific perspective.

"In Assessing the Risk . . . and Determining the Measure . . . Members Shall Take into Account . . . Economic Factors . . ." (Art. 5.3 SPS)

Art. 5.3 not only allows, but actually *forces*, Members ("Members shall") to take into account relevant economic factors when assessing the appropriate level of protection. As relevant economic factors the article mentions potential loss of production or sales from the disease, the costs of control or eradication of the disease, and the relative cost-effectiveness of alternative measures to limit risk.

As will be further discussed later, this article seems to open a wide range of possibilities to rationalize beggar-thy-neighbor type measures. However, the ambit of the article is circumscribed by Art. 5.6, which requires Members to avoid regulatory distinctions that result in disguised restriction of international trade. Art. 5.3 has not been interpreted so far in case law.

It should be noted that the possibility to look for economic factors when enacting SPS measures exists only with respect to risks to animal or plant life or health. No reference to economic factors is reflected in Art. 5.2 SPS which covers risks to human health. Now does this mean that an *a contrario* interpretation is appropriate here and hence economic factors are not a concern when it comes to human health-related SPS measures? Or should we infer that by analogy economic factors are an issue in Art. 5.2 SPS as well? So far, there has been no response to this question in the Appellate Body case law.

"Members Should, When Determining the Appropriate Level of . . . Protection, Take into Account the Objective of Minimizing Negative Trade Effects" (Art. 5.4 SPS)

None of the Appellate Body reports contains in its *ratio decidendi* reference to Art. 5.4 SPS. However, an explicit reference to this Article is to be found in the *Hormones* Panel report which in pertinent part reads:

> Guided by the wording of Article 5.4, in particular the words "should (not *shall*)" and "objective" we consider that this provision of the SPS Agreement does not impose an obligation. However, this objective of minimizing trade effects has nonetheless to be taken into account in the interpretation of other provisions of the SPS Agreement. (§8.166 op. cit.)

This statement read in conjunction with the quoted statement above (that WTO Members can legitimately pursue a zero-risk policy[14]) leads to the inescapable conclusion that the Appellate Body case law does not impose a limit on the appropriate level of protection sought by individual WTO Members.

"Measures Are Not More Trade Restrictive Than Necessary . . ." (Art. 5.6 SPS)

Art. 5.6 essentially reproduces the so-called "necessity test" as we know it from the GATT case law in Art. XX. Art. 5.6 is in close relationship with Art. 5.4 SPS. The latter refers to the objective sought by WTO Members whereas the former deals with the issue of means applied to reach the stated objective. As mentioned above, WTO adjudicating bodies will not put into question the level of the objective sought; all they can do is examine whether the means used are the least restrictive means that a WTO Member could use to reach its objective.

The logical link between means used to reach a particular level of protection and the level sought prejudges the standard of review to be applied by WTO adjudicating bodies: if the level sought is a zero-risk policy, then by definition the means applied will have to be quite restrictive. Hence, adjudicating bodies will have less leeway to examine whether the means used are indeed the least restrictive option than in a case where the objective sought is not as inflexible as a zero-risk policy.

To determine whether "measures are not more trade restrictive than necessary . . . ," we must first answer the question of "to achieve what?" The *Salmon* Appellate Body report made it clear that WTO Members are free to determine their own levels of health protection:

> The determination of the appropriate level of protection, a notion defined in paragraph 5 of Annex A, as "the level of protection deemed appropriate by the Member establishing a sanitary . . . measure" is a *prerogative* of the Member and not of the Panel or of the Appellate Body.
>
> The "appropriate level of protection" established by a Member and the "SPS measure" have to be clearly distinguished. They are not one and the same thing. The first is an *objective,* the second is an *instrument* chosen to attain or implement that objective (§§199–200 op. cit., emphasis in the original.)

The report also dealt with the related question of how to determine the level of health protection applied by a Member enacting an SPS measure, in a situation where the Member has not clearly identified this level:

> We believe that in cases where a Member does not determine its appropriate level of protection, or does so with insufficient precision, the appropriate level of protection may be established by Panels on the basis of the level of protection reflected in the SPS measure actually applied. Otherwise, a Member's failure to comply with the implicit obligation to determine its appropriate level of protection—with sufficient precision—would allow it to escape from its obligations under this Agreement and, in particular, its obligations under Articles 5.5 and 5.6. (§207 op. cit.)

The next question concerns the appropriate test to be applied when reviewing the means used to reach the sought objective. Again, the *Salmon* Appellate Body report contains a relevant passage:

> What is required under Article 5.6 is an examination of whether possible alternative SPS measures meet the appropriate level of protection *as determined by the Member concerned.* (§204 op. cit., emphasis in the original)

Later, upholding the Panel's findings in this respect the Appellate Body provides the test to be used in order to examine whether a means is indeed the least restrictive way to reach the ends sought:

> [T]he three elements of this test under Article 5.6 are that there is an SPS measure which:
>
> 1. is reasonably available taking into account technical and economic feasibility;
> 2. achieves the Member's appropriate level of sanitary or phytosanitary protection; and

3. is significantly less restrictive to trade than the SPS measure contested.

These three elements are cumulative in the sense that if any of these elements is not fulfilled, the measure in dispute would be consistent with Article 5.6. In subsequent case law, the Appellate Body confirmed this finding.[15]

A central issue is what a WTO adjudicating body should do in order to determine whether a less restrictive option exists which would permit WTO Members to reach their objectives. During the *Varietals* Panel proceedings, the United States advanced the argument that Japan could reach its stated objective by using another less restrictive means, namely the "testing by product" method.[16] The Panel weighed the evidence presented to it, examined and rejected the U.S. claim, since it was not convinced that it had sufficient evidence before it to conclude in a definitive manner the issue. The Appellate Body (§§96ff. op. cit.) upheld the result.

It is clear that if presented with evidence by a party to the dispute that a means chosen by a WTO Member to reach a health objective is not the least restrictive one, WTO adjudicating bodies will have to examine the argument. But in case no argument is presented, or in case the presented argument is not convincing, can WTO adjudicating bodies still address questions to the parties in order to determine the degree of restrictiveness of a particular measure? The WTO case law provides some answers in this respect. But we will treat them when addressing the burden of proof issue below.

"Consistency in the . . . Protection against Risk . . ." (Art. 5.5 SPS)

The *Hormones* Appellate Body acknowledges (§213, op. cit.) that "the objective of Article 5.5 is formulated as the 'achieving [of] consistency in the application of the concept of appropriate level of sanitary or phytosanitary protection . . .'." This does not mean that SPS policies always have to be consistent over time. The same report a few lines later explains:

> [W]e agree with the Panel's view that the statement of that goal does not establish a *legal obligation* of consistency of appropriate levels of protection. We think, too, that the goal set is not absolute or perfect consistency, since governments establish their appropriate levels of protection frequently on an *ad hoc* basis and over time, as different risks present themselves at different times. It is only arbitrary or unjustifiable inconsistencies that are to be avoided. (§213, op. cit., emphasis in the original)

According to the same report, three elements must be cumulatively demonstrated for a violation of Art. 5.5 SPS to exist:

> The first element is that the Member imposing the measure complained of has adopted its own appropriate levels of sanitary protection against risks to human life or health in several different situations. The second element to be shown is that those *levels of protection* exhibit arbitrary or unjustifiable differences ('distinctions' in the language of Article 5.5) in their treatment of different situations. The last element requires that the arbitrary or unjustifiable differences result in discrimination or a disguised restriction of international trade. We understand the last element to be referring to the *measure* embodying or implementing a particular level of protection as resulting, in its application, in discrimination or in a disguised restriction on international trade.
>
> We consider the above three elements of Article 5.5 to be cumulative in nature; all of them must be demonstrated to be present if violation of Article 5.5 is to be found. In particular, both the second and third elements must be found. (§§214–5 op. cit., emphasis in the original)

According to the *Hormones* Appellate Body report, the fact that the European Community prohibited the use of some hormones in beef production while authorizing others for pig production was compatible with Art. 5.5 SPS, even if this difference of treatment was found to be arbitrary or unjustifiable, since in the Appellate Body's view, the third element of its three-prong test was not met. §245 of the report states:

> We do not attribute the same importance as the Panel to the supposed multiple objectives of the European Communities in enacting the EC Directives that set forth the EC measures at issue. The documentation that preceded or accompanied the enactment of the prohibition of the use of hormones for growth promotion and that formed part of the record of the Panel makes clear the depth and extent of the anxieties experiencing within the European Communities concerning the results of the general scientific studies (showing the carcinogenicity of hormones), the dangers of abuse (highlighted by scandals relating to black-marketing and smuggling of prohibited veterinary drugs in the European Communities) of hormones and other substances used for growth promotion and the intense concern of consumers within the European Communities over the quality and drug-free character of the meat available in its internal market.

The *Salmon* Appellate Body report applies the same three-prong test when it examines the compatibility of an Australian measure with Art. 5.5 SPS (§140 op. cit.). It further confirms the finding of the *Hormones* Appellate Body report that differences in level of protection are a "warning signal" that the implementing measure in its application might be a discriminatory measure (§161 op. cit.). It thus confirms that differences in the levels of protection as such are not enough to satisfy the third element of the three-prong test: they are a necessary but not sufficient condition to this effect.

The *Salmon* Appellate Body then took note of the fact that the Panel had identified two more warning signals—substantial difference in levels of protection and inconsistency of the SPS measure at hand with Art. 5.1 SPS (§§163–165 op. cit.)—and three additional factors—discrimination between salmon and herring used as bait, the substantial but unexplained change in conclusion between two Reports recommending the SPS measures, and the absence of controls on the internal movement of salmon products within Australia (§§167–174 op. cit.).

The Appellate Body agreed with Australia that the first additional factor was a mere restatement of the first warning signal and hence should not be taken into account (§169 op. cit.). It accepts the remaining part of the Panel's analysis and concludes as follows:

> We have only reversed the Panel's finding on the first "additional factor." We consider, however, that this reversal does not affect the validity of the Panel's conclusion in paragraph 8.159 of its Report, that the "warning signals" and "other factors," considered cumulatively, lead to the conclusion that the distinctions in the level of protection imposed by Australia result in a disguised restriction on international trade. (§177, op. cit.)

At first glance, a discrepancy appears to exist between the two reports although the same standard was applied. There are two distinguishing factors between the two cases, however, which probably explain the difference in the outcome: first, §8.32 of the *Salmon* Panel report states that "the protection of human life or health is not at issue in this dispute." Second, the anxieties of consumers mentioned in the *Hormones* Appellate Body report were reflected in the EC Directive (in its preamble) but not at all in Australian SPS. Indeed, this could hardly be the case since, as Australia admitted, human life or health was not an issue. It appears hence that the Appellate Body is leaning towards a more deferential standard when human life or health is at stake.

> [W]here relevant scientific evidence is insufficient, a Member may provisionally adopt . . . measures on the basis of available pertinent information . . . (Art. 5.7 SPS)

Art. 5.7 SPS reflects the notorious "precautionary" principle that allows WTO Members to take SPS measures even in absence of scientific evidence. But the absence of scientific evidence does not imply that WTO Members are completely unconstrained when enacting SPS measures under Art. 5.7 SPS. The *Varietals* Appellate Body report explains that:

> [A] Member may provisionally adopt an SPS measure if this measure is:
> 1. imposed in respect of a situation where "relevant scientific information is insufficient;"
> 2. adopted "on the basis of available pertinent information."
>
> Pursuant to the second sentence of Article 5.7, such a provisional measure may not be maintained unless the Members which adopted the measure:
>
> 1. seek to obtain the additional information necessary for a more objective assessment of risk; and
> 2. "review the . . . measure accordingly within a reasonable period of time."
>
> These four requirements are clearly cumulative in nature and are equally important for the purpose of determining consistency with this provision. Whenever *one* of these four conditions is not met, the measure at issue is inconsistent with Article 5.7. (§89 op. cit., original emphasis)

Since the Panel did not examine the two elements appearing in the first sentence of Art. 5.7 SPS and based its conclusions only on the elements appearing in the second sentence, the Appellate Body did not have the opportunity to interpret the first sentence.

With respect to the elements appearing in the second sentence, the Appellate Body observed:

> Article 5.7 states that the additional information is to be sought in order to allow the Member to conduct "a more objective assessment of risk." Therefore, the information sought must be germane to conducting such a risk assessment, i.e., the evaluation of the likelihood of entry, establishment or spread of, *in casu,* a pest, according to the SPS measures which might be applied. (§92 op. cit.)

and

> [W]hat constitutes a "reasonable period of time" has to be established on a case-by-case basis and depends on the specific circumstances of each

> case, including the difficulty of obtaining the additional information necessary for the review and the characteristics of the provisional SPS measure. In the present case, the Panel found that collecting the necessary additional information would be relatively easy. Although the obligation "to review" the varietal testing requirement has only been in existence since 1 January 1995, we agree with the Panel that Japan has not reviewed its varietal testing requirement "within a reasonable period of time." (§93 op. cit.)

What emerges from case law is that in case it is relatively easy for a WTO Member to collect the additional necessary information, such collection must have taken place within four years (since the Appellate Body report was issued on 22 February 1999). But, while the additional information must be "pertinent," we are still in the dark, however, as to the interpretation of the term "available pertinent information" as it appears in the first sentence of Art. 5.7 SPS. This term may be the cornerstone of the whole Article: "available pertinent information" is by definition less authoritative than "scientific evidence," but we need to know how much less is sufficient for the "precautionary" principle to be invoked.

Allocation of Burden of Proof Concerning Alleged Inconsistency

The WTO (like most areas of public international law) contains a decentralized system of enforcement, and parties to a dispute in principle carry the burden of proof for their arguments. On the other hand, WTO adjudicating bodies administer the process and are obliged under Art. 11 DSU to conduct an objective assessment of the dispute before them. This raises the question of whether WTO adjudicating bodies have to provide an objective assessment within what has been submitted by the parties to the dispute, or they can/should move to arguments and claims not submitted by the parties.

The discovery process of WTO adjudicating bodies is laid out in a rudimentary form in Art. 13 DSU and Art. 11.2 SPS, and it essentially enables WTO adjudicating bodies to look for outside expertise in order to decide SPS-related cases. However, none of these texts makes it clear whether such expertise should focus on the claims and arguments as presented by parties to the dispute only, or whether it can extend to issues not covered by the parties. These issues have been dealt with in the case law.

The *Hormones* Appellate Body report establishes the rule to be followed when allocating burden of proof:

> The initial burden lies on the complaining party, which must establish a *prima facie* case of inconsistency with a particular provision of the *SPS*

> *Agreement* on the part of the defending party, or more precisely, of its SPS measure or measure complained about. When the *prima facie* case is made, the burden of proof moves to the defending party, which must in turn counter or refute the claimed inconsistency. (§98 op. cit., emphasis in the original)

Hence, it is clear that there is nothing like an *ex ante* control of consistency of SPS measures. Such measures are presumed to be consistent with the WTO unless challenged and proven to be inconsistent before a WTO adjudicating body.

The issue appeared again in the context of the *Varietals* litigation, but this time with a slight "twist" that actually bridges the gap between burden of proof and extent of control by WTO adjudicating bodies: the United States claimed that Japan did not use the least restrictive option to reach its objective, since it should have conducted a "testing by product" in order to ensure that its regulatory objective be met. The Panel sought advice from experts to see if Japan indeed had not chosen the least restrictive option. It did so however, not with respect to "testing by product," as the United States had argued, but with respect of "sorption levels." Hence, the question arose whether the Panel had exceeded the limits of its power by seeking expertise to establish that another (potentially) less restrictive method, not argued by the complaining party, could have helped Japan reach its objective. The Appellate Body dealt with the issue in the following manner:

> We note that the Panel explicitly stated that the United States, as complaining party, did *not specifically argue* that the "determination of sorption levels" met any of the three elements under Article 5.6. (§125 op. cit., emphasis in the original)
>
> And later:
>
> Article 13 of the DSU allows a Panel to seek *information* from any relevant source and to consult individual experts or expert bodies to obtain their *opinion* on certain aspects of the matter before it. In our Report . . . we noted the "comprehensive nature" of this authority . . . to enable a Panel to discharge its duty imposed by Article 11 of the DSU. . . (§127 op. cit., emphasis in the original)
>
> And then:
>
> [W]e note that the present dispute is a dispute under the *SPS Agreement.* Article 11.2 of the *SPS Agreement* explicitly *instructs* Panels in disputes

under this Agreement involving scientific and technical issues to "seek advice from experts." (§128 op. cit., emphasis in the original)

And finally:

Article 13 of the DSU and Article 11.2 of the *SPS Agreement* suggest that Panels have a significant investigative authority. However, this authority cannot be used by a Panel to rule in favor of a complaining party which has not established a *prima facie* case of inconsistency based on specific legal claims asserted by it. A Panel is entitled to seek information and advice from experts and from any other relevant source it chooses, pursuant to Article 13 of the DSU and, in an SPS case, Article 11.2 of the *SPS Agreement,* to help it to understand and evaluate the evidence submitted and the arguments made by the parties, but not to make the case for the complaining party. (§129 op. cit., emphasis in the original)

In a nutshell: the Panel at hand could have sought expertise to ensure that the complaining party's argument with respect to "testing by product" was indeed correct but could not have done so with respect to "sorption levels" since the complaining party did not make a specific argument to this effect. This means that Panels have unlimited discretion to seek outside expertise in order to determine whether a *prima facie* case has been made. This point was further underlined in the *India – Quantitative Restrictions* case where the Appellate Body dealt with the question whether the Panel erred in seeking International Monetary Fund (IMF) expertise when examining whether the complaining party had indeed made a *prima facie* case. There, the Appellate Body held:

We do not interpret the above statement as requiring the Panel to conclude that a *prima facie* case is made before it considers the views of the IMF or any other experts that it consults. Such consideration may be useful in order to determine whether a *prima facie* has been made.[17]

It emerges from the above that a party challenging an SPS measure carries the burden of proof to show that the measure at hand is inconsistent with the WTO contract. WTO adjudicating bodies can seek expertise to persuade themselves about the extent to which the arguments presented by the parties to the dispute are well-founded, but cannot move to arguments not presented by the parties.

The Role of Expert Witnesses

Art. 13 DSU and Art. 11.2 SPS allow WTO adjudicating bodies to select experts in consultation with the parties to the dispute. In the context of SPS, outside expertise is routinely sought since Panelists are rarely sufficiently accustomed with the scientific issues involved.

In the *Hormones* litigation, the Panel first asked parties to the dispute to name one expert each. It then named two experts (from a list prepared by the Codex Commission and the International Agency for Research on Cancer) and one additional expert in the area of carcinogenic effects of hormones (§§6.5 of the Panel report, op. cit.). The European Community appealed the fact that one of the experts was national of a party or third party and had links with the pharmaceutical industry. The Appellate Body, distinguishing the selection of expert witnesses in the context of SPS from expert review groups (Appendix 4 of the DSU), dismissed the EC argument and held that:

> [O]nce the Panel has decided to request the opinion of individual scientific experts, there is no legal obstacle to the Panel drawing up, in consultation with the parties to the dispute, *ad hoc* rules for those particular proceedings. (§148 op. cit.)

It appears that Panels will, in consultation with the parties to the dispute, seek expertise from outside sources following suggestions by the organizations mentioned in the SPS Agreement (OIE, IPCC, Codex). In the *Salmon* case, the Panel chose four experts after consultations with the Office International des Epizooties (§§6.1ff op. cit.). In the *Varietals* dispute, the Panel chose three experts after soliciting suggestions from the Secretariat of the International Plant Protection Convention (§§6.1ff op. cit.). Panels may also allow the parties to name their own experts, as in the *Hormones* litigation, where the parties were given the opportunity to name one expert each.

Panels might also be confronted with unsolicited expertise. Following the Appellate Body report on *Shrimps – Turtles,* Art. 13 DSU has been interpreted in a rather "liberal" manner: outside sources can forward their opinions to WTO adjudicating bodies and the latter have the right to either take into account or ignore such unsolicited expertise. In other words, following this report, Panels have lost their monopoly to the initiative to seek expertise.

In a very recent dispute, the Appellate Body had the opportunity to further clarify this point. In its report it stated:[18]

> The Appellate Body has no legal *duty* to accept or consider unsolicited *amicus curiae* briefs submitted by individuals or organizations, not

> Members of the WTO. . . . We are of the opinion that we have the legal authority under the DSU to accept and consider *amicus curiae* briefs in an appeal in which we find it pertinent and useful to do so. (§§41–42 op. cit., emphasis in the original)

What is good law for the Appellate Body must be good law for Panels as well. Hence, Panels as well might be able to accept unsolicited expertise in an SPS-related case. In such a case, however, due process considerations would oblige the Panel (or the Appellate Body as the case may be) to communicate to the parties the content of such unsolicited expertise and give them an opportunity to react.

When addressing questions to parties, Panelists aim at illuminating themselves on the scientific status of a particular issue. Independently of the issue of how to assess such expertise (we deal with this issue in the next Section), Panels might be confronted with no or seemingly unsatisfactory answers. Can they draw inferences from such cases?

In the recent dispute between Brazil and Canada relating to export subsidies paid to the aircraft industry, the issue came up. Canada refused to provide information sought by the Panel and the Appellate Body was called to decide whether in such a case a Panel can legitimately draw inferences. The relevant passage reads:

> Clearly, in our view, the Panel had the legal authority and the discretion to draw inferences from the facts before it—including the fact that Canada had refused to provide information sought by the Panel.[19]

It is should be emphasized that this passage deals with a case of illegal subsidies. So far, there is no confirmation that the above-mentioned power to draw inferences is also applicable to the SPS context.

Summary

In the light of the discussion above of the case law, the SPS Agreement can be viewed as including the following articles:

1. WTO Members can enact definitive SPS measures provided that a risk assessment has taken place.
2. WTO members can also enact provisional SPS measures in the absence of a risk assessment in the light of available pertinent information.
3. When WTO Members enact definitive SPS measures, their risk assessment must be based on scientific evidence.

4. For evidence to be considered scientific, some minimum methodology requirements must be met.
5. SPS measures can be enacted following a risk assessment based on minority scientific opinions.
6. The scientific evidence does not have to be provided at the moment an SPS measure is enacted; it must, however, be provided when an SPS measure is challenged before a WTO Panel.
7. The scientific evidence supplied must support the view that there is a sufficiently large probability (that is, not a mere possibility) that a particular disease will enter the sovereignty of a WTO Member unless the SPS measure at hand is enacted.
8. WTO Members are free to set the level of risk they are willing to undertake at any level they deem appropriate. When setting their objective, WTO Members can take into account economic factors as well.
9. WTO adjudicating bodies can only examine to what extent the means chosen to achieve the level sought is the least restrictive option.
10. In order to examine whether an SPS measure is in accordance with the SPS Agreement, WTO adjudicating bodies can have recourse to expert witnesses. WTO adjudicating bodies select expert witnesses from the organizations mentioned in the SPS Agreement in consultation with the parties to the dispute. They might also allow the possibility to parties to the dispute to name their own experts in addition to those named by the Panel. WTO adjudicating bodies can decide whether to take into account unsolicited expertise.
11. WTO Members challenging an SPS measure carry the original burden of proof to show that the WTO contract has not been complied with.
12. WTO adjudicating bodies can seek outside expertise, but they can use such expertise only to inform themselves about the validity of arguments as presented by the parties and not in order to evaluate arguments that have not been presented by a party.
13. When a WTO Member invokes the precautionary principle, it must show a plausible relationship between the measure it enacts and the risk it wants to avoid.
14. When a WTO Member invokes the precautionary principle, it must seek to collect any additional information within a reasonable period of time, which in one case was deemed to be four years.

3. Some Reflections on the Case Law in the SPS Agreement

The Interpretation of the Consistency Requirement

What stems from the discussion above is that in presence of scientific evidence, the legality of a measure under the SPS Agreement depends on whether it is the least restrictive measure, and whether the measure is employed consistently. The "least restrictive criterion" can easily be met, since a Member can always insist that it aims at eliminating, to the extent possible, any risk resulting from a disease. Hence, it all boils down to the interpretation of the consistency requirement, and the appropriate choice of interpretation is not a trivial task, as we will argue.

Imagine that country A imposes a sales ban on hormone-treated beef without extending the same treatment to non-hormone-treated beef, or any other product sold in its market. The justification offered by A is that hormone-treated beef is carcinogenic. A imports hormone-free pork from B, and pork and beef are "like" in the GATT sense of the term. A also imports a special kind of cigarette from C, a cigarette that does not cause cancer. Depending on the interpretation of the consistency requirement, both these exporters may lodge a justified complaint against A before the WTO.

The "Like Product" Definition

Country B might argue that consistency requires A to treat all "like products" the same way, where likeness is judged according to the standard criteria used in GATT cases. A should therefore either withdraw its sales ban on hormone-treated beef, or impose a sales ban also on hormone-treated pork. B's interest in this stems from the fact that the expanded intervention would bring B a larger share of A's domestic market.

Now we can imagine two situations: In the first, there is scientific evidence that pork also represents a danger comparable to beef, if treated with hormones. In this case, the judge is on solid grounds to pronounce inconsistency with Art. 5.5 SPS. Such a decision cannot mean, however, that A must strike down its beef legislation. A can perfectly well satisfy the requirements of Art. 5.5 SPS by extending its legislation to pork.

In the second scenario, there is no convincing evidence concerning the danger with hormone-treated pork. It would, in this case, be clearly undesirable for the adjudicating body to require country A to extend the ban to hormone-treated pork, or to drop it. Hence, we see that the consistency criterion *must take health aspects into account* when evaluating the ambit of the consistency requirement; the traditional "like product" definition does not suffice.

The "Like Health Hazard" Definition

Country C argues that standard cigarettes are also carcinogenic. If A is serious about its battle against cancer, then it should address the cigarettes issue as well. Had it done so, C would have captured a large share of A's cigarette market. Like B, C thus has an incentive to construe the consistency requirement as an obligation to act. But, C's argument is not based on likeness in the GATT sense, but from the point of view of *health impact.* According to this argument, consistency of a health measure requires the measure to be taken against all "like health hazards."

Is C's reading of the SPS Agreement a reasonable one? In other words, should we understand the SPS Agreement as adding more than scientific evidence to the pre-SPS world? Intuitively, the problem with the approach advocated by country C is that it seems to impose an unduly heavy burden on health-related interventions. This would tend to reduce health interventions that in themselves are desirable, something that clearly is highly undesirable, given the stakes involved.

On the other hand, in this example there is no good reason why A should not also ban sales of cigarettes. It therefore does not seem an exceedingly onerous demand to require consistency in this case. The question then basically boils down to whether countries should be free to pursue inconsistent policies if they for some reason so wish (a question to which we have no good answer).

One may ask: can two products be like in the GATT sense, and still be different from a health hazard point of view? If one product is hazardous, and not the other, why then do consumers view them as close substitutes? There are several reasons that immediately come to mind. First, consumers may not view the health hazards the same way as may authorities, for instance, due to lack of information on part of the former. Second, the hazards may be externalities, and hence not properly taken into consideration by consumers. For instance, cars with catalytic converters may from individual consumers' point of view be like in the GATT sense to cars without such converters, but they may from a public health point of view not be like products.

The GATT treatment and the SPS treatment must differ in another fundamental way: the treatment of economic aspects. A narrow reading of Art. 5.3 SPS excludes economic factors in the case of risks to human health.[20] It is submitted, however, that not all economic factors can be excluded. Imagine that costs for detecting dangers from hormones in beef constitute only a fraction of costs for detecting dangers from hormones in pork. Would the WTO judge strike down a legislation banning hormone-treated beef because the state at hand does not want to take the costs to undertake the research with respect to hormone-treated pork? Would the WTO judge be immune to the demonstrated adverse impact of hormone-treated beef because similar measures have not been taken in other sectors?

To conclude, it is clear that the consistency requirement must be understood as applying to a wider set of products than to "like products" in the sense of GATT. But it is equally clear that this opens a door that in practice might be deemed to be too wide. Were one to accept the wider definition, health policies would be scrutinized in a much more detailed manner than, for example, antidumping legislation (especially in the presence of Art. 17.6 WTO Antidumping Agreement). The only workable solution may in this case be to restrict the consistency requirement to like (and possibly directly competitive and substitutable) products. Hence, the provision of Art. 5.5 SPS can be appropriately interpreted as a "reverse engineering" process to establish the relevant product market within which the health-based measure should operate. It is also clear that economic aspects cannot be avoided in determining the ambit of the consistency requirement.

Scientific Evidence: Is WTO a Screen against Junk Science?

We will next turn to the issue of how to determine the criteria according to which to judge the degree to which evidence is scientific.

As practice has already shown, in the field of health policy, Panels have to rely on expert testimony. There is a general uneasiness whenever expert witnesses are invited to a court: Posner (1999b, pp. 1536ff.) identifies partisanship of witnesses and intelligibility of testimony as the prime sources of concern. Expert witnesses may be hard to understand for the average judge. This should, however, be less of a problem, since expert witnesses will have an incentive to express their opinions in layman's language, since otherwise their testimony will not be effective. More important may be the fact that witnesses are paid by parties and hence might be biased to testify in a way that suits their clients' needs. This problem might partly be taken care of, if WTO Panels appoint their own experts.[21] Such a system may not eliminate "partisanship to ideas," though, particularly not in fields that are not very well developed.

While expert testimony is associated with problems, it should be emphasized that it is essential. The WTO judge is the hostage of claims made by parties. In denying the scientific proof supporting a certain health measure, the judge will have to pronounce on the inconsistency of the nationally pursued health policy. The judge cannot refer to a "manifestly arbitrary or capricious" standard, as we know it from the U.S. law, or to an "outer limits control" as we know it from EC law, in order to maintain a health policy that has no scientific evidence. Such a standard, in fact, asks the question whether the intervening authority acted *bona fides* when intervening, independently of the soundness of the scientific evidence supporting its measure.

Maybe this is what the Appellate Body had in mind when it pronounced, in its *Hormones* jurisprudence as we noted above, that the "precautionary principle" is not exhausted in Art. 5.7 SPS. The Appellate Body, if we understand it correctly, wanted to give intervening authorities some "breathing space" in case existing and/or submitted scientific evidence does not support a particular measure. This would allow WTO Members to double-check *ex post facto* their regulatory interventions. In any event, it is clear that expert testimony is central to the SPS Agreement.

If expert testimony is essential to the SPS Agreement, the question arises what type of testimony constitutes scientific evidence. The Appellate Body has referred to some minimum methodology requirements necessary to qualify a submission as scientific evidence without contributing any further precision. But the distinction between scientific and non-scientific evidence is very hard to maintain in practice, unless *possibly* one is willing to rely on "objective criteria" for what constitutes scientific evidence, such as publication in top academic journals. For instance, it is hard to conceive of cases where not *some* person with *some* training in *some* relevant field would be willing to stand up—if nothing else for the fame (and possibly money)—to make just about any claim. There is, thus, a clear danger that we will see "scientific evidence" submitted in every dispute for both parties.

It should be noted that in U.S. law, the *Daubert* decision by the Supreme Court argues that an expert witness' evidence is inadmissible if it does not satisfy the methodological standards in the expert's field.[22] In Posner's (1999a) inimitable expression, *Daubert* is a screen against junk science. Such a screen does not clearly exist in WTO case law, although the Appellate Body's rejection of Dr. Lucier's opinion in the Hormones litigation goes some way down this line.

But even if one managed to get rid of the most obvious quacks, the problem still remains for the adjudicating bodies of weighing conflicting claims that each seems to fulfill some minimum standards. First, there are genuine divisions of opinion concerning many important health issues. There are cases where expert witnesses might "cancel out" each other.[23] What to do in these cases? Clearly, there is no way to codify how to perform such an evaluation. Instead, matters have to be left at the discretion of the Panels and the Appellate Body. It is doubtful whether these should be expected to be able to perform such tasks. Of course, the situation is the same in many national courts that rely on expert testimony. Posner (1999b, p. 1540) admits that he can offer no solution to this problem. For example, two reputed economists in the field of industrial organization can be either "antitrust hawks" or "antitrust doves." Their expertise, if appointed by parties one each, might be cancelled out. The solution offered by the Appellate Body, as we saw in the *Hormones* litigation, is, in cases of disagreement among scientists, to rule in favor of the intervening regulatory authority (in favor of the WTO

Member adopting a certain health policy). This is evidence of *in dubio pro mitius.*

Moreover, in the national context there are checks and balances that exist to a much lesser extent at the international level. For instance, the discretion by an "interventionist" domestic judge, if it leads to social uneasiness, can be cut down through enactment of domestic law to this effect. A re-negotiation of the international contract among 139 Members with no certain *ex ante* outcome is a much more difficult and risky task.

Finally, a screen against junk science, of course, has nothing to do with the standard of review to be applied in health-related cases. A screen against junk science will only limit the evidence that will be admitted by the WTO Panel. Once the screen is passed, the standard of review will be exercised against what is deemed to be non-junk science. Hence, the question of the standard of review is not at all prejudged even if one understands the Appellate Body's refusal to consider Dr. Lucier's comments as the WTO screen against junk science.[24]

Synergies between Health Hazards

The danger of a product is often believed to depend on the exposure to other products. For instance, the danger from smoking might depend on the exposure to radiation. Hence, the health impact of an import ban on cigarettes might depend on the importing country's policy vis-à-vis radioactive emissions from building materials. It is also possible that a person can withstand a certain level of exposure without suffering, but once a threshold value is reached, the person becomes sensitive also to lower levels of exposure. For instance, this is to be the case with many allergies: maybe people would not have problems with the gas emitted from the glue used in imported wooden boards if they did not use a particular domestically produced paint?

Such "synergies" between health hazards of different products by themselves cause a fundamental problem when portioning the risk for a certain disease to different environmental factors. But the complexity of these issues involved, of course, also makes the empirical assessment of any probabilities a much more difficult task.

Precaution and Comparability Based on What?

WTO Members can enact SPS measures in the absence of scientific evidence, provided that they have invoked the precautionary principle. As mentioned above, only two aspects of the precautionary principle have been interpreted so far. The most important aspects of the said principle remain uninterpreted. This does not mean, however, that we are in the complete dark as to its meaning.

According to Art. 5.7 SPS, the principle can be invoked on the basis of available pertinent information. "Available pertinent information" must mean something less than scientific evidence, since if scientific evidence exists, it would presumably be used. Then, what is less than scientific evidence? It is reminded that scientific evidence according to WTO case law satisfies some minimum methodological requirements independently of whether it represents a minority opinion. Moreover, scientific evidence must demonstrate that there is a causal relationship between the source of concern identified (i.e., a toxin) and human or animal health. The precautionary principle thus applies when no causal relationship can be demonstrated (and hence no likelihood can be established), or in cases where the scientific evidence is of insufficient methodological quality.

On the other hand, as the Appellate Body notes in the *Hormones* report:

> The principle has not been written into the *SPS Agreement* as a ground for justifying SPS measures that are otherwise inconsistent with the obligations of Members set out in particular provisions of that Agreement. (§124 op. cit., emphasis in the original)

Hence, WTO Members when enacting health regulations based on the precautionary principle, must still respect the coherence argument as laid down in Art. 5.5 SPS, with all the problems this involves, as discussed above.

The control by a Panel however will necessarily be even more hands-off: in the absence of scientific evidence, Panels will be in a much more difficult situation to establish comparability between two situations and hence assess whether the coherence obligation has been complied with.

4. Concluding Remarks

The Appellate Body has so far treated health issues with a rather low profile. It has *de facto* adopted a deferential standard of review when dealing with nationally pursued health policies. There is one important exception to its attitude: the consistency requirement where the Appellate Body has adopted a rather activist approach.

For the reasons examined in this paper, it appears that the WTO system should have a rather low profile with regard to health issues, the consistency requirement included. Our recipe should be relevant in the realm of remedies where Panels, for example, facing a measure inconsistent with Art. 5.5 SPS, should be ill-advised to pronounce revocation of the measure before a "completing the analysis" process, whereby they would request, if reasonably available to the intervening WTO Member, to review the risk presented by other products in the same relevant product market.

Is this a serious problem for the WTO? At the face of it, yes: what is recommended here might give WTO Members the incentive to "cheat." But then, maybe, it is not so serious after all. The system anyway ultimately rests on the willingness of the Members to keep it alive, rather than the (limited) enforcement capacity built into it. Members typically understand that they have to keep the agreement alive by abiding to multilateral rulings. Maybe the same self-interest will prevent countries from exploiting the SPS Agreement for protectionist purposes. But even if it did, one must expect to see some regulations pass that in the eyes of most observers seem unwarranted, due to political pressures. After all, health issues are emotionally and thus politically charged (and the scientific "truths" do change over time). Perhaps a certain amount of "political protectionism" has to be paid in order to save the system from more damaging blows.

REFERENCES

Howse, Robert and Petros C. Mavroidis. The WTO and Europe's Evolving Strategy for the Regulation of GMOS – of Kine and Brine, *Fordham Int'l L.J.*, 24 (2000/2001), pp. 317–370.

Pauwelyn, Joost. 1999. The WTO Agreement on Sanitary and Phytosanitary (SPS) Measures As Applied in the First Three SPS Disputes. *Journal of International Economic Law* vol. 2, No 4: 641–64.

Posner, Richard A. 1999a. The Law and Economics of the Economic Expert Witness. *Journal of Economic Perspective,* 13: 91–99.

Posner, Richard A. 1999b. An Economic Approach to the Law of Evidence. *Stanford Law Review* 51: 1477–1546.

Stein, Alex. 1996. The Refoundation of Evidence Law. *The Canadian Journal of Law And Jurisprudence* IX: 279–342.

NOTES

1. An argument could be made, though, that WTO adjudicating bodies, when dealing with health related disputes, should always start from SPS, move to TBT if SPS is inapplicable and move to GATT only if TBT is inapplicable.

2. This section draws on Howse and Mavroidis (2000).

3. The text of Art. 3.2 SPS does not make it clear whether the presumption established is an irrefutable one.

4. See *EC Measures Concerning Meat and Meat Products (Hormones) – Complaint by the United States,* WT/DS26/R/USA of 18 August 1997 (hereinafter the *Hormones* Panel report).

5. See the report on *Australia – Measures Affecting Importation of Salmon,* WT/DS18/AB/R of 20 October 1998 at §125 (hereinafter *Salmon* Appellate Body report).

6. See *EC Measures Concerning Meat And Meat Products (Hormones) – Complaint by the United States,* WT/DS26/R/USA of 18 August 1997 (hereinafter the *Hormones* Panel report).

7. Surprisingly, the Panel report does not reflect that the term "appropriate level of sanitary or phytosanitary protection" has already been interpreted in Annex A in a way that essentially condones regulatory diversity.

8. Subsequent Appellate Body decisions, like the *Shrimps/Turtles* and the *FSC,* made this point crystal-clear. We should also note that the distinction between "risk assessment" and "risk management" is not unknown, for example, in European Community (EC) law. Indeed, the EC argued along the lines of this distinction before the Panel.

9. See *EC Measures Concerning Meat and Meat Products (Hormones) – Complaint by the United States,* WT/DS26/R/USA of 18 August 1997 (hereinafter the *Hormones* Panel report).

10. Idem at §8.113 (emphasis in the original).

11. L. Brown (ed.), *The New Shorter Oxford English Dictionary on Historical Principles* (Clarendon Press), Vol. I, p. 187.

12. Ibid., p. 477.

13. Pauwelyn (1999) provides an excellent account of all SPS-related cases treated so far by the WTO Appellate Body.

14. Which, as we stated above, is a mere illusion.

15. See *Japan – Measures Affecting Agricultural Products,* WT/DS76/AB/R of 22 February 1999, at §95 (hereinafter the *Varietals* Appellate Body report).

16. See *Japan – Measures Affecting Agricultural Products,* WT/DS76/R of 27 October 1998, at §§8.78ff. (hereinafter the *Varietals* Panel report).

17. See *India – Quantitative Restrictions on Imports of Agricultural, Textile and Industrial Products,* WT/DS90/AB/R of 23 August 1999, at §142.

18. *United States – Imposition of Countervailing Duties on Certain Hot-Rolled Lead and Bismuth Carbon Steel Products Originating in the United Kingdom,* WT/DS138/AB/R of 10 May 2000.

19. See *Canada – Measures Affecting the Export of Civilian Aircraft,* WT/DS70/AB/R of 2 August 1999, at §203.

20. If included, our argument in favor of deference is even stronger. Hence excluding at this stage for the purposes of our analysis does not negatively impair our conclusions.

21. Compare the thoughts of Posner (1999a) and (1999b) in this respect.

22. See *Daubert v. Merrill Dow Pharmaceuticals, Inc.* 509 U.S. 579 (1993).

23. See on this score the excellent analysis in Stein (1996).

24. It should also be pointed out that, whereas in the United States, the *Daubert*-test has led to exclusion of substantial "scientific" expertise, there are no reported cases where a judge dismissed health policies as not corresponding to genuine concerns.

Part IV: Where Do We Go from Here?

CHAPTER 18

The Paradox of Judicial Review in International Trade Regulation: Towards a Comprehensive Framework

Thomas Cottier and Matthias Oesch

Consistency and coherence in the application and interfacing of different legal orders—national, regional, and international—are essential goals of legislation, jurisprudence, and doctrine in a world of increasing economic and regulatory integration. This applies to the substancc of law. It equally applies to procedural aspects, including the issue of standards of review. Should they remain, as they are, different in national, regional, and international law? Or should we seek to overcome such differences with a view to achieving the goals of consistency and coherence? The paper addresses this question. It explores reasons and seeks to explain why standards of review largely differ among countries, and among different levels of the legal order, national, regional, and global, in the field of trade regulation and beyond. We are dealing here essentially with a problem of constitutional law, explicitly or implicitly. Underlying standards of judicial review of administrative action, of lower court decisions, of civil litigation are the constitutional issue of separation and balance of powers within a particular constituted entity. It is equally, in the final analysis, a matter of balance of power among different levels of constituted entities, within nations and among nations. Different standards of judicial review reflect different modes and constitutional traditions. Exploring the question whether a coherent and uniform approach to judicial review, and a coherent role of the judicial branch of government can and should be sought in international trade regulation both on national, regional, and international levels thus amounts to the question whether or not a coherent and common constitutional doctrine should and could eventually emerge.

The paper first addresses the national and regional levels. It then turns to the international level of judicial control in the WTO. What we find is an interesting paradox. Judicial review, in a domestic context, often seems to act in a more restrained manner than on the international level of the WTO. Strong constitutional structures thus show more reluctance than relatively weak constitutional structures in international law. Is this appropriate? Or, is this one of the causes of current tensions and strains on the world trading system? Should it be remedied, and if so, how? We submit and finally discuss a constitutional approach which could bring about a better and well-balanced coherence.

1. Judicial Review at National and Regional Levels

Diversity of Constitutional Models and the Role of the Judiciary

Modern states rooted in the Westphalian system of nation states, the movement of enlightenment, and the discourse of rationality commonly share the ideals of separation of powers and of checks and balances among different statal functions (legislature, executive, and judiciary), all based upon the rule of law. The concept of sovereignty, originally enshrined in an absolute and arbitrary ruler (or a small group of rulers) which has characterized extensive periods of human history, no longer is an almost exclusive legal and political ideal in a world of mutual integration, albeit, of course, it still is a predominant aspiration in many countries, in particular in the developing world. The ideal is rather one of submitting some control of governance to the international system in order to secure lawful conduct and to check and balance the impact of domestic law. This is equally reflected in the WTO. The significant number of provisions in the agreements addressing transparency and requiring judicial review reflect, in the field of trade regulation and thus market access, common and significant minimal standards of good governance.[1]

Beyond this point, however, we witness a large panoply of different models and constitutional traditions under the umbrella of international law. There is no uniformity, a fact which not only applies to forms of government and the rule of law. There is not (yet) a minimal democratic requirement, either, albeit many building blocks exist, in particular in the field of international human rights protection and monitoring of the electoral process.[2] Existing differences stem from different cultural and historical experiences in power allocation. "The life of the law has not been logic: it has been experience."[3]

Equally, the role of the judicial branch considerably varies in different countries. The tradition of common law ascribes a leading role to courts, albeit in democracy subject to legislation. The tradition of continental law, based upon ideals of codification and expressed in a limited canon of rules of interpretation, traditionally ascribes a more modest role to the judiciary. If we add Community law at this point (being domestic law from the point of view of the WTO), diversity is further enlarged. Judicial review of administrative acts relating to external economic relations in the EC reflects, as elsewhere, the constitutional structure and takes into account the leading role of the Council and the Commission in shaping external economic relations. Since World War II, the Western legal systems, however, share a common perception of the leading role of courts in shaping fundamental rights; continental courts today may even be more assertive in this field than common law courts as international instruments, such as the European Convention on Human Rights, play an important role. Outside the transatlantic traditions, the role of courts may again be seen differently. In Western schools, we still know too little about genuine perceptions of the judicial functions in Asian or African traditions. But comparative studies of some detail would provide a picture of great diversity.

Such diversity is likely to exist also in the field of domestic legal review of trade-related measures which fall under the ambit of the WTO. The standards set by the WTO for domestic review are often broadly framed. They do not prescribe details. Whether review of administrative action is limited to law or whether appeals include factual issues is mainly left to countries and respects their constitutional traditions, except for the requirement that there has to be impartial review and transparency. Whether or not courts apply restraint or are proactive, is a matter essentially left to legislation and traditions stemming from the particular perceptions of separation of powers and of checks and balances.

Judicial Restraint in the Fields of External Economic Relations

Common traits, it would seem, are difficult to define in general terms. However, there is one element which many, perhaps all, constitutional models share: When comparing judicial review relating to traditional fields of domestic law with external economic relations, we are likely to detect that review of the latter is characterized by relative restraint. In the context of what has been called the *introverted tradition of constitutional law,*[4] external relations, including external economic relations, were and still are considered to belong mainly to the province of legislation and, first of all, executive government. Traditionally, they are less so part of the core province of domestic courts. This is explained by the fact that external relations have been, and sometimes still are, operating under legally open textured norms of competence, leaving the matter essentially to discretion. Disciplines were developed rather by international (or regional) law than by domestic law. It is not coincidental that discussions about the rule of law or *Rechtsstaatlichkeit,* expounded in the 18th and 19th century for domestic law and internal relations, are only now being seriously discussed for external relations. Trade regulation, from a domestic perspective, is still largely characterized by discretionary and wide textured rules, while it is international (or regional) law which prescribes conduct in more detail. This common trait may also be explained in terms of political economy and public choice. Market access interests are less represented than producer interests in the domestic political process, and the power to bring about domestic guarantees of markets open to foreign competition is domestically limited. Neither is it coincidental that such guarantees are much more advanced in terms of negotiated rights enshrined in international (or regional) law and then partly incorporated into domestic law.

Domestic Review Based on National or Regional Law

We now turn to three jurisdictions, and examine the standards of review as applied by their respective judicial branches in external economic affairs relating to foreign market access. Far from being complete, a few references may indicate that standards of review are generally deferential, with interesting exceptions in civil law matters, in particular intellectual property protection.

European Union

Measures adopted by Community institutions in the field of external economic relations have in common that they are generally based on complex factual assessments and evaluations. In these subject matters, wide discretion is traditionally granted to the executive branch, either stipulated by legislation or developed by case law, and the European Court of Justice has to appropriately limit its judicial scrutiny when "second-guessing" an economic measure adopted by the Council or Commission. Partly, this stems from internal law. The ECSC Treaty contains a specific provision imposing restraints on the European Court of Justice, namely Article 33, whereas in the EC Treaty no equivalent can be found. However, the case law clearly leads to the conclusion that the position under the EC Treaty is now the same as that under the ECSC Treaty.[5] Competition law (which often has a bearing on foreign as much as internal market access) is an example in point. In *Remina,* the Court held that "the court must therefore limit its review of such an appraisal [of complex economic matters] to verifying whether the relevant procedural rules have been complied with, whether the statement of the reasons for the decision is adequate, whether the facts have been accurately stated and whether there has been any manifest error of appraisal or misuse of powers."[6] This doctrine is equally applied to external relations. The wording is almost identical to that in *Fediol* in which an anti-dumping measure was at issue.[7] In *Fedesa,* the Court examined the legality of a measure relating to the ban of the use of growth hormones adopted within the Common Agricultural Policy (CAP). It limited judicial review as to "whether the measure in question is vitiated by a manifest error or misuse of powers, or whether the authority in question has manifestly exceeded the limits of its discretion."[8] The same level of scrutiny was applied in *Piraiki-Patraiki,* in which safeguard measures authorized by the Commission were challenged; once again, the court was guided by considerable restraint.[9]

The same holds true for the EC with respect to the principle of proportionality[10] which is closely linked to the issue of standard of review. It is apparent that the proportionality test can be applied more or less intensively. The case law of the European Court of Justice indicates that, in the field of economic policies, the deferential standard of judicial review as generally developed towards Community measures is also applied to claims based on the principle of proportionality. Again, the Court held in *Fedesa* (and with equal implications for third country relations) that "the legality of a measure adopted in that sphere [Common Agricultural Policy] can be affected only if the measure is manifestly inappropriate having regard to the objective which the competent institution is seeking to pursue."[11]

In light of the foregoing, it is concluded that judicial review of measures adopted by Community institutions in external economic affairs relating to market access is considerably *deferential.* Moreover, the European Court of Justice appears to apply a fairly *uniform* deferential standard of review. The terms in which the Court describes the intensity of judicial review applicable in a present case are often almost identical, and do not vary depending on the subject matter involved. The uniform standard of review can be summarized as "manifestly erroneous standard," and its characteristic criteria are the following: - non-compliance with the relevant rules; - inadequate statement of the reasons for the decision; - manifest error in the assessment of the facts; - or misuse of powers regarding the discretion granted to the Community institutions. With regards to the principle of proportionality, only a "manifestly inappropriate" measure affects its legality. As a corollary, international obligations under the WTO are not given direct effect as a matter of principle, while Member States may do so in their respective fields of competence under a mixed agreement.[12]

On the other hand, judicial review in three fields related to external relations is not characterized by restraint. First, the European Court of Justice has been most powerful in the context of delivering legal opinions under Article 300:6 of the EC Treaty. In examining compatibility of a proposed international obligation with the Treaty, the Court has considerably influenced the law of external relations.[13] The Court, for instance, denied in a case concerning an agreement with the U.S. on cooperation in the enforcement of competition law that the Commission has the power to negotiate and *conclude* agreements with third countries in a field in which it only has the *internal* power to take decisions.[14] These rulings essentially relate to the allocation of domestic power and competence and thus the institutional balance within the level of the Community, and less so to substantive rights and obligations or specific economic policies. Secondly, when the Court has to decide on the territorial ambit of community law relating to external economic relations, it generally does not make reference to the traditionally leading role of the executive but makes its legal findings on the basis of an own assessment of the matter. An illustrative example provides competition law and the territorial ambit of Article 81. It is now well-established, since the landmark decision in *Ahlström,*[15] that Article 81 strikes at any agreement which has an effect, actual or potential, upon trade between Member States whatever the nationality or territorial location of the undertakings concerned (territoriality principle). Thirdly, when a Member State action is being challenged, in the field of external relations, the Court's review generally is searching and thorough under existing regional agreements[16] and, in fact, indirectly amounts to independent *de novo* review. As much as in internal affairs relating to the four freedoms,[17] the Member States are not granted discretionary power in assessing and evaluating relevant facts and determining appropriate measures in order to achieve individually set policy objectives. These decisions do not directly concern the allocation and balance of powers among the Community institutions, but rather shape the *vertical* constitutional framework within the EC, and thus primarily emphasize the promotion of European integration. In conclusion, scrutiny is extensive in matters relating to horizontal or vertical separation of powers among the organs of the Community and vis-à-vis Member States, respectively. It is generally deferential with regard to the implementation of external community policies.

United States of America

The generally applicable domestic standard of review for agencies' interpretations of law is well-known as "Chevron doctrine."[18] Therein, the Federal Courts are to grant deference to agencies' legal decisions if the Congress has not "directly spoken to the precise issue in question." If the court fails to discover such an interpretative intention of the Congress, the standard of review is whether the agency's interpretation of the statute was "reasonable."

Most cases which involve international trade legislation and its implementation in the U.S. occur before the Court of International Trade (CIT).[19] The standards of review which the CIT applies vary, depending on the type of action that is brought before it. In *anti-dumping and countervailing duty* cases, most government measures are judged according to the substantial evidence standard; a few are reviewed to determine whether they are arbitrary, capricious, or an abuse of powers.[20] Thus, the courts are, in general, clearly bound to considerable restraint when reviewing agencies' actions. Indeed, "Canadian trade analysts generally viewed the CIT as extremely deferential to the determinations of the U.S. agencies";[21] while Davey, on the other hand, points out that "it sometimes appears, however, that the CIT accords less deference to those agencies than the Supreme Court suggests should be accorded by federal courts reviewing agency actions."[22] The same substantial evidence standard of review is applied to *trade adjustment assistance* cases.[23] In other cases, such as classification challenges, origin determinations, and protest denials, the Court's review amounts to a *de novo* examination.[24]

Finally, it is interesting to observe that when reviewing matters other than being part of administrative law, the Courts have shown little restraint despite the fact that trade relations are affected. This particularly applies to intellectual property. Assessing parallel trade in the field of trademarks was based upon extensive and ordinary statutory interpretation.[25] The same holds true for the notorious *Alcoa* case in which the Supreme Court established the territoriality principle of U.S. antitrust law.[26] In deliberating on the issue, the court did not defer to the opinion of other branches nor did it make reference to the leading role of the executive in external economic relations. This is curious enough, since the matter goes to the very heart of international trade regulation, and the opinion of the executive might have been expected to be equally relevant for the outcome of the case.

Switzerland

In Switzerland, a medium-sized trading nation, the government has traditionally been in charge of policy-making in external economic matters, and the role of judicial branches, and ultimately of the Swiss Supreme Court, has generally been characterized by considerable restraint. Discretionary powers are often explicitly delegated to the executive authorities, while in matters to which no judicial deference is granted courts tend to appropriately restrict standards of review "due to the very nature" of policy determinations in external economic affairs. It is two exemplary subject matters in administrative law which we first turn to.

For example, in the field of agriculture, broad discretionary power is by law conferred on the competent authorities of the Federal Economics Department in the implementation of the generally outlined policies.[27] In a case in which the regime for auctioning import licenses for meat and meat products was challenged on the ground that it allegedly was a violation of Switzerland's WTO/GATT obligations, the Court clearly pointed out that "it cannot be the duty of the Supreme Court to examine whether the decisions as adopted in the statute are practical from an economic and agricultural policy point of view."[28] The Court later succinctly stressed that "the political responsibility in the field of agriculture lies within the Federal Council."[29]

In competition law cases (again often having a bearing on market access by foreign operators), there is no explicit legal basis for executive discretion; on the contrary, Article 49 of the Swiss Administrative Procedure Act[30] generally requires *de novo* review to be applied by judicial branches. This, in principle, includes the Appeal Body on Competition *(Rekurskommission für Wettbewerbsfragen)* which is the first instance to review decisions by the Swiss Anti-Trust Commission *(Wettbewerbskommission),* the administrative agency primarily dealing with competition law cases. Although its powers of review are very wide, encompassing both factual and legal issues, the *Rekurskommission* has generally been reluctant to *de novo* scrutinize decisions of the *Wettbewerbskommission;* rather, it has been long-standing practice that competition matters mainly belong to the province of legislation and executive government, and less so being part of the core province of judicial branches. The *Rekurskommission* has unequivocally stated that "it is willing to grant a great deal of discretion to the *Wettbewerbskommission,* because it is primarily its job to determine competition policy."[31] The Swiss Supreme Court has confirmed such judicial restraint.[32]

Curiously enough, judicial deference is only applied, in external economic relations, when courts review administrative acts. The role of the judiciaries looks different in *civil law* cases concerning international trade regulation. In the field of intellectual property, for instance, the Swiss Supreme Court had to decide, due to silence on the matter in the respective Acts, on the principle of exhaustion of intellectual property rights. It held in landmark decisions that the principle of international exhaustion applies to trademarks[33] and copyrights,[34] but not to patents for which it only recognized national exhaustion.[35] The Swiss Supreme Court, in every respective case, did not defer to the opinion of the executive branches, particularly the Federal Office of Intellectual Property, nor did it make reference to the traditionally leading role of the executive in external economic relations. Rather, the Court examined the legal questions *de novo,* taking into account economic policy and purely dogmatic methods of interpretation, and subsequently ruled on the basis of its own assessment of the matter before it.

The concept of varying degrees of judicial deference needs to be further examined in relation to the protection of fundamental human rights. Article 27 of the Swiss Federal Constitution guarantees economic freedom as a fundamental right, and it can be invoked before courts when public authorities have unjustly violated it.[36] Domestically, the nature of this right implies full review by the Courts, both of legality and proportionality of a measure taken. There is, and rightly so, the general principle that courts shall *de novo* review whether administrating authorities' measures are in compliance with fundamental human rights. This principle is generally valid in Switzerland and allows only very few departures.[37] Some authors have strongly advocated that the economic freedom also covers external economic activities ("Aussenwirtschaftsfreiheit").[38] The Supreme Court has approved this dimension in passing in *Chanel.*[39] The implications of this statement, however, are far from clear, and they are quite at variance with traditional standards of deference as normally applied in matters relating to foreign economic relations. The matter will need further consideration. It relates to the basic question (denied for example in the United States) to what extent fundamental rights standards can be fully applied in external relations, given its implications on standards of judicial review.[40]

Domestic Review Based upon International Law

The traditions of discretionary regulation of external economic affairs in national and regional law compensated for by increasingly detailed rules in WTO law, of course, renders the issue of relationship between international law and domestic law to paramount importance. While the level of judicial restraint requires still more detailed analysis and research in respect of applying domestic law and its different levels (constitutional, statutory, ordinances), it is clear that multilateral agreements of the WTO are applied reluctantly by most courts in the field of international trade regulation. The general denial of direct effect of WTO law in the U.S. and EC is well-known and does not need rehearsing.[41] While an alleged lack of clarity and density of rules so far established the main argument to reject direct effect of GATT 1947, the doctrine today is denied by the European Court of Justice mainly on trade policy grounds of reciprocity.[42] As U.S. statutory law bars direct effect, this argument is honest, but essentially reflects a power-oriented mercantilist approach. Courts of other, smaller countries such as Switzerland may be more open to direct effect, but little has been achieved so far.[43] Courts limit themselves to the doctrine of consistent interpretation, i.e., to interpretation of national law *as far as possible* in accordance with WTO obligations.[44] They do not overrule national law, even if inconsistent with international law.

In terms of judicial review, this amounts to a doctrine of restraint. Generally, courts have not been willing to overrule domestic legislation which is inconsistent with WTO obligations. This even applies to decisions rendered under the DSU—despite the fact that such rulings, by their very nature, set forth rights and obligations in a sufficiently precise manner. Courts are, in other words, not allowed or not prepared to alter the domestic allocation and balance of powers: giving direct effect would result in shifts towards powers of the court, and ultimately to the executive branch (or commission) which essentially is in charge in the process of negotiations when rights and obligations are shaped. It is interesting to observe that direct effect of agreements is much less controversial where such effects on internal power structures are not likely to occur. The European Court of Justice directly applies regional FTAs[45] or the Lomé Convention,[46] both of which are essentially shaped in accordance with EC law. Moreover, direct effect is likely where obligations are imposed on Member States or foreign countries, but not the bodies of the EC, properly speaking.

The problem of direct effect therefore has to be analyzed and further studied in the context of such effects which are ultimately linked to power allocation and, in particular, to democratic legitimacy of treaty-making. Judicial review of international agreements apparently has to be in line with judicial powers of review allocated under domestic law. To the extent that the balance of powers is not affected, there seems to be a greater willingness to grant direct effect, and vice-versa. A doctrine of direct effect therefore should be built on this type of rationale. It is not a matter of looking at the wording and precision of a text but rather one of examining as to who is best suited to render a decision in the context of a particular legal issue and dispute in the light of domestic allocations of powers in external economic affairs.[47] This also may explain that a provision may be given direct effect in one community, but not another one.

This constellation, again, may provoke imbalances between states and goes to the heart of the reciprocity argument. Direct effect not only affects domestic checks and balances but, equally, international ones. Concerns relating to reciprocity reveal that domestic effect of WTO law no longer is an exclusive matter of domestic constitutional law. The matter has to be looked at in the overall global context. Both aspects transgress the potentials of the present system of nation states each with its own, individual, and independent constitutional settings.

2. Judicial Review in International Fora

WTO Dispute Resolution

Judicial review on the international level operates within a completely different constitutional setting. Panels and the Appellate Body (as other international tribunals) exclusively operate under international law. Relations between different Member States are exclusively defined by this body of law which does not entail (at least explicitly) considerations of balance of powers and checks and balances present in a national and regional context discussed above. Whether or not judges should, or should not, exercise restraint is defined by different underlying considerations.

Contractual Relations

These considerations, it is submitted, reflect the *contractual* basis of relations among different states. Judicial review essentially responds to that and consists of examining and adjudicating whether or not conduct is in compliance with contractual obligations and, possibly, with customary international law or general principles of law. It is a matter of objectively assessing as to whether or not a party has been in breach of its obligations under international law. Considerations relating to separation and balance of powers which have shaped domestic standards of review are not overtly present in this context. There is no room to explicitly consider as to whether a ruling affects the internal or external power relations of Member States and the international system in general. The contractual approach reflects a weak constitutional setting and order which does not allocate powers among different players in a balanced and nuanced manner. This is true with respect to other organs of the WTO itself, and it is equally true with respect to Member States and their governments.

Standards of review therefore are shaped by the rules of treaty interpretation. We all are familiar with these standards, as Panels and the Appellate Body keep religiously repeating them.[48] Defining rights and obligations is based upon the prominent role of the wording, in the context and in the light of the object and purpose of the treaty, and—in our view—upon good faith and thus by protecting legitimate expectations of States emanating from a treaty provision.[49] These rules are characterized by inflexibility. They do not allow—different from constitutional law—for the application of inherent unwritten principles and exceptions within a particular wording. They limit the scope of activist and expansive or restrictive interpretation of rules in light of higher constitutional principles found in domestic or regional law. They reflect the fact that authority and legitimacy of international fora are still comparatively weak—despite the quality of their work—and that acceptability and compliance depends on interpretation closely following the wording of the authoritative texts as agreed and consented to by states.

While it is expected that a weak international order results in judicial restraint applied by its dispute resolution mechanism, the Vienna rules in fact have an opposite effect. Short of appropriate treaty language, there is no legal possibility to grant leeway to domestic rules and practices. And where this is done in effect, it has to be achieved by complicated means and arguments in treaty interpretation. The *Hormones* case comes to mind. Differences between the Panel and the Appellate Body in interpreting the SPS Agreement can be explained in such terms.[50] The Appellate Body resulted in granting more leeway to Members than the Panel which closely followed rules of textual treaty interpretation in order to make its objective assessment under the architecture of the SPS Agreement. We do not argue that the decision of the Appellate Body was not wise. The point we make is simply that, *per se*, there is no room for deference to interpretations given by Member States in accordance with their domestic policies and interests. Treaty language which explicitly directs Panels and the Appellate Body to grant deference to both a Member State's establishment of the facts and its legal findings if they rest upon a *permissible* interpretation can only be found in Article 17.6 of the Antidumping Agreement.[51] But interestingly enough, neither Panels nor the Appellate Body have so far applied a particularly deferential standard of review of both facts and law when reviewing antidumping cases. It seems difficult to articulate a substantive difference to the approach taken under

Article 11 of the DSU and its provision to "make an objective assessment of the facts." The *Thailand – Poland* antidumping case (subject to the Appellate Body's ruling at this time) provides an illustrative example in which the Panel quoted Article 17.6 but did not defer to the defendant's fact-finding or its interpretations at all.[52] Moreover, there is to date no report in which a Panel or the Appellate Body would have determined that a provision of the Antidumping Agreement admits of more than one permissible interpretation and would have dismissed a claim on this ground.

Law and Facts

A second fundamental difference exists between domestic and international review. Adjudication on the level of international law has, in principle, no jurisdiction to construe and interpret domestic rules. Unlike in domestic law, it is not a matter of interpreting both constitutional rules, statutory law (and possibly treaty rules in case of direct effect and consistent interpretation). Here, domestic rules are conceptually dealt with as questions of fact and not of law.[53] Whether or not domestic law is in compliance with international obligations is based on a comparison of national law as reasonably stated by the respective Member and as interpreted by its authorities and of WTO rules construed and applied by the WTO bodies. The distinction, of course, is difficult to draw in practical terms, and poses considerable conceptual problems within a system where review by the Appellate Body is essentially limited to questions of law. Moreover, Panels and the Appellate Body cannot exclusively rely upon the reading of national law as submitted by the defending party (naturally in an alleged WTO-compatible way), and at least apparent misperceptions and interpretations short of a sound rational basis cannot be accepted. The assessment therefore entails legal analysis, but it has to be dealt with as a matter of evidence, i.e., as to whether a defending party is in a position to demonstrate the alleged meaning and scope of its own and domestic law challenged by the complainant.

North American Free Trade Agreement (NAFTA)

Similar effects can also be observed in regional free trade agreements to the extent that they follow (unlike the EC) the structures of international law adjudication. NAFTA is a leading example in point. Chapter 20 includes provisions relating to the settlement of all disputes regarding the interpretation and application of the Agreement, except for subject matters governed by Chapters 11, 14 and 19. The Panels have not yet made explicit statements as to appropriate standards of review; the cases which were brought before a Panel to date and the submissions of the parties seem to indicate that the standards of review *mutatis mutandis* follow those applied by GATT/WTO Panels in the respective subject matters.[54]

The application of the general standards of review similar to those in WTO/GATT dispute settlement reflects the fact that NAFTA equally represents a typical contractual model of international law. It lacks a constitutional approach, its structure is intergovernmental, and its institutional framework is not comparable to that within the EC which is highly elaborated and allows the judicial branches to take into account constitutional deliberations of allocation of powers and checks and balances in a specific case.

Interestingly, things are different in the field of CVDs. Domestic countervailing and antidumping determinations can be brought before an *ad hoc* binational Panel under NAFTA Chapter 19. The standards of review to be applied in these cases follow the respective domestic rules; they are the same as laid down by the relevant statutes of each party.[55] In the case of U.S. countervailing and antidumping decisions, this accordingly requires in most cases that the determinations are based on a "reasonable interpretation" and that the factual findings are supported by "substantial evidence on the record."[56] This standard of review appears to be fairly deferential on its face. However, the binational Panels seem to have ruled in a rather pro-active way, and much U.S. "criticism has centered on the supposedly undeferential treatment of U.S. agency decisions by the Panels."[57] It is interesting to observe that deviation from domestic standards causes concerns as it affects the balance of powers established at home.

3. Towards a Constitutional Approach

The systemic differences between domestic review (including the constitutional structure of the EC) and dispute settlement on the international level leave us with inherently and conceptually different standards of review. Flexibility in practical terms may reduce the tension. International law may be construed with some flexibility, and national or regional law with some rigor. The point, however, is that this does not allow to overcome a fundamentally different starting point under the characteristics of the two legal systems, domestic and international. Domestic review operating under constitutional law and separation of powers allows for more nuanced approaches to review and is embedded in constitutional law. International review, operating under a contractual system which does not reflect balance of powers in legal terms, is more rigid and in the end potentially more intrusive than national review as it lacks a constitutional framework taking into account the balance of powers of various actors, vertically and horizontally. Treaty interpretation in the functionalist traditions of GATT allows for less flexibility in assessing market access than in parallel cases in domestic law. The assessment of hormones within the EC and by the WTO is a striking example in point.[58] Furthermore, the notion of like products is defined more rigorously in GATT than in EC law, for example, when it comes to assess differential taxation.[59] This is a paradox. We would expect a different result. The international order, given its structural weaknesses and the traditions of state sovereignty, would be expected to grant more leeway to Members than is the case within the Member State. Current tensions within the international system, faced with apprehensions of excessive intrusiveness of liberal trade rules at the detriment of other policy goals, can be partly explained by this constellation. It is submitted that the classical canon of treaty interpretation, stemming from a world of purely contractual relations of inter-state coexistence, no longer is in a position to appropriately deal with complex issues of global integration.

At the same time, we recall that judicial review under domestic law and introverted constitutional traditions often is unable to combat rent-seeking protectionism. Again, we would expect a different result. Established constitutional structures, equipped with strong law enforcing powers, should deal with protectionism more rigorously. The paradox thus requires from us to rethink the basis of judicial review both domestically and internationally if a more coherent overall system were to be achieved. It is submitted that we need to find a common constitutional basis for both domestic and international litigation which allows for interfacing the two levels in a coherent manner.

Firstly, the concept and idea of constitutionalism is to be extended to the international level and should replace a purely contractual model of classical international law. We note the caution to extend the concept of a constitution to the trading system.[60] Yet, we would argue that constitutional thinking would allow to accommodate some of the very concerns and needs expressed by Howse and Nicolaidis. Considering all the differences between the EC and the global system, it is nevertheless interesting to observe the process of transformation in European law.[61] The fundamental steps taken in early leading cases reflected a change from a purely international legal system to a constitutional approach, long before it was called that way.[62] The essence was to create a legal order *sui generis* having direct effect and *primauté* over national law, but equally allowing for more flexible interpretation (cf., e.g., *Cassis de Dijon* principle containing inherent, *non-written* exceptions) and taking into account other legitimate policy goals. It reflects a constitutional approach which has left behind application according to rigid principles of international law treaty interpretation. The shift was followed by efforts to enhance democratic legitimacy of rules having such far-reaching effects. In internal trade regulation, the system has achieved strong disciplines while taking into account national policy goals and needs. It has successfully focused on combating economic protectionism.

Secondly, the ideas of constitutionalism developed on the regional level should also apply to domestic trade law under traditional constitutions and would lead to reinforced judicial review of governmental measures. Disciplines of bringing about market integration would be reinforced, and courts would deal with these problems more proactively than in the past.

Overall, the quest for coherent and consistent standards of judicial review both on domestic and global level therefore requires an expansion of constitutional thinking. One of the authors has suggested elsewhere that we should start looking at the overall order in terms of a five-story house of governance.[63] Constitutional structures exist on the local level, the level of federate states, the federal level, the regional level, and the global level. We may work with a simplified model of three levels in Europe for members to the EU, neglecting domestic constellations. We may even work with a model of two levels. It is essential, however, that the global level is being included. Of course, it is not a matter of conceiving this house as a formal constitution, perhaps even in terms of global federalism. It is much more a way of thinking, and an effort to bring about reasonable inter-linkages of different layers of governance. The framework will, in the very end, allow to develop standards of judicial review which are appropriate and consistent among these levels. The global level would equally rely upon doctrines of separation of powers, of checks and balances, and of distributions of powers between the global, regional and, national system. It will allow to address the problem of democratic legitimacy of international trade rules in a broader context. And it will equally allow to define in a more appropriate term the scope of action and conduct which national governments should have within the global system of trade regulation. It will address the proper role of courts. The traditions of leaving trade policy almost exclusively to the executive branch under traditions of introverted national constitutions will no longer fit.

Again, we do not argue that a five-story house will be explicitly created. There are no easy parallels in comparing and combining different constitutional levels. But common and coherent grounds and foundations may eventually emerge on the basis of changing attitudes and perceptions in the process of making and applying the law. The paradox, caused by the dichotomy between traditional national constitutional, administrative, and civil law on the one hand and the contractual foundation of classical international law on the other hand needs to be resolved. The process will shape attitudes towards the role of courts in international economic relations and thus of judicial review both at home and on the regional and global level, reflecting a mutual relationship of domestic and international fora. It is likely to bring about a more nuanced set of tools of interpretation as well as a more nuanced balance between market access rights and other equally legitimate policy concerns on the international level. At the same time, it will allow for a stronger role of market access rights in a domestic context. We need to start with elaborating appropriate theoretical conceptions in the first place.

NOTES

1. Cf. Thomas Cottier, Emerging Doctrines of Good Governance: The Impact of the WTO and China's Accession, in: F. Abbott (ed.), *China in the World Trade System*, 1998, pp. 119–26.

2. Cf. Thomas M. Frank, *The Empowered Self: Law and Society in the Age of Individualism*, Oxford 1999, pp. 255–77.

3. J. Holmes, quoted in: R. W. M. Dias, *Jurisprudence*, London 1976, 4th ed., p. 11.

4. Cf., e.g., Thomas Cottier, Constitutional Trade Regulation in National and International Law: Structure-Substance Pairings in the EFTA Experience, in: M. Hilf/E. U. Petersmann (eds.), *National Constitutions and International Economic Law*, Deventer 1993, pp. 409–92.

5. See Trevor C. Hartley, *The Foundations of European Community Law*, 1998, p. 426; Henry G. Schermers/Denis F. Waelbroeck, *Judicial Protection in the European Communities*, 1992, p. 183.

6. Case 42/84, *Remina,* (1985) ECR 2545, para. 34.

7. Case 191/82, *Fediol,* (1983) ECR 2913, para. 30.

8. Case 331/88, *Fedesa,* (1990) ECR 4023, para. 8.

9. Case 11/82, *Piraiki-Patraiki,* (1985) ECR 207, para. 40.

10. Now incorporated in the EC Treaty, Article 5.

11. Case 331/88, *Fedesa,* (1990) ECR 4023, para. 15. See also Case 265/87, *Schräder,* (1989) ECR 2237, para. 22. Natalie McNelis, in this volume, submits that the standard of review as applied in the *BSE* case (in which the standard of review was identical to that in the *Fedesa* case) "was nearing total deference."

12. See infra II. D. and, particularly, fn. 42.

13. See, e.g., Opinion 1/94, (1994) ECR 5267, concerning the controversy in the Community as to where jurisdiction lay to conclude the WTO Agreement and its Annexes. Cf. generally Christine Kaddous, *Le droit des relations extérieures dans la jurisprudence de la Cour de justice des Communautés européennes*, Bruxelles 1998.

14. Case C-327/91, *France/Commission,* (1994) ECR I-3641.

15. Case 89/85, *Ahlström/Commission,* (1988) ECR 5193. See Bellamy & Child, *Common Market Law of Competition*, ed. by Vivien Rose, London 1993, 4th ed., paras. 2–147.

16. See, e.g., case 104/81, *Hauptzollamt Mainz/C.A. Kupferberg & Cie.,* (1982) ECR 3641; case T-155/94, *Opel Austria/Council,* (1997) ECR II-39; case 12/86, *Demirel,* (1987) ECR 3719.

17. See, e.g., Case 178/84, *Commission/Germany,* (1987) ECR 1227 (*German Beer* case).

18. *Chevron U.S.A., Inc. v. Natural Resources Defense Council,* 467 U.S. 837 (1984). See Steven P. Croley/John H. Jackson, WTO Dispute Settlement Panel Deference to National Government Decisions. The Misplaced Analogy to the U.S. Chevron Standard-of-Review Doctrine, in: E.-U. Petersmann (ed.), *International Trade Law and the GATT/WTO Dispute Settlement System*, 1997, pp. 187–210.

19. Appeals go to the Court of Appeals for the Federal Circuit and, ultimately, to the Supreme Court. See in general John H. Jackson/William J. Davey/Alan O. Sykes, *Legal Problems of International Economic Relations: Cases, Materials and Text on the National and International Regulation of Transnational Economic Relations*, 1995, pp. 158–60. William J. Davey, The United States Court of International Trade and the Court of Appeals for the Federal Circuit, in: Ernst-Ulrich Petersmann/Günther Jaenicke (eds.), *Adjudication of International Trade Disputes in International and National Economic Law*, 1992, pp. 306–12.

20. 28 U.S.C. sec. 2640(b); 28 U.S.C. sec. 1640(b); 19 U.S.C. sec. 1516a(b)(1); see William Davey, in: ibid., pp. 307–11.

21. Michael J. Trebilcock/Robert Howse, *The Regulation of International Trade*, 1999, p. 83.

22. William J. Davey, The United States Court of International Trade and the Court of Appeals for the Federal Circuit, in: Petersmann/Jaenicke (eds.), ibid., p. 308.

23. 28 U.S.C. sec. 2640(c); 19 U.S.C. sec. 2395(b); William J. Davey, the same, in: ibid., p. 311.

24. 28 U.S.C. sec. 2640(a).

25. See *K mart Corp. v. Cartier, Inc.*, et al., 486 U.S. 281, in: Frederick Abbot/Thomas Cottier/Francis Gurry, *The International Intellectual Property System: Commentary and Materials*, 1999, p. 1387.

26. *United States v. Aluminum Co. of America*, 148F.2d 416, in: Henkin/Pugh/Schachter/Smit, *International Law, Cases and Materials*, 1993, 3rd ed., p. 1052.

27. See, e.g., Bundesgesetz über die Landwirtschaft vom 29. April 1998 (LwG), SR 910.1.

28. Decision 2A.496/1996 (14 July 1997), *A. SA v. Bundesamt für Landwirtschaft und Rekurskommission EVD* (own translation; not officially published, on file with authors), p. 10. See also BGE 99 Ib 159, 169.

29. Id., p. 16. We should note, however, that the court went on: "Nonetheless, it still is to examine the compliance with the WTO/GATT Agreements."

30. Bundesgesetz über das Verwaltungsverfahren vom 20. Dezember 1968 (VwVG), SR 172.021.

31. Recht und Politik des Wettbewerbs, 1998, p. 676, *Swisscom v. Weko* (own translation). See Paul Richli, Kartellverwaltungsverfahren, in: SIWR V/2, pp. 511–13.

32. Komm. KG – Gross, Art. 44 Rz. 91; Paul Richli, Kartellverwaltungsverfahren, in: SIWR V/2, p. 514, with reference to BGE 115 Ib 135.

33. BGE 122 III 469 *("Chanel")*.

34. BGE 124 III 321 *("Nintendo")*.

35. BGE 126 III 129 *("Kodak")*.

36. Cf. generally Jörg Paul Müller, *Grundrechte in der Schweiz*, 1999, 3rd ed., p. 632 et seq.

37. Ulrich Zimmerli/Walter Kälin/Regina Kiener, *Grundlagen des öffentlichen Verfahrensrechts*, 1997, p. 90 et seq. and 197 et seq.

38. René Rhinow, Kommentar zu Art. 28, in: Aubert/Eichenberger/Müller/Rhinow/Schindler (eds.), *Kommentar zur Bundesverfassung der Schweizerischen Eidgenossenschaft vom*

29. Mai 1874, loose-leaf, June 1988, para. 67; Thomas Cottier/Remo Arpagaus, Einleitung, Schweizerischen Aussenwirtschafts- und Binnenmarktrecht, in SBVR, para. 39. See also Walter Kälin, Verfassungsgrundsätze der schweizerischen Aussenpolitik, ZSR 1986 II, p. 355 et seq., 368; William Elio Andrich, Die Wirtschaftsfreiheit im schweizerischen Aussenwirtschaftsrecht, 1996, p. 56 et seq.

39. BGE 122 III 469 *("Chanel")*.

40. See Thomas Cottier/Remo Arpagaus, Einleitung, Schweizerischen Aussenwirtschafts- und Binnenmarktrecht, in SBVR, para. 39.

41. The literature on direct effect is legendary, yet the problem is still unresolved. For a comprehen-sive analysis, see in particular John H. Jackson, Status of Treaties in Domestic Legal Systems: A Policy Analysis, AJIL 1992, p. 310; Meinhard Hilf, The Role of National Courts in International Trade Relations, *Mich. J. Int'l Law* 1997, pp. 321 and 337–45; Thomas Cottier/Krista Nadakavukaren Schefer, The Relationship between World Trade Organization Law, National and Regional Law, in: *JIEL* 1 (1998), pp. 83–122; and Thomas Cottier/Daniel Plüss, WTO Law and Domestic Law: An Uneasy Relationship, *Jusletter* 9 October 2000 (www.weblaw.ch).

42. See in particular joined cases C-300/98 and C-392/98, *Dior SA v. TUK Consultancy BV and Assco Gerüste GmbH,* judgment of the Court of 14 December 2000, para. 44. Interestingly enough, the court went on that in a field in respect of which the Community has not yet legislated, it is up to the Member States to decide whether provisions of TRIPs should have direct effect in the domestic legal order, paras. 45–48. This is an interesting finding as it contrasts with the general rationale and qualification that GATT and WTO law is not sufficiently precise and thus unsuitable for direct effect. For previous rulings with respect to GATT 1947, see case 21-24/72, *International Fruit Company,* (1972) ECR 1219; C-149/96, and with respect to the WTO C-149/96, *Portugal/Council,* (1999) ECR I-8395.

43. See Daniel Thürer, WTO – Teilordnung im System des Völker- und Europarechts, in: D. Thürer/S. Kux (eds.), GATT 94 und die Welthandelsorganisation, Herausforderungen für die Schweiz und Europa, 1996, p. 50 et seq. In a decision of the Swiss Supreme Court of 14 July 1997, *A. SA v. Federal Office for Agriculture* (not officially published, on file with authors), the court in fact examined the compatibility of Swiss domestic law with WTO provisions in order to address the claim arguing in part that a national regime for auctioning import licenses was a violation of Article 4 of the Agreement on Agriculture. The court explicitly refrained from deciding *obiter dictum* whether the WTO agreements are to be considered directly effective in Switzerland.

44. For an overview see Thomas Cottier/Krista Nadakavukaren Schefer, The Relationship between World Trade Organization Law, National and Regional Law, *JIEL* 1998, p. 88 et seq.

45. See, for instance, case 104/81, *Hauptzollamt Mainz/C.A. Kupferberg & Cie.*, (1982) ECR 3641; case T-155/94, *Opel Austria/Council,* (1997) ECR II-39.

46. See, for instance, case C-469/93, *Amministrazione delle Finanze dello Stato/Chiquita Italia SpA,* (1995) ECR I-4533.

47. For a refinement of this approach in Swiss law, see Thomas Cottier/Alberto Achermann/Daniel Wüger/Valentin Zellweger, *Der Staatsvertrag im schweizerischen Verfassungsrecht*, Bern 2001.

48. See Article 3.2 of the DSU which is understood as reference to Articles 31 and 32 of the Vienna Convention on the Law of Treaties. See, for instance, *U.S. – Standards for Reformulated*

and Conventional Gasoline, WT/DS2/AB/R, 20 May 1996, Appellate Body report, p. 17; *Japan – Taxes on Alcoholic Beverages*, WT/DS8/AB/R, 4 October 1996, Appellate Body report, D.H.2.c); *U.S. – Sections 301–310 of the Trade Act of 1974*, WT/DS152/R, Panel report, 22 December 1999, para. 7.21.

49. Being, by the way, quite different from expectations under non-violation complaints, see Thomas Cottier/Krista Nadakavukaren Schefer, Good Faith and the Protection of Legitimate Expectations in the WTO, in: Marco Bronckers/Reinhard Quick (eds.), *New Directions in International Economic Law, Essays in Honor of John H. Jackson*, 2000, pp. 47–68.

50. *EC – Measures Concerning Meat and Meat Products (Hormones)*, WT/DS26/AB/R, WT/DS48/AB/R, 26 January 1998. See, particularly, the different approaches in interpreting the term "based on" as stipulated in Article 5.1 of the SPS Agreement, Appellate Body report, paras. 188 et seq.

51. World Trade Organization (Secretariat), *The Results of the Uruguay Round of Multilateral Trade Negotiations: The Legal Texts*, Geneva 1995, p. 168.

52. *Thailand – Antidumping Duties on Angles, Shapes and Sections of Iron or Non-alloy Steel and H-Beams from Poland*, WT/DS122/R, 28 September 2000. The Panel did not elaborate on the standard of review of law but meaninglessly held in para. 7.54: "We are also mindful of the standard of review in Article 17.6(ii), which states: ..."

53. In *India – Patent Protection for Pharmaceutical and Agricultural Chemical Products*, WT/DS50/AB/R, 19 December 1997, para. 66, the Appellate Body seemed to support the view that when examining domestic law for the purpose of determining whether it is in compliance with WTO law no particular deference to domestic interpretations of that law should be applied. The same approach is found in *EC – Regime for the Importation, Sale and Distribution of Bananas*, WT/DS27/AB/R, 9 September 1997, para. 167, although there was not domestic law at stake but the Lomé Convention. In *U.S. - Sections 301–310 of the Trade Act of 1974*, WT/DS152/R, 22 December 1999, paras. 7.18–19, the Panel eventually held that the interpretation of national and regional law should be established "as factual elements," and it required "considerable deference be given to [the Member's] view on the meaning of its own law."

54. See the arguments brought forward by Mexico and the U.S. in the case *U.S. Safeguard Action taken on Broom Corn Brooms from Mexico*, U.S.-97-2008-01, paras. 39–43, at http://www.nafta-sec-alena.org/english/index.htm (visited on 22 February 2001).

55. Article 1904.3, Annex 1911.

56. See Michael J. Trebilcock/Robert Howse, *The Regulation of International Trade*, 1999, p. 84.

57. Ibid., p. 86. For a detailed analysis of the standards of review as applied in the Canada-U.S. FTA, see William J. Davey, Pine and Swine, Canada-United States trade dispute settlement: The FTA experience and NAFTA prospects, 1996, particularly pp. 268–69 for a concise summary.

58. Cf. Natalie McNelis, The Role of the Judge in the EU and WTO, in this volume, p. 225.

59. See Paul Demaret, The Non-Discrimination Principle and the Removal of Fiscal Barriers to Intra-Community Trade, in: Thomas Cottier/Petros C. Mavroidis (eds.), *Regulatory Barriers and the Principle of Non-Discrimination in World Trade Law*, 2000, pp. 171–90.

60. See Robert Howse/Kalypso Nicolaidis, Legitimacy through "Higher Law"? Why Constitutionalizing the WTO Is a Step Too Far, in this volume, p. 307.

61. See Joseph H. Weiler, The Transformation of Europe, *Yale Law Journal* 1991, pp. 2403–83.

62. See, in particular, cases 26/62, *Van Gend en Loos,* (1963) ECR 1, and 6/64, *Costa/ENEL,* (1964) ECR 585.

63. Thomas Cottier, Reforming the Swiss Federal Constitution: an International Lawyer's Perspective, in: M. Butler/M. Pender/J. Charnley (eds.), *The Making of Modern Switzerland, 1848–1998*, 2000, pp. 75–96, particularly 80–84; Thomas Cottier, Limits to International Trade: The Constitutional Challenge, in: *ASIL Proceedings 2000*, pp. 220-22, and the Remarks by John H. Jackson, id., pp. 222-24.

CHAPTER 19

Legitimacy through "Higher Law"? Why Constitutionalizing the WTO Is a Step Too Far

Robert Howse and Kalypso Nicolaidis

Increasingly, fundamental societal choices are being shaped at the global level in the name of trade liberalization. And the question becomes all the more relevant: by whom and on what grounds? One response gaining currency among scholars and even politicians has been to articulate the challenge of global economic governance in constitutional terms. This view typically has both descriptive and normative elements.

Descriptively, its proponents point out that while the GATT lent itself to being viewed as a structure to facilitate mutually self-interested bargains between sovereign states, its successor, the World Trade Organization (WTO), is already performing constitutional functions, *as if* an incipient global economic constitution. They point to the new binding, juridical rigorous dispute settlement mechanism, which provides for virtually automatic authorization of countermeasures in the case of non-compliance; they also point to the explicit role such tribunals play in balancing competing public values, economic efficiency vs. health and safety goals for instance, in the scrutiny of domestic regulation.[1] In terms of the brutal, Schmittean understanding of sovereignty—the sovereign is he who decides—the point of ultimate decision about the balance of public values in a wide range of areas now appears to lie with the WTO and its dispute settlement tribunals.

Normatively, the proponents of a constitutional understanding of the WTO believe that its legitimacy will be enhanced by building on these characteristics and turning the Treaty into a full blown constitutionalized construct. They typically aspire to greater legal certainty for private economic rights, against the depredation of powerful domestic interest groups. Furthermore, there is a minority position that sees the ultimate

---

We would like to thank Thomas Cottier, Steve Charnovitz, Robert Hudec, Andrew Hurrell, Leonardo Martinez, Petros Mavroidis, Eric Stein, Alec Stone Sweet and Joseph Weiler for inspiring discussions on this topic. An earlier and shorter version of this paper was published as "Legitimacy and Global Governance: Why Constitutionalizing the WTO is a Step too Far", in Roger Porter, Pierre Sauvé, Arvind Subramanian and Americo Zampetti, eds., *Equity, Efficiency and Legitimacy: The Multilateral System at the Millennium,* Washington D.C.: Brookings Institution Press, 2001.

implication of WTO constitutionalism as the transformation of the WTO into a progressive economic regulator for the world, bringing into the WTO social rights, environmental and developmental concerns, realizing distributive justice at the global level, so as to make the WTO a transnational economic constitution for *all* the people.[2]

The argument must be analyzed against the backdrop of the broader debate over the legitimacy of international institutions. The connection between constitutionalism and legitimacy is a complex one. Constitutionalization emerges in part as a response to concerns about legitimacy, while the prospect of constitutionalization itself contributes in giving rise to such concerns in the first place. In the short run, at least, the application of the language of constitutionalism to WTO is likely to exacerbate the hopes of globalization's friends that economic liberalism can acquire the legitimacy of higher law—irreversible, irresistible, and comprehensive. At the same time, it is likely to exacerbate the fears of the "discontents" of globalization that the international institutions of economic governance have become a supranational Behemoth, not democratically accountable to anyone. There is thus a real risk that importing constitutional language and concepts into the current debate about the WTO and its legitimacy will increasingly polarize the system's advocates and its critics. This risk exists to a lesser extent with modest or cautious proposals for a constitutional understanding.[3]

The proposed adoption of "constitutional" discourse and understandings as a legitimizing tool for the WTO system has important practical or policy implications. The first and central implication is what is loosely called "direct effect"—constitutional norms are rights, and therefore the WTO system should evolve to a point where individuals rather than states can rely on directly-enforceable WTO law. Moreover, and this is a fundamental point, they would be able to do so not only before WTO dispute settlement Panels or Appellate Bodies, but before domestic courts. Second, constitutional law is generally regarded as higher law, with a presumption against the change of basic structures. Constitutionalization tends to serve a "door-closing" function against claims that in areas such as food safety and intellectual property rights, the WTO has gone too far and may need to be scaled back to give greater scope for democracy at the national level. Third, by characterizing the WTO treaty system as a constitution, one transforms its character from that of a complex, messily negotiated bargain of diverse rules, principles, and norms, into a single structure. Individual elements become less easily contestable—the WTO becomes reified as something one is either for or against, making it harder to broker compromise and adjustment to change in the institution.[4]

The "constitutionalizing" view about the WTO merits careful analysis and critical scrutiny. The present essay is intended as a contribution along these lines. In our view, the question is whether and how the post-war bargain characterized by the political scientist John Ruggie as "embedded liberalism" (trade liberalization constrained by domestic welfare requirements)[5] can be salvaged in the globalization era. We begin by exploring the reasons why the original model has appeared to become increasingly problematic as a means of understanding the WTO. We then examine the claims for the WTO as a constitutional order on the basis of two variants of the constitutional view of the WTO. Both these variants take their inspiration from the evolving debate over whether the European Union has become, is becoming, or should become a transnational constitutional order. To a significant extent, the example of the EU, which began as little more than a trade treaty, and now not only constitutes a new level of governance in Europe but also has permeated *all* levels of governance, has influenced constitutional hopes for the WTO.[6]

The first variant, liberal in the libertarian sense, sees the WTO's constitutional function in terms of pre-commitment by which politicians tie their hands in such a manner as to resist the depredation of economic rights by domestic interest groups, who demand rent-conferring interventionist/protectionist government. This is the model of WTO constitutionalism articulated explicitly by Ernst-Ulrich Petersmann.[7] While Petersmann is the most intellectually forthright and serious of those who accept such a model, explicitly admitting and even endorsing economic freedom as the *telos* and guiding norm of the WTO constitution, this idea is expressed in a wide variety of contemporary scholarship on the WTO. It is inspired by a minimalist reading of European integration as driven and constructed by judicial review of expansive Treaty commitments. The conception of constitutionalism at operation here is one that understands constitutionalism as a means, indeed the means, of placing law, or the rule of law above politics. WTO constitutionalism is a solution to the limits of domestic constitutionalism in achieving such a result with respect to *economic* rights—limits that are attributed to the capture of domestic politics. While this variety of constitutionalism aims at using a constitutionalized WTO to place economic freedom above politics, we argue that just the reverse is necessary to address the legitimacy crisis of the multilateral trading order—more politics, not less. As we will argue, the evolution of the EU itself is a case in point.

The second variant of WTO constitutionalism is not pre-occupied like the first with pre-commitment and property rights, but builds on the internal EU debate about the Union's status as a polity, and its future. It also, however, is based on an inaccurate assessment of the EU's own constitutionalizing path and its underlying federal model. This variant recovers the function of constitutions as formalizing the distribution of power among governmental institutions while establishing a permanent link between these institutions and societies; and, at least in federal contexts, as establishing the basis for the division of power among and the relationship between levels of government. It is nevertheless philosophically more modest in that it identifies WTO constitutionalization with the adjudication of competing values in WTO dispute settlement.[8] The largely unspoken premise in describing such a function as constitutional or constitutionalizing is that these trade-offs (say between freer trade and protection of human health and safety) are made, not so much in the framework of international law generally, but in light of the WTO "constitution," the principles of trade liberalization taken as constitutional norms, and with a view to the *telos* of the WTO itself—economic freedom. Thus, competing human values enter into the picture as narrow, and carefully policed exceptions or limits, to the overall constitutional project of freer trade. (To be sure, there can be a progressive view of WTO constitutionalism—one which is more ambitious as to the requisite degree of institutionalization—that sees the WTO as transforming itself into a socially just global economic government, by assimilating social and environmental governance under its remit. Such a view is consistent nevertheless with the second variant, in the role attributed to Courts in the process of integration and in the belief that tensions between conflicting values at the global level can be resolved short of political give and take.)

This second variant of constitutionalization is largely based on a belief in the transferability of the EU model to the global level, not so much in its pragmatic innovative features but its most ambitious constitutional *telos.* But does it really take on board the full implications of such a logic? In the EU model, constitutionalism is increasingly seen as closely connected to democratic self-determination, the autopoesis of a citizenship which has not only economic, but also political and social dimensions. There has been intense debate as to whether European law and regulation is a sufficiently direct expression of democratic will to possess a legitimately constitutional status, whether European institutions need to have for their foundation a European *demos,* whether a demos is possible at all beyond the confines of a community defined in terms of sub-political ties such as race, language, or cultural heritage; and to what extent a shared constitution requires shared social responsibility, including functioning redistributive mechanisms. Whatever the responses given, there is no avoiding the fact that intense polity-building has and will continue to take place in the EU as a pre-condition to its formal constitutionalization.

So neither the first nor the second variant of constitutionalization seems to provide an adequate or realistic response to the WTO legitimacy conumdrum. As we elaborate in the final section of the paper, we believe that just the opposite response is needed if the legitimacy of the WTO is to be preserved and enhanced. The EU itself, we argue, can remain an inspiration in this matter, since the spirit of embedded liberalism can be recovered by applying at the international level a kind of "global subsidiarity" adapted to the structure of the international system. At the global as well as the regional level, we need to *bring politics back in,* not seek to transcend it. This means first that WTO judges show *political sensitivity* and deference to views defended outside the WTO, a kind of "horizontal subsidiarity". In this, we endorse the approach taken—at least at times—by the WTO Appellate Body in interpreting WTO rules that engage competing or divergent human values. Instead of presupposing that the treaty text is animated by a constitutional *telos* of freer trade, or looking primarily *within* the WTO for the relevant structural principles, we emphasize the importance of non-WTO institutions and norms in treaty interpretation, which represent values other than free or freer trade. The WTO dispute settlement organs must display considerable deference to substantive domestic regulatory choices as well as draw on and defer to other international regimes whose rules, policies, and institutions represent and articulate such values, whether in respect of health, labor standards, environment, or human rights. Thus, we advocate a kind of diffuse externalization of what Cottier identifies as the constitutional dimension.

In addition, the WTO ought to promote the principle of *political inclusiveness* at the national, transnational, and supranational levels. It should emphasize procedural obligations rather than normative constraints on the conduct of lower level policies, and support mechanisms for the participation of actors inside and outside states' jurisdiction. Inclusiveness also implies moving beyond notions of representative democracy at the supranational level. Although the notion of a global *demos* seems implausible, there are elements of democracy that can be realized, at least partially, at the global level, by facilitating greater access to WTO processes for non-governmental actors and more transparency and deliberation within those processes—not so much with view to creating eventually a world democracy, but rather to enhancing the connection between WTO decision-making and domestic processes of accountability.

Finally, a renewed spirit of embedded liberalism may require that global institutions not only *let* the state go about its protective business, but also *empower* the state (and sub-national units) to do so, in a manner compatible with its international obligations. Such an approach may, in the long term, create the conditions for federalism at the world level, but one which, as Kant envisaged, builds on the sustained legitimacy of its constituent units.

To the extent that its Member States and Courts are ready to act in the spirit of global subsidiarity, the WTO need not have the kind of legitimacy that it would require if it were to act as the final authority in the prioritization of diverse human and societal values. Nevertheless, by aiming for such a less ambitious role, it is likely, paradoxically, to serve the cause of free trade better than by following a constitutionalizing logic.

1. From Interstate Bargaining to the Demand for Constitutionalism: "Embedded Liberalism" in Disrepair

Of all the post-war economic institutions, the multilateral trading order would seem to be the one most amenable to explanation and justification in terms of "cooperation under anarchy."[9] While many other multilateral institutions (the World Bank, the International Monetary Fund or specialized agencies of the United Nations) could appear as projections of the U.S. post-New Deal constitutional order,[10] the GATT was born from the failure of an ambitious project for a global trade regulatory agency (the International Trade Organization), and was little more than a bare-bones structure for progressive negotiated reduction of tariffs on a reciprocal basis among sovereign states—subject to the MFN and national treatment rules. The story of how it evolved beyond its modest beginnings has often been told.

The Underlying Assumptions of "Embedded Liberalism"

Based on the notion of comparative advantage, standard economic theory of trade supports unilateral trade liberalization as an optimal policy for all countries, in most circumstances, i.e., regardless of whether others liberalize trade. Why would states, if they are rational, have to bargain to get others to do what economic theory says is in their interest to do anyway? And what would they seek to achieve through cooperation? Realists argue that states might be deterred from liberalizing trade, either unilaterally or through cooperation, even when doing so yields absolute gains, if the result were that this openness resulted in greater, i.e., relative gains for *other* countries.[11] Even if one recognizes that relative gains may matter in certain circumstances (e.g., positional goods), we need a more differentiated account of the puzzle of reciprocal negotiated trade liberalization and how the characteristics of the trade regime sought to address the configuration of incentives that gives rise to this puzzle.

First, states will behave strategically, in order to *maximize* absolute gains over time.[12] When they assess that the distribution of the surplus generated by free trade is too skewed, they may withhold liberalization now in the hope of a greater share of the pie later. The GATT was conceived as a system based on diffuse reciprocity and expectations of iterated negotiated rounds which allow for liberalization in the face of such strategic posturing.

Secondly, even though unilateral free trade would normally be the first best policy for every country from the perspective of wealth maximization, asymmetric distributional consequences internationally and domestically, combined with the lack of adequate compensatory mechanisms in either sphere lead to pressures to employ protectionism as a response to the needs of certain economic actors, or in order to sustain the existing social contract under changed or crisis economic conditions. In this light, the GATT can be seen as a set of commitments that limit protectionist responses to such pressures, which is only sustainable if predicated on the assumption that a wide range of alternative policy responses to social demands is available and legitimate. This includes the recognition that adjustment pressures might be such that, at least in the short term and under commonly agreed conditions, some scope for recourse to trade-restrictive, discriminatory policy instruments might be needed. Thus, while the GATT contained no requirement to eliminate tariffs at any given rate or pace, allowance was made for temporary balance-of-payments-based import restrictions (Arts. XII-XV), for safeguards in response to the injury to domestic industries from sudden surges of imports (Art. XIX), and for negotiated rebalancing of concessions (Art. XXVIII).

Thirdly, even given these reasons for coordinated liberalization, cooperation may be hindered by mutual fears of cheating on liberalization bargains. For one, quantitative restrictions on trade were largely prohibited, while tariffs were subject to successive rounds of binding reductions. On this basis, the rules of the GATT could be largely explained as sustaining negotiated commitments to tariff binding; thus, the National Treatment obligation (Art. III) was a means of preventing Member States from instituting discriminatory domestic policies that would distort competition between domestic and imported products in a manner similar to the effects of tariffs or other discriminatory border measures (i.e., from cheating on the negotiated bargain), not an instrument for liberalization *per se.* At the same time, the dispute settlement practices that developed out of the general language in Art. XXIII of the 1947 GATT was means of identifying instances of cheating on the trade liberalization bargain, thereby sustaining Member States' confidence that defection from the cooperative equilibrium could be clearly and rapidly ascertained and appropriately sanctioned, by allowing withdrawal of concessions.

Last but not least, unilateral or coordinated liberalization might be withheld because it might conflict with other policy goals. To address this concern, ample room was made for policy autonomy. States were constrained by the distinction under GATT between permitted and prohibited forms of domestic intervention on discrimination grounds. The flip side of National Treatment as "cheating prevention" was that it seemed to cover as legal most non-discriminatory policies. Actually, even discriminatory domestic policies might be permitted, provided that they did not entail *arbitrary or unjustified* discrimination, and could be linked, more or less tightly, to superior public policy goals such as the protection of human life or health, the conservation of exhaustible natural resources, or the protection of public morals (Art. XX).

This core bargain to allow for a kind of multilateralism molded by domestic requirements rather than the other way around is what John Ruggie has aptly called "embedded liberalism."[13]

2. The Embedded Liberalism Bargain under Stress

The embedded liberalism bargain came under sustained stress in the 1970s, as the gold standard collapsed and with it the structure for managed macroeconomic adjustment foreseen by the Bretton Woods system. The 1970s recession and the mounting intellectual as well as practical (stagflation) challenges to the Keynesian consensus, led to increasing emphasis on microeconomic interventions of various sorts for adjustment purposes, as well as to new kinds of trade restrictions—"voluntary" export restraints negotiated under threat of unilateral action—of dubious legality under the GATT.[14] For various reasons, the safety valves for adjustment written explicitly into the GATT did not prove to have the appropriate kind of flexibility to deal with the political economy of adjustment in the 1970s.[15]

As for the domestic microeconomic interventions, especially subsidies but also technical regulations, they challenged the stability of the GATT's non-discrimination norm as a means of distinguishing normal legitimate domestic policies from cheating on the trade liberalization bargain.[16]

Domestic technical regulations raised claims that even facially neutral regulatory requirements constituted disguised protectionism, with regulations creating obstacles to trade by forcing foreign producers to adapt to distinctive requirements of the importing country not obviously justified by non-protectionist regulatory objectives.[17] By the end of the 1970s, it was evident that the post-war multilateral trade liberalization system needed fine-tuning in order to sustain a cooperative equilibrium. The Reagan Revolution brought a radically different outlook on the problems at hand, and their solution. The problem, at least for the United States, was no longer that the rules of the game did not ensure adequate scope for America to adjust, consistent with the adjustment of other major industrialized powers. In fact, the normative basis for interventionist adjustment policies was put in question by a moral laissez-faire outlook of the ascendant political right, abetted by widely accepted "public choice" accounts of interventionism as the payment of rents to concentrated, entrenched constituencies.

3. Beyond the Border: Economic Liberal Ideology and the New Negotiating Agenda

By the 1980s, the focus of the policy community in the U.S. and eventually in Europe thus shifted from trade measures *per se* to the inherent worth of such interventionism itself and from cooperation based on liberalization bargains under diffuse reciprocity to the management of competition between policy norms. As perceived, the multilateral rules of the game had enabled Germany and Japan, the United States' wartime enemies, to compete successfully in the U.S. market for industrial products; they had also enabled the newly industrializing developing countries to compete successfully in highly labor-intensive industries such as textiles. On the other hand, the U.S. faced many barriers worldwide to exploiting *its* apparent comparative advantage in knowledge-intensive industries and services. Intellectual property was largely unprotected. Competition in network service industries, such as telecoms and financial services, was severely restricted. In many industries, Byzantine and archaic regulatory requirements existed. And often, while a business presence in the other country was necessary, American firms faced severe foreign investment restrictions. These disparate non-tariff barriers had to be eliminated.[18]

This new agenda became the core of the Uruguay Round concluded in 1993, and, whatever its merits, would, in many ways, prove a greater threat to the sustainability of the multilateral trading system than any of the adjustment pressures of the 1970s. Unlike the traditional GATT rules constraining tariffs, quotas, and discriminatory domestic regulations,[19] the new WTO rules, while clearly enhancing market access, have much more ambiguous welfare effects, both domestic and global. Take the case of intellectual property protection. For developing countries in particular it is easy to imagine how the gains in terms of incentives to efficient innovation from enhanced patent protection will be far outweighed by the welfare losses to consumers deprived of affordable generic pharmaceuticals. To be sure, countries like India or Brazil are slowly becoming players on both sides of the fence—selling as well as buying patents. But the developing world as a whole and even these countries for the foreseeable future are no doubt net debtors in this realm. In short, trade liberalization is no longer a positive sum game *across* countries with the need to compensate losers *within* countries. Some countries gain from increased patent protection and some lose; aggregate welfare may increase or decrease.[20] The picture is even starker if one includes certain types of cultural, regulatory or policy diversity in one's concept of welfare.

The developing countries did, formally, sign on to the new system. Why did they do so if it was not unquestionably welfare-enhancing? First, due to the debt crisis in the 1980s, many of these countries had been required to engage in unilateral trade and microeconomic policy reform anyway as a condition for IMF support for debt rescheduling. Secondly, there was the notion that while developing countries might "lose" from some of the agreements, they gained from others, such as commitments to agricultural and textiles trade liberalization. The Uruguay Round was a grand bargain like other previous trade rounds. But this is a kind of reciprocity quite different from that under the previous multilateral trading order where, assuming appropriate scope for domestic adjustment policies, all countries stood to gain from *every* liberalization measure. Reciprocal liberalization served to sell the deal at home much more than to get efficiency gains. Linkage politics in the Uruguay Round may even have convinced developing country leaders that the overall package was in their interest since there was little way to tell. But more than ever before, the potential costs and benefits of the various agreements were obviously indeterminate. What if it were to turn out that for certain countries gains (say from textiles or agricultural trade liberalization) were to prove elusive, while costs (say of implementing TRIPs or GATS obligations) were proving, if anything, greater than expected? The bargain itself would become highly unstable.

Similarly, we can also ask why a great majority of free trade advocates so easily bought into this agenda to use trade rules to narrow regulatory diversity in the area of goods and services standards, given their hostility to such an agenda in the environmental and labor areas, as we will come to below. Surely, in both realms, regulatory convergence would stem protectionist pressures motivated by perceived "unacceptable differences" between national systems, rules or standards; and regulatory diversity in the former can be accommodated more easily than in the latter through proportionality requirements. There is, of course, a simple—if not simplistic—conceptual response to this puzzle. Addressing the former does not directly impinge on the "territorial principle" of classical jurisdictional attribution. Home standards need to converge but the products in question actually *penetrate* on the host country's territory; they need not, however, be disturbed when the processes they address never take place outside the home country's boundaries. But this is, at best, an overly legalistic argument that does not do justice to the intertwining of production processes and product characteristics in the modern information economy. A more powerful reason for this asymmetry is that many free traders were independently attracted to what might be crudely described as the "reinventing government" revolution. Given the intellectual trends predominant in the 1980s, it seemed fairly obvious that improved protection for property rights, deregulation and privatization of network industries, and the use of risk assessment and cost-benefit analysis in regulatory choice, would in and of themselves improve domestic welfare in the countries changing their policies, thus preserving the win-win nature of the linked domestic and international bargains. The enthusiasm for promoting the adoption of these policy prescriptions *on their own merit* led to considerable blindness as to the implications for the multilateral trading order of making the promotion of free trade depend upon adoption of such policy prescriptions *universally.* And such blindness was fueled by elation at the death of communism, as the world seemed to be converging on a single legitimate model of liberal capitalism. Fukuyama's "end of history" may not have been synonymous with the end of all conflicts around the globe, but it surely confirmed the "technocratization" of world politics, which meant that diplomats were now engaged in the sacred mission of engineering globalization through homogenizing the characteristics of all that moved across borders.

In fact, aside from salient cultural and ideological differences which persist, the technical economics of regulatory choice is messier and more complex than suggested by the enthusiasts of the regulatory reform revolution.[21]

To be sure, the WTO rules in the areas negotiated in the Uruguay Round contain a balance of rights and obligations that still permit a great deal of regulatory diversity. There is a non-constitutional way of applying these rules: they can be applied within the framework of general international law, and not in light of a *telos* of economic liberalism as the constitutional concept of the WTO. However, it is also true that the spirit in which the rules were made at the time reflected over-enthusiasm for economic liberal ideology, not mere free trade, as the basic economic objective of the system. This explains why the new system could easily appear to create higher law rather than simply treaty law. In fact, the new WTO rules are such, whether under SPS, IPRs or GATS, that they lend themselves to a range of interpretation, from classic national treatment to "enhanced policed regulation" incorporating tests of dis-proportionality, necessity, equivalence, and balancing into WTO law.[22] This "creative ambiguity" may have been a covert way for pushing the domestic liberal agenda onto WTO without taking on counter-arguments upfront. But as with all such ambiguities, they merely served to delay confronting hard questions. Similarly, the switch from positive to negative consensus for adopting Panel findings served an important functional need to avoid deadlocks and national vetoes motivated by blatant protectionist concerns. But at the same time, the other functional need addressed by the post-war system—to provide political safety valves—is still with us (and, as we will argue below, could be fulfilled by the DSU if wisely used). Such safeguards would prove crucial for the second factor contributing to the legitimacy challenge facing the World Trade Organization.

"Trade and . . .": The Left Strikes Back with Its Own Beyond the Border Agenda

The adoption of the Uruguay Round package would probably have been enough to create intense interest in finding a constitutional basis for WTO law—a basis that would prove more solid, given the new scope and structure of WTO law, than the notion of mutually self-interested interstate bargains. However, two developments in the last decade contributed significantly to the challenge to "embedded liberalism," as its meaning became subverted to underpin a multilateral order apparently hostile to social non-economic values.

First, at the beginning of the 1990s, GATT dispute settlement Panels had to examine certain kinds of measures that did not fit within the normal, post-war model of domestic policy interventionism, yet did not resemble old-style protectionism, either. These measures were to be scrutinized against the non-discrimination norm crucial to "embedded liberalism" without clearly fitting extant interpretations of this norm. Thus, in the *Tuna/Dolphin* dispute, two GATT Panels had to decide the legality of a U.S. trade embargo against tuna fished in a manner that killed dolphins at high rates. As they extended a domestic scheme to imports the measures in question did not, arguably, constitute discrimination against imports. Yet, the scope for domestic policy intervention which was attached to the post-war "embedded liberalism" bargain did not necessarily encompass actions of this nature, aimed at influencing behavior, or at least addressing various non-commercial consequences of behavior, outside the boundaries of the intervening state. Free traders were quick to label the action as an instance of "regulatory imperialism" where the U.S. bully sought to impose its way of life onto the rest of the world. Defenders of the ban retorted that U.S. consumers did not want to tell consumers in other countries what preconditions they should adopt for buying tuna in their own market. Only they themselves did not want to contribute to the depletion of dolphins through their own consumption pattern. Unilateral application of the importing country's norms, in this case, was aimed at altering the very nature of the object consumed (e.g., the quality of dolphin-friendly tuna) rather than—as the unconditional free trade advocates would argue—at altering competitive conditions that might have presumably favored Mexican fishermen.

Sorting out how to deal with such measures within the explicit "embedded liberalism" bargain, while preserving the centrality and coherence of the non-discrimination norm, is not an insuperable intellectual challenge,[23] as became evident in a similar instance, the *Shrimp/Turtle* case, where what was at issue were measures prohibiting methods of fishing shrimp which killed sea turtle. In this case, and unlike the Panels in the *Tuna/Dolphin* cases, the Appellate Body of the WTO accepted the view that such measures could be justified under Art. XX of the GATT, subject to the conditions of the chapeau of Art XX, in particular that they not be *applied* in such a way as to constitute arbitrary or unjustified discrimination. But the GATT Panels in *Tuna/Dolphin* were not up to it, and instead read into the GATT various kinds of limitations on such measures that would exclude them entirely from the legitimate scope for domestic policy intervention. The Panels might have thought that they were merely preserving as best they could the implicit parameters of the post-war "embedded liberalism" bargain—since they were upholding the sovereign lawmaking rights of the exporting country. But because they denied consumer-citizens their collective pro-conservation choice, and on the technical front, because of the lack of textual foundation for the rulings, and the apparent flouting of the explicit hierarchy of norms in Art. XX (which allows even explicitly discriminatory policies on the part of the importing country for conservation purposes), the Panels were understood to be making a choice that trade liberalization should trump environmental values. To many, the Panels had blown up what they had been trying to preserve—the notion of trade liberalization as consistent with deep regulatory diversity, accommodating a full range of non-economic public values.

A second set of developments in the last decade also put pressure on the "embedded liberalism" bargain. In the wake of the debt crisis, a range of developing countries removed or modified restrictions on foreign investment and other domestic policies that constituted disincentives to attracting foreign capital, either because of IMF conditionality or because, with access to debt markets now limited, attracting equity investment from abroad seemed the only plausible means of financing economic growth. As a result, fears of "social dumping" and, as a consequence, fears of a "race to the bottom" between domestic laws became prominent in the developed world. Developed countries, the reasoning went, would not be able to sustain high environmental and labor standards, or rates of taxation needed to finance the redistributive policies of the welfare state, if they had to compete with developing countries for the location of capital investment. To be sure, there are wide disagreements among economists about the causal link between footloose industries and social standards, and between trade and the immiseration of the working class in developed countries.[24] And, to this date, the "race to the bottom" argument remains unsubstantiated, except with regards to high differentials in corporate taxation.

Whatever the limits of the empirical evidence, the "race to the bottom" gave a new, non-protectionist normative foundation to traditional "level-playing-field" concerns about fair trade. First, because it put in question the sustainability of "legitimate" policy interventionism which was the domestic side of the "embedded liberalism" bargain. Second, because the "race to the bottom" conjured up images of the kind of beggar-thy-neighbor competition that the international side of the "embedded liberalism" bargain was aimed at constraining. In fact, matters were much more complex, since given their levels of development, and even taking into account appropriate discount rates for the costs to future generations and transboundary externalities in the case of the environment, it was far from clear that for many developing countries, the "bottom" was not an optimal place to be. The trading system was, to a large extent, being made to take the rap for the effects of liberalizing capital movements. Yet, by making investment liberalization part of the official multilateral trade agenda, the free traders could, to some extent, have been said to have thrown in their chips with what Susan Strange has called the casino of free global capital markets. It did not help that free trade was being lumped together with all the other liberalization measures being sold to developing and transitional countries by Bretton Woods institutions as a formula for economic success.

In this context, the new social movements protesting in Seattle were not necessarily contradicting each other when they called for both global standards in certain areas (environment, labor) and for the protection of local standards in others (food, culture, intellectual property). Both sets of demands reflected considerable unease at the increasingly "disembedded" character of the international liberal order, and fears that either lack of international minimum standards or imposition of foreign standards threatened the sustainability of the domestic social contract under conditions of globalization. The stability of the bargain that underpinned the post-war model of “embedded liberalism” had been subverted by the combination of domestic ideological change, economic forces and international policy prescriptions. The bargain needed to be revisited.

4. Responses to the Legitimacy Crisis: The Fallacy of Constitutionalism

How then can the "embedded liberalism" bargain be sustained? To many, the WTO in its present form appears to constrain some domestic policies too tightly, while not constraining others tightly enough. In a world of ad-hoc sequential or linked bargains, no one seems able to provide an overarching rationale to explain these apparent inconsistencies. It is not surprising, under these circumstances, that a constitutional route to the legitimization of WTO rules and institutions would prove attractive. Especially to those well accustomed to the "madhouse" of trade and contemporary trade politics and less accustomed to the complexities of constitutional politics, this option may seem to offer greater stability. Why?

Constitutionalization means different things to different people. In traditional terms it refers to a constitutional moment which defines the founding or refounding of coherent polities or nations. This is not what advocates of WTO constitutionalism have in mind. Instead, some simply seek the constitutionalization of market access rights, while others seek to redefine the regulative functions and the organizational structures of the WTO itself as a global quasi-federal system. To be sure, those explicitly affirming a belief in the appropriateness of constitutionalism for WTO, in either guise, only represent the top of the iceberg. This belief is actually shared by a broad spectrum of the trade "epistemic community" and reflected in their evolving conception of the role of the judge and how adjudication ought to be conducted in WTO and of the relationship between the respective role of law and politics in the international trading system. It is not only the former's proclaimed agenda but also the latter's implicit assumption that we have in mind in our discussion below.

The Libertarian "Constitutional" Alternative

Libertarians have their Utopia. If the WTO can be understood as a charter of economic rights, conferring enforceable claims on non-governmental actors, then balancing the welfare effects of its rules on different groups and different countries over time seems unnecessary. The complex welfare effects of beyond-the-border trade rules (intellectual property, etc.) need not create significant challenges for democratic legitimacy, nor even be the subject of explicit democratic deliberation. Constitutionalism is often said to be about principle, not policy, about rights, not interests. In its libertarian version, it is about individual economic rights. Thus, according to Ernst-Ulrich Petersmann, one of the leading advocates for constitutionalizing the WTO: "The time has come to recognize that human rights law offers WTO rules moral, constitutional, and democratic legitimacy that may be more important for parliamentary ratification of future WTO Agreements than the traditional economic and utilitarian justifications."[25] When a WTO dispute settlement Panel invalidates an environmental protection scheme (which affects imports albeit indiscriminately), this can be understood not as replacing the policy balancing of domestic democratic institutions with its own policy balancing[26] (of environmental vs. trade costs and benefits), but rather as enforcing a higher legal norm, with which *all* domestic policy balancing must be consistent. WTO members must protect intellectual property rights, for example, not because doing so necessarily maximizes global or domestic welfare (in many cases, it may be welfare-reducing for a given polity) but because these are private rights, with a moral foundation independent of predicted welfare effects. In this view, the WTO, with its binding system of dispute settlement and with its persuasive compliance mechanisms, already provides a far more effective protection for individual rights than do the human rights organs of the UN institutions.[27]

Why would states agree to the protection of such individual rights at the international level, when in many cases they are not recognized in their own domestic constitutions? And even if they did—due to various kinds of positive and negative incentives—how would these rights be enforceable in their own jurisdiction? Indeed, Kant saw a transnational constitution as possible only once the members of the juridical union had themselves adopted domestic liberal republican constitutions.[28] And one does not need to agree with the Virginia school of (domestic) libertarian "constitutional economics" to recognize that constitutions are commitments about incomplete contracts that lead to impossible dilemmas in democratic contexts, as constitutional courts for equally good reasons should and should not follow the legislative "last word" on any given topic. In response, Petersmann suggests that there are forms of hands-tying or precommitment that can be effective internationally even while not possible domestically. A government acting in the public interest may make effective precommitments at the international level that tie its hands because these international precommitments impose a new set of costs (retaliation from trading partners, in particular) associated with giving in to rent-seeking demands for protection.[29] If advocating such a process seems to beg the question of how the constituencies that will lose once the government ties its hands would permit hands tying in the first place, the nature of international trade negotiations provides an answer: the prospective benefits from reciprocal liberalization bring new constituencies to the fore that have an interest in increased access to foreign markets and the government can depend on these new constituencies to counterbalance the impact of constituencies seeking rents from interventionist government policies. Thus, the logic of negotiated trade liberalization provides opportunities for the protection of economic rights against interest group depredation that are not available within the domestic political process.

In our view, this approach is problematic, first because it underestimates the conditions under which hands-tying can be made legitimate in the WTO context. Mechanisms of hands-tying are relevant to all situations whereby individuals or collectivities create conditions that will help them resist temptations to act in a manner that they regard as contrary to their longer-term self-interest, but would otherwise appear irresistible in the short term. Jon Elster has recently reconsidered the complexities of understanding constitutional arrangements in terms of such precommitment since "in politics, people never try to bind themselves, only to bind others."[30] Clearly, what Petersmann characterizes as the precommitment of a public-interest-motivated government to tie *its own* hands in the future in dealing with interest groups, is really a commitment to tie the hands of its political opponents and the groups they represent, should they win a democratic victory. Indeed, this realization has been the ground of much of the criticism of constitutionalism at the national level from Locke to Paine who thought that the only concern that legitimates any form of government is the consent of the living. But, of course, national constitutions provide grand narratives which are both the product of and made possible by extant political communities.

Wherever one may fall on constitutional debates at the national level, it is fair to argue that hands-tying is much more problematic internationally. As Elster describes, at the level of domestic constitution-making, an important hedge against the antidemocratic feature of hands-tying is to require extraordinary levels of democratic consent in the first place to the rules that will tie the hands of future governments—such as referenda, super-majority votes, elected constitutional assemblies. But judging hands-tying through WTO law against this standard only puts into high relief the questionable democratic *bona fides* of WTO rules. Domestic deliberation of these rules is perfunctory and constrained by information and agency costs. This process produces a mass of general and often ambiguous rules, whose effects cannot easily be debated intelligently *ex ante* in national legislatures, and which must be accepted or rejected as a single package.[31]

To be sure, in the "embedded liberalism" view, the GATT itself could be understood as hands-tying. But the same democratic difficulties did not arise to the extent that the rules could be rightly understood as providing sufficient leeway for adjustment policy, and regulatory diversity generally—so that the domestic policy sphere could address and balance the claim of all constituencies through non-trade measures. Libertarians like Petersmann are consistent: they are confident that economic rights can best reflect the public interest *because* they believe it is possible to achieve legitimate public goals adequately and most efficiently in a manner that does not violate these rights. If the government intervenes in a protectionist manner or excessively interferes with these rights, this is because of public choice considerations. Politics must be sacrificed on the altar of the "general interest"—albeit a certain conception of the general interest. Ultimately such a vision is little more than "disembedded liberalism" in pseudo-Kantian dress. This approach may have had merit in the crusade against border measures, but it cannot easily be applied to the new rules about intellectual property, food safety, labor standards and so forth. Yet, it is these new rules that call for a "constitutional" justification.

The tension is more fundamental, however, if one disagrees with economic libertarians about the range of legitimate policy objectives, and the capacities of different policy instruments to achieve such objectives. Then one would not share the conclusion that the level and manner of intervention in the market characteristic of domestic polities is due solely to interest-group rent-seeking, and one would not draw the implication that economic rights require protection through hands-tying at the international level.

Beyond the problematic advantages of hands-tying, we also believe that libertarian liberalism is flawed in its implicit assumptions on the traditional sources of economic rights in voluntaristic political constructs. Petersmann claims that "the dynamic functions of human rights and fundamental citizen rights have prompted many courts (notably in Europe) to adopt functional and teleological interpretations that have progressively extended individual freedoms across frontiers and beyond narrower interpretations. The jurisprudence of the EC Court of Justice on the free movement of goods, services, persons, capital, and payments, and the judicial protection of these freedoms addressed to states as *individual rights* of the 380 million EC citizens, illustrates the legal, political, and economic importance of individual rights and of their judicial protection for international economic integration."[32]

Does Petersmann really draw the right lessons from the EU experience? For one, and to the extent that the European bargain can be seen as a legitimate one, this is due in the first instance to a mutual hands-tying between social democratic and Christian democratic traditions based on a unique combination of ideological convergence and concessions after the war; a configuration that can hardly be replicated at the global level. The Member States' tolerance for elements of supranational governance—from ECJ rulings to the partial delegation of authority to the Commission, to the Coreper and to non-consensual intergovernmental decision making—are expressions of this continued compatibility.

Furthermore, the EU Treaties contain no enumeration of fundamental rights, economic or otherwise. Instead, such rights had to be inferred by the Court from the general obligations of free movement included in the Treaties and derived through a progressive transfer to the EU of the principle of proportionality. To be sure, such piecemeal constitutionalization is what most trade lawyers advocating an expansive interpretation of WTO articles have in mind rather than a "constitutional moment." However, is it irrelevant that, in the EU context, economic rights have not been justified on their own merit, but framed by the Court as a by-product of the pursuit of a "common good," a single market in Europe? If the teleology served as the justification for encroachment of trade on competing collective values to be collective goals rather than individual wants in the EU context, on what basis are we led to believe that individual rights would do more for legitimacy at the global level? To the extent that there are inferred individual economic rights in the EU, history has shown that they cannot stand alone and benefit from a monopoly on constitutionality. When the ECJ stated in *Wachau* (ECJ 1989) that it was balancing individual rights against the interests and policies of governments, it did so in the name of social rights, not of market access rights. Even if this minimalist vision of European integration was correct, we would argue that constitutionalization (as the inference of market access rights by the ECJ) was made acceptable in Europe by characteristics whose functional equivalent does not obtain today at the WTO level.

In the end, the first phase of EU development did not suffer from acute legitimacy problems because it was successful in balancing the need for stability in its constitutional rules with the need for flexible adjustment in the system. Successful federal arrangements develop forms of flexible governance to allow the federal balance to shift with various social, economic, ideological trends. The question is how to best develop an institutional commitment to flexibility and adaptability under constraints of democratic legitimacy. One major basis for such flexibility is the complex relationship between constitutional politics and legislative politics in the EU.

The very reason why the EU process of constitutionalization progressively turned from the first to the second model discussed below is because constitutionalism based solely on economic libertarianism did not provide the kind of democratically grounded flexibility that allows for cycles of centralization and decentralization in the regulation of free trade.

The European "Federal Vision" Alternative

At least as influential as the idea of libertarian precommitment in most discussions of the WTO constitutional trajectory, is an idea akin to evolutionary federalism advocated by those who call for a shift from current international law to a new "global law." Such a law would define and integrate a series of legitimate goals and entrust the WTO with the task to enforce them.[33] This progressive internationalist version of WTO constitutionalization is more consistent with the standard conception of the actual constitutional trajectory of the European Union.[34]

The European example is obviously appealing to WTO constitutionalists in that while some of the founders of the European project, such as Jean Monnet and Robert Schumann, might have discerned at the outset a constitutional *telos,* European constitutionalism appears to have evolved organically. Joseph Weiler observes: "[T]he Treaties have been 'constitutionalized' and the Community has become an entity whose closest structural model is no longer an international organization but a denser, yet nonunitary polity, principally the federal state. Put differently, the Community's 'operating system' is no longer governed by general principles of public international law, but by a specified interstate governmental structure defined by a constitutional charter and constitutional principles."[35]

Particularly persuasive to proponents of WTO constitutionalization is the European Court's transformation of the European treaty system into a constitutional order. This account is of special interest since, in the Uruguay Round, the membership of the GATT rejected the invitation to reconceive the global trade system in constitutional terms, that is, as an autonomous level of governance, despite proposals to create regulatory powers in the WTO.[36] Law*making* in the WTO was to remain consensus-based interstate bargaining and no autonomous or independent lawmaking or regulating institution was created within the organization. On the other hand, the Uruguay Round produced a dispute settlement of a judicial sort whose workings were made largely independent of the political preferences of the membership. The European example suggests that a conventional treaty regime, once endowed with a judicial mechanism for interpretation and enforcement, can be converted by degrees to a genuine constitutional order.

The European Union, however, possessed the prerequisites for these developments that the WTO lacks. The Treaty of Rome, from the outset, conferred upon Community institutions the explicit power, in the case of regulations, to create law that was directly applicable in the Member States (Article 189). Thus, already implicit in the treaty was an idea of *federal* governance, transcending the confederal notion of a pact among sovereigns (to merely pool, or limit, exercises of sovereignty as among each other) and creating a direct relationship between the individual and the orders of governance established by the treaty. The logic of applying the ideal of the rule of law to that direct relationship was a doctrine of direct effect that was then extended by the ECJ beyond the limited, special case of regulations.

Yet in the case of the WTO, there is *no* basis in the treaties for finding such direct effect. As a WTO Panel recently noted, the fact that WTO law *indirectly* protects the economic opportunities of individual traders, and that many of the benefits from the treaties flow from such protection, cannot be bootstrapped into the notion that WTO obligations are owed directly to such traders. As the Panel suggested: "Neither the GATT nor the WTO has so far been interpreted by GATT/WTO institutions as a legal order producing direct effect. Following this approach, the GATT/WTO did *not* create a new legal order the subjects of which comprise both contracting parties or Members and their nationals."[37] In a cautious footnote to this passage, the Panel rightly did not dismiss the possibility that in some instances the only way of effectively *implementing* a WTO obligation to other *Members* might be to create court-enforceable rights for individuals within the domestic legal system in question; but it equally rightly appears to have perceived that, even if this were the case, the individuals in question would have these rights, not by virtue of a direct relationship to an autonomous WTO legal order, but merely as a consequence of what would be required to implement obligations as between Member states.

In contrast, analysts have shown how the so-called constitutionalization of the EU treaties would not have been possible without the continuous stream of referrals from national courts on the basis of article 177 and the ensuing cooptation of national systems and actors. The characteristics of the legal community in Europe contributed to legitimizing the ECJ approach from the bottom up and embedded it in deeper national level evolutions. National constitutional courts, albeit reluctantly, were eventually sucked into this process. National and supranational judges together participated in the construct of a new system of higher law that was compatible with their mutual understanding of their roles. It is hard to see how such a congruence of interests could work at the global level. Admittedly, advocates of WTO constitutionalization would argue that institutionalizing direct effect in the WTO would contribute to, and not only be, the result of creating such a congruence of interest. But such an argument relies on heroic assumptions regarding the relevance of the EU's historical dynamics to the WTO context.

Indeed, the flip side of the role of the ECJ in European constitutionalization is the complex connection that has existed between judicial developments and political dynamics in the process of integration. Often enough, the Court actually refrained from deploying the full measure of direct effect, laying out instead a roadmap for others to follow. In the EU, "the progressive elaboration of constitutional rules generated an expansionary dynamic tending to recast policy processes and outcomes."[38] Moreover, the legitimacy of judicial rulings against the application of domestic regulation was predicated upon the existence and development in Europe of a political and administrative system for "compatibility assessment and enforcement"—including the institutional foundations for mutual regulatory monitoring—which enabled the legislative and administrative process to take over from the judiciary in sensitive areas of economic integration.[39] ECJ rulings often provoked policy reforms—from the liberalization of the telecommunication regime to the invalidation of price fixing—through a combination of argumentation and threat of future censure. The Court even envisioned a social policy in Europe through its rulings on non-discrimination which drove the conversion of article 119 on equal pay for equal work into the 1970s directives on equal pay, equal treatment (1976), and social security (1979), and the conversion in turn of these directives into expansive new social rights for European citizens. Member States, as it were, constituted themselves as a constituent assembly to these decisions of the court by amending the so-called "Barber protocol"—on the question of entitlement to pensions—to the Maastricht Treaty. In this case, the Member States clearly selected among one of the possible options suggested by the Court thus being informed but not bound by its rulings.

In short, the ambitious interpretation of direct effect by the Court helped establish the credentials of the Council of Ministers and the Commission as autonomous institutions of governance, encouraging them, at least indirectly, to deliver on the promise of a federal level of governance implicit in the Treaty of Rome. But since such a promise does *not* exist in the WTO treaties, and if the dispute settlement organs were to create such expectations among the citizens of contracting members through the creation of a doctrine of direct effect, they would likely undermine the legitimacy of the WTO system as a whole, making it seem to promise something that it does not have the institutional structure to deliver.

Proponents of constitutionalization argue that this is precisely why the promise needs to be introduced and an institutional structure appropriate to constitutional status needs to be created at WTO level, since trade liberalization "inherently starts to require, rely upon and develop positive integration."[40] Indeed, because the WTO treaties do not create any institutional mechanisms for positive integration, there is no means of balancing a court-ruling against a certain type of regulation through harmonization or some version of managed mutual recognition which includes working out the conditions for safeguards at the domestic level. These routes may be taken by subset of actors acting in conformity with the WTO but not directly under its umbrella.[41] While WTO law allows for the *constraint* of policies that interfere with the trading rights of members, it does not provide a mechanism for the creation of new, agreed policies that can rebalance such trading rights with other legitimate policy objectives. Thus, even if not intended (unlike the libertarian approach), a constitutionalizing reading of trading "rights" by the WTO dispute settlement organs, inspired by the teleological interpretation of the European Court would necessarily have a libertarian bias in the case of the WTO, whereas in the EU context it could be taken as a challenge and even a mandate to the Commission and the Council to perform their positive integration responsibilities. To the extent that proponents of WTO constitutionalization do not advocate an EU-like regulatory state at world level, their approach, even if less ideologically explicit than the libertarian one, would likely lead to the same legitimacy problems.

It may be argued that other international fora exist for positive integration, and indeed in the WTO Sanitary and Phytosanitary Agreement (on food safety measures) and the Technical Barriers to Trade Agreement, there is a formal link between WTO rules and harmonization in some of those fora. However, they do not make up part of the purported constitutional order of the WTO; their relevance to how WTO law is interpreted simply points to the need for greater openness to other institutions and integration of WTO law in the broader framework of international law and institutions as a whole, rather than a notion of normative self-sufficiency implied by the constitutional idea. In short, the institutional incompleteness that some decry with regard to the WTO cannot be easily perfected from the inside, and points instead to the need for greater openness to other institutions and fora on the outside.

Of course and alternatively, if we take the constitutionalization argument seriously, the question is whether such constitutionalization driven by the judicial branch of the WTO could be recommended as a strategy of building pressure for formal institutional change (that is the creation of an explicit level of federal governance at the WTO, with the regulatory powers required for positive integration). Why this is unlikely to happen, or more precisely why legitimacy difficulties would arise if it *were* to happen, is illuminated by developments in the European Union once Europeans became widely conscious that the Community institutions were indeed behaving as an autonomous federal order of governance, acting directly on the citizens of Member states. These developments display the danger of, in Weiler's words, "adopting constitutional practices without any underlying legitimizing constitutionalism."[42]

In short, even in the European Union context, profound legitimacy problems have arisen from the so-called "democratic deficit." Pinder ably describes the problem:

> The system of representative government locates legislative authority in an assembly of representatives chosen in regular free election. This is not how laws are made in the Community. Community laws are enacted by the Council, to which each member government delegates "one of its members" according to the subject being dealt with at that particular Council meeting . . . The Council does, indeed, when legislating, behave like an executive body rather than an elected assembly. It negotiates behind closed doors and approves without debate many of the texts prepared by officials . . .[43]

A direct relationship between the federal level of governance and the individual implies a direct *democratic* relationship which even in the EU is lacking. At least in the European Union, there is an institution that could plausibly establish that relationship—the European Parliament—if given the appropriate powers and capacities. By contrast, the option of a directly elected WTO Parliament is far-fetched. The current Director-General of the WTO has suggested that one could nevertheless create some kind of WTO assembly composed of national parliamentarians. One must take seriously, however, the critique that the European Parliament is not effective in creating a direct democratic relationship between the European level of governance and individual citizens because there is no corresponding EU-wide political space which could feed into and in turn be fed by its own deliberations—or, as the German Constitutional Court first articulated, there is no European *demos* or democratic community whose considered will the Parliament can express. The communitarian Right explains that a democratic community must be constituted on the basis of a *Volk,* united by prepolitical bonds such as religion, race, and culture, a condition that does not or cannot hold at the European level (except through the most ominous kind of development—the construction of a "European" *Volk* in distinction or opposition to the "non-European"). We are skeptical of this view for many reasons, but rejecting it does not dispense with the need to articulate the civic conditions of a democratic community based on a deliberative public sphere.[44] As a minimum, this arguably requires, as Eric Stein has recently articulated, "a certain community of a common good and common expectations of the people that bridge the cultural differences."[45] We will come back below to some suggestions as to how such a community within Europe can be built and how these suggestions could well be applied to the WTO, thus enhancing its democratic legitimacy *without* going down the road of constitutionalization. Nevertheless, the very consideration of what constitutes a political community and how institutions may and should reflect its characteristics make it amply clear that the regional and global scale of democracy are indeed incommensurable.

Finally, it may also be a condition of a democratic community that it shares equitably the benefits and burdens of the common community project, particularly as deeper integration reveals more sharply a distribution of such benefits and burdens. The evolution of the EU in the 1980s and 1990s has shown clearly enough how every bargain over economic liberalism needed to be accompanied by side payments to regions, groups, and countries in order to be sustainable. Moreover, it has become increasingly clear that democratic legitimacy cannot be ensured under conditions of regulatory competition short of a proactive engagement on the part of the federal level to allow states to deliver on their welfare function. Member States of the European Union have become irreversibly committed to a pervasive program of European economic integration whose very success is now confronting national welfare states with the same kind of regulatory competition that had impeded the development of social policies in the American states.[46] National problem-solving capacities seem to be most severely affected by the economic and legal constraints of economic integration and conflict between states with regard to precisely those instruments of market-correcting policy that have been of critical importance for the legitimization of the welfare state. In Europe, the fact that effective control of economic outcomes at the national level has not been compensated by a concurrent shift of resources at the federal level means that other compensating mechanisms need to be found. And indeed, there are ways in Europe to address such problem-solving gaps, albeit imperfectly, that could not be plausibly introduced in WTO—from coordinated policy reform and "shaming" methods to the monitoring by the Commission of "unfair regulatory competition" or the introduction of minimal social standards.

In sum, the conditions for constitutional legitimacy in the EU accepted even by those on the pro-European constitutionalist side of this debate, to say nothing of those on the nationalist side, include integrative institutions that can be accountable for the policy and value tradeoffs that they make; a commitment to flexible structures and procedures that can respond to ideological, technological or economic shifts by allowing reallocation of power through bargaining or other agreed-upon procedures short of constitutional "revolution" and mechanisms for co-opting and compensating potential losers.

If we examine these conditions it becomes apparent that the WTO lacks, and will lack in the foreseeable future, the sources of legitimacy that would need to underpin a "constitutional" status. Most obviously, one must not underestimate the distance between members of the WTO on the appropriate conception of distributive justice, if any, to govern the operations of the multilateral trading system. A large part of the membership resists the idea of the WTO having any social agenda at all; neither are these members seriously seeking to address the issue in other international institutions. Part of the problem here is that the decision-making structures of the WTO do not easily allow a flexible approach to cooperation, the kind of integration *à deux ou à multiples vitesses* which played such a key role in sustaining the forward movement of EU integration. The old GATT was arguably more accommodating of such approaches, with its plurilateral codes which some contracting parties signed and others did not, but which were not a condition of membership and thus did not require full consensus in order to work. There are still some plurilateral elements in the WTO system, and it is not entirely inconceivable that a social charter could evolve in the WTO on a plurilateral basis. However, the divergence of values and circumstances among Members of the WTO is immensely greater than that among the Member States of the EU. The WTO commitment to universalism does not square easily with requiring, as a condition of WTO membership, not merely the recognition of a set of common values, but a high threshold of reflecting those values in the domestic legal system of all members.

In sum, constitutionalism—if it is to solve rather than exacerbate the legitimacy difficulties of the WTO—would require *constitutional* sources of legitimacy. Admittedly the rule of law is one of these sources and WTO dispute settlement displays now important rule of law features.[47] But as the European experience illustrates, the rule of law as a source of legitimacy is not self-sufficient or self-sustaining outside a framework of public institutions of governance that are a direct expression of democratic self-determination, in other words, outside democratic federalism. In short, to get legitimacy through the constitutional route would require something like a world democratic state, and this in turn would require the end of politics as we know it. We have shown how deep structural features of the multilateral trading order create constraints that make the satisfaction of such demands close to impossible. In fact, we merely seek to provide a reminder of the crucial role of politics in constitutional legitimacy, and to show that one cannot and should not lightly adopt the discourse of constitutionalism, without thinking through the nature and fate of the political at the international level.[48]

5. Non-Constitutional Means of Strengthening the Legitimacy of the WTO System: Adjudication and Politics within a Model of Global Subsidiarity

Imposing the constitutionalist spirit on the World Trade Organization is not the answer to its current crisis of legitimacy. Policymakers do not need to settle the question of the desirability of Hegel's "universal and homogenous state," before addressing the apparent obsolescence of the original "embedded liberalism" bargain. The solution is unlikely to come "from above"—from a new normative super*structure*. Rather, the spirit of "embedded liberalism" needs to be recovered and reinterpreted "from below," under the new conditions of globalization. This can be done again in part through inspiration from the EU, not in its constitutional guise but by incorporating some of the institutional and political features associated with the thinking on subsidiarity. A model of global subsidiarity can help take into account the *process* dynamics and the kinds of conflicts present in the WTO and assumed away by constitutionalism. Such a model can provide a framework for revisiting the politics of "embedded liberalism" by suggesting functional equivalents to traditional "safeguards" for the state while acknowledging other legitimate loci of governance than the state.

A model of global subsidiarity would incorporate throughout the workings of the WTO three basic principles: institutional sensitivity, political inclusiveness and top-down empowerment. We now examine each of them in turn.[49]

Institutional Sensitivity

Subsidiarity, in its most straightforward sense, calls for ensuring that debates and decisions take place at levels and within fora of governance that are most likely to reflect in a balanced fashion the interests, aspirations, and opinions of all actors concerned. It thus calls for balancing the centralizing bias inherent in the need to deal with "global public goods" with a decentralizing bias inherent in the demands of "democratic proximity." To be sure, such a balancing act may still end up pointing to the superiority of global governance mechanisms, if only because many actors are best represented at the global rather than national or local level. But even then, the question remains: which global forum? which global norm?

In the case of WTO, we believe that *global subsidiarity* requires accepting the logic and development of a plural, decentralized, and multi-centered system of global socio-economic governance of which the trade organization would be but one of many nodes. This, in turn, requires that WTO political agreements and judicial rulings display appropriate sensitivity to the superior credentials that other institutions of governance may have in deciding the substantive trade-offs entailed in domestic policies that the WTO dispute settlement organs are, necessarily, required to review from the perspective of WTO rules on trade.[50] This includes, but need not start with, a presumption of deference to the states themselves. The WTO dispute settlement machinery cannot substitute itself for domestic democratic processes which have often painstakingly shaped fundamental trade-offs between economic, social, political cost-benefit considerations and values.

To be sure, institutional sensitivity should not amount to mere or unconditional deference. Such sensitivity is not only consistent with, but positively calls for, strict scrutiny of national compliance with general trade regime norms such as nondiscrimination, and especially procedural norms such as transparency and due process in the formulation and implementation of trade-related policies. When it comes to ensuring domestic due process, the WTO dispute settlement organs *are* the institutions of superior competence. We will discuss below the broader political corollary to this legal principle.

Deference to the states in their collective as opposed to simply individual expression is the second aspect of institutional sensitivities. Within the WTO, the judges need, more often than not, to defer judgment to the politicians either with regard to bilateral disputes or with regard to multilateral rule-making. This may mean that in crucial cases, courts simply provide roadmaps for future political settlements rather than rulings that are directly preemptive or prescriptive of policy. As a corollary, the states themselves can less afford to rely on general standards (as opposed to specific rules) when they make law internationally rather than domestically.[51] In the end, conflicts of interpretation which involve primary conflicts of values (in the Kojevian sense) ought to be solved through political negotiations, whether bilaterally, to resolve a dispute, or multilaterally, to create a new base line for resolving future disputes. In the same vein, institutional sensitivity implies favoring transnational or bilateral solutions to supranational solutions when conflicts of jurisdiction arise.

Third, deference on the part of WTO law enforcers needs to be expanded to other issue-area regimes such as environmental, health or labor regimes. There does not exist at the global level any alternative means of making trade-offs between values and priorities which is the essence of politics domestically, and even to some (still limited) extent in the EU. Institutionalized linkages between segmented regimes must play the role of the Cabinet at the national level or the Coreper (Committee of Permanent Representatives) in the EU. Inter-institutional linkage must be "institutionalized" at the global level where there is not, nor should be, an integrative government-like institution. But there is no reason why this linkage should happen solely under the terms spelled out by WTO. Short of building a functioning democratic community, all institutional externalities cannot and should not be internalized. Checks and balances need to remain and be fine-tuned *between* as well as *within* institutions. We illustrate these general points through a discussion of recent case law under the WTO dispute settlement system.

The first step requires no changes of the WTO law. It is to interpret those provisions of the WTO agreements that are not easily understood as a straightforward "win-win" deal for all Members in a manner sensitive to the inadequacy of constitutional sources of legitimacy *within* the WTO system itself. For one, while the treaty text requires the dispute settlement organs necessarily to adjudicate between conflicting values, there needs to be *prima facie* recognition of outcomes from more democratically legitimate political and regulatory institutions. In *Hormones,* the Appellate Body displayed considerable sensitivity along these lines, for example, when it stated:

> [A] Panel charged with determining, for instance, whether "sufficient scientific evidence" exists to warrant the maintenance of a particular measure may, of course, and should bear in mind that responsible, representative governments commonly act from perspectives of prudence and precaution where risks of irreversible, e.g., life-terminating, damage to human health are concerned.

Furthermore, the Appellate Body has substituted such lacking sources of legitimacy by placing WTO law in the framework of general international law—externalizing, as it were, the constitutional dimension. Thus, in the *Hormones* case, it questioned an interpretation by the Panel of a requirement that Members (in this case the EU) not take trade-restrictive sanitary and phytosanitary measures unless they are "based on" international standards. The Panel had said that such measures needed to conform with the international standards, thus assuming a strict meaning. In a more lenient interpretation of the implied obligations—allowing for diversity of domestic standards—the Appellate Body noted the crucial importance of weighing all the details of the negotiated political text, reflecting as it does a "delicate and carefully negotiated balance . . . between these shared, but sometimes competing, interests of promoting international trade and of protecting the life and health of human beings."[52] Thus, the Appellate Body opposed the tendency of the Panels to *assume* a certain purpose prior to careful textual interpretation, in order to prevent the interpreter from having to "test" their view of purpose against the exact words used in the treaty, a necessary safeguard against the importation of a single purpose into a legal text crafted to balance diverse and possibly competing values.[53]

Should there be much doubt that following these general public international law interpretative norms ought to enhance the legitimacy of the dispute settlement organs in adjudicating competing values? Crucially, these norms are common to international law generally, including regimes that give priority to very different values, and are not specific to a regime that has traditionally privileged a single value, that of free trade.[54]

Another interpretive issue in the *Hormones* case highlights this significance. In the traditional GATT-specific canon of interpretation where a provision of the treaty allows for an exception to a trade-liberalizing obligation, the burden of proof falls on the party invoking the exception—an approach that clearly privileges free trade over other, competing values, assuming that the latter, embodied in the exception, cannot easily dislodge the former, regardless of the nature of the matter in dispute. Such an asymmetry, however, was compensated by the relatively narrow scope of GATT free trade obligations. Significantly, when in *Hormones,* the Panel applied this traditional GATT-specific approach to a provision of the Sanitary and Phytosanitary Agreement, the Appellate Body reversed its finding on burden of proof. It emphasized instead that "merely characterizing a treaty provision as an 'exception' does not by itself justify a 'stricter' or 'narrower' interpretation of the provisions than would be warranted by examination of the ordinary meaning of the actual treaty words, viewed in context and in light of the treaty's object and purpose . . ." (para. 104).

Moving one step further on the "sensitivity scale," the *Vienna Convention* calls for the consideration of *non*-WTO international legal rules in the interpretation of WTO treaties—rules that may reflect other values and interests than those of trade liberalization.[55] Signaling its willingness to abide by this norm, the Appellate Body referred to international environmental law in the *Shrimp/Turtles* case when interpreting the provisions of Article XX of the GATT (the article refers *inter alia* to the possibility of justifying otherwise GATT-inconsistent trade measures aimed at protecting endangered species). Assessing the alleged "unjust" or "arbitrary" nature of U.S. measures, and thus their possible character as "disguised restriction on international trade," the Appellate Body did not simply invent its own limitation on unilateralism as a means of protecting the environmental commons, as had been done by the *Tuna/Dolphin* Panels. Instead, it referred to a baseline in international environmental law contained in the *Rio Declaration.* Principle 12 of the *Rio Declaration* called for the avoidance of unilateral measures, preferring a solution based on consensus whenever possible. Thus, the Appellate Body could find that the failure of the United States to negotiate seriously with the complainants towards a consensus-based solution, while having already negotiated successfully with other members, constituted "unjustified" discrimination (paras. 168–172). Deference to the substance of U.S. law was hence compensated both by strict procedural requirements and horizontal subsidiarity or deference to a non-WTO regime.

However subtly the dispute settlement organs apply the tools of institutional sensitivity, the most delicate interpretation of such rules will not legitimately resolve the dispute in all cases. The *Beef Hormone* case is an example whereby the parties may simply need to agree to disagree, as the U.S. and the EU have, without escalating into a more general trade war. Neither European non-compliance in this case, nor U.S. insistence on retaliation signals a wavering commitment to a cooperative equilibrium in international trade. Rather, the trading system has not evolved institutionally or structurally to the point where all such disagreements can be legitimately resolved above the level of domestic politics. In a case like this, the outcome of non-compliance can be system-supporting, avoiding inordinate pressure on rules that do not yet have an institutional context that would confer on them the legitimacy needed for supremacy. Here, however, in order to forestall risk of escalation, the parties, we suggest, should seek alternatives to withdrawal of concessions by the winning party (such as negotiated rebalancing of concessions). While withdrawal of concessions is an obviously logical response to non-compliance, compensation (the losing party offering *additional* concessions in some other area) is a more optimal approach to dealing with unsolvable conflicts. It serves consumers on one side and opens markets on the other. And by not engaging in a tit-for-tat approach it signals a recognition that it is not defection that is being addressed by the very limits of the system. However, there is little doubt that the political economy of such an approach is tricky, if only because of the new import-competing groups that come to be affected in the process. Moreover, from the perspective of international law, we do not believe that compensation could be seen as adequate to discharge the duty of good-faith implementation of the treaty. Thus, a rather different mechanism might be required, one that allows a legal rebalancing of concessions, which is what was already provided in Art. XXVIII of GATT, at least with respect to tariffs on goods.

Finally, the progress made on the discussions for reform discussed above should strongly determine the speed with which further economic-liberalism-oriented negotiations are undertaken, whether in competition policy, domestic regulation in services, rules on intellectual property protection, or investment. This might mean a standstill on some significant new disciplines until the legitimating structures "catch up." Time may bring about the necessary convergence across polities in regulatory perspectives, scientific assessment, public demands for regulations or lack thereof, and attitudes towards risks. This may make it possible in turn to develop new, legitimate institutions and norms of global governance. In the meantime, what is needed is a system for the peaceful management of policy and political differences, which need not entail a complete halt to progressive liberalization of trade. Moreover, states may legitimately choose to embark in exercises of regulatory cooperation and mutual recognition for the purpose of plurilateral liberalization, under the express conditions that they respect procedural obligations of openness and inclusiveness as outlined below.

Political Inclusiveness

The second guiding principle that can serve as a model for global subsidiarity is political inclusiveness. Classic "embedded liberalism" was predicated on the assumption that democracy happened inside, while bargains happened outside between national representatives who were the sole representation of these domestic processes. How and to what end state-society relations were to be conducted were the sole prerogative of the sovereign state. This view mirrored the sharp distinction between inside and outside and the role of the border in the territorially-based conceptions of trade law. While the economic and, to some extent, legal reality has moved on with the interpenetration of domestic systems of production, laws, and regulation, indirect representation is still the basis of the politics of WTO and its claim to legitimacy. It is time to unbundle traditional concepts of territoriality, as Ruggie has called for.[56] Or, as Robert Keohane and Joseph Nye have discussed, international regimes, like the trade regime, were conceived as decomposable hierarchies governing specific issue areas, and they were designed to keep out the public as well as officials from branches of government other than the executive.[57] The undoing of the "embedded liberalism" bargain suggests that this club paradigm needs to be adapted.

First, at the *national* level, the WTO can encourage greater inclusiveness in trade-policy-making. After all, indirect accountability remains the first requisite for improving democracy beyond the nation-state, and perhaps the most straightforward way of dealing with the problem of a democratic deficit at the global level.[58] National citizens, groups, or parliaments can more truly and meaningfully participate in trade policy decision-making under obligations of domestic consultation. We could imagine that WTO Member States commit to "political codes of conducts" reflecting general principles of democratic accountability in the conduct of trade-related policies without imposing specific means of implementing them.[59]

Second, at the *supranational* level, it has become much harder to pretend that governments adequately represent all relevant interests in a given trade issue. There are epistemic communities, transnational issue networks, and global advocacy NGOs that do not find any adequate point of entry at the domestic level. The irony of the Seattle Ministerial is that it revealed the beginnings of a global civil society with regard to trade matters, as both a product and a reaction against globalization.

In the judicial and political spheres, limited progress has already been made. The Appellate Body has made clear that *amicus curiae* briefs by non-governmental actors may be considered in WTO dispute settlement cases and rulings are made widely available on the Web immediately after their release. A process of consultation regarding trade and environment has been going on for the last five years. But this is not enough. It is also necessary to underpin greater inclusiveness by amending dispute settlement rules, which currently provide for secrecy in WTO dispute settlement proceedings themselves, both in the written pleadings and oral argument. It is also important to explore ways of giving greater voice to non-governmental actors during political negotiations. This is justified normatively since corporatist notions of democratic legitimacy may be warranted beyond the nation-state, given economies of scale of organization and the fact that some groups may be given access previously denied to them at the national level.[60]

But for a long time this kind of inclusiveness is bound to fall short of the direct democratic relationship required for constitutionalization. And, given the persuasive arguments about the lack of representativeness of NGOs and the like (as compared to democratic governments), there is something to be said for caution. NGOs and civil society can play a crucial role by publicizing and opening the process—more than they can by pretending to represent a significant stake in the final outcome. Countless useless debates would be avoided if decision-makers were to recognize that their inclusion is justified on grounds of deliberative democracy, even if it does not fit with the classic model of representative democracy.[61] Here, inclusiveness—more inclusive public participation in shaping the system—should also be contrasted with the constitutional idea of private litigants' rights in the WTO, with private parties being able to sue on WTO treaty provisions on the understanding that these provisions create "rights" as with the libertarian constitutional model. As long as one understands the non-constitutional role of participatory opportunities in dispute settlement (amicus-type intervention, right to attend hearings, etc.), such opportunities need not and should not be viewed as the first step towards private rights of action. Similarly, participatory opportunities in political debates need not be understood as rights of representation. In this area, the use of the Web could be greatly enhanced along the lines suggested by Joseph Weiler for the EU—for instance, that all deliberations of the European institutions be put on the Internet.[62]

In addition, the WTO could help enhance obligations of *transnational* inclusiveness in domestic rule-making processes. While we have argued that WTO Panels should refrain from interfering with substantive choices between values at the domestic level, there might be less pressure for this type of interference if people felt that they had had their say at the input stage of decision-making in other countries—to the extent that the decisions in question concern them. This puts a greater onus on the WTO to design and enforce procedural constraints on the exercise of their prerogatives on the part of states. A first step in this direction was taken in the Uruguay round with the creation of contact points and enquiry points through which information about trade-relevant domestic regulations is disseminated by the WTO. The approach needs to be generalized through more stringent and direct obligations of transparency borne by the contracting parties themselves. More radically, obligations of inclusiveness could be applied in certain areas to earlier stages of law- and regulation-making, whereby a notice and comment procedure could be required in areas of extraterritorial effect. The EU has pioneered this to some extent in the field of environmental law. On the judicial front, *inclusiveness* calls for a focus on *due process* elements of WTO rules, including participation and transparency as opposed to substantive balancing. As de Burca and Scott argue, and as we mentioned above this is an important feature of the *Shrimp/Turtle* ruling. Instead of engaging in some sort of scrutiny of the trade off between free trade and environmental protection embodied in the U.S. scheme, once the Appellate Body had assured itself that there was a *bona fide* non-protectionist rationale for the scheme, i.e., that it was "in relation" to the protection of exhaustible natural resources, they went on to examine whether its application was consistent with various due process values of transparency, fairness, non-arbitrariness, and prior negotiation/deliberation with all affected interests.

Another aspect of transnational inclusiveness is the role the WTO must play in ensuring fair access by non-OECD countries to both formal and informal negotiations by the OECD, or between OECD countries, in particular in negotiations or applications of Mutual Recognition Agreements (MRA). Admittedly, inclusiveness has become more complicated than unconditional MFN and automatic non-discrimination since an increasing amount of liberalization has become conditional (on regulatory compatibility) without being discriminatory.[63] Emphasis on due process rather than on substantive assessment of "equivalence" ought to characterize judicial review in assessing compliance with "procedural MFN."[64] These constraints can be requirements, for instance, to give third parties to an MRA a chance to prove their case, and even reversing the burden of proof of regulatory compatibility in their favor.

This proceduralist focus on the interpretation of WTO rules necessarily involves some review of delicate domestic policy choices, and complements the notion of institutional sensitivity. A crude rule of deference could be destabilizing if it led to excessive tolerance of cheating. In addition, any such general rule would risk being in tension with general international law principles, such as effectiveness in treaty interpretation. Institutional sensitivity in reviewing substantive policy trade-offs, combined with a strong or relatively strict approach to due process and obligations of inclusiveness, both enhances the democratic pedigree of policies, rendering them more contestable in domestic and international discourse, and preserves the confidence that protectionist cheating will be disciplined.

Top-Down Empowerment

Finally, the *permissive* interpretation of “embedded liberalism” needs to be progressively supplemented by a *proactive* interpretation that lays some of the responsibility on the global community to help states fulfill the functions that the original bargain was meant to protect. Globalization has made it harder, for at least some states, to deliver the goods that citizens have come to expect of them, or at least for many states to recast or redesign the domestic social bargain so as to respond effectively to the new pressures and opportunities of globalization. It is because the state is still the greatest buffer against the effects of globalization that the more open countries are also the biggest welfare states.[65] The WTO can not simply allow or restrict states in their rights and obligations to their respective citizens. In this vein, global subsidiarity does not need to be interpreted as shifting functions away from the center but instead as conceiving of those functions as means of empowerment of the sub-units including, but not exclusively, the state.

Here again, the WTO may be able to borrow from the EU experience. Fritz Scharpf and others have proposed implementing a "European law of unfair competition."[66] Why not create a version of such a law at the global level to curb extreme instances of social or environmental dumping or of tax competition? And why not introduce differentiated applicability of such a law depending on the level of development of the country concerned, for instance, or on the type of economic actors? It may enhance the legitimacy of the system to require Multinational Corporations to apply minimum social standards across countries before this is required from local producers. Differentiated applicability, including opt-out for very poor countries, will ensure that such a regime focuses on curbing welfare-reducing or beggar-thy-neighbor regulatory competition and does not amount to a surreptitious harmonization of domestic policies or imposition of a paradigm of global distributive equity, both of which require, to be legitimate, federal democratic governance. In other words, we can address the "race to the bottom" concern within the "embedded liberalism" model, whose major function is to provide constraints against beggar-thy-neighbor interstate competition. Some of the poorest countries in the world may not accept being so constrained, and perhaps quite justifiably, but there is little empirical evidence that the importance of such countries in global markets is such as to induce movement downward of regulatory standards elsewhere. Thus, countries for whom a standard lower than the "bottom" to which others might legitimately wish to commit is optimal from the perspective of domestic welfare, would not have to be tied to such commitments. On the other hand, a major player in the global marketplace that refused to be so constrained would bear a heavy burden of proof that it was not simply a free-rider (a hold out from a bargain that would benefit everyone). Thus, we could envisage a plurilateral code at the WTO on environmental and social dumping. Adherence to the code would not be a requirement of membership in the WTO, nor would existing benefits under the WTO system be conditioned on joining the code.

There is, however, an important condition for such an approach to actually result in empowering not only states but also the peoples within it. When the WTO envisages obligations with real financial consequences, it needs to support state efforts to adjust to those obligations. The European proposal for a joint WTO-World Bank-IMF approach with regard to the social clause should be seen in this context, while operationalizing the kind of regime linkages called for by political sensitivity. Trade conditionality can be made easier and more legitimate if backed up by a real "agenda of empowerment" in the aid and project finance field. If child labor is to be progressively banned from the production processes of exported products—starting with those made by MNCs—then local communities and families need to be assisted in these efforts through combined schooling-training programs. To be sure, the best remedies in this vein may be those already implemented from the bottom-up such as micro-financing, but there is no reason why the resources of the international community should not be brought to bear more systematically in this context. Again, however, we do not see such an initiative in constitutional terms as a form of federal global governance, but as a means of returning to the adjustment focus of the "embedded liberalism" model, while adapting it to global monetary and financial arrangements very different from those presupposed by the adjustment features of the original Bretton Woods arrangements. Here, the role of financial assistance should not be viewed as based on the kind of aid conditionality premised in the so-called Washington consensus—the imposition of a governance model on the countries concerned—nor as premised on a global conception of distributive justice, but rather as underpinning the political economy of a world trading system still based, for the foreseeable future, on mutually beneficial interstate bargains.

Clearly, such an approach to top-down empowerment should not be conceived or perceived as an allowance for international economic institutions to supersede local democratic processes and bypass domestic institutions. On the contrary, the WTO, in our case, ought to play a role in enhancing these domestic processes by helping strengthen indirect democracy and accountability and by supporting the creation of political spaces for local actors who might have been hitherto disempowered in their respective domestic contexts (women, children, minorities, consumers, unions, migrants). In this, requirements of political inclusiveness and empowerment converge and complement each other. If governments need to be accountable for what they decide collectively at the international level, then national actors and groups in civil society need to be empowered to exercise indirect control. Local democracy is the ultimate key to our model of global subsidiarity.

6. Conclusion

In this essay, we have analyzed the conceptualization of the judicial role in the WTO in the broader context of the overall challenge of reshaping global economic governance. We have argued that constitutionalization is not the right answer to the WTO's legitimacy crisis, and that the practice of the WTO

Appellate Body can be best understood in non-constitutional terms. We based our analysis of the current situation on the fate of "embedded liberalism" in the GATT and then WTO in the last fifty years, and the difficulty of balancing over time progressive trade liberalization and the notion that when in doubt, the imperatives of domestic welfare should trump the requirements of laissez-faire. The challenge today is to recover the spirit of embedded liberalism under conditions radically different from those at its inception. In doing so, we argue that we need to *recover* rather than seek to *transcend* the primacy of politics and recognize that, at least at the global level, no single authority or principle can legitimately adjudicate between conflicting local values. When rational discourse, persuasive argumentation, generalized deliberation or peer pressure are not enough, human society needs recourse to political mechanisms of interaction to deal with the inherent tensions entailed with living together and interacting in pursuit of the individual as well as collective good.

In our critique of the use of the European Union as a model for constitutionalizing the WTO, we do not belabor the self-evident point that the two settings are too different to warrant a direct transfer in mode of governance. Nor do we lose sight of the fact that constitutionalization in the EU has been a long incremental process which is still in the making and indeed still highly contested. Instead, we have sought to highlight the critical political assumptions behind either formal or informal constitutionalization and to point to the qualitatively different nature of the global system and the balance between diversity and convergence that it implies. Our prescription is to retain some but not all of the lessons provided by the EU through the use by WTO judges and diplomats of a "global subsidiarity" model as guidance for their action.

It might be objected that, if all the proposals that we make were fully realized, especially those on inclusiveness, empowerment, and deliberative democracy, we might indeed bring about the very conditions for global democratic federalism that we have been arguing are structurally incompatible with the multilateral trading system. It might further be argued that, with *enough* global subsidiarity of the right kind(s), some of the normative objections to a world state or government, based upon concerns about democratic deficits, about the destruction of desirable human diversity and the risk of technocratic tyranny, might no longer have significant weight. Indeed, the prescriptive guidelines that we have suggested could ultimately result in creating some conditions for constitutionalism in the long run—because integration of human rights and environment into WTO law as higher norms that shape and limit specific trade liberalization commitments would give it more of the kind of normative structure consistent with constitutional status.

There is force in these claims, and certainly we do not wish to foreclose the possibility that the conditions for a legitimate global federal government might eventually *emerge*. Indeed, in terms of achieving some kind of overlapping consensus about the future direction of the multilateral trading system this self-limiting feature of our critique of constitutionalization bears an advantage—for we would say even to those who are already committed to the ultimate goal of WTO constitutionalism that the best means of bringing about those conditions are non-constitutional ones, which have coherence and legitimacy on their own terms within a revised understanding of the "embedded liberalism" bargain. The problem with the constitutionalists, however radical or moderate their proposals, is that, when understood properly, their trajectory presupposes the very conditions of legitimacy that they want to create. But constitutionalization of non-constitutional structures cannot itself create the conditions of constitutional legitimacy; rather, legitimate constitutionalism depends on those conditions, both conceptually and temporally.

NOTES

1. Thomas Cottier, Limits to International Trade: The Constitutional Challenge, in: *The American Society of International Law, Proceedings of the 94th Annual Meeting, April 5-8, 2000, Washington, DC*, Washington, DC 2000, pp. 200-22.

2. G. R. Shell, "Trade Legalism and International Relations Theory: An Analysis of the World Trade Organization", 44 *Duke Law Journal*, pp. 829–927.

3. Thomas Cottier, n. 1.

4. Dan Tarullo uses the expression "constitutional" to refer to or denote issues or doctrines that are "fundamental to the nature of the WTO." See D. Tarullo, "The Relationship of WTO Obligations to Other International Arrangements", in M. Bronckers and R. Quick, eds., *New Directions in International Economic Law* (Kluwer Law International: The Hague, 2000), pp. 155–56. Understood purely descriptively, such usage appears to be innocuous. However, it can also be used (or abused) normatively to resist change and transformation, by ruling out certain options and certain kinds of claims as incompatible with the "nature" of the WTO, the idea being if you want a WTO at all, there are certain structures that you have to accept. But if we look, for instance, to what on any account are, and which we ourselves would call, fundamental characteristics of the GATT, such as MFN, these have always been accompanied by exceptions, limitations, and balancing rights and obligations. *Dépeçage* of WTO rules and structures into those that are fundamental or constitutional and those that are not may well be based on an assumption that what is fundamental are the pro-free trade principles and rules and what are peripheral or less fundamental are the exceptions, limitations, etc.

5. J. Ruggie, "International Regimes, Transactions, and Change: Embedded Liberalism in the Postwar Economic Order", 36 *International Organization* (1982), p. 379.

6. "Constitutional" talk about the WTO has spilled out beyond these two variants, which represent serious understandings of the WTO, its telos and future, into trivial or intellectually sloppy use of the terms constitutional or constitutionalism. For example, Deborah Cass has chosen to speak of the constitutionalization of the WTO because WTO jurisprudence is

developing some rules and principles that share characteristics with those in constitutional law. However, the rules and principles are mostly characteristic of traditional public international law; only ignorance of the latter could lead someone to think that notions such as proportionality or of delimited competences or powers are peculiar or specific to constitutional bodies of law. See D. Cass, The "Constitutionalization" of International Trade Law: Judicial Norm-Generation as the Engine of Constitutional Development in International Trade, 12 *European Journal of International Law* (2001), p. 39. Many of the characteristics of WTO law that lead scholars such as Cass to cry "constitution" are, in fact, as David Palmeter points out in an excellent article, merely characteristics that we think of as belonging to a legal system as such. See D. Palmeter, "The WTO as a Legal System", 24 *Fordham International Law Journal* (2000), p. 444.

7. Ernst-Ulrich Petersmann, Trade Policy as a Constitutional Problem: On the Domestic Policy Functions of International Rules, 41 *Aussenwirtschaft*, pp. 405–39.

8. Thomas Cottier, n. 1.

9. Robert Keohane, *After Hegemony: Cooperation and Discord in the Modern World Economy* (Princeton University Press, 1984). Kenneth Oye, ed., *Cooperation Under Anarchy* (Princeton University Press, 1985). Robert Axelrod, *The Evolution of Cooperation* (Basic Books, 1980).

10. A.-M. Slaughter, "Regulating the World: Multilateralism, Internationalism and the Projection of the New Deal Regulatory State", in Robert Howse, ed., *The World Trading System: Critical Perspectives on the World Economy* (Routledge, 1998).

11. Stephen Krasner, "State Power and the Structure of International Trade", 28 *World Politics* (1976).

12. M.J. Trebilcock, M.A. Chandler, and R. Howse, *Trade and Transitions: A Comparative Analysis of Industrial Policies* (Routledge, 1990).

13. According to Ruggie: "The task of postwar institutional reconstruction, . . . was . . . to devise a framework which would safeguard and even aid the quest for domestic stability without, at the same time, triggering mutually destructive external consequences that had plagued the interwar period. This was the essence of the embedded liberalism compromise: unlike the economic nationalism of the thirties, it would be multilateral in character; unlike the liberalism of the gold standard and free trade, its multilateralism would be predicated upon domestic interventionism. If this was the shared objective of postwar institutional reconstruction for the international economy, there remained enormous differences between countries over precisely what it meant and what sorts of policies and institutional arrangements, domestic and international, the objective necessitated or was compatible with. This was the stuff of the negotiations on the postwar international economic order." J.G. Ruggie, "International Regimes, Transactions and Change: Embedded Liberalism and the Post-War Economic Regimes", 36 *International Organization* (1982).

14. See Jagdish Bhagwati, *Protectionism* (Cambridge University Press, 1988).

15. M.J. Trebilcock, M.A. Chandler, and R. Howse, *Trade and Transitions: A Comparative Analysis of Industrial Policies* (Routledge, 1990).

16. Daniel Tarullo, "Beyond Normalcy in the Regulation of International Trade", 100 *Harvard Law Review* (1987), pp. 546ff.

17. See Alan Sykes, *Product Standards for Internationally Integrated Goods Markets* (Brookings, 1995); Kalypso Nicolaïdis, "Mutual Recognition of Regulatory Regimes: Some

Lessons and Prospects", *Regulatory Reform and International Market Openness (*OECD Publications, 1996).

18. William Drake and Kalypso Nicolaïdis, Ideas, Interests and Institutionalization: "Trade in Services" and the Uruguay Round, 46 *International Organization*, no. 1 (Winter 1992), 17–100.

19. Alan Sykes, "Regulatory Protectionism", 66 *University of Chicago Law Review* (1999).

20. Alan Deardorff, "Should Patent Protection be Extended to all Developing Countries?", 13 *World Economy* (1990), pp. 497 ff.

21. See generally Steven Vogel, *Freer Markets, More Rules* (Cornell University Press, 1996).

22. Kalypso Nicolaïdis and Joel P. Trachtman, "From Policed Regulation to Managed Recognition: Mapping the Boundary in GATS", in Pierre Sauve and Robert Stern, eds., *Services 2000: New Directions in Services Trade Liberalization* (Brookings Press, 2000).

23. See Kalypso Nicolaïdis, "Non-Discriminatory Mutual Recognition: An Oxymoron in the New WTO Lexicon?", in T. Cottier, P. Mavroidis, P. Blatter, eds., *Regulatory Barriers and the Principle of Non-Discrimination of World Trade Law: Past, Present and Future* (Michigan University Press, 2000).

24. Jagdish Bhagwati and Robert Hudec, *Fair Trade and Harmonization* (MIT Press, 1996).

25. E.-U. Petersmann, From "Negative" to "Positive Integration" in the WTO: Time For "Mainstreaming Human Rights" into WTO Law?, *Common Market Law Review*, Vol. 37 (2000), No. 6, p. 1377.

26. J. Dunoff, "The Death of the Trade Regime", 10 *European Journal of International Law* (1999), pp. 733–62.

27. Petersmann, n. 25, p. 1370 *et passim*.

28. Hedley Bull, "Society and Anarchy in International Relations", in Butterfield and Wight, eds, *Diplomatic Investigations* (1966). M. Wight, "An Anatomy of International Thought", *Review of International Studies* (1987). A. Hurrell, "Kant and the Kantian paradigm in international relations", *Review of International Studies* 16 (1990), pp. 183–05. H. Reiss, *Kant's Political Writings* (Cambridge University Press, 1970).

29. Petersmann, n. 25, p. 1369.

30. J. Elster, *Ulysses Unbound* (Cambridge University Press, 2000), p. ix.

31. See E. Benvenisti, "Exit and Voice in the Age of Globalization," *Michigan Law Review* (2000). Marco Bronckers, "Better rules for a new Millennium: A warning against undemocratic developments in the WTO", *Journal of International Economic Law* (1999).

32. Petersmann, n. 25, p. 1376.

33. Thomas Cottier, n. 1.

34. We recognize that those advocating the European analogy do not deny the obvious point that the WTO is different from the EU. But their methodological premise relies on two types of arguments: 1) This is an evolutionary process: the WTO is simply at the point of the EU in the early 1960s; 2) Even while the two are different, many of their institutional and procedural features are functionally equivalent. On the first point, we argue that the EU was different at

birth and thus cannot be emulated on path dependency grounds. On the second point, we show that such functional equivalence does not obtain.

35. J.H.H. Weiler, "The Transformation of Europe", Yale Law Journal Vol. 100 (1991), No. 8, p. 2407.

36. John H. Jackson, *Restructuring the GATT System* (RIIA, 1990).

37. *United States—Sections 301–310 of the Trade Act of 1974,* Report of the Panel, 1999, para. 7.72).

38. A. Stone Sweet, *Governing with Judges: Constitutional Politics in Europe* (Oxford University Press, 2000), p. 189.

39. Kalypso Nicolaïdis, "Mutual Recognition of Regulatory Regimes: Some Lessons and Prospects", *Regulatory Reform and International Market Openness* (OECD Publications, 1996).

40. Thomas Cottier, n. 1.

41. Kalypso Nicolaïdis, "Mutual Recognition of Regulatory Regimes: Some Lessons and Prospects," *Regulatory Reform and International Market Openness* (OECD Publications, 1996). Kalypso Nicolaïdis, "Non-Discriminatory Mutual Recognition: An Oxymoron in the New WTO Lexicon?", in T. Cottier, P. Mavroidis, P. Blatter, eds., *Regulatory Barriers and the Principle of Non-Discrimination of World Trade Law: Past, Present and Future* (Michigan University Press, 2000). Kalypso Nicolaïdis, "Regulatory Cooperation and Managed Mutual Recognition: Developing a Strategic Model", in George Bermann et al., eds, *Transatlantic Regulatory Cooperation: Legal Problems and Political Prospects* (Oxford University Press, 2001).

42. J.H.H. Weiler, *The Constitution of Europe: "Do the New Clothes Have an Emperor?" and Other Essays on European Integration* (Cambridge University Press 1999), p. 298. Indeed, building on this formula, one could say that what the constitutional enthusiasts for the WTO draw from their reading of the European experience is that one can *create* the underlying legitimizing constitutionalism, which the WTO now needs, given the problems with the "embedded liberalism"/ interstate bargaining model described above, only if one begins to assert boldly enough *constitutional practices* at the WTO.

43. J. Pinder, "The European Community, the Rule of Law and Representative Government: The Significance of the Intergovernmental Conferences", *Government and Opposition* (1991), p. 204.

44. For a discussion on this point and other dimensions of the EU debates, see Kalypso Nicolaïdis and Robert Howse, eds. *The Federal Vision: Legitimacy and Levels of Governance in the United States and the European Union* (Oxford University Press, 2001).

45. E. Stein, "Panel Statement on Democracy without a "People," *European Studies Association Meeting*, Pittsburgh, June 1999, p. 10.

46. F. Scharpf, *Governing in Europe: Effective and Democratic?* (Oxford University Press, 1999).

47. See J.H.H. Weiler, *EU, WTO and NAFTA: Towards a Common Law of Economic Integration?* (Oxford University Press, 2000).

48. Alexandre Kojeve, Frost and Howse, trs., *Outline for a Phenomenology of Right* (Rowan and Littlefield, 2000).

49. The formulation of this model of global subsidiarity is inspired by our analysis of some of the existing or incipient characteristics of the EU developed in Kalypso Nicolaïdis and Robert Howse, eds. *The Federal Vision, op.cit.*

50. Robert Howse, "Adjudicative Legitimacy and Treaty Interpretation in International Trade Law: The Early Years of WTO Jurisprudence", in J.H.H. Weiler, *EU, WTO and NAFTA: Towards a Common Law of Economic Integration?* (Oxford University Press, 2000).

51. M. Bronckers, "Better rules for a new Millennium: A warning against undemocratic developments in the WTO", *Journal of International Economic Law* (1999). See also Kalypso Nicolaïdis and Joel P. Trachtman, "From Policed Regulation to Managed Recognition: Mapping the Boundary in GATS", in Pierre Sauve and Robert Stern, eds., *Services 2000: New Directions in Services Trade Liberalization* (Brookings Press, 2000).

52. *EC—Measures Concerning Meat and Meat Products (Hormones),* Report of the Appellate Body, supra n. 76, paragraph 177.

53. As Cass Sunstein notes in the context of domestic public law adjudication, "Statutory terms—not legislative history, nor legislative purpose, nor legislative 'intent'—have gone through the constitutionally specified procedures for the enactment of law. Largely for this reason, the words of a statute provide the foundation for interpretation, and those words, together with widely shared conventions about how they should be understood, often lead to uniquely right answers, or at least sharply constrain the territory of legitimate disagreement. Resort to the text also promotes goals associated with the rule of law: the statutory words are available to affected citizens, and it is in response to those words that they can most readily order their affairs. An emphasis on the primacy of the text also serves as a salutary warning about the risks of judicial use of statutory purpose and of legislative history, both of which are, as we will see, subject to interpretive abuse." Cass Sunstein, *After the Rights Revolution: Reconceiving the Regulatory State* (Harvard University Press, 1990), p. 114.

54. Nichols discusses some of the GATT-specific interpretive canons that evolved before the WTO adoption of customary interpretive rules in public international law: for instance, on exception to trade-liberalizing obligations is to be interpreted narrowly and whenever an exception is at issue the party that seeks to invoke it bears the burden of proof so that it meets the specific criteria for the exception. Clearly in both these cases, these canons assume the primacy of trade liberalization as a value in treaty interpretation. "GATT Doctrine", 36 *Virginia Journal of International Law* 379 (1996), supra n. 73, pp. 434–35.

55. See Article 31(3)(c) of the *Vienna Convention,* which provides that "any relevant rules of international law applicable in the relations between parties" shall be brought to bear on the interpretation of a treaty.

56. John G. Ruggie, "Territoriality and Beyond: Problematizing Modernity in International Relations", 46 *International Organization* (1993).

57. See Robert Keohane and Joseph Nye, in Roger Porter, Pierre Sauvé, Arvind Subramanian and Americo Zampetti, eds, *Equity, Efficiency and Legitimacy: The Multilateral System at the Millennium,* Washington DC: Brookings Institution Press, 2001

58. Robert Howse, "Transatlantic Regulatory Cooperation and the Problem of Democracy", in G. Bermann et al., eds., supra n. 41.

59. We would like to thank Leonardo Martinez for an enlightening discussion on this issue.

60. Ibid.

61. However, as one of us has argued, these groups can serve as monitors of the agency costs of representative democracy, ensuring that the negotiating behavior of the people's agents or agents of agents (diplomatic bargainers, for instance) represents the interests of principals rather than those of the agents themselves as a special epistemic community (the trade policy elite). R Howse, "Transatlantic Regulatory Cooperation and the Problem of Democracy", in G. Bermann et al., eds., supra n. 41).

62. J.H.H. Weiler, note 42, p. 351.

63. See Kalypso Nicolaïdis, Non-Discriminatory Mutual Recognition, op. cit., fn 22.

64. Kalypso Nicolaïdis, Mutual Recognition of Regulatory Regimes: Some Lessons and Prospects, *Regulatory Reform and International Market Openness* (OECD Publications, 1996). Kalypso Nicolaïdis and Joel P. Trachtman, "From Policed Regulation to Managed Recognition: Mapping the Boundary in GATT", in Pierre Sauvé and Robert Stern, eds., *Services 2000: New Directions in Services Trade Liberalization* (Brookings Press, 2000).

65. Dani Rodrik, *Has Globalization Gone Too Far?* (Institute for International Economics, 1997).

66. F. Scharpf, *Governing in Europe: Effective and Democratic?* (Oxford University Press, 1999).

CHAPTER 20

Concluding Remarks

Thomas Cottier and Petros C. Mavroidis

Where do we go from here? This is the question we ask at the end of every Forum. The answer, of course, heavily relies upon what we managed to establish at the Conference. As usual, it is not an easy task to draw conclusions from the many thoughts and ideas which are expressed in the papers and discussions. As usual, they produced a mixture of overlaps, of convergences, and of divergences. Both angles offer valuable insights into where we stand, all with a view to take matters a step further in coming years.

1. Assessing the First Five Years

The agenda of the World Trade Forum 2000 was mainly induced by increasing allegations in civil society and diplomacy that panels and the Appellate Body engage in proactive legislative jurisprudence under the new Dispute Settlement Understanding of the WTO. Many argued that these bodies should limit their work to clarification of rules and principles. They should not engage in interpretation *per se* (let alone activist and creative interpretation). Such statements clearly are wrong. Where does one draw a line between interpretation and clarification? All application of the law entails interpretation, whether this is in domestic, regional or international law. This stands firmly in legal theory. The type of political statements made, however, shows the tendency of perhaps a majority of WTO Members and in civil society towards international judiciary.

In this climate of suspicion, we felt it appropriate to examine and discuss the problem of the proper place of the judiciary in the overall legal process in the WTO. The problem entails the relationship to the diplomatic process and to the Member States. It is on the later aspect that the studies of this conference and volume focus.

The studies and comments examining the jurisprudence of the Appellate Body and panels and the process of trial and error entailed rebut allegations that dispute settlement in the WTO has overreached and trespassed its boundaries under its mandate of making an objective assessment under Article 11 DSU. These findings were approved at the conference and did not cause substantial discourse. The view cannot be substantiated that the rulings created new rights and obligations and unduly curtailed sovereignty of

Members protected under Article 3:2 DSU. Subsequent views and studies published in the meantime further confirm this view.[1] General allegations as to the intrusiveness of the WTO and its agreements therefore would need to rest on the set of substantive rules and obligations negotiated by the political process during succeeding trade rounds. Allegations may be found on the fact that dispute settlement now is of a mandatory nature and findings are subject to obligations to implement.[2] Both these elements, however, need to be distinguished from assessing the conduct of the judicial branch, properly speaking. This branch should not be blamed, and there are no reasons in our view to curtail its role and achievements during the first five years of its operation.

These findings are important with a view to demystify not only dispute settlement, but WTO as an organization. Allegations and wide-spread public perception conceive the WTO as a powerful body on its own. True, we read in the press that the WTO has ruled against country X. But this creates a wrong impression. The WTO has remained a member-driven organization. Rights and obligations reach just as far as Members have agreed by consensus, including enforcing these rights. If they are perceived to be one-sided, it is primarily a matter of negotiations to change them. And it is a matter to assess the composition of interests involved in negotiations and to enlarge, if necessary, the representation of constituencies in the negotiating process. Panelists and Judges are aware of their limitations. They know that rules are difficult to achieve and to change. The question arises in this context to what extent they can and should take into account deficiencies of the political process, weaknesses and lacunae of agreements and seek rebalancing, where appropriate, within their rulings in order to accommodate the sensitivities of Members and their public opinion. It would not seem possible to give a general answer to this question. We therefore chose a sensitive regulatory area: protection of public health.

2. The Dumb Duck Disease or the Respect for Well-Founded Health Policies

The Conference, based upon a hypothetical case study (Dumb Duck Disease case, Appendix), focused on the issue of health protection which clearly is a prime function of all Member States. Three points may be emphasized by way of conclusion.

First, and again, there was consensus that health protection on all accounts is a prime public good which deserves priority and may justify trade restrictions. This, however, does not dispose of the prime problem as to how legitimate health concerns can and should be identified and assessed in judicial review. How to separate wheat from chaff? The problem was examined on a comparative basis. It is far from well-settled in law. Different models developed in national and regional law were discussed. Diverging views were expressed and remained. Under the U.S. Constitution it is not simply a matter of balancing interests under the interstate commerce clause, both aims or purposes of a measure as well as effects are conceivable tests on substance, while procedural requirements play an equally important role (standing, intervention, *amicus curiae*, evidence and burden of proof). In the European Communities, the assessment is based upon proportionality. The Court would examine appropriateness and necessity to achieve the intended purposes and among possible alternatives the least restrictive measure would be chosen. It is interesting to observe that here much less emphasis was given to procedural devices than on the other side of the Atlantic.

Another point of contest was the place for economic analysis in WTO jurisprudence. Within the expressed disagreements, there was an overlap: that, if at all, economic analysis should first make its way into other areas (mentioned candidates included the causal link in contingent protection instruments, the place for simultaneous regression analysis, the relevant product-market definition, and the place for cross-price elasticity). The disagreement expressed had to do both with the question whether existing breakthroughs in economic science can serve as generic example and with the question whether the WTO judge is appropriately equipped to incorporate such analysis in his or her reasoning.

Second, there was recognition that a more deferential standard is warranted when trade is restricted for non-economic motives. This should be the case even if the judge is called to establish the appropriate standard of review in the absence of a clear legislative mandate to this effect. A deferential standard of review is warranted both because, in such cases, it is often scientifically impossible to distinguish wheat from chaff and because a certain amount of political protectionism is necessary in order to provide a shield against attacks on the institution: the WTO, especially at the current juncture, needs to show to the world that it fully understands its mandate which in Art. XX GATT clearly establishes a hierarchy whereby health/ environmental concerns have primacy over trade liberalization.

Third, it is interesting to observe that the delicate problem of delineating public health and economic, rent-seeking protectionism is equally faced on all levels of governance, national, regional and international. The structure of the problem is the same for all these levels whether or not the problem is addressed in constitutional, regional or international law. In particular, they all face the problem of multiple motivation of measures and unholy coalitions which do not allow to clearly allocate and determine the motif of a particular measure. Different methods are possible and may be combined in achieving the goals of delimitation. What national experience shows is that aims and effect tests and balancing are being employed in health matters and may be complemented by European traditions of proportionality tests, entailing necessity. All of this experience provides an interesting background also for the WTO where aims and effects have been ruled out in relation to fiscal matters only, but not health under Article III GATT. Whatever tests are being applied, it is evident that results must show a comparable level of coherence short of which the legitimacy of institutions is put at risk. There is a need to develop a common doctrine, perhaps a common law, relating to health measures management which can be understood globally, despite the existence of cultural diversity and different consumer preferences. In particular, it would seem necessary to square the tests applied in the United States and in the European Community in order to assess differences and commonalties. It would be necessary to think further about the impact and implication of economic theory. In depth comparative and interdisciplinary analysis therefore needs to be pursued in the field. The contributions of the volume may provide assistance in further work.

The Forum's consensus for respect of health measures subsequently has been affirmed by the Appellate Body's ruling in the *Asbestos* case.[3] The concern of preserving public health was retained in the determination on likeness of hazardous, carcinogenic and artificial fibres in the context of existing border tax adjustment criteria, i.e. physical properties and consumer preferences. The crucial test employed by the majority on the bench was whether this quality altered the competitive relationship of the two types of product. It was held that given these properties they are not to be found in a competitive relationship. While this approach sought to remain within the bounds of existing criteria, a dissenting opinion favored direct reliance on established and uncontested health hazards as determinate for unlikeness under the circumstances of this case. It is unclear where this ruling leaves us in relation to aims, effects and proportionality tests and which impact this will have for the application and interpretation of the SPS and TBT Agreements. Whichever method and route is chosen, however, it confirms the critical importance and predominance of well-founded health measures over market access rights and interests.

The case, however, also illuminates the problem of judicial restraint or activism. All too often, judicial deference is sought to equal judicial restraint, and judicial activism is equated with excessive defence of market access rights, to the detriment of non-economic goals. This relationship cannot be sustained. Standards of review are unrelated to the objective and thus employed both in favour of non-economic goals as well as of the pursuit of market access rights. While the latter were dominant under GATT 1947, the cases discussed and in particular *Asbestos* show that judicial activism and innovative interpretation beyond the text of an agreement work to the benefit of non-economic concerns. The same was equally true when the panels adopted the aims and effect test or when, in *Hormones*, a procedural approach beyond the wording was suggested under the SPS Agreement to offer a solution to a complex regulatory problem.[4] In both cases, judicial activism was sought in order to protect non-economic concerns.[5]

Fourth, there was also consensus that the paramount importance of health measures requires some deference vis-à-vis determinations by legislation and the executive branch yet for another reason. There was overlap in the view that the degree of integration should influence the standard of review. The judge, in other words, should operate according to his or her mandate which is decisively prejudged by the tone of the integration process itself. Economists focusing on agency costs, lawyers and political scientists focusing on the amount of sovereignty transferred and the question of democratic legitimacy agreed that the judge should be well aware of the institutional parameters within which she is called to operate. Consequently, *in dubio* we should expect more daring judges at the domestic rather than at the international level.

One of the interesting observations in various contributions to the volume consists in the finding that national and regional courts employ a higher degree of deference than panels and the Appellate Body are entitled to exercise under the DSU. One would expect the opposite as judicial review normally increases in proportion to higher levels of integration. This paradox is mind-boggling as standards of review applied follow the logic and structure of the polity concerned. In comparing, none of the different standards applied can be discarded as being irrational. It is not irrational to exercise constraint under domestic administrative law review, whether it is a test limited to arbitrary and capricious decision or the Chevron doctrine. And it is perfectly rational, in applying the Vienna Convention on the Law of Treaties, to engage in full review under a contractual system of classical international law; yet, the overall interplay of different layers of governance shows signs of irrationality as levels of higher integration show more deference than levels of low integration. At this stage, we lack adequate tools to bring about overall coherence in terms of standards of review and levels of deference required. This brings us to the second theme.

3. The Problems of Constitutionalization and the Scope of the WTO

It is not astonishing that assessing the role of the judge in international trade regulation inherently triggered a debate on the problem of constitutionalization of the WTO. The function and position of the judicial branch, both in relation to the political branch of the WTO and its Members and in relation to national authorities, implies questions of allocation of powers. Standards of review, in the very end, depend upon constitutional structures and the design of interplay of different bodies of a given polity. There was, however, no agreement at the Forum whether or not we should depict these relations in terms of constitutional relations. The problem is primarily one of definitions. There is no agreed understanding on what a constitution does and should mean in the context of an international organization and multi-layered governance. The Forum shows different competing perceptions. They range from comprehensive importation of models of constitutionalism essentially inspired by the traditions of the liberal nation state to the idea of constitutional thinking as opposed to contractual thinking, all the way to the rejection of constitutionalism going too far and being replaced by "embedded liberalism".

This is not the time to discuss the pro and cons of these different approaches.[6] In terms of conclusion, we are interested in exploring the common ground of these schools of thought and in asking to what extent they all together may assist in answering the question raised at this Forum: what is the proper role of the judicial branch in the WTO? Two points may be discussed by way of conclusion.

First, it is submitted that the schools may offer more common ground than one expects at first glance. The critique of applying constitutional doctrines essentially relies upon the assumption that fundamental market access rights and rules are given priority in terms of hierarchy and impact as they are prime tools to combat welfare-reducing protectionism. This, in return, is sought to frustrate the pursuit of non-economic concerns, such as public health, and excludes deferential standards of review. With the subsequent import of the entire spectrum of human rights and the claim to take these into account, for example in the interpretation of Article III and XX GATT, it would seem that a proper balance becomes possible under Article 31(3)(c) of the Vienna Convention on the Law of Treaties. The model of embedded liberalism, on the other side of the spectrum, takes these concerns into account and offers an alternative. It is interesting to observe, however, that this model equally engages in constitutional analysis. It purports to suggest concepts of global subsidiarity, institutional sensitivity and the concept of checks and balances and political inclusiveness which entails far-reaching proposals with a view to enhance democratic legitimacy of the process. The merit of embedded liberalism is to give us a warning that constitutionalism taken seriously requires underlying legitimacy which may not even be attained at the level of the EU, but is certainly lacking on the global level. The interesting point, however, is that the issues, the regulatory problems encountered and their structures remain the same for both schools of thought. Importantly, both seek to establish a proper balance between market access and non-economic concerns, such as health. This is certainly the prime goal of limiting constitutionalism to constitutional thinking which somewhat covers the middle ground: Moving away from a contractual to a constitutional model serves the purposes of bringing about an overall balance, including vertical coherence of judicial functions, assessing both restraint and activism, on different levels of governance. Whatever the terms employed, therefore, we can detect a common goal of bringing about a well-balanced system which allows to take into account competing values and concerns of national policy-makers other than market access rights.

The problem of standards of review, at national, regional and international levels, ultimately is part of the problem of the appropriate role of the judicial branch on these levels. We cannot escape from discussing it in a broader context and theoretical framework, whatever term we employ. We agreed on the prime importance of health as a public good, we agreed on the need to exercise deference in assessing such measures, but we have not found and agreed upon an appropriate underlying intellectual framework based upon which the proper role of the judiciary and practical problems relating to competing policies on all levels of governance alike can be properly rationalized and simplified.

Second, divergent views were expressed as to the optimal mandate of the WTO and the place for economic analysis in the reasoning of the WTO judge. The view was expressed that the WTO substantially needs to develop a world trade constitution—i.e. a constitutional approach—where trade will have its place along societal values revealed at the domestic level. A clearer relationship should be established so that the judge would be aware of what importance to accord to trade when it conflicts with other societal values. A clarification in this perspective is necessary not only for the world community to have a clear road map which reflects a consensus in this respect but also for the institution itself which will be further protected against unwarranted attacks.

The arguments against this position can be summarized as follows: some participants voiced their dissatisfaction with the way the discussion on the WTO mandate had been taking place. To their mind, there is nothing like a systematic discussion on the criteria under which the WTO agenda should be enlarged. Others maintained that the WTO should remain focused on its market access perspective and should not move anywhere else. In doing that, respecting its mandate, it should accept the primacy of trade-obstructing legislation on non-economic motives over trade liberalization. Finally, others simply failed to grasp why an extension of the WTO mandate is necessary for the WTO judge to adopt a deferential standard of review when dealing with health/environmental issues.

We do not think that the mandate of the WTO is directly linked with standards of review and judicial restraint or activism. The Appellate Body and panels were able to make steps in the right direction of balancing market access and non-economic concerns. The well-known cases of *Shrimp/Turtles* and *Asbestos* are cases in point, demonstrating that the balance can be found irrespective of the breath of coverage of the WTO. There are sufficient ports of entry to allow an overall balancing of diverging interests. Yet, is the current situation acceptable to all? Apparently not. A number of commentators, and indeed many in the Forum, expressed their dissatisfaction with the current state of affairs, in particular from the point of view of smaller countries. Constructing the current contract as a negative integration instrument means that country X can block trade from country Y when the latter does not conform to X's health/environmental standards; X, however, cannot impose on Y its own standards (since we do not deal with *jus cogens* here) if country Y is not trading with country X. Moreover, even in presence of trade with X, Y will adopt X's standards only if the persuasive power of X's countermeasures matters to Y.

The above-described scenario is inevitable under the present circumstances and evolution of WTO law. At the same time, it is an illustration of the limits of negative integration. In order to move beyond what is described above one would need to re-construct the WTO mandate and adopt more TRIPs-like agreements where a particular behavior will be requested from all states upon joining the WTO. This is the road to positive integration. The decision to move down this road, however, is not the judge's prerogative; it lies within the margin of appreciation of sovereign governments. Until this happens, if it does, the WTO judge will be called upon to apply the WTO contract as it now stands, taking into account the context in which the law operates. He or she will be well-advised to continue the deferential pattern she has already adopted in respecting non-economic concerns, and probably to even strengthen this approach while remaining firm in defending market access against undue rent seeking protectionism. To conclude: "First do no harm" should be the leitmotiv of the WTO judge when dealing with separating wheat from chaff, and this should apply not only to domestic regulatory policies but also to the WTO itself.

NOTES

1. Claus-Dieter Ehlermann, *Some Personal Experiences as Members of the Appellate Body of the WTO*, European University Institute, Florence 2002. For a detailed analysis of standards of review in case law see Matthias Oesch, *Standards of Review in WTO Dispute Settlement: A Contribution to the Balance of Power between the Judiciary of the WTO and its Members*, Oxford University Press, Oxford 2003 (forthcoming).

2. See Claude E. Barfield, *Free Trade, Sovereignty, Democracy: The Future of the World Trade Organization*, Washington, D.C., 2001.

3. European Communities – Measures Affecting Asbestos and Asbestos-Containing Products, Report of the Appellate Body, 12 March 2001, WT/DS135/AB/R.

4. An approach discarded by the Appellate Body, see European Communities – Measures Concerning Meat and Meat Products (Hormones), Report of the Appellate Body, 16 January 1998, WT/DS26/AB/R, WT/DS48/AB/R paras. 188-191.

5. See generally Thomas Cottier, Risk Management Experience in WTO Dispute Settlement, in: David Robertson/ Aynsley Kellow (eds.), *Globalization and the Environment, Risk Assessment in the WTO*, Edward Elgar, Cheltenham 2001, pp. 41-62.

6. Since the Forum took place, the literature on constitutionalization of the WTO has considerably grown, see e.g. Armin von Bogdandy, Law and Politics in the WTO – Strategies to Cope with a Deficient Relationship, 5 *Max Planck Yearbook of United Nations Law* 609-674 (2001); Deborah Cass, The 'Constitutionalization' of International Trade Law: Judicial Norm-Generation as the Engine of Constitutional Development in International Trade, 12 *European Journal of International Law* 39-75 (2001); Steve Charnovitz, WTO Cosmopolitics, 34 *New York Journal of International Law and Politics*, 299-354 (2002); John H. Jackson, The WTO 'Constitution' and Proposed Reforms: Seven 'Mantras' Revisited, 4 *Journal of International Economic Law* 67-78 (2001); Markus Krajewski, *Verfassungsperspektiven und Legitimation des Rechts der Welthandelsorganisation*, Duncker & Humblot, Berlin 2001; ibid., Democratic Legitimacy and Constitutional Perspectives of WTO Law, 35 *Journal of World Trade* 167-186 (2001); Jens Ladefoged-Mortensen, WTO in an Era of Globalisation: Imperfections in the Global Economic Polity, 6 *European Law Journal* 176-204 (2000); Eric Stein, International Integration and Democracy: No Love at First Sight, 95 *American Journal of International Law* 489-534 (2001).

The Moot Case

Arimania (a WTO Member/U.S. State/EC Member State) adopts legislation banning sales of ducks (and duck meat products) treated with growth hormones into its territory. The reason invoked is that there is widespread fear that its citizens will be contaminated by the so-called "Dumb Duck Disease" (aka DDD) if they consume such food. The legislation reads:

Article 1

All sales for food consumption of ducks (and duck meat products) treated with growth hormones are prohibited in the territory of Arimania.

Article 2

There is no obligation to exterminate ducks treated with growth hormones if they are not aimed for food consumption.

Article 3

The sales ban is non discriminatory; it applies to sales of both domestic and imported ducks.

Arimani producers typically do not use growth hormones. They take pride in the fact that their ducks are "meaty" anyway. An old Arimani saying goes like this: "An Arimani duck's good food and good luck."

Some Arimani producers use growth hormones and they protest to their government. They first put into question the authenticity of the saying about duck and luck. But then they produce an unofficial document apparently signed by an authority on DDD, Prof. Dr. Dr. h.c Helmut von Entefleisch, according to which DDD is a mere fiction or something close to that. The relevant passage reads:

> I never understood all this noise about DDD. First, the last victim of DDD dates from September 2, 1902 (Mick Duckinduck, 62, farmer, Duckville, Missouri). Then, it is common knowledge that by consuming water and fruits every day, even the most remote danger to contract DDD is eliminated. So where is the problem? Responsible governments should simply recommend their citizens to consume a certain amount of fruits and water on a daily basis and forget about import and sales bans of ducks treated with growth hormones.

Few scientists would contest von Entefleisch's expertise. Hence, the Arimani government is looking for some back-up to its legislation. It finds two:

1. the governmental Institute for Public Health issues a report which explains in a very systematic manner why DDD can be dangerous and even deadly if certain conditions are met;
2. the domestic Industrywatch points out that only 88.12% of the domestic production is hormone-free, meaning that the sales ban does hit hard on domestic producers as well.

Karponia, a neighboring state, does not have a similar legislation on growth hormones. Karponi producers use such hormones since they are a safe way to maximize their welfare. Some Karponi radicals, though, continue in the old-fashioned way and produce hormone-free duck meat. They represent a very small minority (less than 2% of the total production). Hence the large majority of Karponi producers is affected.

The competent authorities of Karponia protest. But their protests do not lead anywhere. In a goodwill effort to persuade their counterparts they request a neutral institution ("Free your mind," a very reputed organization specializing in diseases and having its headquarters in Neutronia, a nearby state) to examine the issue.

The report of "Free your mind" is unambiguous. There is no danger at all from eating hormone-treated duck meat. DDD belongs to the past. If at all, a person consuming at least 3 kilos of duck meat daily for an uninterrupted 5 years has a less than 2% chance to incur fever for a week (the so-called 'duck fever').

Arimani authorities are not persuaded by the report. They point out to the fact that their own institute is based on sound evidence. Karponia and Arimania submit their dispute to you. How do you decide the case? You are welcome to present your thoughts and we would kindly request you to address, among other things, the following questions, to the extent you think that they are relevant:

1. Does the fact that we deal here with a *de facto* and not *de jure* discrimination issue already make you adopt a more pro-deference stance?
2. How many of the above-mentioned facts do you find relevant for yourself to adjudicate the case?
3. Do you think that all cases of *de facto* discrimination (even remotely so) should be punishable in the legal context where you operate?
4. Follow-up to Question 3: can causality help you exonerate some *de facto* discrimination cases like, for example, these cases where only a weak

indirect link can be established between the intended objective and the outcome observed in the market?

5. Assume that DDD is also contracted by being close to ducks (i.e., feeding them in the national park) and Arimania is taking no action against this possibility: would such a fact be relevant in your judgment?
6. Follow-up to Question 5: would it matter if feeding ducks is responsible for 2 or 82% of all DDD casualties?
7. Do you think that the role of the judge is to impose an obligation to governments to be efficient? Is such role justified in the letter of the existing legal text that you apply? Is efficiency a *prima facie* case for finding in favor of the intervening state (in our example, if watching ducks is responsible for only 2% of DDD casualties and Arimania decides to start eliminating the main source of the externality, that is eating ducks)?
8. In an international context, would you give precedence to democratic legitimacy (not interfere too much with domestic sovereignty) or to efficiency considerations?
9. Would the seriousness of the externality be an issue? Would you adopt a different attitude if DDD is deadly or simply causing slight fever?
10. What if growth hormones are also used in beef meat and no action is taken against such practices? Would this fact matter in your judgment?
11. How would you evaluate the report by a scientific institution? What in case where you simply lack the expertise and cannot evaluate it at all?
12. Follow-up: what would you do in presence of conflicting scientific reports? Where do you place the accent? On the craftsmanship of the report? On the reputation of the house issuing the report? On the fact that one litigant chose a national house whereas the other litigant chose a non-national house?
13. Do you think that in issues of scientific conflict it is maybe wiser to adopt a pro-deference stance?
14. How well-suited is the so-called precautionary principle to deal with cases of scientific conflict? Do we need something more? Should there be, once the precautionary principle has been invoked, an obligation imposed on invoking states to periodically re-examine the issue?
15. Do you think agency costs explain a more pro-deference stance when we move from the domestic to the international judge?
16. Is absence of, or limited, democratic legitimacy a consideration mandating a pro-deference stance for the international judge?
17. How much do, or should, political acceptability concerns weigh in your judgment? Should the judge always take into account the context (public opinion)? If yes, how can this be possible at the international plane where there is nothing like domestic WTO politics (private citizens remaining passive observers, if at all)?

18. Would evidence from other constituencies be relevant to your judgment? For example, what if in a different state with food habits very similar to Arimani consumers have been consuming for decades hormone-treated duck without running into any trouble?
19. Assume that you cannot prejudge the level of enforcement wanted by the intervening regulator, and you can only put into question the instrument used: how would you conclude that the option adopted by the intervening state is, or is not, the least restrictive one on international trade? Would you construct the counterfactual?
20. Follow-up: can you *ex ante* be sure that another less restrictive option can achieve the same result? Would, for example, the level of education of Arimania count for you in inducing you to decide that a simple labeling campaign against DDD by and large suffices? Is knowledge of local circumstances crucial in that sense? If yes, how can the international judge be presumed to have good knowledge of local circumstances? Is the opposite, that is, a presumption of absence of knowledge of local circumstances, reason enough to recommend a pro-deference standard for the international judge?
21. What in case where the regulating authority deviates from an international standard? What evidence is necessary for the judge to decide that the deviating authority has met its standard of proof?